Parachuting for Gold in Old Mexico

Jim Hall

NPJR License #A-82

PCA License #B-33

USPA License C-68

Mexico License #1

Senior Riggers EX-9

Parachuting Publishing
www.ParachutingAssociates.com

Books may be purchased in quantity and/or special sales by contacting the publisher:

Parachuting Publishing
PO Box 461377
Aurora, CO 80046
303-680-3560
Fax 303-627-4718 or email at
Info@ParachutingAssociates.com

Published by Parachuting Publishing, Aurora, Colorado
Design by WESType Publishing Services, Inc., Boulder, Colorado
Illustrations by Charles Stoeckle; Artwork by James J. Broome;
Cover Design by Robin Zgurski

Hall, James, 1926–
Parachuting for Gold in Old Mexico

Library of Congress Control Number: 2009912511
ISBN-13: 978-0-9842790-0-5

10 9 8 7 6 5 4 3 2 1

Parachuting, Adventure

First Edition   Printed in the USA

For Georgann, Jennifer and Jim "Eagle"

You've been the wind beneath my wings ...

PAYING TRIBUTE TO BRIGADIER GENERAL JAMES C. HALL

STATEMENT OF
HON. JON C. PORTER

Madam SPEAKER: The chair recognizes Mr. Porter from Nevada.

Mr. PORTER: Madam Speaker, I rise today to honor the life of Brigadier General James C. Hall, Colorado National Guard (Retired).

James C. Hall was born into a coal mining family with 10 children in Wilkinsburg, Pennsylvania on April 14, 1926. He is the youngest son and followed in the footsteps of five of his older brothers when he joined the Army during World War II at age 17. He served as an airborne radio operator and later a flight engineer throughout his service in the Pacific theater. After returning from World War II, Mr. Hall re-enlisted in the Army Air Corps and was awarded a direct commission into the new United States Air Force. Mr. Hall received his Bachelor's degree from the University of New Mexico and is a graduate of the Army Parachute School at Fort Benning, GA, the Advanced School at Fort Bragg, NC, and US Forest Service Smoke Jumper's School.

Throughout 36 years of military service and the rest of his civilian life, he became a pioneer in parachuting. Mr. Hall is a Master Parachutist with more than 1800 jumps. He started the parachuting program at the United States Air Force Academy which is the safest program of all similar service schools. In 1959 Mr. Hall and a partner organized the first professional parachuting firm in the world which led to many innovative advances in its field. His hit television show "Ripcord" has been noted as starting the modern conception of parachuting as a sport. He pioneered the "Buddy System" for free falling and the "4-line-cut" for emergencies in parachuting. Mr. Hall has been honored and cited numerous times. He has received such accolades as the AFA Medal of merit, the Citation of Honor for his MIA/POW program, the Exceptional Service Plaque, the AFA Presidential citation, the Colorado Man of the Year, Leo Stevens Parachute medal, and the Colorado Meritorious Service Medal. As a founding member of Colorado's Wright Brothers Memorial foundation, he was inducted into the Colorado Aviation Hall of Fame in 1985.

Madam Speaker, I am proud to honor Brigadier General James C. Hall. I thank him for his honorable service to our country. I now yield the remainder of my time.

Jon C. Porter
Member of Congress

Tribute to Jim Hall

BG R. Steven Ritchie (USAF, Ret.)

During service in Southeast Asia in the Vietnam war, Brig. Gen. Steve Ritchie became the only Air Force jet pilot ace by downing five MIG-21s. After completing 339 combat missions totaling more than 800 flying hours, Ritchie returned as one of the most highly decorated pilots of the war, having received the Air Force Cross, four Silver Stars, 10 Distinguished Flying Crosses and 25 Air Medals.

Steven Ritchie

I have spent a major portion of my life either flying a high performance military jet fighter or sitting in a ready room reading about how to get out of one of these aircraft in case of an emergency. During this time I had never given much thought to the "experts" who write these briefs and manuals until I met "the best of the best" of them at an Air Force reception.

The name, Jim Hall, matched with the master parachutist's badge on the blue Air Force uniform, clicked in my mind that this was the man, a pioneer in the escape field, whose name and picture I had seen on many, many parachuting safety articles.

Over a career that spanned 36 years, Jim was at the forefront of the "experts" who wrote about and demonstrated how to survive an emergency bailout. From his invention and perfecting of the "Buddy System" of free fall parachute training that teaches aircrews and astronauts to successfully freefall from high altitudes to his assistance in designing, jumping and live testing of American's first zero-zero ejection seat, Jim Hall has helped the United States lead the way in emergency parachuting.

He has been awarded the parachuting industry's highest award, the Leo Stevens Medal, has been inducted into the Colorado Aviation Hall of Fame, retired as a Brigadier General in the Colorado Air National Guard and was honored with the Air Force's Legion of Merit.

I am certain you will enjoy this exciting book about Jim's early parachuting experiences before he devoted his energies to helping save the lives of our aircrews.

Foreword

Bill Owens
Governor of Colorado, 1999–2007

Jim Hall has been my friend, mentor and hero for more than 30 years—and from the first time I met him I knew I was in the presence of an American patriot, the "Greatest Generation" personified.

Without Jim Hall, I would not have been Governor of Colorado; and without Jim Hall and heroes like him, our country would not be the shining beacon of hope and liberty it remains today.

I first met Jim in the 1970's shortly after I moved to Colorado. I was a young businessman and father wanting to participate in the public policy debate.

He was a Colonel in the Colorado Air National Guard; his wife—Georgann—was a Republican activist. It was through Georgann that Jim and I soon became the best of friends.

Since Jim was in the military, he was limited from working in politics, but—from the sidelines—he was a constant source of advice and counsel as I moved up the ladder in state government. And later, after his retirement as a General in the Colorado Air Guard, Jim's assistance was both much needed and dramatically effective, as I moved from State Representative to State Senator to Treasurer and, finally, to Governor.

I could not have done this without Jim and Georgann by my side. They advised me on issues, strategy, personalities and policies, all the while doing the tough work of organizing, building and cajoling through hundreds of meetings, conventions, assemblies and caucuses.

What Jim, as a close personal advisor, gave to me *most* however, was a maturity and common sense, which he had in deep reservoir, filled as it was by a lifetime of experiences and drama often requiring great courage.

It was during my long-shot, 1998 race for Colorado Governor that the idea of this book emerged. Jim helped me during the early days of that campaign not only as a friend and mentor, but also as my volunteer driver, helping me get to Colorado's 63 counties, across its mountain passes and lonely plains. He would drive while I would work next to him, preparing speeches, reading research and making calls to the next town on our itinerary.

Often, after the last event of the day, as we'd be heading back to our homes in Aurora, Colorado, I would ask Jim about his amazing life—sometimes about B-29's over Japan, or training U-2 pilots to eject, or Chuck Yeager or his experiences with Che and Castro—his time in Hollywood—the list and stories would go on and on.

Jim would never tell these stories unprompted, but would reminisce upon request as the time and the miles passed by.

I then suggested—way back in 1998—that Jim write a book—a memoir—outlining his life through the stories which tie together so much of America's history of these last 60 years.

And even after my upset victory in 1998, I kept encouraging him to write his book. He'd drop by my office in the Capitol, or stop by the Executive Residence and the first thing I'd ask him was . . . "How's the book coming?"

In 2006, he contracted MRSA, a potentially fatal "staph" infection while in the hospital for an operation to repair some of the injuries incurred during his early parachuting days in Mexico. Jim underwent years-long treatment with a broad-spectrum antibiotic, suffering severe weight loss and amputations and spending three years in nursing homes including, at the last, a Veteran's home, when eventually his doctors gave up on him, expecting him to die.

Jim survived—he was not ready to die—and he finally decided to write what I had first suggested to him over a decade ago while we drove together through Colorado's night—a book on his life filled with amazing, dramatic experiences . . . as a WWII airman, as a mining engineer in Mexico and as a pioneer working with the military in developing new techniques in the science of parachuting.

The result is *Parachuting for Gold in Old Mexico,* about his early years, his family, flying in the war and his life in Mexico. It is a wonderful account of a "life well-lived," of how a poor boy born in the hardscrabble hills of rural Pennsylvania went on to accomplish so much, all the while living a life that would seem to be fictional— except it is all true. I hope it will be the first installment of the full story of his amazing life and career.

Today, Jim Hall is doing much better physically, thanks to modern medicine and his indomitable spirit and the love and support of his wife of 38 years, Georgann, and their two children, Jennifer and Eagle.

The United States is fortunate to have sons like Gen. Jim Hall to defend and protect it, and I am fortunate to have Jim as my friend.

Acknowledgments

The parachutist, or skydiver, lands smoothly to a sea of applause. As he glides through the crowd and signs autographs for thrill seeking admirers, he knows there are people behind the scenes without whose help, he could never get off the ground.

I would like to acknowledge the technical advice and wise counsel I received from three of my closest friends. Col. Jim Hagenson, USAF, for his teaching skills that brought me into the computer age; Trent Castor, a leader of the Patriot Guard Riders, who kept me focused on telling my story; and Rich Bristol, President of Bristol Botanics, who could and did fix any problem encountered when I would push the wrong button and lose my writing when I forgot to hit "save as."

To Howard White (D-29650), a fellow parachuting pioneer, for grasping my story and beginning the process it needed to be relevant to today's jumpers.

And last, to be sure I hit the correct drop zone with a perfect PLF, the top book production team in the business provided expert ground support to bring it to publication. Book Shepherd Judith Briles came to the rescue and assembled the team that allowed for the perfect landing. John Maling spent countless hours making sure that dates matched, my stories flowed and the reader could jump in with relish; Ronnie Moore designed the interior to allow the reader's eye to appreciate the ruggedness of the terrain and transition from adventure to adventure with ease; Mike Daniels and the team at Sheridan Books for their attention to detail that only a printer sees; and Robin Zgurski captured my parachuting pal Ace and created a cover that is me, my rugged life and parachuting.

1
Welcome
to Mexico

It was a bright sunny June morning in 1956 when I pulled my Jeep off the main highway and stopped in front of the military checkpoint about 50 miles west of Chihuahua City, Mexico. A tall, well-dressed, young Mexican soldier stepped from the guard shack with his polished M-1 rifle held at high port.

"Your papers, señor," he said.

This was something new. A Mexican military checkpoint where you were not going to be asked for a bribe even before you were identified. I handed the guard my letter of introduction with Gen. Rodriguez's signature scrawled at the bottom of the page and with the general's official seal imprinted over it. The soldier took the paper, looked at it closely and said, "I'll have to show this to my sergeant," as he turned and re-entered the guard shack.

In Mexico, the country outside the cities is controlled by military, or paramilitary, forces. They are the law. In order to manage their areas, military checkpoints are established to determine what is happening and this is reported back to the regional commander.

The commander is usually a two-star general. He can either be a veteran of the last revolution or a political appointee. Commanders usually have the last say on who gets permits to cut down the forests, mine the hills, and establish businesses in their regions, and they have authority over their area of responsibility. The officers and soldiers under their command are quick to act if they think there is anything that is going to happen that will make their boss look bad, as their boss has a lot of power over what can happen to them if they screw up.

Each checkpoint is manned day and night by two soldiers and a sergeant. Their word is the law. When they shout, "Stop and be recognized," they really mean it. Their tempers are short and your hearing had better be good, as they don't yell twice before they shoot. These soldiers are conscripts, and most of them are mad at the world.

In Mexico at that time, every male over the age of 18 was subject to the draft. When your name came up, you appeared before a board which would determine if you had to serve in the army and, usually, where. As your paperwork wound its way through the system, a gift of a couple of hundred dollars, presented in the right place and at the right time, could cause the paperwork to disappear. So the young men manning these checkpoints were the poor and the less intelligent of the Mexican citizens.

But most of them were smart enough to realize that there are worse places to serve in the Mexican army than these checkpoints—such as the jungles of Yucatan—so they err on the side of keeping people out of areas where they shouldn't be. Occasionally they get chewed out for overreacting, but that is better than letting someone slip by and, as a result, getting shipped off to the boondocks. Now and then an American tourist, or an American engineer, gets shot, but that can be covered up.

As I waited anxiously for permission to proceed, the door to the guard shack flew open and a bleary-eyed, unkempt, obviously drunk guy in a rumpled brown, uniform lurched out of the shack and threw my identification papers in my face. He staggered and fell against my Jeep to regain his balance and puked on the hood. His sweaty face was contorted with an unknown hate, and he gasped for air.

"I should kill you, you gringo son of a bitch. You think you can make me a fool with fake papers signed by my general," he screamed. He stuck his head inside the Jeep and as I turned my head to avoid his stinking breath, I noticed a very big .45 automatic pistol hanging loosely from a low-slung holster on his right hip. His bloodshot eyes locked on to mine and I felt my skin crawl.

"Get your ass out of here pronto"—he spit the words out—"or I will blow your damned head off."

Wow! This guy was sure angry. I was not used to being talked to in this manner and I was slow to react. As I hesitated, I saw the sergeant's hand creep towards his pistol. If he touched the butt of that .45, a chain of events would kick in that would change my life forever.

I was completely unprepared for this! This morning, before we left the hotel, Fr. Pat, a Catholic priest who was visiting with me in Chihuahua City, had insisted that I take his small .22 caliber pistol, his Saturday night special, he laughed. "You'll need some protection if you run into any bears," he laughed again.

I jammed the pistol into the right side pocket of my jacket and forgot about it. A lot of good this thing is going to do me, I thought—until now. Talk about being outgunned—my .22 caliber pistol against a .45 automatic and an M-1 rifle that I now noticed was pointed at my head. I could probably beat the drunken sergeant to the draw and as close as I was, I couldn't miss putting a couple of rounds into his gut, but the soldier with the rifle—I was a dead duck.

Time stood still. I'm sure I stopped breathing. The sergeant's right arm quivered and suddenly shot forward as he reached to catch the top of the Jeep's roof to check his fall. He missed and fell flat on his face in the dirt. I eased the gearshift into low and very slowly began to turn around and move toward the highway, all the while with my eyes focused on the soldier with the rifle. Inch by inch we got closer to the highway. My neck muscles were stretched beyond their limits. In my mind I could hear the crack of the rifle and feel the .30-30 slug tearing into my back.

But, wait. Not yet!

Our front wheels were on the pavement. I slammed the gear shift into second and jammed the accelerator all the way down. We burned rubber for about 50 feet and the Jeep leapt forward. I began to breathe again, and I was laughing like a fool. Whew! Damn, that was close. We stopped at La Mesa, the little village about two miles south of the checkpoint, had the puke washed off the hood, and were on our way back to Chihuahua City.

The young Mexican sitting next to me had not moved or spoken a word during the entire episode. When I attempted to talk to him, he stared straight ahead. He was paralyzed with fear, and I had to punch him on the shoulder to get his attention. This guy isn't going to be much help if we ever get in a jam, I thought.

"We will get new permits and try again tomorrow," I reassured Julio.

"Please, Jefe, let's go back to Deming," he pleaded.

Surprised, I said, "No can do, Julio. We came to Mexico to find the gold, and you are the only one who can lead us to it. You will be a rich man if we find it. No more working in the fields, many muchachas, a fine car."

I was beginning to unwind and I guess I was trying to build up his enthusiasm as well as mine, as it was starting to sink in that we had almost been shot and killed—and for what? What series of events had placed me in the foothills of the Sierra Madres in the State of Chihuahua, Mexico on June 4th, 1956?

2
Pre-1956 ...
My Life
Before Mexico

F or starters, my name is James Carl Hall—"Jim"—and I was born in the small town of Muckelrat in the coal fields of Western Pennsylvania at the start of the great depression in 1926. I was the seventh son of seven boys and three girls.

My dad was a coal miner and a union organizer for John L. Lewis, the big boss of the United Mine Workers. He started working underground when he was twelve years old and was one tough guy. All he knew was work and sleep and getting drunk on the weekends. He was up at four o'clock in the morning, worked around the house, then walked three miles to his coal mine or five miles if he was working at the steel mill, then came home, worked in the garden, and went to bed. As far as I know, he never owned a suit or a tie or a dress shirt. We never had a one-on-one conversation. He talked, or commanded, and I listened.

During the election cycles, he worked for the Democratic Party. As a ten-year-old kid, I accompanied him as he went from mining town to mining town to buy votes in exchange for a half pint of bootleg whiskey. I carried the whiskey in pockets my mom sewed in a long overcoat to keep the booze out of sight of the union members, as they would try to roll the old man after he had drunk too many of the bottles reserved for the undecided voters.

My mother was a gracious and gentle southern lady who worked 24 hours a day raising ten kids during very difficult times. She was the kindest and most generous person I have ever known, and I would do almost anything for her. My dad had married far above his station in life and how he and my mom ever got together is a mystery to me.

I attended school off and on while working, along with my brothers, in a bootleg coal mine operated by my old man. The coal we stole provided my family, and several others who were too poor to buy it, with fuel to keep us warm during the cold Pennsylvania winters.

I also worked in a garage, which gave me excellent experience with engines and all things mechanical. In 1943, at age 17 and at the height of World War II, I joined the Army Air Corps to be a fighter pilot. At basic training in Biloxi, Mississippi, my ego received a severe shock when the sergeant who was interviewing me for my assignment after basic laughed when I told him the recruiter who had signed me up said that I could go to pilot training.

"Kid, the Army already has a long line of grown men who want to go to pilot training, and you have quite a bit of growing up to do before you can join that group," he said. "How about being a gunner, a radio operator or, maybe a flight engineer?" I left that room feeling that perhaps the Army really didn't think that I was as special as the recruiter had led me to believe.

After basic training, the new recruits were permitted to choose a career field, and if they passed the qualification tests and the Air Force thought it would be in the best interests of the service, they were sent to a technical school to sharpen their skills. I chose the career field of flight engineer and passed the qualification tests with flying colors, chiefly because of my work in automobile garages plus the hours and hours I spent fixing the old junkheaps I drove to school.

The Air Force thought that it was in the best interests of the service that I go to flight engineer school, so they sent me to their best.

One day, after a couple of months of training, I was directed to go to the first sergeant's office for an interview. I was informed that it was no longer in the best interests of the service that I remain in flight engineer school, although I was doing well, and that now it was in the best interests of the service that I be sent to radio operator's school. In radio operator's school, the promise was made that if you graduated in the top ten percent of your class, you could choose the type of airplane you would work on and where you would serve. I graduated first in my class and I chose the B-17, and I said that I wanted to serve in the European Theater of War.

The Air Force decided that it was in the best interests of the service that I serve on the new B-29 and that I go to the Pacific Theater of War. So it was off for training in the brand new B-29s at a place called Pyote Army Air Force Base out in the wastelands of western Texas. I was matched up with ten other guys, and we became a top-notch bomber crew. After intensive training in the art of delivering ten tons of high explosives to a target located fifteen hundred miles from our base and then returning to our base, we picked up a brand new B-29 from Fremont, Nebraska, and headed to the Pacific Theater of Operations for the good of the service. The place from which we delivered the high explosives was called Tinian Island and the place to which we delivered the high explosives was called the Empire of Japan.

The Air Force had decided that the job we were doing was in the best interests of the service and the job we were doing resulted in the defeat of Japan and the end of World War II, and we were sent back to the United States. I liked what I was doing in the Air Force and, with the encouragement of recruiters, I reenlisted to serve one more year in the United States Army.

Again, the Army asked me what I would like to do and where I would like to do it. I told them I would like to fly on a B-17 aircrew, and I would like to do this in the European Theater. The first sergeant informed me that the Army decided it was in the best interests of the service that I fly on B-29 and C-47 aircrews and I do it in the Pacific Theater. I asked the first sergeant, "What about my best interests?" He replied, "Sarge, the service's best interests are your best interests. Shove off."

The next year turned out to be a pretty good deal. Everybody was pushing to get home, so there were never enough flight engineers or radio operators to man the airplanes, and I got to fly as much as I wanted. I racked up hundreds of hours of experience flying all over the Pacific Theater to places I had read about and to places I had never heard of, and I learned a lot about places and people that would prove invaluable later in life.

One of the missions that my crew was assigned was making the monthly "Rum Run" to the Philippines, where we would pick up a C-47 load of booze for the officer's clubs on the island of Guam. During this time I established a friendship with a young captain who was on the general's staff and was in charge of the liaison airplanes assigned to the Wing Headquarters. These aircraft were small, single-engine prop jobs that were used to deliver paperwork throughout the islands and also to train new pilots. I had always wanted to be a pilot and I saw a way to accomplish my dream with my friendship with the captain. I traded a case of Scotch whisky for flying lessons and flying time in one of the headquarters L-5 aircraft. By the time I left the islands, I had racked up over a hundred hours of stick and rudder time, some of it in tough weather conditions.

When I returned to the States, I was asked to reenlist in the new Air Force Reserve. I had been offered a direct commission from staff sergeant to second lieutenant during the war, but I had turned it down. The step up from the enlisted ranks to that of an officer was one I did not want to take at that time.

Lt. Jim Hall

Things were a lot different now. The service had made me grow up and I saw that if you worked hard, you could rise above your lowly beginnings. If the new Air Force would honor the offer they made me during the war, I would reenlist. The new Air Force decided it was in the best interests of the service that I become a second lieutenant, so I did.

When I returned to Pennsylvania in 1947 after my second tour in the Pacific, I found I was the last of the servicemen to return to the old home town. It seemed as if everybody was married and having children and settling down into the same rut they were in before they went off to war. My six older brothers and two remaining sisters were all married and having kids, left and right. My oldest sister, Mary, died when she was three years old. My parents couldn't afford to have a doctor come to our rural home to treat her during the flu epidemic in the early twenties.

I loved my mother with all my heart and thought of her as a saint for living through hell being married to an alcoholic and raising ten kids. She was an oldschool Catholic mom. "A man should be married and raising kids or in the priesthood," and that was her firm and loudly-stated opinion.

From the moment I tossed my duffle bag down on the floor of what used to be a storeroom—my old room was now occupied by one of my married brothers and his pregnant wife—mom's main objective in life was to get me either married or shipped off to the seminary. The girl next door was her closest and first target. But even two tours in the south Pacific without seeing many females couldn't convince me that Betty was the mate for me. She was short and overweight, and I could see that it was only going to get worse. (Three years later, when I came home on a visit, I saw that those years of Polish cooking had proven me right.)

When I told mom that this match was not going to work, she shifted her efforts to the pool of remaining eligible females. This was a small town, and that pool was extremely limited and the pickings were poor, and it looked like mom was going to have a hard time finding me a mate.

Some form of possible relief came when a friend of one of my brothers announced that he had passed all the tests to qualify for a new program that the Catholic church was putting into place. A seminary in the northern part of the state was offering a program that would enable a young man to sign up for a nine-month, or shorter, trial to see if the priesthood was for him. You would take all the same courses and live the same life as a regular seminarian, but you could quit at any time if you saw that you didn't like it, no questions asked. And you could use the time as credit toward college.

Ever since my discharge from the Army, I had been trying to get into college, but I did not have a high school diploma, and I saw that this program might be a way around this problem. I took the tests, passed, and in due course found myself in a cell—that's what they called it, and rightly so—in a small seminary in the little town of North East, Pennsylvania.

From day one, it was worse than Army basic training. The physical part was OK, but the mental chicken crap was perfected

by guys whose intelligence and cunning were several steps above
the backwoods D.I.s we had in basic training. We were up at
0400 and scrubbed floors or anything else that needed to be
scrubbed until 0600, then religious service until 0700, then wait
on tables and other kitchen chores until 0900. It was a welcome
relief to have studies from 0900 until 1600 and then kitchen
duties and study until lights out at 2200.

During the war, I had contracted a painful disease called "jungle
rot" while I was serving in the South Pacific. It caused running sores
on the legs and feet and the only known cure for it at the time was
to sit under an ultraviolet lamp for several hours a day. That
was out of the question under these monastic conditions, so whenever I could during the day, I would sneak away from my chores or
studies and sit in the sun and let the sun dry up the sores. It was
not long until the novice master, a little weasel of a 4-F, and I were
on a collision course. Not only did he put a stop to my visits outside,
he piled on extra duty after lights-out. I began to spend more time
figuring out how I could put his lights out than I did in studying the
Bible. This routine got old real quick, but I needed time to receive
replies to the letters I was sending to colleges I thought might admit
a guy without a high school diploma—preferably a college far away
from Pennsylvania.

I had to get away from mom, but I had to have a good, solid
reason. I got excited when I received a letter that said I was accepted by the University of Melbourne in Australia, but my
hopes were dashed when I learned that since that school was
south of the equator, their school year didn't start until next year.

Finally, I got a letter from the admissions director of the University of New Mexico, and it said that their school year started
next month and I was accepted. The University needed the
money the GI Bill would bring and they would worry about the
lack of a high school diploma later.

Now I had to find a reason, other than this was a dead-end
position, to resign from this place. A reason came the very next
morning when our seminary was hosting a group of priests and
a bishop from a nearby diocese. We novices, or people on pro-
bation, were serving breakfast to the group, and we were not
permitted to eat what was left over until after the guests had
departed. I was serving the bacon, and I really liked bacon, and

the last person to be served was the bishop. The four of us servers were looking forward to a hearty breakfast as nothing was left for us to eat after last night's meal, and we went to bed with empty stomachs. I was following the novice who was serving the fried eggs—it looked like there were four or five left—and I gulped when I saw the bishop exchange his plate with the plate the server was carrying and wave him on. Well, there was enough bacon left on my platter to give each of the novices four pieces each, and that was enough to make my mouth water.

When I presented the platter to the bishop, I damn near dropped the dish when he scraped the entire mess of bacon on to his already full plate. I stopped in my tracks and looked at him. He looked at me and said, "Yes?" When it sunk in to my hungry brain what had just happened, I uttered an un-Christian like epithet, threw the platter to the floor and stomped out to the kitchen and out the door. I walked to my cell, picked up my overnight bag and was outside the gate of the seminary waiting for a bus when the novice master ran up, breathing hard, and said, "We must learn obedience. That test was part of our vow of poverty, chastity and obedience, and you have failed."

As I boarded the bus, I replied, "I never believed in the first two and I'm damn glad I flunked the third and, you had better get the hell out of my way or I will kill you."

So ended my brief encounter with the life of the religious. My mom was not happy when I walked into our house and dropped my overnight bag on the floor of the store room. My brother and his wife and new baby were still living in my room. Living accommodations remained tight for returning GIs, and my brother was not very pleased that he could not afford his own home. I could see that this was going to be a sore subject and this gave me an added incentive to get out of town as soon as possible. I immediately confirmed that I was accepted by the University but was told that classes didn't start for three more weeks. That meant that I still had to dodge mom's last-ditch efforts to get me married off to one of the locals, so I took a night job as a laborer on the Union Railroad in East Pittsburgh and stayed out of sight until it was time to leave for New Mexico.

Before I left my hometown for good, I did get close to the marriage scene, but as a spectator. My best friend since childhood,

Bud Plack, had just returned from service as a Marine in the South Pacific. I had last seen him on the island of Saipan about two years ago and over a couple of beers we had discussed how we were never going to give up our freedom and get married. Well, old Bud had found the girl of his dreams and had changed his mind and mom said, "See every one is doing it. Why don't you stay home and start a family?" I didn't take her advice, and I was glad that I managed to escape what would have probably been a very mundane life.

I spent the next four years at the University of New Mexico and my World War II service earned me a double degree in engineering and geology under the GI Bill. The years passed quickly and although there were lots of dull periods, I had more than enough activities to keep me busy. I played some sports, but they were too regulated to excite my interest, unlike the sandlot brawls back in Pennsylvania. I was accepted into the Sigma Chi Fraternity and found out that rich guys, most of them, can be just as nice as poor guys. I did a lot of growing up and growing out of the shell of being a poor boy from a little coal mining town.

During my first year at the university, I was introduced to parachuting by a former paratrooper who was my roommate at the student housing project we were both assigned to when we arrived in Albuquerque. He taught me to parachute, and we made very good money making exhibition parachute jumps at county fairs, rodeos, open houses and sporting events in New Mexico and Texas during my years at the university. I spent a lot of my time with the Air Force Reserve unit headquartered at Kirtland Air Force Base in Albuquerque.

The unit was commanded by a lieutenant colonel, but the guy who controlled the day-to-day operations was a tough old master sergeant named Mitch O'Brian.

Sgt. O'Brian had been a squad leader and later a platoon sergeant with the 82nd Airborne Division and had the distinction of having made all four of the combat jumps the 505th Parachute Infantry Regiment participated in during World War II—the low-level jump in Sicily, the jump at Salerno, Italy which culminated in the bloody battle of Arnone, the D-Day jump at Normandy and the capture of Ste. Mère-Église in France, where he was awarded the Silver Star, and the Operation Market Garden jump in Holland where he received the Distinguished Service Cross for gallantry while capturing the Nijmegen bridge from the elite German SS troops. He also had five Purple Hearts to go with his other medals.

This old soldier had done it all. He was out of his element assigned to "babysitting" a bunch of young officers. He never missed a chance to apply for any first sergeant's job that became open in a combat Airborne unit. I thought I had experienced some close calls while flying combat missions over Japan, but I was not in the same ballpark as this trooper. When we started telling "war stories" at beer call, I kept my mouth shut, as should have the rest of the group, when Sgt. O'Brian, after several rounds of Coors beer, began to tell of the hand-to-hand battles he had fought with the best of the Nazi storm troopers.

Our reserve unit was made up of about 150 lieutenants and captains from the southwestern part of the United States, most of whom had avoided overseas duty during World War II by virtue of being in ROTC or other education-related programs. The old sarge disliked them for their lack of guts, just as he disliked any other serviceman who avoided combat. So we got along just great. We had a special bond because of my parachuting activities, and he treated me as the little brother he never had.

These were exciting times. All reserve officers had to spend at least two weeks every year, usually more, on active duty attending some sort of technical school, and Sgt. O'Brian was in charge of these quotas. He would show me the list and let me pick out the schools I would like to attend and when I would like to attend them. I, of course, chose the special schools the Airborne forces were establishing for counter-insurgency operations. This enabled me to keep up with anything new in the parachuting world in the United States.

This fit in perfectly with Sgt. O'Brian's plans to be aware of any new advancements and developments in the parachuting field. He put me in for secret military and government clearances, appointed me as the unit's intelligence officer, and I was off to school. These technical schools and the different types of parachute jumping I was exposed to were a real eye-opener, and I quickly discovered that the day-to-day life of an ambitious officer was much different from that of an enlisted man. As an

officer, even a lowly second lieutenant with a secret security
clearance and several glowing letters of recommendation from
Sgt. O'Brian to old combat buddies now in key leadership positions in the paratroopers, I had access to classified reports from
military attaches in embassy offices in France and Russia, as well
as Yugoslavia and Czechoslovakia, who were the world-wide
leaders in innovations in parachuting.

I eagerly read these reports from front to back, and I learned that
a new sport called skydiving was becoming popular in Europe, and
France and Russia were leading the way in developing procedures
to control the parachutist's body in long delayed freefalls. This was
of special interest to me, as I had experienced problems with my
body sometimes rotating rapidly after I had reached what I called
"the wall," or the airspeed that I felt was where I was falling as fast
as I was going to fall and the air became "heavy." Sometimes I
would start spinning one way and when I reached in to pull my
ripcord, I would start to spin in the other direction.

On several occasions I felt I was going to black out and I had
to pull the ripcord before I wanted to and screwed up what
would have been a good jump and missed my target. Later, whenever I had a chance to try some of these freefall procedures, I
would experiment—sometimes they worked and sometimes they
didn't. But I did discover that the more I practiced, the easier
it became to obtain a face-to-earth position when doing a long
delayed freefall.

My attendance at these schools, and an occasional ankle or leg
injury, caused me to miss some classes and my grades to drop
somewhat, but my association and training with the elite paratroopers of the 82nd and the 101st Airborne Divisions gave me
the experience and credibility to earn a very good living making
exhibition parachute jumps while attending college, and I still
graduated with my class in 1952.

At school's end I didn't even stop to pick up that piece of paper
that said I was an engineer before I headed north for Butte,
Montana, to take a job as a junior mining engineer for Anaconda
Mining Company—a plum job for a kid just out of college.

When I was mustered out of the Army, I used part of my pay
to buy a big old used 1941 dark green Cadillac. It was a sturdy,
well-built machine. Four doors and a V-12 engine. Lots of room

and power—and I spent many a night sacked out in the rear seat, my home away from home. I, and my friends, affectionately called the beast the "Green Hornet."

I had stored my civilized possessions, good clothes, books, papers and the like—also my parachutes and associated equipment—in the basement of my landlady's house, so all I had to do was toss my traveling gear in the "Hornet" and take off. After driving all night, I rolled into Butte about 7:30 the next morning and the place was jumping. The miners from the night shift were crowding the streets, some already well on their way to getting drunk. It was like a scene from an old 1880s western. I'm going to like this place, I thought.

I scored a room at the local "Y," ate breakfast, and checked in at the Anaconda headquarters. It was a busy place. I was told to report at the mine shaft at 6:45 the next morning. I met the engineer I was supposed to be working with at the appointed time. He was a short, pudgy guy, not too much older than I was. He looked like a nerd, with new boots, pressed pants and a clean shirt. He glanced at his watch and said, "You're late. Grab that surveying transit, and let's get going."

We crowded into a packed elevator, the gate clanged shut, and we dropped like a rock. Five thousand feet later, we jerked to a stop.

This was a first for me, a mile underground. I didn't know if I was claustrophobic or not, but I sure was impressed. It was pitch black—the only light was that from the head lamps on the miners' hard hats. The heat was suffocating and the air was heavy with the smell of sulfur and sweat. There was a mad rush to get off the elevator, and the equipment I was carrying got tangled with some of the bodies.

After much cursing and shoving, I finally broke out of the pack. The engineer was waiting for me, clipboard in hand and tapping his foot. "Hurry, hurry, we don't have all day. There is work to be done." The shift hadn't even begun and this clown was about to have this transit shoved up his rear end. I could see that darkness was going to be my friend.

The rest of the day was about as exciting as watching a checkers game—basic surveying that I had mastered my first week in Engineering 101 and other routine crap. In fact this stuff was so routine that in college I spent most of the outdoors classes watching, through the instrument, the sorority girls sun bathing. The only saving grace is that I did have a chance to talk to miners as they did their jobs and I learned a lot about the life underground.

After three days of this, I was sure that this was not what I wanted to do the rest of my life. The next morning I stopped the shift boss and told him that I came here to get some experience and any dolt could do what I was doing. He suggested that I partner up with one of the old miners and get into the more dangerous and interesting parts of mining.

Great idea, but I didn't know any of the old guys, with the exception of a Polish guy I had met on my first day on the job. The shift had ended, and there was a rush for the elevator. This old fellow had stumbled and was in danger of being run over. I grabbed him by the collar and dragged him into the elevator and pushed him into a corner. He had trouble standing up. I thought, "The poor guy, he is working too hard." Then I smelled his breath. He was dead drunk. He said to me, "Boy, get me my lunch bucket." I shoved aside a couple of bodies and picked up his bucket. The damn thing weighed about 20 pounds. He grabbed it and held it tight.

"What the hell ya got there?" I asked. "Dynamite?"

His face twisted into a sly grin. "Yep," he said.

Damn! This drunk had enough explosives in his lunch bucket to blow himself and the other forty miners in this elevator, me included, to hell and back. My first reaction was to back away from him as far as I could, in this case, only about a foot or so. That wasn't going to work. I reached out and hugged him, and the lunch bucket, as tight as I could. Don't drop it! Please don't drop it, I screamed to myself! The old miner gave me a funny look. "What's the matter, boy? It won't go off. I have the blasting caps in my pocket. At least, most of them are in my pocket."

The ride to the surface seemed to take a long, long time. When we stopped and everybody got off, I was still holding on to the old man.

"Let me go, boy," he said. "Come, let me buy you a drink."

I turned down his offer, but after my talk with the shift boss, this guy seemed like a good place to start looking for a partner. The next morning I waited for the old miner to show up and got on the same elevator with him. I said I would take him up on the offer to buy a drink after work. He said, OK; meet him at the New Moxom Café this afternoon.

We met and I explained to him, as best I could, as he was half drunk and spoke very limited English, what I would like to do. After about six beers, my limit, we finally came up with a rough idea of what we would do. A handshake, and we were partners. He was the brains, I was the brawn. Split the profit 50-50.

At the beginning of the shift, before he started drinking, we would go to our work location, he would tell me what we wanted to accomplish and how to do it. We would set up the drilling machine, he would retreat to the relative safety of a bend of the drift, and I would start to work. From time to time he would check on how I was doing. We would make a few corrections, he would go back to drinking, and I would go back to drilling.

About an hour before quitting time, the dynamite cart would roll by and my partner (his name was Stanislaw Vodeak) would wake up, take the number of sticks of explosives he thought we would need to blast the correct number of tons of copper/silver/lead ore from the ceiling for this shift, plus a number of sticks of dynamite he would need to work his bootleg mine this weekend, and send the cart down the line. The powder monkey (the boy who was responsible for the explosives) took no note of the amount of explosives we off-loaded and trudged off into the darkness.

Stan crimped the caps on the fuse, punched a hole in the sticks of dynamite, inserted the combination, and handed the finished product to me. I placed the dynamite in the drill hole and, using a long wooden pole, rammed it home. The tighter you can pack the dynamite, the better results you get when it explodes. This I understood, but it always gave me a thrill when I hammered this high explosive stuff into the hole. What if? I'd close my eyes and wouldn't start breathing regularly until we had backed off and lit the fuses.

This setup worked well for the next three months. I learned a lot about the basics of mining—stuff you could never encounter in the textbooks—and practical geology my teachers never heard of. I also made very good wages. Old Stan and I made an excellent team. We could really move the ore and make the money.

One cold October morning, Stan did not show up at the mine shaft. Later that day, the timekeeper said that they had found him over the weekend inside the entrance to his mine. He was dead. Face down with a shovel in his right hand and his lunch bucket tucked under his left arm. He had worked his last shift.

3
Jump into the Kern River

The Montana winter was getting a hold on the land, and I was getting restless. I had talked to hundreds of miners who had worked all over the world while downing hundreds of gallons of beer. That was the social life of Butte, Montana. It was time to move on.

I packed my gear into the old Green Hornet and headed south to Pioche, Nevada. I landed a job at a silver/lead mine about ten miles out of town in an area that had once held promise of a big strike. It became apparent after a few weeks that this property wasn't going anywhere—also, the weather wasn't much better than Montana—so I moved on.

Next stop was a placer gold project in Kern County, California. I had never worked placer before, so I welcomed the experience. Also, the weather was more to my liking; it was great to feel the warm sun on my face again. I learned the ins and outs of gold panning—it hasn't changed much since the days of the fortyniners—how to find the most likely places for gold deposits in stream beds, the thrill of seeing the dull gleam of real gold appearing from a pan of dirt, mud, sand and clear, cold mountain water.

One day, while working a tributary of the Kern River, I received a letter from an old friend, a scuba diver, who had invented a mechanical gold pan that was small enough to be packed in, or better yet, air-dropped into remote areas of the high Sierras. This would enable even a novice gold panner to work several tons of sand and gravel per day. A magazine would do a story on the operation if he could get someone to drop the equipment, then jump in and make the machine work as advertised. That sounded like a fit, so I said, "I'll do it." Things were getting dull and I needed some excitement.

When I left college for work in Montana, I had stored my parachute gear in the basement of my landlady's house for safekeeping. I wired her to ship me one of my parachutes in care of the Kern County Airport.

Somewhere along the line, somebody had slit open the parachute bag and replaced my custom-made rig with a ratty old World War II surplus parachute. Not a good situation, but we would have to make do, as the jump was to take place tomorrow and the camera crew had been on the trail for two days. I yanked the ripcord and popped the chute. I inspected the canopy closely, tightened the connector links and very carefully repacked the chute.

Next morning we took off from the Kern Airport in a rented Cessna 180 and climbed to altitude. We reached the drop zone— a double bend in the river—about an hour later and were able to make radio contact. After establishing the wind direction and speed we dropped the cargo from 300 feet. The drop was good and we climbed to jump altitude, three thousand feet AGL— above ground level. I added an extra thousand feet to play with in case I ran into any unexpected winds aloft.

The jump run was OK, but I was slow getting out of the door. I corrected for a less than perfect spot by maintaining my freefall a few seconds longer. Bad move. I was now at terminal velocity, faster than I wanted to be when the chute opened. I yanked the ripcord and braced myself for the opening shock. Not as bad as I had expected, I thought as I glanced upward to check my canopy. No wonder. I had blown about five panels and the damage was putting me in a slow turn to the right.

Damn the bastard that stole my parachute rig. The rag they replaced my canopy with could not withstand the maximum shock of my body slowing down from 125 miles per hour to 20 miles per hour in three seconds. Oh well, I was looking for some excitement and it looked like I was going to get some.

I tossed aside any idea of hitting my intended spot and kicked into Plan B. The name of the game was to get on the ground without getting too badly hurt. The ground was coming up fast and I was still in a turn. Feet together, knees bent, eyes on the horizon.

Jump into the Kern River

I hit in a rock pile and I felt my left ankle bend and my left knee hit hard. The wind started to drag me toward the river but a dead tree branch snagged the canopy and the jump was over without further damage.

Was it a successful parachute jump under adverse conditions? I guess so. I was still alive, but it was going to be uphill from here. I was going to have trouble walking in a very short while and my contributions to the mission were going to be less and less as time went on. The crew rushed up, untangled me from the parachute and started to unlace my jump boot. I stopped them and told them to leave the boot laced because if we took it off, we would never get it back on.

"Let's get set up and get the filming done as soon as possible, and fake as much as we can," I said. "Shoot the long shots and background and we'll get the closeups later and closer to home."

We did the filming in record time and were soon on the way down hill and out of the mountains.

I had a badly sprained left ankle and a bruised left knee, but nothing broken. I was able to walk with the aid of a homemade crutch and was relieved from carrying any equipment on the trip home. The two-day journey gave me ample time to reflect many times over on my handling of all phases of the operation.

In my mind, it was a wash. I took too many chances, but I learned from my mistakes. I'll have to be more careful and think things through. I was laid up for about a month. No big deal and it gave me time to catch up with my book reading, swimming, sun bathing and girl watching.

4
A Death
in the Family

O ne of the things I did to pass the time while my injuries
healed was to visit the more popular sites where an as-
sortment of wanderers, vagabonds, drifters, amateur gold
panners and just plain people who had nothing else to do, used a
variety of devices to slosh about the mud and sand they found along
the banks of the Kern River in search of the stray flecks of that
magic mineral, gold, that had been overlooked by the forty-niners.

One of the interesting characters I encountered was a rugged
Australian named Tony Hawkins. During World War II he served
with the British Commandos who fought against the "Desert Fox,"
the famous German general, Erwin Rommel, in North Africa.
Among the many tales he spun while we shared a few beers was
that of the legendary "Lost Dutchman" gold.

One night, after he had consumed more that his normal ration
of Coors, he boastfully showed me a "genuine" map that revealed
the location of the lost gold. He had purchased the wrinkled map
from one of the great grandsons of the Peralta brothers who had
discovered, and then lost, this incredibly rich deposit. Would I
like to help him find it?

Of course I would, so the next morning the old Green Hornet
was heading south on the road to the Superstition Mountains, the
place where the lost treasure was located. I did give the adventure
a second thought, as I was waiting for a check from my last job
in Nevada, but Tony assured me I could have my mail forwarded
to a trading post called Florence, Arizona, the place where we
would pick up food and water for the trek into the mountains.

We pulled into Florence the next morning and as we were paying for supplies and I was writing a check, the owner said, "Boy,
you are in luck. I just got a telegram for you that has been forwarded twice. It's from Pittsburgh. That's from back east, ain't
it? Pennsylvania?"

This was strange, and I had a bad feeling as I ripped open the
envelope. I always tried to tell one of my brothers where I was
and how to reach me, but this was the first time I had ever received a telegram from back home.

I was dumbfounded when I read the words. I really couldn't
believe what it said.

BROTHER HONUS DIED TODAY.
BURIAL FRIDAY MORNING.
COME HOME.
RAY.

Honus dead! It couldn't be. He was ... he was bigger than life.
My big brother. My very favorite brother. He was my idol. I
measured myself against Honus in everything I did. He taught
me everything I know. How to play baseball, football, how to box
and he would kick me around if I didn't do it right. He was there
for all my firsts. My first bloody nose. "Well, what the hell do
you expect when you try to catch a line drive with your face."
My first broken rib or ribs. "Whaddya you think is going to happen when you try to block a big guy like Fat Ass Leske without
first trying to trip him?" The first time I got stood up by my very
best girlfriend, Sweet Elaine. I had a case of puppy love, and I had
it real bad. I moped around the house. "Kid, girls are like buses.
Another one will be along in a couple of minutes."

This was the wise counsel of Brother Honus. He could also be
kind and gentle. "What the hell is the matter with you? Let that
black kid use your mitt! Do you want to see him break his hand?"

"Don't you dare shoot that rabbit? Can't you see he's already
hurt? Take him home to Sister Grace or Sister Pat. They will take
care of him."

Mom named him John Emory Hall, but he was known in our
circle of friends and enemies as Honus Hall, after the famous
hard-charging, no-holds barred, aggressive base stealer Honus
Wagner of the Pittsburgh Pirates. There was nothing Honus, the

kid, could not do on the baseball field. He was the first baseman of the Muckelrat Rats and he guarded that sack like a hungry dog guarded a juicy steak.

With Brother Fritz as our pitcher, the pair would entice a base runner to try to steal and then drop the hammer on him. When the guy tried to get back to the base, Honus slugged him with the baseball wrapped in his leather mitt. He used it as a black-jack. Many an unwary opponent was carried off the field and it was the cause of an occasional dust-up at first base.

On the other side of the coin, it would be a rough day for any second or third baseman who tried to tag out Honus after he had earned enough money to buy a genuine pair of baseball shoes with spikes. With his new shoes, freshly sharpened spikes gleaming in the sun, Honus would barrel down the base paths and take out any one who got in his way—sometimes including the umpire.

For him, the name of the game was winning. "What in the hell are we playing this game for, anyway?" "Ain't we keeping score"? "Attitude kid, you gotta have an attitude if you ever intend to amount to anything in this world." That was Brother Honus's attitude.

With football, it was the same deal. Honus, a born leader, was, of course, our quarterback. Football always was personal to him. If he had a beef with a lineman or a back on the opposing team, he would call a play on that side of the line. In the pile up that followed, if you heard a scream of pain or a lot of cursing, you knew that Honus was bending back someone's finger or he had an enemy by the balls.

When World War II came, most of the young men in our town went to war. Honus joined the outfit he said were the real fighting men—the United States Marine Corps. He was probably one of the few recruits almost sent home because they were too eager to fight. When they shook down the new guys at basic training at Parris Island Marine Base they found that Honus had brought with him a gun, a knife and a pair of brass knuckles. After fighting the drill instructors all the way through boot camp, he wound up in the First Marine Division, the first Marine unit to see action against the Japanese on the island of Guadalcanal in the South Pacific. I almost felt sorry for the Japs—but not quite.

On the "Canal" he was with a machine gun squad led by a famous Marine named Manila John Basilone, who won the Medal of Honor during the battle of Bloody Ridge. Honus said that Manila John deserved everything he got, except for the honor of being killed on Iwo Jima.

Honus also fought on Iwo with the Third Marine Division and, in a roundabout way, may have saved my life. The Marines captured the island at a great loss of life but it gave the B-29 bombers a place to land if they were shot up on a bombing mission over Japan. If you didn't land on Iwo Jima then you had to land in the ocean, and that was usually fatal. My bomber had to land on Iwo on five different missions and my chances of surviving five water landings were not very good.

Honus ended the war fighting against our so-called allies, the Russians, in North China and Manchuria while trying to prevent them from looting the Japanese factories and sending the machinery back to Russia.

My last memories of Honus were of one night after we had both returned from the war. We were double-dating twin sisters from our town and were parked in the local lover's lane. I was driving—I lost the coin toss—and Honus was in the back seat with his girl. The windows were steamed up and the breathing was heavy. Honus said, "Quiet, I hear something."

The Marines had taught him some good skills. Suddenly, the rear door was yanked open and a large guy lunged into the car and grabbed Honus by the coat. The two of them tumbled out and landed in a heap by the side of the car. The guy had a knife and I could see it gleam in the moonlight as he raised it above his head. A shot rang out and blood spurted from the guy's face.

Honus had a .32 caliber pistol in his jacket pocket. ("Kid, if you ever find yourself in a fair fight, you haven't done your homework.") Thank you, Honus, for those words of wisdom and thank you for living by them. The knife went flying and the guy grabbed his face and fell to his knees. Honus landed a solid kick square in the middle of his head. The guy rolled over and Honus proceeded to stomp the guy into the ground. All was quiet except for the screaming of the girls and the crunching of the guy's face bones. (Honus had picked up the habit of wearing cowboy boots when he was in the Civilian Conservation Corps. in New Mexico and now they came in handy.) There was another guy with the first guy but he had split when the gun went off.

The first guy was curled up in a ball, holding his head and crying like a baby. Honus said, "Let's get the hell out of here," and we did. We looked in the papers the next morning, and for a week or so after, but there was no mention of any problem in lover's lane.

I sat down on a bench with a thud. These were some of the memories of Honus, Brother Honus. How can you be replaced? Tony came over and placed his hand on my shoulder.

"What now," he said.

"I'm going home," I replied.

Engine Fire On DC-6

Today is Thursday. Honus is to be buried on Friday morning. Less than 24 hours to get back to Pennsylvania. Can't drive it, so flying is the only way to go. Tucson, Phoenix? Connections no good. How about El Paso? Maybe I can catch a military hop out of Biggs Field. I have a lot of friends with the B-25 outfit there. If I can't connect, go commercial. But I had to get moving.

I called my bank in Albuquerque. What a hassle to get through from this outpost. I had a thousand dollars wired to me and I picked it up in downtown Florence. I gave five hundred dollars to Tony. "Hey, friend, what can I give you as security?" he asked. I shook his hand and told him," you paid that security on the desert sands of North Africa and the jungles of South East Asia, Mate. Good luck until we meet again." I telegraphed the funeral home in Pittsburgh and told them I was on my way home. I jumped in the "Hornet" and was on my way to El Paso.

Six hours later I was at Base Operations at Biggs Field. They had no military flights going east. I drove to El Paso International and booked a flight to Pittsburgh, via Chicago. Sixteen hours to go. My flight was a DC-6, scheduled to land in Chicago at 2200 hours.

We took off on time and all went well until about an hour after wheels-up. I was sitting on the right side of the airplane, just aft of the wing, and dozing, when number four engine started throwing sparks. Suddenly, the engine erupted into flames. The fire was streaking past the window and lit up the sky. My seatmate, a mouse of a guy, was screaming and leapt to his feet and joined several other people in the aisle.

The stewardess, a small, good-looking blonde, was trying to calm the passengers, who were milling around. Things were getting out of hand. We had probably blown a jug—that is, a cylinder had ruptured and raw gasoline was spraying on the hot engine and fueling the fire.

As a combat B-29 flight engineer, I had encountered this emergency many times and it was no big deal if you got on the problem right away. The pilot would cut the fuel to the engine and feather it to shut it down. Easy to do, if all goes according to plan, but disastrous if the pilot screws up. If the fire burns too long it can eat through the wing into the main gas tanks and the plane blows up. The engine was still blazing and it seemed like the pilot was having trouble cutting off the fuel.

I thought to myself, "OK, Buddy, feather the damn engine and let's get on with it." I saw the fear in the stewardess's eyes and I felt sorry for her. She was in charge and there was nothing she could do. Fortunately, the flames began to retreat back under the cowl flaps of the engine and the fire was going out.

Now we had another problem, and probably a bigger one. The propeller was turning faster and faster and if the pilot could not slow it down or stop it, it would twist itself off the shaft and crash through the side of the airplane.

The stewardess knew what could happen and her eyes pleaded with me to help her. We had to get the passengers out of the danger zone in the middle of the airplane. I motioned for her to push some of the passengers toward the cockpit and I would push the rest toward the rear. The hub of the propeller was glowing a dull red and it looked like it was going to tear off. I held my breath.

Suddenly, the prop began to windmill—some of the internal gears had sheared off, but the shaft was still intact. The prop caused a severe drag on the right side, but that was something that could be controlled by the pilot—at least by a good pilot, and I hoped we had a good one, maybe an ex-military one with a couple of thousand hours of three-engine time.

Boy, another close one. What a helluva way to die, in an airplane surrounded by a bunch of salesmen and housewives. Over Japan, flying combat missions, I thought of being blown out of the sky, but over Missouri?

Things settled down and the little stewardess regained control, and somewhat embarrassed, she yelled, in a squeaky voice,

"Everybody sit down, fasten your safety belts and shut up, please. If any of you know God real well, say a prayer for all of us."

The pilot declared an emergency and we were vectored to St. Louis Municipal Airport. Ten minutes later we were on the ground, greeted by the mandatory meat wagons and fire trucks. As we deplaned, I got a big hug and a kiss on the cheek from the blonde stewardess. I wish I had time to pursue this further, but I was faced with a change of plans again, and I had to move on.

Goodbye To Brother Honus

I couldn't get a flight out to Pittsburgh until the next morning so I tried to get some sleep on one of the airport's "comfortable" benches. The plane left St. Louis on time and I got into Pittsburgh at 9:30, a half hour before the scheduled funeral Mass. A friend picked me up at the airport and we arrived at the church just as the priest was buttoning up the casket. He motioned to me to come forward if I wanted to view the body. I did not. I would rather my last thoughts be of Honus walking on water. I rode out to the cemetery with family and it was a solemn trip. Everyone still seemed to be in shock. Little was said. I had some time with the brothers and sisters and everything was muted.

Honus's death cast a pall over the family. No one wanted to talk about how a strong, young guy could suddenly be gone. From what I could gather, he died of a heart attack in a Pennsylvania snowstorm while trying to free his car from a snowbank. What a lousy way to die for a tough fighter like Brother Honus.

The weather was raw and windy. It certainly befitted the occasion. As I left the grave site, I had a chance to talk to Brother Ralph, our second brother. In addition to working as a bridge painter—a job that required both skill and lots of guts, considering he only has one leg—he worked as a part-time grave digger He lost his leg to a German mortar shell in the Battle of the Bulge and is credited with wiping out a Nazi patrol, while wounded, during the house-to-house fighting. I'm sure he did an extra special job in preparing the last resting place of a fellow warrior.

Ralph was drafted into the Army before the start of World War II and rose to the rank of tech sergeant in the infantry. He was in one of the first waves to hit the beach at Normandy with the 29th

Division, the Blue and the Grey, on June 6th, 1944 and fought across France to the Netherlands. When I think of the term, dog-face Soldier, I see Tech. Sgt. Ralph Hall slogging through the mud and snow at Bastogne. He really was an outstanding example of the common man who won the war for the United States. God bless him and those like him. I shook his muddy hand and slapped him on the shoulder. No embracing in this family.

"Ralph, I admire you with all my heart." He half smiled and said, "Give 'em hell kid, or should I say, lieutenant, sir."

"Sarge, you have earned the right to say any damn thing you want to."

I never saw him again—he died the next year. I guess he worked himself to death. I sure miss him.

There was a reception after the funeral but I had had enough sadness for the day and after chatting with some old friends I bummed a ride out to the airport with Big Red Stratemeier, my brother-in-law and the father of a cute little redheaded fireball that had the honor of being the namesake of the very first min-ing claim that I ever staked—the Patty Jean in Grant County, New Mexico. I checked in and found that I could get a non-stop to Chicago, but the schedule looked pretty grim for anything going south to El Paso unless I wanted to take short flights via DC-3s (old military C-47s). I passed on that one. I had been a crew chief on a '47 for a couple of months while island-hopping in the Pa-cific, and that barely beat walking. I elected to wait for a DC-6 that would arrive late that night.

This settled, I called my bank in Albuquerque and asked them to send a thousand dollars to my mom to cover the cost of the fu-neral (she could ill afford that expense, in fact, the family mem-bers would have to chip in to pay for it) and I was glad, and proud, that I could take care of that. I also asked the clerk to wire me three hundred dollars to cover my airfare. He said "Wait a minute." A banker got on the phone and informed me that three hundred dollars would just about wipe me out. I told him to send it along anyway, and I would figure it out later.

The flights were on time and uneventful and we arrived in El Paso about two in the morning. I got to the "Hornet" in the park-ing lot, climbed in the back seat and went to sleep. I was beat.

5
Arrive in Deming, New Mexico

I awoke at dawn, went into the terminal and washed my face and then jumped on highway 10 and headed north to Las Cruces, New Mexico. While I was gassing up in Las Cruces—the old "Hornet" took 17 gallons, she sure was a gas hog—it dawned on me that I was at a crossroads, both literally and figuratively. If I kept on going north on Interstate 25, I would end up in Albuquerque, where I had lots of friends, including two girlfriends. If I went west on Interstate 70, I would end up in Tucson and maybe hook up with Tony and take another stab at the "Dutchman's" gold or keep on going and make some new friends in California. What to do? I decided to head west.

About fifty miles west on Interstate 70 and ten miles east of the little town of Deming, New Mexico, the "Hornet" began to act up. She bucked a little, the transmission clanged a little and she became hard to handle. I eased up on the gas—I had been cruising about 80—and that seemed to help. As I pulled into the outskirts of Deming, she jumped into neutral gear and coasted to a stop, fortunately in front of a gas station. I got out and looked under the car to see if I could spot what was the matter.

It didn't look good. A puddle of fluid was beginning to form beneath the transmission. The gas station attendant strolled over and said "something wrong with your car?"

"Probably, "I said.

"Let's push 'er over and I'll take a look see, but I can't get to her for a while," he said. I went to the pop machine, got a coke and looked around.

"What's that across the highway?" I asked, looking at a few big buildings and a lot of machinery.

"The Allied Chemical and Dye Company fluorspar mill," he said. "Sure makes a lot of dust when the wind blows."

Always on the lookout for knowledge, and with time on my hands, I walked across the highway and through the guard gate.

"What the hell do you want?" a Mexican laborer asked.

"I want to see the boss."

"Over there," he said. I didn't thank him. He was a jerk.

The guy behind the desk was tall, thin, smoking a pipe and looked mad.

"Yeah?" he said.

"I'm just looking around. I have never seen a fluorspar mill before. I am a mining engineer."

"Are you looking for a job? If you are, you may be in luck. What's your experience?"

"I'm not looking for a job, but I would like to see what you do," I said.

He called out the door. "Hey Pete, show this guy around."

Surly Pete came over and said "Follow me."

Pete, I thought, "you are damn lucky I am not looking for a job, for if I were hired and were your boss, I would can your ass on the spot."

I got a half-hour tour, and it was interesting, but it didn't particularly impress me. This time, I thanked him and went back across the highway to see what gives with the "Hornet."

As I had feared, the transmission was shot. "A new tranny will cost you twice what this old heap is worth," the guy said. I bristled; now I am on foot and I was not happy with this hick calling the "Hornet" an old heap. So here I am in a strange town, I have no car and my bank says I'm going to be broke pretty quick. All thoughts of Tucson vanished.

My thoughts flashed back to my conversation with the mill boss. What did he say? "Are you looking for a job?" Well, I guess I am now.

I helped the mechanic push old "Hornet" into an empty field next to the gas station and hat in hand, figuratively speaking, I trudged back across the highway, entered the boss's office and said, "Why yes, I was looking for a job."

"Good, I had to fire the midnight foreman last night. He was having an affair with the wife of one of the workers and they got into a knife fight. He won, but it was best that he hit the road. We've got enough problems around here without the cops bothering us. Go to the timekeeper's office and fill out an application and we'll work out the details later."

"You look like a smart guy and can handle the job and I can also probably use you up at our mine. Work two jobs. Get lots of experience. Be back here at 11:30 and I'll show you what has to be done. The shift starts at midnight, but we'll make up the time later."

After filling out the application, I hitched a ride and asked the driver to drop me off downtown.

"This is it," he said as he stopped at the single traffic light at Main and Ash. I thanked the driver and got out and looked around.

There was some activity in the intersection so I checked it out. It seems like a local service organization called the 20/30 club was having a raffle and a fundraiser for some community project. After observing the action, I noted the leader was a burr-headed young man, tall and about 28 or 29.

I approached him, put out my hand and said, "my name is Jim Hall. I'm a new guy in town and I'm looking for a boarding house. You know of any such animal?"

He said, "Hell yes, my name is Sonny Voiers and there is a top-notch place right across the street from my plant, the Pepsi bottling plant. Run by a lady named Molly Brown. She serves up real good food, too.

"Say, you look like a good guy. How would you like to join us, the 20/30 club?"

"Maybe I would," I said, "but first I need to find a place to stay."

"You play baseball?" Sonny asked. "We got a game with Lordsburg this afternoon at three o'clock and maybe we could use you. It's at the City Park."

The Pepsi Cola plant was right around the corner so I walked over and knocked on the door of an old, but well kept up house.

"Come on in," a voice with a soft southern drawl said. "Ain't no locks on these doors. What can I do for you, son?" Molly was a short, pleasant lady who looked as if she consumed a lot of her famous cooking.

"I'm looking for a place to stay for a while, don't know how long," I said.

"Well, you sure are in luck. We had a fellow just moved out this morning. Soon as my daughter fixes it up, it's yours. It's fifty dollars a week, and that includes breakfast and dinner. In advance. You want to see it?"

"Naw, Sonny said you run a good business and that's good enough for me."

Now I've got a place to stay. The next thing is transportation. We had passed a bicycle shop about a half a mile out of town so I started walking. It will be back to basics, but it will give me a chance to sort things out. The shop had a good selection of used bikes and I picked out a simple one—and it was green. I called it the "Green Hornet" the second.

I showed up at the park a little before three and Sonny introduced me to the team manager. He was a pompous little runt—sold insurance and was big in the social life of the town—and I didn't like him right off.

"What position do you play, Bud?"

"Anything you got," I replied. "Plug me in where you need me."

"Well, I'm going to stick you in right field. That's where you can do us the least harm, out there. You got a glove? "

I said no. He walked off and no one offered to loan me one, and as numbnuts said, probably no one will hit a ball to right field. So I played the game bare-handed. I batted last, even after the pitcher, which was another nod to my probable ineptness, and when my turn came—the bases were loaded—there was a low moan from the hometown crowd. The pitcher threw two high, inside fast balls at my head and I ended up on my butt on home plate.

"You are going to pay for this, you son of a bitch," I muttered to myself. The next one was straight down the middle and I blasted it out of the park. After a hushed silence the crowd voiced their approval by some scattered applause. They must have thought this new guy might actually know how to play the game and do more than fill a hole in the lineup.

The game was a dull affair through the seventh inning. The Lordsburg Lions were bush league and the Deming Wild Cats were just as bad.

Their pitcher was wary of me by now and would have walked me if I had not gone after two lousy pitches and turned them into base hits. I was aching to get another one over the plate so I could drive it through the box into his beer belly. Finally, I got a good pitch and lined it to the second baseman. He muffed it and it rolled into center field. I had a double for sure, but decided to stretch it into a triple and they caught me between second and third.

The shortstop, a real hot dog and the captain of their team, was blocking the base and had the ball firmly in his glove. He had me dead to rights, was a pretty big farm boy and was just not going to let me get past him.

What would brother Honus do in a case like this?, I thought. So, naturally, I lowered my head and smashed into him at full speed. Just before I hit him, I noticed the fear in his eyes and he took a step backwards. A fatal mistake, boy, a fatal mistake. The short-stop went ass over tea cups and as I ran over him, I saw the ball, his glove and his hat follow him. The third baseman was standing over the bag, his mouth agape and his gloved hand hanging limply by his side. I tumbled and took him out as I straightened up. The infield was a shambles with "Lions" scattered all over the ground. I practically walked across home plate.

I could hear Brother Honus say, "Pretty good kid, keep it up and one of these days you may be half as good as your brothers." Damn, I sure miss his praise and encouragement. Deming won 17 to 1; their first win of the season.

At the mandatory beer bust after the game, I was treated like the second coming. I had been accepted. The beer flowed and I didn't have to buy a round. Good thing. I only had three bucks and some change in my pocket.

I pedaled out to the mill and arrived just as the boss drove up in his truck and saw me on the bike. He gave me a sidelong glance. You're traveling kinda light, ain't you," he said.

"I need the exercise," I replied.

The boss's name was Mike Scharnhorst. Burly, tough looking and acting and pretty well fitting the image of a German immigrant.

"Follow me" he said, "and be prepared to get dirty."

After a half hour of instruction, I saw that this job wasn't going to take the skill of a rocket scientist, and by midnight, I was ready to take over. The night passed slowly and Mike popped in about four in the morning to see how I was doing. Either he was an early riser or he just didn't quite trust the college kid the first night on the job.

I Meet Father Pat

At eight o'clock the next morning I clocked out and pedaled back to the boarding house. As I was washing up I heard a church bell tolling. It was Sunday and I thought it might be a good idea to start off my new life in this town by going to Mass. I didn't bother changing my clothes and walked a couple of blocks to Saint Michael's, the Catholic church. I walked in and sat down near the front.

As the church filled up, I noted I was getting some mean looks. I realized that perhaps I was sitting in a pew that was reserved for a regular parishioner. Then it struck me. I was still in my work clothes and I looked a rather shabby sight among the well dressed town folk. I made my way out a side door with the intent of going back to the boarding house, talking a shower and returning for a later Mass.

As I walked off I passed a group of Mexican farm laborers, dressed no better than I, milling around the door to the basement of the church. One was strumming a guitar and they seemed to be having a good time. An altar boy, dressed in his robes, opened the basement door and the men filed in.

"What the heck, "I thought, "I might as well hear the Mass, and not have to go back to the boarding house and dress up. I really needed the sleep. It had been a long day, the ball game, the beer bust, and then working for eight hours. I followed the group and took a seat in the rear.

When we got settled, one of the Mexicans came over and asked me what I was doing in here. I told him I was going to hear Mass. What of it? He said that I should go upstairs with the Anglos. He muttered something and walked away. I felt a chill in the air. The priest walked in and the talking and moving around stopped.

He was a big, rough-looking guy with the map of Ireland on his face. Fr. Pat O'Hara was his name. Born and reared in the seaport town of Oakland, California.

He played in and roamed the mean streets until he found God and became a priest. I didn't realize at the time that he would play a large part in my life. His commanding gaze swept the room and in a booming voice and broken Spanish he said, "Nosotros necesitamos un persona que pude serve Mass."

No one moved and no one volunteered. I had done my time before the altar and at the side of priests while growing up and still could mutter the Latin, at least good enough for most priests. I raised my hand.

"I'll give it a try, Father," I said.

"Go get some vestments and get back here," he said. I went behind the curtain in back of the altar, through a door and into the vestry. The altar boys were preparing for the Mass upstairs and I walked in just as the kid who seemed to be charge finished downing a big gulp of communion wine.

"How about trading with me?" he asked. "I have to serve Fr. Kenennly, who is visiting from El Paso, and he is a real pain in the butt. Everything has to be just right. One day I would like to stick out my foot and trip him. It would be a laugh to see him fall on his fat behind. Here, take these things. They are good enough for those guys."

Fr. Pat was a pro. He moved fast, and I had a hard time keeping up with him. After the Mass he said, "you're a little rusty, but we can get you back in shape, if you're interested. I see you are a new guy in town. I would take you upstairs for the gathering after church, but you are not dressed for it.

"Come by at seven this evening. We have a young people's coffee. You might meet someone who would be of interest to you. What's your name? I understand you're staying at Molly's. Good choice."

"My name is Jim Hall and thanks, Father. I'll take you up on your invitation and see you tonight."

I came back to the church at 7:30 and the coffee was in full swing. But it was a pretty grim scene. All the foxes were off to college and the local girls were not much into conversation. I left early, went back to Molly's, read part of a book and went to sleep. Life settled into a pattern and, finally, pay day on Friday. A pay check and I could breathe a little freer. I went out and splurged on a double hamburger and a tall coke. Molly's food was good, but I needed a change.

Frank Wilson

Of particular significance was a situation with one of my fellow 20/30 poker players. He was a member of one of the elite families who owned cotton land outside of the city. His name was Frank Wilson and he was engaged to a young lady who was away at a Christian college in Texas. Her father was on the city council and owned several large businesses along Main Street. He often boasted that she would inherit all her father's possessions, as she was an only child and her father doted on her. He would be the biggest wheel in the city and would be happy to give any of the 20/30 guys a job.

One weekend, the lady in question, Linda by name, came home on spring break, I was downtown shopping at one of her father's stores and I ran into the girl, literally. I rounded a corner in the store and brushed into her. She dropped the book she was carrying and bent over to pick it up. She was wearing a very low-cut blouse and no bra. It was lust at first sight. What a fox! This was what I had been waiting for ever since I arrived in this town.

I introduced myself and asked her if she would like to go to the show tonight.

"You're new around here," she said. "I've been watching you for a while. Tonight is a bad time, but how about Sunday night?"

"That's a go. Pick you up at seven thirty, your house," I said.

"Fine, gotta split," she said as she bounced out of the store.

We hit it off from the start. She was fun, romantic, a daredevil, an adventurer. My kind of girl. She extended her vacation for a week and I used every excuse I could think of to stay in town at the mill instead of going up to the mine in the mountains. Frank Wilson couldn't even get a phone call answered.

One of the 20/30 guys said that Wilson was really mad and that I had better watch out, particularly my back. He was mean and used to getting his way. At the next poker session at Sonny's house, the boy friend showed up with a chip on his shoulder and looking for a fight. That was OK with me. I had given up recreational fighting when I left the coal fields of Pennsylvania, but I had boxed—was captain of the boxing team at UNM and never lost a fight—so I could probably beat him without any problem in a fair fight.

But when he showed up at Sonny's house, he left no doubt he was carrying a gun. I could see the outline of a gun in the right rear pocket of his Levis. More than likely, a .22 automatic. Small, but big enough to cause some damage if he hit you in the back, upper left side.

I remembered Brother Honus's admonition about being in a fair fight, so when the beer was passed around, I always kept a long-neck bottle of Lone Star beer close at hand. Sonny sensed the tension in the air and closed down the game early. We all went home with no harm done.

The small-town rumor mill got hold of the gossip that there was bad blood amongst the young Turks of the 20/30 club, and they waited with anticipation for the outcome. The next week passed quickly with Linda and I being together every night. When Friday came around, I was going to the poker game. I wasn't going to let the word get around that some nerd was scaring me off.

When I walked in to the conference room of the Pepsi bottling plant—I guess Sonny didn't want to get blood on the carpet in his living room—I was prepared for a fair fight. I had my .32 revolver taped to my right paratrooper boot, something I had learned at the 82nd Airborne Advanced Killing School at Fort Benning. I got to the game early and reserved a seat with my back against the wall (another thing I learned from Brother Honus.)

Frank arrived shortly there after and he was half drunk. He was probably working up his courage for what he might do. The atmosphere was electric and as the night wore on, I began to see how ridiculous the situation was. But it still was fraught with the possibility of somebody getting hurt, maybe seriously.

I remembered a scene from a movie about Wild Bill Hickock's last poker game in Deadwood, South Dakota. I was waiting, and half expecting, to be dealt the hand of aces and eights, the dead man's hand.

The beer flowed freely and finally, Frank just passed out. That ended the tension and the poker game. Our differences would have to wait to be resolved later.

Linda went back to college and our romance cooled off. It had run its course, but it sure was interesting while it lasted. Frank quit coming to the poker games and our paths never crossed again.

6
Cave-In ...
a Life Changing
Moment

Three weeks after I took the job at the mill, Mike called me into his office and said, "I'm going to send you to the mine in the mountains for a while. The pay is better and I think you will work well with the miners. It will also give you a little more experience and a change of scenery."

I said "fine," got my gear together, checked out of Molly's and caught the next ore truck to the mine in the Burro Mountains, about 80 miles north of Deming. The switch to working underground was OK at first, but I shortly became concerned with the safety program that Allied had in place. Allied was a big company and I thought they would stress safety, as they couldn't afford even the smallest accident. This, I found out, was not the case. Just before I arrived, they had a cavein and two miners were badly injured. They almost died before they got to the hospital, thirty miles away.

Still, the mine foreman had not tightened the safety procedures and I told him I was going to write him up if he did not take some action. From his attitude, I got the impression that he thought that I, the boy engineer, was throwing my weight around. They were doing just fine before I arrived on the scene, and the foreman didn't like it.

About the second week of my posting at the mine, Rico, a Mexican helper, and I were surveying at the face of a new drift. Suddenly, and without warning, the ground shifted and there was a cave-in that trapped us up against the face of the drift. We were cut off from the outside world. It was very dark, very dusty and very quiet. In a little while we could hear the noise of miners digging into the mound of dirt separating us from the main shaft.

Good. But how much of the roof had caved in? How much dirt are they going to have to move to get to us? They were going to have to do it by hand, with shovels, as they couldn't get any machinery into the narrow drift. Being in the dark, and realizing that our lives were depending on our fellow miners whose will and ability to save us was suspect, scared the hell out of me. We didn't have any communication with the rescue party, but we continued to hear them digging.

When they stopped for lunch, or whatever, and did not start up for an hour or so, I got excited. We did not have shovels or anything else so we started to move the rocks by hand. I knew this was futile, but I had to do something to help save my life. What if they had given up the rescue effort and gone home? I imagined that the air was getting bad and my breathing became labored.

Damn it! Why hadn't I treated those miners better? Why had I yelled at Jose for being a lazy bum? Why had I chewed out Edwardo for sleeping on the job? Why had I told the mine fore-man that I was going to write him up—and maybe he would lose his job, and couldn't take care of his family?

Maybe it would not be such a bad idea if the nosy boy engineer didn't get dug out. They could say, we just couldn't get to him in time. Maybe they had thought, "the hell with that gringo engineer. I'm tired. I need a break." Better still, "Let's knock it off and go home. Come back tomorrow—but wait. My cousin Rico, he is be-hind that pile of dirt. If I don't work to get him out, my uncle will kill me. So I will keep on digging."

I didn't know it at the time but my life was entirely in the hands of others. If I were going to be saved, it would be because of Rico. Then and there, I made up my mind: if I made it out of here, I would not put myself in this situation again. At last, the sound of the digging began again and in another hour, they broke through. Almost five hours, my watch said.

But that can't be right. It should have been at least twenty hours, or maybe a couple of days. The hell with my thoughts, I was just glad to see them. They pushed by me and embraced Rico. They had saved their cousin.

I played it cool. "Just another day at the mine," I said to the mine foreman as I strolled nonchalantly down the drift to the main shaft and got on the elevator. Up, up to the sunlight and fresh air.

"Here's my metal I.D. tag," I said to Mike who had driven up to the mine from town when he heard that they had had an accident. "How about hanging it on the peg and punching me out. I think I'll go back to the bunk house and lie down for a while."

Recovering The Transit

I was at the mine shaft at six o'clock the next morning. I had assured Mike that I would go down into the mine and bring the surveying transit back so he could take it with him this afternoon. The company was buying the property next to the mill and he wanted to check the city's measurements and make sure Allied Chemical did not get cheated.

As I waited for the elevator to take the first load of miners down—a half a mile below the fresh air and the bright sunshine of this crisp, clear day—it hit me. Fewer than twelve hours ago, I was looking at a very painful and slow death from suffocation in a dark, dank hole in the bowels of a mountain in New Mexico that I had never heard of a month ago. And worse than that, my life depended on people I really didn't care for and I knew damn well didn't like me too much.

I stepped aside and indicated that I would take the next elevator down. While I waited, I got to thinking: is this the way you would like to end your life? I had always prided myself on taking the big chances, but in the back of my mind, no matter how daring or dangerous it might look to others, I always had a way out—my ace in the hole. Part of this job I was now doing was putting myself in situations where there was no possibility of having an ace in the hole.

You are a man and you have a big ego. Is your big ego worth the price of putting yourself in situations where you don't have too much control of the outcome? Your big ego has made you stand out in many areas where you weren't that good. Is it worth the chance? Well, are you going to go back down in that pit? The answer is yes, but reluctantly, and I am not going to show that reluctance to anyone. I'll have to go back into the drift where the cave-in took place and retrieve the surveying equipment, but we will be doing no surveying today.

My helper, Rico, had handed in his hard hat and badge as soon as he got off the elevator yesterday. "No mas," he said. "I'll go chop cotton in the valley with the rest of the Mexicans, but never will I go underground again. I'll starve first."

The elevator arrived and when I got on it, along with a full load of miners, I noted—the first time I had bothered to look—that nobody was smiling and all their eyes were closed. We stopped at several levels and when we got to the bottom, I was the only one left on the elevator. I rang the bell and sent the elevator back up to the surface.

I walked down the main drift to the area where we had been working and, there on the right, was the mound of dirt that had trapped us. I would have to crawl through the tunnel the miners had dug to get us out.

It looked a lot smaller that it did yesterday. It sure is lonely down here. What if there is another cave-in and nobody knows I'm down here by myself? The surveying transit, the measuring tapes and other pieces of equipment were on the other side of the cave-in. Can I make it through the tunnel with my heavy jacket on? It's cold down here. What if I get stuck? I'll surely freeze without the jacket.

I would gladly buy the damn transit—a month's wages—if I didn't have to crawl through that tunnel. I hesitated, ran through my options and decided, "Oh well, here goes. I'll leave the jacket on and take my chances. At least I'll die warm."

I got about a third of the way through the tunnel when some rocks began to move. I held my breath and when nothing moved any more, I inched forward.

Finally, I was up against the face of the drift. What a difference a day makes. An hour ago, I was safe and sound and now I am back in the same damn place I was yesterday. I picked up the transit and carefully and slowly shoved it down the tunnel before me. I left the other crap. I could replace that stuff at little cost, and I didn't want anything extra that might hang up on the loose rocks. I inched my way over the rocks and finally I reached the end of the tunnel. I pushed the transit out of the tunnel and it fell to the ground with a thud.

It was probably damaged, but at that moment, I really didn't give a damn. I felt like a Marine at the battle of Iwo Jima. Brother Honus had told me that the Corps had a tradition. "We never left a Marine on the battlefield, be he dead or alive."

I had upheld the tradition. This transit was my Marine. I had brought his body back. I rang the bell for the elevator and while I waited, I dusted off the transit. If it got knocked out of calibration, I can blame it on the cave-in. The insurance claim can say "Act of God." I started thinking that my decision—I had pretty much made up my mind not to go back to work underground—was an "Act of God."

The engine fire on the DC-6, the cave-in. Maybe the good Lord was trying to tell me something. I'll give it some thought when I have more time. Right now, I have to write up a report on the cave-in and the conditions that led up to the accident for Mike to take back to the mill. I have a feeling that after the managers upstairs read the report, I will not be too popular around the mine.

Bull Session at the Church

The report was in Mike's hands by three o'clock. I told him I would like to come down to Deming for the weekend and I would take the last ore truck that left from the mine on Friday. When I got to Deming I checked in at Saint Michaels, got my sleeping quarters in the church basement, had a short talk with Fr. Pat and headed off to the Friday night poker game at the 20/30 club.

I looked forward to these poker sessions, as I usually fattened my bank account after a couple hours of playing. I don't know where these boys learned their poker skills, but I owe their teachers a great debt. I had to try to lose, which was a good thing, because winning too much made enemies and I still wasn't totally accepted by the community.

Every Saturday night, Fr. Pat would have a bull session with the Mexican farm workers who also slept in the church basement when they could not get back to their living quarters on the region's cotton farms. I liked to sit in on these meetings as it gave me an opportunity to practice my Spanish—although the Spanish they spoke was chiefly slang and wasn't much use in polite society.

I found particularly interesting, as did Fr. Pat, the stories they would tell of the fabulous gold deposits their fathers, or their uncles, or their cousins, or sometimes themselves (if they had had a couple of shots of tequila before they came to the session) had discovered in the high Sierras of Mexico. If only some rich Americano would come back with them to old Mexico to see these treasures. One night, shortly after the accident at the mine, the BS was flowing hot and heavy in the church basement. One young Mexican named Julio was spinning a tale of a gold deposit in Chihuahua, the land and territory of the great Gen. Pancho Villa.

Julio was sharp, smooth and crafty. He looked as if he should be selling tickets to a girlie show on the streets of Tijuana or Juarez instead of chopping cotton in Deming, New Mexico.

"The vein, she is as far as you could see. Seguro, Padre," he said. "I see it with my very own eyes."

Fr. O'Hara's round, pleasant, open face lit up. He said he was going to El Paso in a week to perform a wedding for a wealthy Mexican family and they had invited him to the reception in Chihuahua City. This would be a fine time to visit the gold deposit that Julio was talking about. If it was anything like Julio said, we would all be rich.

This was how the great adventure started. Fr. Pat said "Let's all go to Mexico and check this out," and it was a go.

I didn't give Julio's story much credence, but Fr. Pat was fascinated by the story of lost gold. He contacted Morris, a parishioner at St. Michael's and the owner of the cotton farm where Julio worked, for permission for Julio to be gone for a week. I asked Mike for a leave and he said OK, but for no more than seven days. We borrowed various camping items, and on Wednesday morning, Fr. Pat, Julio and I were on our way to El Paso.

Fr. Pat officiated at the wedding at noon while Julio and I bummed around the city. Then it was off to Chihuahua City where we arrived about six o'clock. Fr. Pat and I checked in at the Plaza Hotel as the guests of Señor Alonzo Ortega, the father of the bride and a very wealthy businessman from Juarez. Julio said he would stay with relatives.

The reception was at eight o'clock and the elite of Chihuahua City were present. Señor Ortega had made arrangements for us to meet with the regional army commander and a member of his staff, who would give us a letter that would authorize us safe passage to anywhere in the Sierras. Señor Ortega said this permission was necessary as there were many bad hombres out there.

The general was a short, pudgy man who had absolutely no military bearing and obviously had received his appointment through political connections and not for service during the revolution. The general signed the letter with a flourish and wished us well. Señor Ortega had a new Jeep, complete with two five-gallon jerry cans filled with gasoline, delivered to our hotel the next morning.

"Oh yes," he said, "There is one thing that is wrong with the vehicle, but it is no big deal. Several days ago, someone tried to steal the Jeep and they broke the ignition. The mechanic did not have time to fix it, but all you have to do is put the two wires together and it will start."

After a few delays we were finally on our way to that encounter at checkpoint #81.

7
Back to Chihuahua City

We were now back in Chihuahua City after almost being shot at the checkpoint and I was still upset and nervous. I was beating myself up for being so naive and ignorant as to have exposed myself and my friend to what could have been a life-ending situation. How could I be so stupid for not thinking ahead? I vowed that this would never happen again. What started out to be a lark—a vacation among a simple people who usually went out of their way to be kind to Americans—almost ended in tragedy.

When I got to our hotel, Fr. Pat was on his way to a dinner party with Señor Ortega and his friends from Juarez. They were in a festive mood and he was surprised to see me. He was even more surprised when I told him what had happened at the checkpoint. Well, his friends in high places would take care of this right away. Señor Ortega sent a messenger to the commander's office and requested a stronger letter from the general. Fr. Pat added that it should include a gun permit. The general was outraged that one of his soldiers would not honor a letter signed by him and in a show of authority, assigned one of his aides to accompany us to the checkpoint to reprimand and place the sergeant in jail. These guys moved fast when they wanted to.

I begged off from attending the dinner and went to my room. I took a shower and went out to the nearest gun shop and bought a .357 Magnum pistol and a .30-0-6 rifle. At first the clerk said "no way," but lost his reluctance when I showed him the letter from the general. I told him if he didn't believe me, call the general. I had just left him at a party and I was sure that he would be glad to hear from him. The clerk said, fine, it was OK with him and he really didn't want to disturb this important man for such a minor matter. He took my money, tossed in two boxes of cartridges and said "adios."

I stuck the .357 in my belt and covered it with my shirt. A carrying case concealed the rifle and I walked back to the hotel. The next morning, at six o'clock sharp, a captain, the general's aide, met me and Julio at the front door of the hotel. He was dressed in his uniform and I noticed that he was wearing a .45 pistol, prominently displayed. He was definitely not a happy soldier.

On the ride west, I tried to engage the captain in conversation but all he seemed to want to do was stare out the window and mumble to himself. He did say the sergeant we were going to see had worked in the sugar beet fields in Texas for one season and had been treated badly by several of the farm owners. One time, they had cheated him out of his wages and told him to move on or they would turn him into immigration as an illegal—a wetback. He returned to Mexico very bitter and with an intense hatred for all Americans, especially Texans or anyone that he thought looked like one.

When we reached mile post 81, the same sharp young soldier stepped from the guard shack and leveled his rifle at us. When he saw the captain, he immediately snapped to order arms and yelled "Attention!"

The captain jumped from the Jeep, brushed aside the soldier and entered the guard shack. Julio cowered in the back seat and crossed himself a couple of times. Much loud talking and shouting came from the open door of the shack. The captain had yanked the sergeant out of bed and pushed him out the door. The officer had drawn his pistol and was waving it about. I was nervous and Julio was scared stiff. The sergeant had not changed his clothes from the day before and he was a sorry-looking sight. The captain was giving the sergeant a tongue-lashing that would make a Marine drill sergeant proud, all the while hitting him with the pistol, which was cocked and ready to fire.

I caught some of the words, "You are not fit to represent the general, I had to leave an important party early because of you, you low-life peon. I had to get up early and you embarrassed the general in front of a bunch of gringos." He paused long enough to catch his breath, turned to us, and screamed out, "Get out of here, now!"

We did, just that. (I was learning that losing face was a very big thing among the Mexican military and I would encounter the problem again.) About a hundred yards past the guard house was a small cluster of shacks. The commotion had drawn all the inhabitants, mostly women and young kids, out to the side of the road to see what was happening. They watched us go by, without a word and blank faced. One or two of the little kids waved, their skinny hands peeking out from under the tattered sleeves of their ragged hand-me-down coats. I stopped the Jeep and gave them two candy bars I had bought at the hotel. I could see that they wanted to be friends, and so did I.

Julio and the Snake

Both Julio and I breathed a sigh of relief as checkpoint number 81 faded into the billowing dust behind us. Before us stretched miles and miles of barren waste land that disappeared into a light blue haze that housed the Sierra Madres. I had uncovered the .30-0-6 from under the sleeping bags and other gear in the back seat and I placed the .357 on the transmission cover between us. Julio retrieved several bottles of tequila he had stashed under his ground cloth and was gulping it down. I thought he probably needed a little shot of courage after getting past the checkpoint. I felt sure we wouldn't see any more Mexican Army troops until we came to the next fair-sized city and that would be several hours from now, according to the maps we had.

It was beginning to get hot and the heat waves rose in shimmering waves from the desert floor. It was sixty miles to San Francisco de Borja, the little village where we could get some water if we needed it. (Say, I had better start thinking in meters. Let's see, one mile equals roughly one and six tenths kilometers. So it's ninety-six kilometers to San Francisco.) We pressed on, mostly in second gear, until we passed a small cluster of sunburned buildings that was San Francisco de Borja. According to the maps—the best that AAA could give us from the downtown office in Deming—the road, or what passed for one, ended about four miles south of here. We would then head due west until we came to a dry river bed. We would cross this and continue west into the foothills for another three miles, or four point eight kilometers. Then we would come to a canyon and we could drive no farther. This was it, or maybe it was the next canyon.

Julio was not quite sure, but he would know it when he saw it. I noticed that Julio's eyes were not making contact with mine and he was becoming nervous. When we came to the canyon, where we could go no farther, Julio said, "stop here." He took another big gulp of the tequila and threw the bottle away.

"We're here, at last. Let's go." I said.

"Isn't it getting a little late?" asked Julio. "The sun will be gone pretty soon. We wait until tomorrow?"

"No," I said, "we still have a couple more hours of daylight. These could be the most important hours of our lives."

We took two canteens of water, a prospecting pick and sampling bags, as well as my .357, and trudged up a fairly steep hill to a knoll overlooking a steep canyon.

"Down there," Julio says.

We descended into the canyon with great anticipation. As we climbed down the side of the narrow valley we lost the light of the sun and after about an hour, I decided to call it quits. So much for our first go at finding the lost Mexican gold mine.

We walked down the valley floor to a point where we thought we had left the Jeep. As we started up the slope, Julio was about twenty feet in front of me, I heard a blood-chilling sound that— once you have heard it—you will never forget. I froze in my tracks and Julio bolted up the slope. He took one step, slipped on a loose rock and landed face down on the ground, his head less than a foot from a coiled four-foot sidewinder rattlesnake. The rattler had been sleeping in the shade of a large rock and we had scared him. Julio let out a scream and that seemed to startle the snake and it coiled tighter. I drew my .357 Magnum and fired it as fast as I could pull the trigger. Julio was still screaming when snake meat and dirt filled his mouth. I must admit these were lucky shots, as I had not had a chance to zero in my weapon.

I remembered a truism I learned in the desert of Arizona. If you run into one rattler, there is always another one nearby. I didn't bother looking before I grabbed a blubbering Julio by the collar and kicking the still-squirming carcass of the snake out of the way, I half dragged and half pushed him up the incline. When we reached the top, I yanked him to his feet and shoved him toward the Jeep. He slumped against the vehicle and then fell to his knees.

"We go home," he whined?

"Hell no," I said, "We have gone to a lot of trouble to get here, and I intend to find the gold."

"There is no gold, señor," he said. "I lied to the padre. We go home now," he pleaded. He crawled into the back of the Jeep and curled up.

The sun had set and it was very quiet. I sat on the hood of the Jeep, with my feet off the ground, and ran through my options. Was Julio's admission true or false? If he was stringing us along, why? Did his big, bragging mouth get his butt in a situation he could not handle and was he going to say anything to get out of this mess? Rats! What to do? Well, I was going to stick it out, at least for another day.

It was getting chilly, so I pushed Julio out of the way and snatched a sweatshirt from the back seat. Julio had found another bottle of tequila and was slugging it down. It was going to be a beautiful night and the rising moon cast long shadows of the cactus on the parched ground. It had been a rough day, and tomorrow was probably going to be worse.

It was time to turn in. With some misgivings, I spread out an old tarpaulin I had brought along as a ground cover, beside the Jeep. The thought of waking up and finding a rattlesnake as a bed partner did not appeal to me but, what the hell, I needed to get some rest and trying to sleep in the Jeep wasn't an option. Julio could make his own decision as to where he wanted to bed down.

I walked off into the sagebrush to relieve myself and when I returned, Julio was nowhere in sight. As I bent down to unroll my sleeping bag, I caught a glint of polished medal off to my right. It was the barrel of the .30-0-6 I had bought back in Chihuahua City and holding that rifle was a wild-eyed Julio. His whole body was shaking and he was crying.

"Now we go home?" he demanded.

Damn. I had had enough adrenaline rushes for a day. Now this! I slowly turned to face him and I felt my .357 pistol heavy on my hip. I thought I had emptied the weapon at the snake, but had I? Julio was going to shoot me if I said no, and probably if I said yes. If I could distract him for a moment, I might be able to get off a shot. I had proven to myself this afternoon that I was a good shot, but that was with a loaded gun. What if...?

I stared at him for an instant and said "We go. Give me your hand and help me up, right now!" I counted on Julio's training to obey orders and as he reached down to grasp my hand, I grabbed his arm and threw him over on his back, hard. In an instant, I had a death grip on his throat and was squeezing the life out of him. But I was wasting my strength. He was as limp as a wet rag. The combination of fear and tequila had taken all the fight out of him.

I picked up the rifle and pointed it at his head. I had an intense desire to kill him on the spot. Why not kill this worthless bastard? He was nothing but trouble. He had scared the hell out of me and that made me mad. He had discovered a chink in my armor, and I didn't like what I saw. Go on, kill him! I could get away with it. I could make up a story that we were jumped by bandits.

Fr. O'Hara's friends in Chihuahua City had told us there were still lots of unemployed guys running around in the mountains in this part of the country. The revolution had only been over for about twenty years and every peon or laborer had a gun. That's it! We had been surprised by a group of guys and they had robbed us and they took Julio for ransom. Maybe I could bury him in the canyon where we were looking for the gold Julio said was there.

Naw, bad idea. I should keep on going farther into the mountains where I could find a better spot. These thoughts raced through my mind as I looked down on this miserable hunk of humanity who had lied to us—lied in fact, to a priest—and besides that, he had wanted to kill me.

What to do with Julio? I dragged him to his feet and stuffed him into the right seat. I tied his hands behind his back and lashed him to the seat. He was weeping all the while and I was beginning to feel sorry for him. He did look uncomfortable and if it were this bad now, what would it be like by morning? What the hell. The SOB deserved to be uncomfortable.

Well, maybe not. I untied him, tied his hands in front of him, retied him to the seat and gave him a marijuana joint, one of several I saw in his shirt pocket. Maybe this will calm him down. I was hungry but I was too hyped up to bother to eat. I lay down on my sleeping bag and stared into the night.

Julio Steals the Jeep

I slept fitfully, if at all, that night. The dawn broke with a brilliant display of yellow and red streaks across the bright blue sky. As the sun rose out of the desert waste land, I rolled up my sleeping bag and ground cloth, picked up my pistol—I had loaded it last night—and went to the other side of the Jeep. I tossed the bag and the cover in the back of the Jeep and put the pistol in the holster on my belt. Julio was wide awake and wide eyed.

"Water please," he said. "And, please untie me, I have to go out there."

I untied him from the seat, but left his arms still tied in front of him. I loosened his ropes and told him to go. When he returned, I tied his legs together and had him sit down in the Jeep. I gave him his canteen and a couple of tortillas and watched him wolf them down. I put a marijuana cigarette in his lips and lit it. I grabbed a canteen of water, an apple and an orange and was ready to start out for the day.

But first, I had to tie up Julio. I waited until he had finished the joint. His eyes were beginning to get glassy. The stuff hit him pretty hard on an empty stomach. I secured him to the seat and left the rope around his wrists a little looser as he complained that they hurt and were cutting off the blood to his hands.

He begged me not to tie him so tight. He pleaded with me, "Please don't hurt my arms. I wouldn't try to run away. I promise you Jefe, on the Bible, I will be here when you return. You can trust me."

I did trust him. I climbed up the hill and down into the canyon. I wanted one last good look to see if I could find any trace of a geologic formation that could possibly contain gold.

I spent the next two hours searching from one side to the other in the canyon to find any trace of gold-bearing rock or any place where someone might have started a mine to look for gold. I had given it my best shot. There was no gold here. Fr. Pat had been conned, and so had I, I guess.

Oh well, I'll chalk it up to experience and press on. The main thing now was to get back to Chihuahua City, get a shower, a good meal, a couple of beers and check out the social scene. A young stud like me should be able to scare up something. The sun was getting high in the sky and I was getting tired. I was looking forward to sitting down in the shade, but there was no shade. No matter, the Jeep would offer some relief, and when we got moving, some breeze. I topped out of the canyon and looked around to get my bearings.

I did not see the Jeep, but no sweat, I had walked several miles down the canyon and maybe I had misjudged my distance. The Jeep was probably just over the next sand dune. I stood on top of a rise where I had a clear view of the desert and I still did not see the Jeep.

Then a sickening thought hit me right between the eyes. Had Julio, that sniveling peasant, got loose and took off in the Jeep. Impossible. He didn't have a key. Damn it! He didn't have to have a key. I remembered the broken ignition and I had a sinking sensation in the pit of my stomach. That ignorant peon had out-smarted me again!

I continued walking to where I had parked the Jeep. Yes, you idiot. He stole the Jeep, and right now, you are in deep crap!

OK, smart guy. Just standing here isn't getting you anywhere. You had better move out. Follow the tire tracks. Put your head down and trudge on. Left right. Left right. I was muttering to myself and imagining all sorts of things I would do to Julio when I caught up with him.

Left right. Left right. It was getting hotter. I only had a few swallows of water left in my canteen. I had used half a canteen of water to wash off a rock this morning. You fool! Don't drink it now. Save it. It is priceless. Left right. Left right.

I can see a vision of a newspaper article. There is Julio, sitting at a table in the best restaurant in Chihuahua City. His feet are up and he is smoking a big cigar. The headlines read, "Local Boy Finds Big Gold Strike." He is drinking a cold beer.

I stagger and fall and get to my feet again. I am sweating, my mouth is as dry as cotton and I am getting dizzy. My .357 is getting heavy. There's a big rock. I'll hide the gun under the rock and come back for it later. I won't need it to kill Julio. I'll use my bare hands.

Left right. Left right. I am back at Fort Benning and the jackass of a drill instructor is saying. "OK you misfits, we are going to double-time it into the parade ground and past the reviewing stand. Sgt. Sweeney, help that Air Force lieutenant with his pack and weapon. I don't think he can make it."

"The hell I can't," I snarl. "Get your damned hands off my gear, dogface. I can do any damn thing you grunts can do, only better."

"OK, let's hear it. Double time," shouts the D.I. "Pick up the cadence."

I can feel the taste of a cold beer. "H'mm, that tastes so good." Left right. Left right. I stagger and fall again. As I get up I see a length of rope and the earth is torn up around a pile of rocks and the tire tracks make a sharp turn to the left. There are scrapes— white marks on some of the rocks—and the ground appears to be wet. I stagger to my feet and trudge on, following the tire tracks.

Left right. Left right. A vision of a beautiful girl, wearing a low cut peasant blouse, floats in front of me. Her soulful brown eyes have that come-hither look, and her blonde hair cascades over her ample bosom. She is carrying a pitcher of cold beer. How I would like to have a drink of that beer.

Left right. Left right. As I come to the top of a sand dune, I see it! At least I think I see it. The Jeep, and it's not a hundred yards away! I fall to my knees and look again. Well, I'll be damned. It is the Jeep. The merciless sun beating down mesmerizes me and the dark shadows fade in and out. It just sat there. No Julio. No anyone.

I retreat back behind the crest of the hill. I have to think this through. This came on so suddenly that I had a hard time switching my mind from fantasizing to what's happening in the real world. All I had was Brother Honus's KA-BAR knife and I was in damn poor shape to fight anybody. But I had to make a move. The thought of that Jeep moving away from me again panicked me.

At that moment, I didn't know what I was going to do, but my legs started to move forward and I crept up to the Jeep and looked in the back window. Julio was passed out in the front seat, and a canteen was on the seat beside him. I went to the passenger's side of the Jeep, reached in and grabbed the canteen. It seemed like it was empty. I unscrewed the cap and turned it upside down. It was empty! Crap!

Julio stirred—what should I do? I was too weak to do battle with anyone—even this sorry hunk of humanity. I went to the driver's side and put a rope around Julio's body. I put a slip knot in the rope and threaded it through the steel supports of the seat. The tighter he strained against the rope, the tighter it would bind him to the seat. With all my strength I pulled the rope tight. Julio awoke with a start, glassy eyed and incoherent, and passed out again.

I noticed that the two ignition wires were tied together. That meant that the key was still on and draining the battery. I hoped that there was still enough juice to turn the engine over. I hit the starter button and the engine clicked a few times and stopped. I hit it again and it painfully cranked over. Well, at least I still had some battery power but something else was terribly wrong. I disconnected the ignition wires, shut down the engine and got out and raised the hood. The engine was hot and some of the rubber gaskets were smoking.

My heart sank as I put two and two together and realized that the dumb jerk had high-centered on the pile of rocks, punched a hole in the radiator and kept driving until all the water drained out. It didn't take too long before the engine became so hot that it froze up. I looked under the front of the Jeep and saw that the center of the radiator had a hole gouged in it, but not too deep.

Maybe I could repair it. I jammed about a foot of duct tape in the hole and hoped for the best. Next problem. It would take ten quarts of water to fill the radiator. We didn't even have a canteen's worth. But we did have two five-gallon cans of gasoline. I had never heard of using gas as a coolant before, but it was worth a try. It might cause the engine to catch on fire, but that was couple of catastrophes down the line.

First, I had to move Julio over to the passenger's seat. I had thought of just leaving him here by the side of the road, but my better instincts took over. I tied his feet together and pulled him over the center aisle. I tied him securely to the seat with several slip knots and cinched them down, tight. No more mister nice guy.

I poured a little gas into the radiator to see if it would leak. It did, but not too badly. I filled the radiator to the top and now the big test. I put the ignition wires together and the engine did its best to crank fast enough to start. No luck.

I tried again. It coughed, caught, wheezed and chugged into life. The engine was running, but for how long? I shoved it into low gear. We moved a few feet and we stalled. The overheating must have really screwed up the internal workings of the engine. I got it started again and eased it into gear. We were wounded, but we were moving and it sure beat walking.

I nursed the Jeep forward, yard by yard, toward the village of San Francisco de Borja. We were leaking water, or gas, from the radiator and I had to stop and empty the jerry can into the radiator about fifteen minutes after I got the Jeep started. The duct-tape plug was still holding and I kept my fingers crossed. Finally, the village came into view. One big hurdle had passed, but what would we find here?

Buying a Carbine from Viejo

The Jeep limped into San Francisco and I stopped at the biggest adobe structure in the village. The temperature gauge was pegged as far as it could go to the right and steam poured from under the hood. Our Jeep looked like a spent horse that had done its best but just couldn't take it any more.

There was total silence in the village. The heat was oppressive and nothing moved. As I walked up to the open door a very old, wrinkled man appeared.

"Señor, I would like to buy some water from you," I said. He gave me a very long, hard look.

"Americano, why do you have my countryman tied up?" he asked.

"He tried to kill me," I replied.

"Untie him and I will give you both water."

I untied Julio and he bolted for the door and inside the house. The viejo invited me into his house and gave me a drink of tepid water. It tasted wonderful. I gulped it down and asked for more.

"I will pay you, señor," I said.

"You no pay," he said. "You are my guest. I have invited you into my home, please sit down."

"You have troubles with your car, señor?" he asked.

In my broken Spanish, I told him the whole story, including the troubles with the Jeep and with Julio.

"Maybe I can help you," he said.

"I will pay you."

"No, that is not necessary. I think I owe something to you Americanos."

"How is that?" I asked.

"Have you heard of the Mexican General, Pancho Villa?"

"Of course I have," I said.

"He was a great leader, but he did some bad things," the old man said. "One time I was with Pancho when we attacked your country. We broke into stores. We took things that did not belong to us. I did not hurt anyone. I had a rifle, but I could not buy any bullets as I had no money to buy them."

"Pancho, he was mad at a storekeeper who had cheated him He said, ride, and we followed. He was our leader. I rode with him in many battles. But I am sorry that we took things from the Americanos. Maybe I can help you and repay your countrymen for my bad deeds. I am an old man and I will die soon. I do not see any Americanos to say I am sorry for the bad things I did in your country."

Many times in Mexico, particularly in the states of Chihuahua and Durango, I encountered old Mexicans who said they rode with the legendary bandit Pancho Villa. One time I asked a Viejo, an old man, if he had known the General.

He said "I knew Pancho very, very well."

"How was that?" I asked.

He replied, "One day I am riding my horse along the trail to Chihuahua City. I meet up with another horseman who is riding toward me. The trail is very narrow and we come together, nose to nose. Neither one of us would move over to let the other one pass. The other horseman pulled a big pistola and said, 'get off that horse.' My horse becomes frightened and he make a big dump in the middle of the trail. The other horseman said, 'Now, you eat that dump or I will kill you.' I eat the dump and the other horseman thinks it is so funny that he laughs so hard that he drop his pistola."

"I pick up the pistola and I say to the other horseman, 'Now, you get off that horse and eat that dump or I will kill you.'" The other horseman, he get off his horse and eat the dump. "You ask me if I know Pancho Villa"? "Hell yes, I know Pancho Villa. We had lunch together on the trail to Chihuahua City."

"Come with me," he said to Julio, and they walked off into the desert. They returned with their arms loaded with cactus branches. I am still drinking the warm water. The old man beats the cactus in a pulp and then boils it into a paste. I stuff more duct tape into the hole and we pour the mixture into the radiator. I crank up the engine and after a couple of minutes, the leak becomes smaller, but is still dripping.

"I must pay you for your help, my friend," I say.

"No, señor, consider my help to you as payment for the things I took from your country."

I filled the jerry can I had emptied into the radiator with water and gave the gas in the other can to the old man for his small generator. We filled this can and our canteens and were ready to be on our way back to checkpoint 81. I was beginning to think that we were going to make it after all. As I shook hands with the Viejo and thanked him, I noticed an old .30-30 hanging on the wall. It was a beat-up carbine, lever action with a chunk taken out of the stock.

I asked him, "Where did you get that rifle?"

He said, "It belonged to the general. He gave it to me after our last battle."

"I would like to buy it from you. I need a weapon exactly like that in my work. I will treat it with great respect," I said.

"I will sell it to you, as I need money to send to my son so that he can come to visit me before I die."

"How much," I asked him.

"One hundred pesos," he replied. "And I have one bullet for it."

"I will give you two hundred because I want you to see your son and you are a good man."

"No, señor, that is too much."

"Please take it. I have always wanted something that belonged to that great general, and this will probably be the only chance I will have something like his rifle."

He said, "Bueno," and took it down from the wall and handed it to me. He rummaged around in a box in a corner and came up with a cartridge that looked like it would fit the carbine. The tip of the lead was covered with a blue-green oxide—he had had this cartridge for a long time.

I handed him the two hundred pesos and said "Would you like to shoot it one more time?" A strange look came over his face, he paused and, almost in a reverent tone, he whispered, "Si señor, por favor."

I handed him the weapon. He hefted it up and down a couple of times and raised it to his shoulder. I scraped the oxide from the bullet with my KA-BAR and handed it to him. He expertly slipped the cartridge into the feed and cranked the lever to chamber the round. He smiled broadly—the first time since I met him—at the sound of the brass and steel slamming together.

"Pick a target," I said. He held the carbine to his shoulder and moved it from side to side until he focused on a large, squat barrel cactus. For almost a full minute he held a bead on the plant, and then he pulled the trigger. The bullet sped from the muzzle of the gun, followed by a puff of blue smoke and a loud report. The cactus blew apart into a thousand pieces. The kick of the gun knocked the old man back, and he laughed. I'll bet that was the first time he had laughed in years. Slowly, he handed me the gun.

"No," I said. It is my gift to you."

He shook his head, "No, mi amigo. It is my gift to you. Vaya con Dios."

Julio climbed into the Jeep and I didn't tie him up. I put the ignition wires together, the engine spit a time or two, and we were on our way to checkpoint 81.

Alacrans!

The engine was making all kinds of weird clanking sounds, but each turn of the pistons brought us closer to checkpoint 81. The duct tape patch and the viejo's cactus paste had pretty well stopped the leak and I only had to bring the Jeep to a halt twice to refill the radiator. The desert seemed to stretch forever and the sun's radiation turned what breeze there was into a very warm wind. The Jeep ground along in second gear until the shapes of the small adobe shacks outside the checkpoint came into view. It was a welcome sight, as the sun was just setting.

Up ahead, by one of the shacks, a man was chopping wood. We pulled over when I recognized the young soldier who had stopped us at the checkpoint. I wanted to ask him about what happened to the sergeant of the guard.

The soldier laughed. "The captain took him away, but he was much too valuable to the general to have been put in jail." The sergeant was an expert at forcing bribes from the timber men and others who worked the nearby farms and forests and had to pass through the checkpoint. He would split the bribes with the politician who managed this area, who in turn would give a cut to the general. If some people got hurt or angry, so what. That's life outside the big cities.

As we were talking, we heard a great commotion from inside the hut. A young, very pregnant, woman dashed out the door. She was hysterically screaming, "Alacran, alacran." The soldier dropped his ax and rushed into the hut. I leapt from the Jeep and followed on his heels.

Inside, a toddler lay on a mat, squirming about and screaming at the top of his lungs. The soldier picked up the child in his arms, whirled and carried him outside in the fading light. The woman had dropped a flashlight and I reached down to pick it up. I felt one sharp prick on my right hand, then another. Immediately my hand started to throb. Damn, that hurt! In the beam of the flashlight I saw several many-legged, light-colored insects about three inches long squirming and writhing on the dirt floor. Damn, I had stuck my hand into a nest of scorpions, and here in this iron-rich soil, the bite of a scorpion can be deadly.

I rushed outside, shaking my hand. Boy, that really hurt! The soldier was holding the little boy who was quivering and beginning to sweat. His leg was red and swollen and he was having trouble breathing. The soldier had a look on his face of complete helplessness. His wife continued screaming and the child was strangely silent.

I ran to the Jeep. Along with the gear I had brought with me from Deming was a first aid kit. In the first aid kit was a vial of an anti-scorpion serum that was recently discovered by a doctor from the University of Arizona. I shook the vial and loaded its contents into a syringe. I looked the soldier in the eyes and nodded my head. He gave me a blank stare for a minute and then said, "Si."

I jabbed the syringe into the ever-growing red spot on the boy's leg. He let out a loud yelp and began crying again. The child was twitching and having convulsions.

It was time for action. "We go to the doctor in Chihuahua City," I said. The soldier told his wife to get in the back of the Jeep and gave her the child. He ducked into the hut and brought out a serape and gave it to the woman to wrap around the baby. As we took off, the guard stepped in front of the Jeep. The soldier rattled off some instructions to the guard, whose rifle was at the ready, and we shot past the guard shack and our wheels hit the pavement.

It wasn't until we had gone about a half a mile down the road when I thought, "Where's Julio?" At that moment, I didn't know and I didn't care. My right hand was tingling and getting numb and I was having a little trouble breathing. I had the gas pedal to the floor and the engine was clanking and making grinding noises as if it would tear itself apart. There was no traffic on the road, so we could just press on until the engine quit or we reached Chihuahua City.

We barreled through La Mesa without stopping. My hand was now completely numb, no feeling at all. The soldier turned to talk to the woman from time to time and every now and then gave me a sidelong glance. He motioned to my hand. I said it was OK. The child was moaning softly and we sped on into the night.

About half way to Chihuahua City, the temperature gauge began to creep up into the red zone. I didn't want to, but we pulled over and I emptied the remainder of the jerry can into the radiator. We were on the road again, and we were racing against time. By now, the gas gauge was hovering a little above empty— maybe we should have gassed up back at La Mesa—but it was too late now. My hand was like a solid rock. It felt strange to bang it against the gear shift and not be able to feel it.

I was getting sleepy. The adrenaline was keeping my foot pressed down hard on the gas pedal and the engine was now making a high-pitched whine.

"Come on baby, I shouted to the Jeep! Just ten kilometers more and we can all go to sleep."

Up ahead was a traffic circle where a uniformed policeman was arrogantly directing the cars this way and that. I knew we were going to have trouble with this guy, but we had to stop. I slammed on the brakes and the cop stomped over to the Jeep. A car skidded to a stop behind us. The cop's face flushed and he made a move to draw his pistol. I shouted, "Hospital, Hospital!"

Without thinking, he said "Turn right at the next circle." I jammed on the gas and we cut back into traffic. The cop was dumbfounded and burst out with a string of profanities, but we were gone before he could draw his pistol. Another thing that I was learning was that some of the cops are unpredictable. It must be something about carrying a gun.

In two minutes we were at the circle and a quick right turn put us in front of the hospital. We jerked to a stop and the Jeep bucked and gasped and just quit running. Smoke poured from the engine and steam bathed us, and several onlookers, in vapor. The soldier grabbed the baby and we rushed through the door. A whitecoated intern was walking down the corridor and we stopped him. "Emergency," I told him. "Alacran bite." He nonchalantly pointed down the hall.

No one was in the emergency room. I frantically looked around for a doctor. The soldier, with a stoic look on his face, held the child and did not say a word. It came to me that I was not in charge of the situation.

"Calm down, you jerk," I thought to myself. I had been running on adrenaline for the past couple of hours and I was now beginning to think of where we go from here. My hand was beginning to get some feeling in it and it was throbbing. A doctor strolled in and said, "Put the child on the table and get out. I'll call you when I need you. It will be a while."

The soldier and I walked down the hall to a bench where his wife sat. Her head was bowed and she was crying softly. She hid her face. "He is my baby," she sobbed. "Please don't let him die." The embarrassed soldier put his hand on her shoulder and said, "He is our only baby."

A nurse rushed up and excitedly asked, "Who will pay for this?" I reached in my pocket and pulled out my cash. Forty five pesos. Not much. I took off my watch and said to the nurse, "Please take this until I come back with more money. These are my friends, they work for me. I will pay all the bills. I am Ingeniero Jaime

Hall. I am the guest of Gen. Hernando Rodriquez." She took the watch and went back to her desk.

"Thank you very much, señor," said the soldier. "I will pay you back."

"That's OK ," I said. I stuck out my hand and said, "My name is Jim Hall."

He eagerly grasped my hand and said, "My name is Juan Ochoa. I am Yaqui."

My hand was beginning to have some feeling returning and his firm grip almost brought me to my knees. I gasped, "I have heard of your people. I understand they are very brave and are very good fighters."

"Thank you, señor," he said. I handed him my forty-five pesos.

"Please take this until I see you tomorrow morning. I am staying at the Plaza Hotel. Call me if I can help you tonight. I'm sure that your son is going to be all right." I walked past the nurse and out the door.

The Jeep reluctantly started and I slowly drove through the back streets of Chihuahua City. The engine was making such a racket that I was embarrassed and I did not want to be stopped by the police. I had no money for a bribe and I was in no mood to be hassled. I drove into the garage at the Plaza and waited for Alfredo, the bell boy, to come help me. He looked at me for an explanation, but I was too tired to give him one.

I motioned to my gear in the back of the Jeep and said, "Bring it all up to my room." I picked up the two rifles and said, "but first, bring me a couple of beers and some aspirins." When I got to my room I placed the rifles on an overstuffed chair and took my boots off. Boy, did that feel good. Alfredo arrived and I downed the first beer in one giant gulp. I lay down on the bed and all the tiredness seemed to drain out of my body. It had been one hell of a day. Welcome to Mexico!

At the Hospital

I didn't even bother taking a shower; I just climbed into bed and conked out. I was up at five o'clock, as I was worried about Juan's little boy. My hand was still sore and throbbing and I was a little sick to my stomach, but all in all, not too much the worst for wear. I guess my body weight and my good physical condition weakened the scorpion's poison and I was able to fight it off. After a quick shower, I was on my way to the hospital.

Juan was still on the bench where I left him last night and his wife was asleep beside him.

"How's the boy?" I asked him.

"The doctor told me he was going to be all right and we can take him home this afternoon." The anti-venom shot had saved the boy's life, he added, and we were "very lucky to have such a good friend who would risk his own life to save the life of a little boy. You could have very well have died from the scorpions."

His wife awakened and she had been crying. "Thank you señor, oh, thank you," she said. Juan also had tears in his eyes and said, "I will do anything, absolutely anything, to repay you. Tell me, señor, I will do it."

I was embarrassed and told them that just having their child well was payment enough for me. "Señor," Juan said and dropped his head, "it would be a great honor if we could name our child after you."

"Certainly," I said. "The name Jaime Ochoa sounds fine with me." We shook hands and he smiled broadly. The hand felt much better than it did last night.

"I would like to come to work for you, at any wage, even for nothing," he said. I explained to him that I did not have a company and I came to Mexico as a favor for a friend and would be going back to the States in a few days. However, if I ever returned to Mexico to work, I certainly would look him up and we would work together.

"How much longer do you have to serve in the Army," I asked him.

"Two more months and I will be free," he said.

"Well, I must be going," I said as I turned toward the door.

"Take good care of little Jaime," I said.

"Señor, your pesos?"

"Please keep them," I said. "You will need the money for bus fare back to La Mesa. You can repay me when we meet again."

With a shrug, he accepted. No matter what his pride said, he had to have bus fare to take him and his family back home.

I walked back to the Plaza Hotel and as it was still early morning, I decided to eat breakfast alone. I had not contacted Fr. Pat last night, as it was going to take a lot of talking to explain the absence of Julio, the complete destruction of Señor Ortega's Jeep and, last but not least, what happened to the lost gold mine in Julio's story.

At about ten o'clock I called Fr. Pat's room and a sleepy voice said that the wedding party had celebrated far into the wee hours, but he would be down for breakfast in about a half hour. He was, of course, surprised to see me back long before I was expected and he was eager to hear the details of what happened. I was determined to fulfill yesterday's dreams of "a nice cold beer" and ordered several to last me during what promised to be a lengthy narrative. Fr. Pat listened intently and asked few questions.

All in all, the story was pretty simple. Two bright, well-educated Americanos were completely hoodwinked by an ignorant, grade school dropout, Mexican laborer. A little greed, mixed with a hint of adventure plus too much time on their hands lured the Americanos to take a trip to an exotic foreign land.

"Forget about the Jeep," Fr. Pat said, "Señor Ortega can well afford the loss, and he can take it off his income tax. As for the gold mine, he is still going to listen to the tall tales spun at the Saturday night bull sessions and, who knows, maybe he will hear another one that will lead us to another lost gold mine in Mexico."

The padre changed the subject. "How would you like to join the wedding party and spend a few days on the beach at Acapulco?"

"That sounds great," I said. "Let's go."

We went to the telegraph office and I sent a message to Mike telling him that I would not be back in Deming for another week. I could just see his explosive reaction when he read it. He would blow his stack. But this shootout was going to happen anyway when I would tell him I was not going underground any more. What the hell, it was getting time to move on, so why not enjoy the Mexican sunshine and worry about what happens in Deming after the trip to Acapulco?

8
Don Diego's Request

It was party time again tonight and this time I would have a chance to meet the wedding entourage. I spent the afternoon touring Chihuahua City and was showered and suited up by eight o'clock. It was another fancy affair and Fr. Pat introduced me around to a lot of big wheels. I don't know if a priest can go to hell for lying, but he was pushing the limits in his praise and embellishments of my talents and accomplishments. I had several businessmen ask me if I was available to inspect mining properties they were interested in. I had to tell them I was just in Mexico on vacation and I did not have the work papers required by the Mexican government.

As the evening wore on, I noticed a very beautiful young lady, about 21 or 22, who was always on the edge of the groups of people who were having conservations. She was approached by young men but she brushed them off and remained aloof.

She was going to be hard to impress. I was interested in her; she was by far the pick of the group of the females my age, but I didn't want to approach her and do anything that would make me look like a fool if I violated protocol. I was going to be with this group for the next several days and I did not want to be looked on as the ugly American. So I asked Fr. Pat to introduce me to her. He did, with the usual buildup, but she dismissed me before I even had a chance to make a move on her.

She was Tina, the younger sister of the bride, and she was sulking because all the attention was being focused on her sister. I wasn't looking for any lost causes, so I said, "Glad to meet you," and went searching elsewhere.

Over in a corner was a tall, distinguished looking white haired gentleman. He seemed to be like a noble holding court. Fr. Pat offered to introduce me to Don Diego Ortega, the patriarch of this wealthy family. He made his fortune as the owner of a string of nightclubs in Juarez and was also very big in political circles in Mexico City.

"I've told him all about you, so try to be humble," Fr. Pat said, laughing.

We waited our turn to get the old man's attention and he greeted us warmly. In Mexico, as in Italy, the title "Don" is not casually bestowed upon a man in the public arena. It means that this man is known in his community as a very nice guy or as a very bad guy and he is to be feared and, most of all, respected.

"Young man," he said, "I have been wanting to meet you. I have an idea I wish to discuss with you."

"Any time, Don Diego," I said. "I am at your service."

"How about now," he said. "Let's go in the next room where we won't be disturbed." We went into the adjoining room. He called the waiter and ordered two beers for each of us. Ah, a fellow beer drinker; he must be a very good guy.

He got right to the point. "Tomorrow night we are holding the grand reception for my daughter and her husband at my home in Acapulco. I will be giving them a gift of a new Corvette, and I want to do it, not in an ordinary manner. I want to remind my family I am still the master of the surprise. Fr. O'Hara tells me you are the world's greatest parachutist. Is that correct?"

I said, "I'm probably one of the best. There aren't many people who do this for a living."

"What I want for you to do is parachute into a small area at my home and deliver the keys of the Corvette to my daughter. Can you do that?"

"Yes," I said.

"Have you done it before?"

"Yes," I replied.

"Good. My considerable contacts are at your disposal and expense is no problem, within reason, of course. I want to see it done, successfully, with style. It is worth a thousand dollars to you."

"It's a deal," I said.

He called the waiter over and told him to find his grandson and bring him to our meeting. When the young man arrived, we got down to business. His name was Jesse, and he was more than eager to be part of his grandfather's scheme. In fact, it was nauseating to see how he flattered and bowed to the old man. This fellow knew where his next paycheck was coming from. He was going to bust his butt to see that this project was a success and we all looked good, especially him. That was OK with me and I was going to push him to the limit.

First, I was going to need an airplane ticket to Acapulco. He would need one, also. We would take the first flight out tomorrow morning. He would be my shadow for the next day. I would need a place to stay, probably at the grandfather's house. Jesse would be my chauffeur and instantly available whenever I wanted him. Through Don Diego's contacts, he would arrange a meeting between me and the State of Guerrero's police commander as soon as possible.

He would also call Don Diego's pilot at the local airport and set up a meeting with him at his hangar at the airfield. He would also rent a one thousand candlepower searchlight and have it delivered to the Don's house, and would get a white jumpsuit for me.

We left from the Chihuahua City airport at eight o'clock the next morning and arrived in Acapulco two hours later, rented a car and drove to Don Diego's house, or should I say, mansion? The entertainment business must have been very good in Juarez. It was easily a million-dollar layout. The reception was to be held outside overlooking an immaculately-maintained lawn that was a natural drop zone. A north-south jump run would keep me clear of any major obstructions and we could set up the searchlight at the edge of the woods, and out of sight.

The state police commander had driven in from the capitol at Chilpancingo to meet with us at the don's mansion. He brought his deputy commander, a Capt. Roberto Camerero, with him and ordered him to stay in close touch with us until the project was completed.

Don Diego had clout and it became more apparent as we put the operation together. The state police cars had the radio net we

needed and they were portable. We could station one car on each
side of the drop zone and they would shine their spotlights, with
a red cover over the lens, to converge with the beam of the big
spotlight at about 500 feet. The police captain would direct the
jump aircraft from his command car and make sure the airspace
was clear before the drop.

We met the pilot, Felix Mendoza, at his hangar at a small civilian airport west of the city. He had never dropped a jumper before, but he was willing to learn. One of his aircraft was a Cessna
180, an excellent aircraft to jump from. We removed the right
hand door of the 180 and taped over anything that might cause a
hangup.

We went into the pilot's office and carefully discussed the procedures several times to make sure we were both on the same
page. He was concerned that what he was going to do was against
the Mexican Aviation Agency's regulations, but felt sure Don
Diego's influence would cover him. We checked his radio against
the police radios and everything was five by five.

Next, and the most important thing: a parachute. None of the
pilot's emergency parachutes were suitable so we went to visit
the military detachment at the big international airport serving
Acapulco. The Mexican Air Force had three AT-6 trainer aircraft
stationed there and they all were equipped with the standard
United States Air Force back and seat pack parachutes.

One of the AT-6 aircraft was assigned to the State Police and it
was flown by a Maj. Manuel Morales who, as a young pilot, had
flown with the small Mexican detachment attached to the U.S.
Army Air Force during World War II. They were known as Es-
cuadron 201 and flew P-47 Thunderbolt fighters against the
Japanese in the Pacific. They had an outstanding record and, as
I was to learn while working with the major on future projects,
he was a good example of their flying ability. Maj. Morales was
a close friend of the deputy police commander, Capt.Camerero,
and as they wanted to keep this operation as quiet as possible, he
was an ideal guy to work with.

I looked over the major's parachutes and ruled out the seat
packs. Those things opened like the kick of a mule and they had
the habit of malfunctioning if you had a bad body position when

you pulled the ripcord. And on this jump I didn't want any problems, as I would not be wearing a reserve parachute.

I chose a standard 28-foot flat circular canopy with a B-4 harness. I checked the parachute record log and it indicated that the chute had been repacked about sixty days ago and had not been repaired. Nevertheless, I was going to inspect it carefully and repack it.

"How are we going to work this?" I asked Maj. Morales. "You won't be able to use it as an emergency parachute after I jump it."

"No matter, I will write it off as salvage," he said.

I spread the parachute canopy out on the hangar floor and inspected it carefully. When I

Jim and Felix Mendosa

asked Maj. Morales for a pair of sharp scissors, he gave me a quizzical look. He went into the office and returned with a large tool that was used to trim bushes.

I said, "No, something small, like you would use to cut paper."

This time, when he came back he had a small pair of scissors a little bit bigger than fingernail clippers. I said, "OK this might take a little longer, but it will do." I asked the Air Force major and the police captain to grasp the parachute canopy at gore number 28 and hold it tight while I cut the two panels from the canopy.

Maj. Morales looked at me as if I were nuts. "You're crazy. You're loco, Señor Jamie."

I told him not to get excited; I knew what I was doing. The modification to this canopy was called a "blank gore," something relatively new in the parachuting world. I had seen drawings of this modification in a report from the French Embassy, and I was looking forward to testing it. It would give the jumper some control of the direction the parachute was drifting and help him land much closer to the spot he was trying to hit.

I toyed with the idea of finding a seamstress to reinforce the cut material with tape, but we were running out of time, so I would take my chances. I very carefully repacked the parachute and included about a pound of gold glitter particles I had borrowed from the wedding decorators. They would reflect nicely in the searchlight's beam. I buttoned up the parachute pack and our end of the operation was ready to go.

The guests and the wedding party had been arriving all day at the mansion. The champagne began flowing at six o'clock and the gift presentations started about seven.

My "entrance" was to happen at eight. I would land, walk up to the stage and present the key to the couple, and someone would drive the red Corvette across the lawn and to the stage. The happy couple would enter the Vette, crank up the engine and drive off into the night. The party would continue until the wee hours. This group didn't need the wedding couple to continue celebrating.

Our team had been set and ready to go at seven o'clock. The engine had been run-up, radios checked, the police cars placed at the four corners of the drop zone, and Jessie was manning the searchlight. The Cessna was airborne at seven thirty and we climbed to altitude above the hills north of the city.

With the Pacific Ocean to our west and the lit-up city of Acapulco in the foreground, it was a spectacular sight. We were at altitude and flew back across the DZ and had the police cars turn on their red lights to see if they were working. The north and west light looked good but the east and south lights did not show up. I radioed the police captain to have them rotate their lights, but they still were not visible by the time we passed back over. No problem. The mansion and lawn were a slash of light that stood out in the dark of the foothills.

I had briefed the pilot that when we were caught by the searchlight, he would cut the power on the engine and as the aircraft speed dropped below seventy miles per hour, give me the signal to bail out.

At 7:55 we were over the ocean and ready to start our jump run. I radioed the police captain for clearance and he said it was

"Go." We passed over the beach at 7:58 and at exactly eight
o'clock Jessie switched on the searchlight.

It held steady about ten degrees to our right and as we entered
the full beam of the light, our whole world changed from one of
pitch black darkness to blazing white light.

This came as a shock. Suddenly I was thrown back almost
eleven years to the day when the B-29 bomber on which I was the
flight engineer was caught by a trio of Japanese radar-controlled
searchlights over the naval arsenal in Osaka, Japan. Our crew was
on a fire raid at an altitude of seventy five hundred feet and the
searchlights we were unlucky enough to encounter were part of
the high-tech equipment the Germans had smuggled into Japan
by submarines after Germany had surrendered. They were state of
the art and once they latched onto a bomber, their synchronized
anti-aircraft batteries opened up and you were very likely going to
be shot down.

We were on our bomb run and the bombardier had turned the
aircraft's course, straight and level, over to the Norden bomb
sight. Suddenly, the B-29 was bracketed by a rain of high explosive artillery shells. At that moment, the bombardier yelled,
"Bombs away," and our aircraft leapt skyward as 20,000 pounds
of napalm tumbled from its bomb bays.

The voice of the panic-stricken left waist gunner screamed over
the inter phone, "We've been hit hard, and there is a big hole in
the wing between number one and number two engines."

The central fire control gunner yelled, "We've got wounded
back here."

The calm, cool southern drawl of the pilot, Lt. Charlie Barber,
broke through the noise and he said, "OK, you guys. Calm down
and get the hell off the damn intercom!"

The B-29 was in a steep dive to the right and it was shaking
violently, but the radar searchlights still held us in their tenacious
grips. The pilot's voice came over the intercom, "Prepare to bail
out! Bail out!"

My daydreaming was broken by the yelling of my jump pilot,
Felix Mendosa, above the roar of the air rushing by the open door
of the Cessna. "Bail out, bail out," he was screaming. I hit the
wheel of the Cessna and almost smashed into the strut of the aircraft as I leapt from my place in the door. The pilot had forgotten

to lock the brakes, a common but stupid mistake of first-time jump pilots.

I dropped into the warm sky over Mexico and thanked God that it wasn't the extremely hostile cold sky over Japan. I free fell about 500 feet to make sure I had plenty of airspeed before pulling the ripcord, and the chute opened with a sharp crack. The opening shock was a little harder that I expected, but when I checked the canopy, everything was as I wanted it to be.

The sky sparkled with a thousand points of light as the glitter I had packed in the parachute was released into the night air. It was a good touch. That was the first time I had tried that gimmick, and it looked good.

I had lost the searchlight but I could see the drop zone clearly. I turned the parachute canopy and ran toward the target. "Damn, that was a good spot," I thought as I was directly over the stage at about a thousand feet.

Just then, Jessie found me with the searchlight. I was completely blinded by the light and couldn't see a thing. The light was so bright and intense I thought I could feel the heat.

"Turn off the damn light, you moron," I screamed to myself. But the moron couldn't hear my thoughts, and the light blazed on. I hadn't had time to determine the wind direction and speed, but instinct told me to make a 180 degree turn and hold it. Better to land short than to crash through a window of the mansion. I assumed the position for a stand–up landing—a very dangerous maneuver in these conditions—but my reputation was on the line and I had to look good.

Thankfully, Jessie could not depress the search light any closer to the ground than permitted by an automatic stop and I broke out of the beam of light at about a hundred feet above the ground— less than five seconds before touchdown. I braced myself and made a perfect stand-up landing. There wasn't a sound from the crowd as I punched the quick release on the parachute harness and stepped from the rig. (I would remember this jump as one of the best of my career.)

I walked up to the bride, bowed and presented her with the spare key to the Vette, as the red machine pulled up—running right over my parachute. The crowd cheered! I walked into the shadows beside the stage and slipped out of my jump suit.

Suddenly, a girl rushed out of the crowd and planted a big kiss square on my lips. It was Tina, the little sister. She must have been impressed, or wanted to gain some attention.

I had to wait while the bride and groom zoomed off in their magic carpet before I could retrieve my parachute. I field-packed it and tossed it under the stage. If someone stole it, as they probably would, so what? It had paid for itself.

Tina had watched me closely as I field packed my parachute. "I would like to try that sometime," she said.

Coming from her, it was just so much baloney. It was no more than small talk, and didn't ring true. My senses were telling me, watch out buddy, but nothing ventured, nothing gained. This young lady was going to be trouble, but I'll go along with her to see where it leads.

She took me by the hand and led me into the mansion. There was a ballroom right in front of us, and that's where we were heading. I didn't want to dance; I wanted a beer. Tina wanted to dance, so it looked like we were going to dance.

I am far from being a classy dancer; in fact I am below average and I demonstrated that to her very quickly. I am an observer. I like to stand on the sidelines and watch the girls. Wearing paratrooper jump boots didn't help me at all.

We got through the number and as we walked off the floor, we ran into Capt. Camerero.

"That was absolutely one of the greatest things I have ever seen," he said. "You are really good. I would be honored if you would have a drink with me."

Of course I said yes.

Tina pouted and said "Oh, you can do that later. There are so many people I want to introduce you to."

The captain gave me a sly look and said, "Perhaps we can do it later?"

Tina dragged me around like a prize dog at a pet show and it got to be old—real fast. Most of the people I was introduced to were polite, some even overly so, but with some, particularly the younger males, I sensed a reserved coolness, maybe hostility. Kinda like, what is this Americano doing with one of our fair maidens? Perhaps the fairest of them all. I suggested that we go out on the terrace and get some fresh air.

Tina probably thought that I was going to make a move on her, but I really wanted to get away from the crowd.

We were enjoying the million-dollar view of Acapulco when a body slammed into me from behind. I was knocked down, and before I could get up, two guys piled on top of me. I tried to defend myself and I thought I was doing a pretty good job until one of the jerks landed a solid sucker punch to the side of my nose.

Blood and snot flew everywhere, and it dazed me for a minute before I managed to get hold of a couple of fingers that belonged to the guy who had landed the blow. I bent them back and the guy screamed as he tried to jump to his feet. He pulled me with him as he got up and I kept my grip on his hand. I bent the fingers further back and I heard them crack.

I dropped him and looked for the other guy. He was just getting to his feet and he had a large knife in his hand. I caught him on the side of the head with a well-aimed kick and he flew about three feet through the air and slammed into a concrete flower pot. Score one more for my genuine American-made paratrooper jump boots. They ain't much for dancing, but they sure are great for fighting. I think I am beginning to forget how to fight with my fists.

By now we had attracted a small crowd. From the corner of my eye, I could see someone shoving the people aside and trying to get to the center of the action. It was Capt. Camerero and he acted like he was on official business.

He expertly disarmed the guy with the knife and slammed his face into the cement floor for good measure. He turned to take care of the guy with the fingers but stopped when he saw that Tina was cradling his head in her lap and running her fingers through his hair and cooing sweet nothings in his ear.

The captain said, "Let's get out of here, get you cleaned up, and have that drink."

My ego was kind of bruised. I had won the fight, sort of, but lost the girl. We went into the kitchen and the cook put a cold rag on my nose and stopped the bleeding. My shirt and pants were a mess so I excused myself and went to my room and changed clothes.

When I returned, I joined the captain and his wife, or girl-friend—he didn't say which—for a beer.

"Do you want to press charges?" he asked. "The guy did have a knife."

"Hell no," I said. "It seems as though I got caught, and was used, in a lover's quarrel. You guys down here sure take losing a girl friend really hard."

Don Diego sent word that he was very pleased with my performance and he would like to have breakfast with Fr. Pat and me at nine o'clock tomorrow morning. My head was beginning to hurt, so I said good night and went to bed.

9
Get Papers in Mexico City

Fr. Pat and I showed up at Don Diego's private dining room at ten minutes to nine. We were warmly greeted by the don and we went out on the patio and had our coffee while overlooking the city and the bright blue Pacific Ocean. It wouldn't take much to get used to this life. There was no limit to the praise Don Diego had for last night's parachute jump and the professionalism that it took to make it work. He gave me an envelope that contained ten one hundred dollar bills, American, and repeated his thanks.

"I am indebted to you for helping make my daughter very happy and for making her reception a great success," he said. "Have you ever considered starting a business doing exhibition parachute jumps and using your skill and education to explore for mineral deposits in the remote regions of Mexico?" he asked.

"The thought has entered my mind," I said, "but the possibility of getting the necessary permits and all the paperwork involved with the Mexican government seems too much to overcome."

"Not at all," he said. "With my connections we could accomplish it very easily. My lawyers could draw up the necessary papers in less than an hour, and I will pay for it."

It sounded like a good deal to me. It would be nice to have these papers and permits in my back pocket if I ever did decide to do some business in Mexico.

"Let's do it."

"Fine," said the don. "I will call my law firm in Mexico City and you can pick up the papers on your way home."

In an hour, we were on our way north in the rear seat of Don Diego's chauffeur-driven Cadillac. As the don had promised, his lawyers had all the paperwork completed and all I had to do was sign them and have my passport stamped to certify I was legal to make money in Mexico.

I asked the lawyer if I could get a Mexican parachutist's license and he said he didn't know, but he would find out. I showed him my United States National Parachute Jumpers-Riggers license and my more recent Parachute Club of America licenses, as well as my senior parachute rigger's license. He put in a call to the director of the Secretaria de Comunicaciones y Obras Publicas, the Mexican equivalent of the Fédération Aéronautique Internationale, the body that issues worldwide parachuting and pilots licenses.

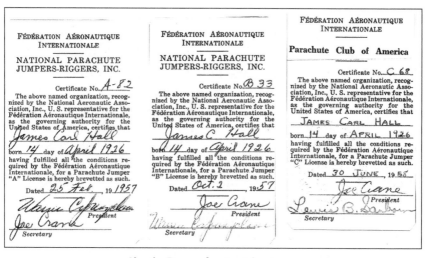

Jim's Parachute License

The Secretaria's office said that they didn't know if they had the authorization to grant a license for someone to make a parachute jump in Mexico, as the government viewed the parachute as a weapon of war and such a permit would have to be issued by the military. And they seriously doubted that they would grant one to an American. As this was a large law firm, and probably represented a lot of money, the secretary said that he would look into the matter and get back to them.

This would turn out to be a rather lengthy and expensive procedure, but finally, after traveling up and down through every Mexican government agency that had any authority in the realms of aviation or military affairs, I, an American, was awarded the very first parachutist's license issued in Mexico.

The First Mexican Parachuting License

After my bout with the Mexican legal system, the chauffeur took us to Mexico City International Air Port and we were back at the Plaza Hotel in Chihuahua by nine o'clock that night. Fr. Pat and I cleared out of the Plaza early the next morning, passed through customs at the border—there was no trouble with Pancho's rifle—and were back in Deming in time to eat dinner.

We had lots of time to dissect the entire adventure on the road trip from Chihuahua City. Fr. Pat had made a lot of new friends and I had gotten a lot of experience, some good, some bad. Fr. Pat probably would not have to go to hell for all the lies—exaggerations—he told about my parachuting abilities, as I had, with a little luck, proven him to be right.

All in all, a very interesting trip. One thing we both agreed on was that the chances that Julio would show up at one of the Saturday night bull sessions in the basement of Saint Michael's church were pretty remote. But, if you were ever in Juarez, you might see Julio on one of the side streets selling tickets to a girlie show or, maybe snake oil.

Deming and a Call from Don Diego

I did not relish the thought of my meeting with Mike. Although I was only gone a week, I had broken my promise when it looked as if I had an opportunity for a greater adventure than I could get working at the mine and mill.

Let's face it. At this stage of my life, I'm not ready to settle down doing a routine nine-to-five job. However, working at the mine did occasionally cause my heart rate to jump up. I entered the front office, walked past the time clock—I don't think I will be punching that thing any more—and knocked on Mike's door.

"Come in," he snarled.

I opened the door and walked in. Mike had his head down, working on some reports and vigorously puffing on his pipe. The smoke wreathed around his head and he appeared very angry. He looked up, surprised to see me, and said "When the hell did you get back?"

I immediately realized that my timing was terrible and I wished that I could erase the last few minutes and come back later. It wasn't that I was afraid of Mike or his anger, it was that I was uneasy around him. Physically, I was more than a match for him and, I don't know, maybe it was because he reminded me of my old man, and, at the time, I hadn't resolved where I stood with my dad.

"Sit down," he half ordered and half asked. "What do you want to do? I have a feeling that you want to move on and you have outgrown this job. If that's the case, I will give you a letter to cover your time here. You have done a good job and, by the same token, you have gained a lot of experience. A fair exchange. Both sides made out OK."

I thanked him for the opportunity to work for Allied Chemical and Dye. I had put a lot of effort into the job, and I had certainly gained a lot from the experience.

We shook hands and as I walked out the door he said, "Thanks for recovering my transit. It was a little scratched up, but it works just fine. By the way, we had another cave in at the face of that drift. It got to be just too dangerous so we just blocked the damn thing off. Your report on the accident was not to my liking, but it was fair."

I hadn't had breakfast yet so I decided to stop by the Pepsi plant and see if Sonny wanted to have a bite to eat. He was in a production meeting so I left word with his secretary that I would call him later. Well, here I was again, unemployed, but not too worried. I had an extra thousand bucks in my pocket that I didn't have before I went to Mexico and I didn't have to punch that damned time clock in the morning.

I walked back to Saint Michael's, and, although Fr. Pat had signed a note for me and I now drove a '50 Chevy, I needed the exercise.

I met the padre as he was going out the door and asked him if there were any chores I could do around the church to help pay for my sleeping quarters.

He said, "Well, yes there is. How are you at running a paint brush?"

"I could handle that," I said, and I spent the next five days painting and doing carpentry work around the church. By Friday, I felt that I had paid this week's rent and I was getting restless. When I gassed up at the Texaco service station in downtown Deming, I picked up a map of the southwestern States. I think I will drive to California and visit some of the old gold mining districts I had read about in the books I studied back at UNM. I would try my luck in some of the rivers and see if I could pay expenses by panning gold and, at the same time, soak up the culture. I would leave first thing Monday.

The Saturday night bull session was a dull affair. Most of the workers had been there before and they told the same old stories. Of course they wanted to hear about how the trip to Chihuahua went and where was Julio. I told them that we couldn't find the gold deposit Julio told us about and that he had decided to stay back home. No more questions were asked, and I didn't volunteer any more information.

Sunday evening, I found a note on my bed to call Don Diego, collect, in Juarez. When I reached the don, he was excited and greeted me warmly. He said that a very good friend of his had a gold mine—or at least they were digging on his property—and one of his workers had found a very rich rock that was solid gold. But the rock did not come from his property, but from another place in the mountains nearby.

The worker had found the gold while he was prospecting on his own time, after work. Before he knew it, the sky clouded over and it began to rain and got very dark and he got lost. He wandered around for several hours before he saw a campfire that his companions had built to help him find his way. His boss got very mad at him for getting lost and causing all this trouble so he did not show the boss or his fellow workers his find until they got back to Juarez to take a few days off.

The don's friend, who had been in the mining business for many years, said that this rock, with a chunk of solid gold in it, was the biggest he had ever seen, even in the big museum in Mexico City. The friend said that he didn't want to tell anybody about the gold find until he could go back into his claim with an experienced mining engineer—one he can trust—and try to find the place where the gold came from.

The don said he owed this old friend a big favor from when they were growing up and this was the first time he has had a chance to pay it back. If I would come to Juarez and go to his friend's mine with him, and help him look for the gold, he would pay all my expenses and a healthy fee, and the friend might also give me something extra. Anyway, with my new work papers, this would be a great way to start out my business.

"I will be in Juarez by ten o'clock tomorrow morning," I told the don.

So, it's Monday morning and instead of traveling west to sunny California, I am heading east and south to sunny Mexico. I met Don Diego at his office in downtown Juarez and we took a cab to the home of Señor Ruben Hernandez, the don's friend.

Señor Hernandez is a likable guy, but very intense and too timid to be the hardcharging businessman that Don Diego described to me. He was born in the Mexican state of Zacatecas, the same state in which his claim was located, about 800 miles south of the border on the way to Mexico City. His gold mine—it was little more that a claim located on the outskirts of what was once a profitable silver mining district in western Zacatecas—was passed down to him by his father.

Señor Hernandez explained that some prospecting work had been done on the property and there had been some sign of gold found in what had been an ancient stream bed. With the increase of the price of gold, he thought it would be a good business investment to do some exploration work on the property. He had sent four construction workers who were employed in his business in Juarez to Zacatecas to dig trenches and dry pan the dirt in selected spots that might yield traces of gold.

There was a possibility that water could be found fairly close to the surface, as a small stream flowed at times during the year in a gully about a hundred yards to the west. However, he wasn't going to spend any money looking for water until he was sure the investment was worth it.

This new development changed the whole game plan. He was really pumped up; he could barely contain his enthusiasm and was eager to get moving. However, he had scheduled an important business trip to Los Angeles for five days and was going to leave this afternoon. Before he left, we were to meet Miguel, the laborer who found the fabulous chunk of gold, and he was going to show me the treasure, and tell me, as much as he remembered, where he found it. Miguel and I were to drive to the city of Zacatecas in the morning and we would buy all the supplies we would need for our trip to the mining property. While we waited for Sr. Hernandez to return from his trip and meet us in Zacatecas, I could visit the museums and some of the government offices to learn more about the geologic formations we would be exploring.

Noon came and Miguel did not show up for our meeting. By twelve thirty, Miguel was still a no show and Señor Hernandez was becoming agitated. At one o'clock, he summoned his secretary to find out where Miguel was and how dare he make his boss wait. At two o'clock, Señor Hernandez had to leave for the airport to catch his flight to Los Angeles. He was very angry and told his secretary to express his displeasure to Miguel and warn him that if he wasn't on time to leave with me in the morning he was fired.

Don Diego showed me some of the high spots, and some of the low spots, of Juarez and I retired early. Tomorrow was going to be a long day. I was to meet Miguel at the office at eight o'clock the next morning.

When I arrived, the secretary was distraught and crying. Miguel had been located, and he was dead! The police said his body had been found in a vacant lot outside of Juarez early this morning. His corpse showed signs of torture, his hands were tied behind his back, and he was shot in the back of the head, execution style. And the chunk of gold was missing.

We located Señor Hernandez at a meeting in Los Angeles about noon and told him what had happened. He was shocked and said that this called for us to move quickly. He would try to cut short his meetings and be home as soon as possible. He asked me if I would drive to Zacatecas by myself and make the preparations and buy the supplies that we would need for our trip into the mining property.

I, of course, said "Yes." He would call an old, close, family friend, Fr. Ramon Lopez, the rector of the church of Santo Domingo in the heart of the city of Zacatecas, and ask him to help me in any way he could.

"You will like him," Señor Hernandez said. "He was educated in your country and speaks English very well."

That afternoon, the police reported that they had traced Miguel's movements last night and said that he had visited several cantinas and was drinking heavily. He told anyone who would listen that he was celebrating because he had found a rich gold mine and he would be gone for several weeks to help bring the treasure out of the back country. He showed everybody a large piece of gold he carried, but he would not let any of his drinking buddies hold the gold as he was afraid they would run away with it and his boss would fire him.

He was last seen at the Tres Amigos de Sinaloa bar about two o'clock in the morning. No more information was available, but they would keep the investigation going, as Señor Hernandez and Señor Ortega were very powerful men in the community of northern Chihuahua.

I picked up a new Jeep—it had twenty miles on the odometer—at the dealership in El Paso and hoped it was as good as the one Señor Ortega had loaned us. I was on the road to Zacatecas at six the next morning. The trip was a little slower than I had anticipated, as the farmers and ranchers were driving their cattle and goats along and sometimes on the highway, and I didn't want to bang up this Jeep so early in the game.

I had lots of time to think about my new job. There were now some unknown, serious people interested in Miguel's gold find and this could get interesting.

Meet Father Lopez

Señor Hernandez was right. Fr. Lopez was a good guy. Young, about thirty, he had attended eight years of religious schools in five different cities in the States, from his novitiate to ordination, and spoke perfect English, and understood it, including the slang. He was into backpacking, river running, mountain climbing and auto racing, but he had never tried parachuting. I had a feeling he would be one of my future students.

After an excellent dinner, including a fine wine, we strolled through the narrow streets and alleyways. I did not expect the first-class tourist treatment on a trip that was supposed to be spent in the back country. The weather was perfect, almost a slight chill in the air, and I was beginning to get a little winded. I forgot that we were at an altitude of more than eight thousand feet, or, to use my new units of measurement, two thousand four hundred and eighty five meters, and the air was a little thinner than it was where I had spent the past several months.

Fr. Lopez met me for breakfast and asked for a list of the things that we would need for our trip into the wild and desolate country of west Zacatecas. I had made one up the night before, and handed it to him. He, in turn, handed it to a young man who appeared out of nowhere.

"This is Luis. He knows where everything is in Zacatecas, and how to get it."

I shook Luis' hand and I noted that although he was small in stature and weight, he had an air about him that said he had a lot of guts. After Luis left to buy our supplies, the padre told me Luis was the son of a German woman who had been brought to Mexico by a wealthy family as a nanny. Luis was fathered by the head of the family and when he would not claim the child, Luis was raised in a Catholic orphanage, but he sometimes lived on the streets. His mother had since died and now he lived at the church of Santo Domingo. "He is not strong, but he is a good, loyal worker," the Padre said.

By the end of the day, Luis had rounded up most everything we needed except for a four-man tent. We finally located a used one and had to settle for that. Señor Hernandez arrived by air from Juarez on Sunday afternoon. Fr. Lopez drove out to the airport with me when I went to pick him up. Señor Hernandez was wearing some new work clothes that he had obviously bought for the trip and he looked uncomfortable. It had probably been a while since he had not worn a coat and a tie.

He had been away from Zacatecas for too long. It had been a few years since Fr. Lopez and Señor Hernandez had last seen one another and they spent the ride into town from the airport catching up on old times. They spoke in Spanish, of course, so I enjoyed the scenery while I was doing the driving.

Fr. Lopez had arranged for a room for Señor Hernandez at the same hotel where I was staying so we would have little trouble getting together in the morning. At dinner I briefed Ruben—we were now on a first-name basis—and I told him everything I had learned about the area we were going to be exploring.

Frankly, the reports I had studied didn't lead me to believe that the gold sample Miguel had showed him had a high probability of being found within a mile or a mile and a half from his claim. However, we would have to get our boots on the ground before we could make any credible observations or decisions. The maps the government could provide me showed the geologic formations were pretty well jumbled up, so anything could happen. We would know a lot more tomorrow at this time.

Earlier in the day, Fr. Lopez asked me if I would take Luis along with me on the trip. It would be a big adventure for him, he would work hard and be a lot of help in running errands.

I said I thought it would be a great idea and I would pay him for his time. We agreed to meet for breakfast at six o'clock the next morning and that finished our day. The itinerary for the trip was the road north to Fresnillo which was very good, the road southwest to Lobatos, which was good, the road west to San Mateo, which was fair, and the road to the mine, which was very poor, like "you will be riding a mule up a mountain trail for ten miles."

"San Mateo is a small village where we can leave the Jeep and rent three mules to ride and two burros to carry the equipment," Ruben said.

He hadn't been to the mine for a few years, but he said we would have no trouble renting the animals. The campesinos, or rural people, used mules and burros as we used trucks and cars and they would gladly rent them to us to get the extra money, he assured us.

Luis was up before dawn and had the Jeep loaded and ready to go. The cook at the hotel had made us several large sandwiches and some hot coffee—and hot tea—and we were on our way. It took us less than an hour to drive to Fresnillo, an hour and a half to Lobatos, and a half hour to the village of San Mateo.

The road, or what passed for a road, ended in a small clearing in a solid grove of trees. This must have been one of the jumping-off points for the mining district many years ago. The trees were the only living things visible for as far as we could see. To the right was a small hut surrounded by a log fence. On the left was a large rambling adobe structure, also surrounded by a log fence.

Suddenly the yard of the adobe house was filled with kids of all shapes and sizes, and they converged on our Jeep like a swarm of locusts. Within a few minutes they had grabbed everything that wasn't tied down. The kids scattered when an old man burst out of the house followed by a pack of mangy dogs. Pandemonium reigned as the aged campesino kicked the kids and the dogs out of his way and made a path to the Jeep. He screamed to the kids to bring back everything they had stolen and, after dropping a large heavy machete to the ground, offered me his gnarled hand in friendship.

"My apologies, señor. The children do not see many strangers out here and they don't know how to act with people they have never seen before."

I had been eating a sandwich the hotel cook had made for me when we drove up and I placed it on the hood of the Jeep when I got out to shake the old man's hand. There was a flash of black and white as a large mongrel broke from the pack, made a giant leap, and snatched my sandwich. All talk and action stopped as the dog returned to the front of the pack, dropped the sandwich and stood defiantly over it, daring any and all to take it from him.

The old man was the first to react to this Mexican standoff as he scooped up his machete and ran toward the pack of dogs. The mongrel let out a menacing growl and bared his fangs. The campesino drew up short and cursed the dog.

I decided it was time for me to exercise some leadership and I picked up a stick one of the kids had been using when they played hockey and advanced on the defiant dog. I had made one step when the dog made a huge leap for me. He landed short and as he quickly got to his feet, I managed to land a good, solid kick to his head. He rolled over a couple of times and slowly got to his feet. With glazed eyes he looked at me for a full minute, picked up the sandwich and walked away. It was the beginning of an understanding that would prove to be very important later.

The show was over and the kids and dogs wandered off to play. We got down to business and I told the old man that we would like to rent some of his animals for a trip into the mountains.

"So sorry," he said. He had no more animals left, except for some very old and tired mules. Just yesterday afternoon three rough-looking men had arrived and rented all his good mules and burros. These men did not look like regular Mexicans. They were dressed in city clothes and they did not even know which side of the mule to get on. They wanted to pay me with money made of paper, but I wanted only money made of metal.

"Oh yes," he said, "Some of them had guns. Why? There is nothing to hunt or kill around here. We had much trouble getting them on top of the mules and getting their things on the burros. They also had mucho tequila with them. Finally they left and the autos that brought them drove off and the drivers said they would be back in three days.

"I sent my oldest son with them to take care of the animals. I also sent feed and water. I do not know what they will find to feed the mules wherever they are going. Perhaps you, also, should take something for the mules to eat. If you want them to work, they must eat."

These new strange events caused us to reconsider our plans. Should we try to go on, or should we go back to Zacatecas? We discussed our options and I decided that first we had to find out if and where we could get mules and burros that could make the trip. I asked the old man if we could see the mules he had left.

He sent the biggest of the kids into the trees to find the animals. They returned shortly with six of the most worn-out beasts of burden I had ever seen. We looked them over and they sure didn't add much to the option of going forward with the trip. But we had put so much time and effort into the preparation of getting to where we were that I didn't want to give up so easily.

I voted to take these mules and press on to the claim. Ruben consented, but only after I showed him the .25 caliber revolver I had in a shoulder holster hidden under my shirt. Luis said nothing, but looked ill at ease.

We took four of the mules, three to ride and one to carry our equipment and the feed and water the old man had suggested. It dawned on me that we had not prepared as well as we should have. At this moment, I would have wagered even money that we would be on foot and walking before we reached the claim.

We didn't have any metal money to pay the old man, but we were going to leave the Jeep as collateral, and anyway, he didn't think the mules were worth stealing. Luis proved that he knew his way around the animals, and in short order, we were on our way down, or rather, up the trail.

The terrain was unremarkable, similar to that described in the reports I had read, but the trail was in good condition and the mules performed reasonably well. The stamina of the beasts was amazing and I began to think they were faking being worthless to fool the old man and avoid hard work. Score one for the mules.

It took us about three hours to get to the claim and when we got there, Ruben was surprised, and angry, that his workers had accomplished so little while they were out here. We picked a spot, not the one used by the workers Ruben had hired, smoothed out the dirt and set up the tent.

Ruben proposed that we take a nap before we started our exploration. Not a good sign for what was going to be some tough days. We rested for about an hour and then walked the boundaries of Ruben's claim. There was a lot of evidence that someone had been digging in the dirt here and there, but no sign that they were looking for anything in particular.

Before we began our exploration for the source of Miguel's gold, we first had to find extra water for the mules. Luis hobbled the mules and tied them to some of the strong scrub that was plentiful near our tent. He stayed with them as Ruben and I took off in the direction where I thought we would find water. The gully on the west side of the claim shown on the maps was the logical place. We dug down about two feet before the hole began to fill with water. We dug deeper, widened the hole and called it OK. It didn't look too good, but the mules would probably drink it in a pinch.

We continued looking for a geologic formation that might have been the source of Miguel's find, but after a couple of hours, we came up with a blank. Ruben was totally exhausted after the first series of up and down hikes, and it would get to be that I would leave Ruben in any shady spot we found, I would scout ahead, and he would follow as best he could. Finally it got so that I could not keep him in sight, and we certainly did not want to get separated, and perhaps lost, so we made our way back to camp.

The light was fading when I caught sight of Luis and the mules, and I breathed a sigh of relief. To myself, of course. I didn't want Ruben to have any idea that I was anything less than Don Diego had told him, and I was beginning to feel that Ruben wishes that he was somewhere else right about now. He looked a little pale and was nervous and jumpy.

The night came on suddenly, and all three of us just sat there on our sleeping bags, deep in our own thoughts. Ruben was bushed and kept nodding and jerking his head. But he was also scared, worried about the unknown. Who were those guys that rented the mules? Where were they going? What if they were the guys who killed Miguel? What if?

After a long period of silence, Ruben said, "I am thinking that maybe we have gotten ourselves into a situation where we could get hurt. Those guys out there with the guns and the booze could mean trouble, and we are no match for them.

"I am no quitter. I have fought for everything I have and I have made enough money to last me for the rest of my life. I don't need any more money. I'm afraid that we could get killed. Let's get out of here as soon as the sun is up. When we get back to Zacatecas, we can figure out what to do over a stiff drink. What do you say?"

"I'm with you one hundred percent," I said. "I'll wake you at dawn," I said with a nervous laugh. Luis said nothing, but I kind of thought he had already had a taste of the adventure he was looking for and didn't like it.

No one got much sleep that night and I kept my .25 at my right hand. The dawn couldn't come quickly enough and with the light we packed in record time and were on our way. The old man had a surprised look on his weathered face after his dogs announced our return at eight o'clock that Tuesday morning.

"Did you find what you were looking for?" he asked.

"No," we said, "but we will be back. Give those mules some extra feed; they did a good job. Charge us for it the next time." I paid him in paper money. He took it and I said that I would bring him money made from metal when I came again.

We made the trip back to Zacatecas, mostly in silence, each with our own thoughts of the personal demons we had faced.

Fr. Lopez was walking down the street on his way to do some good deed when our paths crossed in front of our hotel.

"How did it go?" he inquired. I expected Ruben to answer, but he just sat there and stared into space and his whole body was shaking. Fr. Lopez suspected that something was wrong and after I briefly told him what had happened, he said, "I think Ruben should lay down and get some rest."

We put Ruben to bed in the hotel and outside his room Fr. Lopez said, "I am going to get Dr. Alvarez. Ruben seems to be in shock, and maybe he is having a heart attack. Perhaps on the trip back from the mine he got to thinking what could have happened to you guys and it overwhelmed his system."

The doctor arrived and, after attempting to talk to Ruben and getting no response, he called an ambulance and took him to his clinic where he could be observed by his staff. I asked Luis to unload the Jeep, gave him some pesos for helping us, and told him to check back with me this evening and see what we were going to do.

On Hold

Our expedition was on hold until we could talk to Ruben. Fr. Lopez asked me if I wanted to go to lunch after he had finished running his errands and I accepted. We had an excellent meal at a small restaurant with a fantastic view of the valley and its approaches to the city. This young man really had his finger on the pulse of the city of Zacatecas. He asked me to call him Ramon in all but formal settings, and I welcomed this, as I found it awkward to call a guy father when I was probably older than he.

Tonight there was going to be a meeting of a group of young people who were going on an outing to do some mountain climbing tomorrow morning. I was more than welcome to join them this evening and possibly go with the group in the morning. That sounded interesting to me, as I had done some mountain climbing myself. My chief conquest was a climb to the top of the Grand Tetons while I was training with the smoke jumpers in Missoula, Montana. I had mastered the tallest peaks in New Mexico, but the Grand Teton climb would probably put me in a class above the local climbers.

I was right. The level of experience of this group was in the novice class, but I kept my mouth shut. What interested me most was one of the group. She was a female, and what a female! Much taller than the average Mexican girl and very solidly built. She had long, raven dark black hair and light olive skin. My preference in women had always been sharply skewed towards blondes, but here was a gal who could reorient my entire thought process. When Fr. Lopez introduced us I remarked on her choice of mountaineering clothes, how well she looked in outdoors garb.

She politely acknowledged the compliment and brushed me off. Boy, she is the master of the cold shoulder, I thought. This group looked like, and acted like, the cream of the young, rich people of Zacatecas. Ramon showed a French movie on mountain climbing, of which I did not understand a word, but the members of the group nodded and laughed at all the right places, so I guess that they did. A question and answer session followed in Spanish, so you could say that the evening was a blank for me, except I did have a chance to talk to the raven-haired one.

Thankfully, she spoke perfect English, and that removed a major impediment to a relationship right away. I think she felt a little sorry for me and was going to give me a break. Not so with the male members of the group. They did not seem to want to give me that break, as far as she was concerned—here we go again with the Mexican machismo—and they kept interrupting our conversations. I did find out that her name was Raquel and she was from the State of Durango, but that was about all.

10
Emergency

Fr. Lopez ended the meeting by saying, "See you all at six o'clock tomorrow morning in front of the church, and come prepared for a long day."

When I arrived back in Zacatecas after the trip to the mine, or claim, I considered myself off Ruben's payroll until he decided on what he wanted to do. I was a free agent. So, at six o'clock the next morning I joined the group that had met last night, in front of the church, prepared for a day of mountain climbing. We were waiting for a straggler to show up when an alter boy rushed from the church and pulled Ramon aside. After a brief discussion, Ramon approached and said "A Major Morales from the Mexican Air Force urgently needs to talk to a Lt. Jaime Hall. Could that be you? I didn't know that you were working with the Mexican military."

I told him I had met Maj. Morales a couple of weeks ago while I was in Acapulco and I was probably the guy he was looking for. I excused myself and followed the boy into the church.

I picked up the phone and Maj. Morales greeted me with a sigh of relief. "Boy, am I glad to get hold of you. We have an emergency and I think you can help us."

"Tell me about it," I said. I'll do anything I can for you. I owe you a favor."

He explained that an American businessman had purchased a motor-sailboat in the southern Mexican State of Chiapas and was powering it back to Acapulco. The new owner and his passengers had decided to go deep sea fishing about two hundred miles off the coast of Guerrero when they collided with something that damaged the propeller of the boat and they can't use the engine. No one on the boat has experience in sailing so they are dead in the water.

"The real emergency is that the wife of the owner is a diabetic and she has used all her insulin. Unless she has the medicine, she can go into insulin shock and will probably die. We tried to air-drop a new propeller and some scuba gear to the boat yesterday just before dark and we missed the boat. They launched a small life boat to retrieve the drop but the current swept it away before they could reach it. I feel real bad as I was the pilot and I should have known that a parachute drop from an AT-6 was a risky operation at best. But it was worth a try because we knew that if we missed we could send a power boat to deliver another prop in a few days. But that was before the boat declared an emergency with the woman and the insulin.

"Now, time is of the greatest importance and, although we are having a coast guard cutter dispatched immediately to take the insulin to the boat, it will be at least eighteen hours before they locate the boat, and the lady could possibly die. Minutes count. We need someone with your parachuting expertise to help us. Incidentally, the owner is a friend of our commander. What do you say?"

"Count me in. I'll be waiting for you at the Zacatecas airport just as soon as you can get here," I said.

"I can push it and I will there in less than two hours," Morales replied.

"Whoa, there are a few things I will need from you. First, a chest-pack parachute and a quick release harness, a single tank scuba rig—I will make a harness for it here. I will jump with it. I don't want to take a chance of losing it. I will need a parachute bag to put the prop in, a Mae West to keep it afloat, a 30-foot piece of half-inch nylon rope, and a Mae West life jacket for me. Bring the parachute and harness with you. I will modify it here and I will supply the scissors," I said.

"I somehow feel that you are making fun of me. Am I correct, Señor Jaime?"

"You are correct, Maj. Morales. You Air Force types catch on fast."

"Have Felix Mendoza and his Cessna 180 standing by, warmed up and ready to take off as soon as we land. If you can't get Felix, get me another 180 with a good pilot. Maybe you can fly it. And be sure they take off the right door and tape over anything that I might snag my gear on. And when you talk to the medics, have them double the amount of insulin they think will be necessary so I can split it into two packages."

This is one area in which we can increase our chances of success. It is always best to have a backup. In parachuting, the adage is if something can go wrong, it will.

"I can have one of my men handle these details while I am on my way to pick you up. One very important thing, if you can attach all your equipment to your body, do so. The currents are very strong, as we found out, and if you cargo drop anything, it will probably drift away before you can recover it."

"No sweat," I told him. "I have some experience in this area. In fact I probably have more experience than any other parachutist in parascuba except an outstanding professional parachutist named Dave Burt."

Dave was my mentor and was, in my opinion, the number-one professional parachutist in the world. Right now, he was in Alaska, and I was hoping I could hook up with him and do some exhibition jumping in the States. Dave did all the test work in parascuba and developed a workable system. The Army claimed they were the leaders in this field, but they were wrong. I had made five jumps with scuba gear, and I would use the method Dave pioneered.

I hung up the phone and explained to Fr. Lopez in detail what had to be done before Maj. Morales—Manny—arrived at the airport in his AT-6.

"What can I do to help you?" he said.

"Plenty," I replied.

Fr. Lopez turned to the group and said, "Lt. Hall needs our help for a very important mission. Carlos, you take charge of the activities for today and let's meet back here when you return. I will take the lieutenant to the airport and help him pick up the things he needs."

He grabbed me by the arm and we started toward his car. Raquel picked up her back pack and announced, "I would like to go with you. I can help and it sounds like an interesting project."

Fr. Lopez looked at me and I nodded my head, yes. This good deed might have some side benefits, I thought to myself.

Ramon asked, "What do we do first?"

I said, "I will need a tight-fitting pair of coveralls and size eleven tennis shoes. Also, some sharp scissors. Do you know anybody in town who is a scuba diver?"

Ramon said that he had a friend, a professor at the Museo Rafael Coronel who liked to explore caves. Maybe he has scuba gear.

Ramon was right. He did. He had a single air tank unit that was just what I needed and he willingly agreed to let me use the tank as a model when I built a harness and also to let me use his tank for the actual jump if the one that Maj. Morales was bringing did not work out. Raquel picked up the tank and carried it to the car. She was out to prove that she wanted to be a working member of the team.

"Is Luis available?" I inquired. He was, and when I asked him to find a shop that had big sewing machines; he took us through the back alleys to a canvas shop that had the webbing we needed to make the harness for the scuba tank.

Good boy! The harness was built and fitted and we were on our way to the airport in less than an hour. We stopped at a small market by the side of the road and I bought a couple of candy bars and a bottle of water—my lunch for the day. I hoped they would serve a more substantial meal on the boat. At the airport, we staked out a place where I could modify and repack the chute, and waited.

While we were killing time, Ramon asked me if I thought he would be capable of making a parachute jump.

"Certainly you are in good physical condition," I said, "and your mental attitude is positive. I would be happy to teach you after this job is over. I will send a message to the lady who is storing my parachute gear and I will ask her to ship the parachutes we will need."

I had decided I had better have my professional equipment on hand if I am going to accept any more work jumping out of airplanes. I thought I might as well do it right now, so I wrote a note to Mrs. Breen in Albuquerque to ship to me, collect in care of Fr. Lopez, the two parachute bags tagged the "Best" and the "2nd Best," that I had left in her basement, as soon as possible. This time, she should take the bags to the shipping department and have them construct a box to ship them in. This way, no one can steal part of the shipment, as they did the time she shipped a parachute to me in California.

I gave Ramon the message to be sent after our AT-6 left for Acapulco. Maj. Morales greased the T-6 onto the runway at Zacatecas and taxied up to where we were waiting. The airplane canopy was pushed back and before he climbed down from the cockpit, he adjusted his white scarf. I think he must have seen Raquel. Manny looked every bit the dashing fighter pilot.

Here we have a double negative, I thought. A macho Mexican, who is also a white-scarf-wearing fighter pilot who merits the honor of having accomplished something. He is going to be hard to handle, but I will try because I genuinely like the guy. I introduced Maj. Morales around and, as I suspected, he turned the charm way up when he met Raquel. He passed me the parachute and harness and the scuba tank. The tank was exactly like the one the professor loaned us, so we put it aside and went to work on the parachute canopy.

It was equipped with a pilot chute, which was not good as it would increase the chance for a malfunction with the gear I would be wearing. I removed the pilot chute. The canopy was new and had been repacked recently, but I was still going to pack it. My life was going to depend on it, so if it failed, it was going to be my fault. I spread the canopy on the floor and Manny grabbed one side of panel 28 and Raquel pulled on the other. As I cut the fabric, Manny said "I still think you are crazy to cut holes in the very thing that is keeping you from falling to the ground very fast." I was going to make a blank gore again. I was very pleased at the ease with which it handled on the jump at Don Diego's mansion.

We were airborne in fifteen minutes and arrived at the Air Force side of the Acapulco airport in record time. As I mentioned to Maj. Morales this morning, if anything can go wrong with a parachute mission, it will. And it did, double. Pilot Felix Mendoza and his Cessna 180 were not available so we would have to rent a 180 and supply our own pilot. No big problem there, as Manny could fly it, and very well, as I had noted on the flight down from Zacatecas. He was an excellent pilot. A little on the "hot dog" side, but a good stick and rudder guy.

The second problem was the Coast Guard cutter was involved in an accident with a water-skiing boat and had to return to the

dock with its cargo. It was replaced with another boat but it cost
us four hours of valuable time. The Cessna was ready to go, and
after getting an update on the weather and the location of the boat,
we took off, heading southwest. One of the Air Force AT-6's would
accompany our Cessna and, using a homing device, lead us to our
target. This unit of the Mexican Air Force had the latest in radio
equipment, and plenty of it. They were involved with the United
States in trying to stop drug runners flying off the coast to the U.S.
from South America, and their gear was first rate. We were lucky
to have the AT-6 guiding us, as the navigation and electronic equipment on the Cessna was much less than "state of the art."

We were in constant contact with ground control, the bird dog
AT-6, and the boat. The AT-6 picked us up as we crossed the coast
and hung on our left wing as best he could, considering the difference in our airspeeds. We settled down to what was going
to be a dull flight of about two hours when I noticed the AT-6
edging closer to our Cessna. I have always been intrigued by the
thought of flying in formation. Having two huge hunks of metal
hurtling through the air while being supported only by the air
flowing over their wings excites me. It is a thrill to see another
plane pull in close to yours and fly wing-tip to wing-tip, close,
but not too close, as the AT-6 pilot was doing right now. Formation flying requires a lot of practice and teamwork and I was sure
that our two pilots had never practiced before.

I yelled in Manny's ear to tell that clown to knock off the grand-
standing—this was no time for a midair collision, particularly
since Manny was not wearing a parachute. In the States, it is
mandatory for any pilot flying formation or dropping parachutists
to wear an emergency parachute. We were doing both! But in
Mexico, many times the regulations are winked at.

After a moment of sheer terror, the AT-6 pilot pulled up and
over our Cessna and resumed his position on our wing at a safe
distance. I breathed a sigh of relief and I'm sure Manny also did,
but he was too macho to admit it.

So it was back to boring holes in the beautiful Pacific sky. The
noise of the air rushing past the open door of our aircraft made
communications between Manny and me difficult, but since we
had discussed the jump procedures several times on the flight
from Zacatecas, we both knew what had to be done, and when.

Finally, the boat was in sight. The AT-6 pilot waggled his wings and did a couple of barrel rolls. This guy was a showoff, but a good pilot. Manny turned and grinned at me. I could read his mind. He wished that he was flying that plane instead of this old Cessna.

OK, enough horsing around. Time to get down to work. The boat was drifting with the current. That gave me a excellent wind line, so we didn't have to use a drift indicator. The forward speed of my canopy could make up for any small error I might make from my jump altitude. We descended to three thousand feet and started a long, slow, level approach to the point where I would leave the aircraft. I would exit upwind of the target and rely on the wind to carry me to the boat. The forward speed of my parachute canopy would be used to compensate for the changes in the wind as I got closer to the boat.

This jump was going to be different than a normal one. It would be a static line jump for several reasons. I was wearing a chest chute with no reserve and jumping an equipment bag with the propeller, tools, one half of the medical supplies and a partially-inflated Mae West life preserver between my legs. I needed one hand to protect my face in case I had a bad position when my chute opened and the other hand to hold on to the bulky equipment bag.

I had removed the ripcord of the chest chute and replaced it with a forty-pound break cord threaded through the locking cones that holds the pack closed. This break cord was attached to a two hundred pound break cord and both were attached to a ten foot static line which was attached to the pilot's seat in the aircraft. I had put duct tape over the protruding valve of the tank to prevent the suspension lines from snagging on the valve.

I would exit the aircraft with my back to the open door and, hopefully, the chute would deploy while I was on my back, preventing the parachute canopy from hitting me in the face or the suspension lines from tangling with my feet or the equipment bag between my legs.

We were almost to the exit point when I slammed my fist down on Manny's shoulder, the signal to cut the engine and hold the aircraft straight and level. My exit was perfect and I got a good solid opening and no hang-ups with the equipment I was carrying. I checked my canopy. Everything was as it should be so I held into the wind, reached down and pulled the toggle on the CO2 cartridge to inflate the other half of the Mae West on the equipment bag, pulled the quick release and dropped the bag to hang below me. It cut down on the oscillations and I was fat, dumb and happy.

I pulled hard on the right riser and spiraled down above the boat. I could have landed on the deck but, wisely, chose to land in front and have the boat drift to me. They didn't even have to use the dinghy.

Another good jump! I hope my luck continues to hold. I hit the quick release on the harness and shrugged out of the chute. The guy in the dinghy didn't know how to handle the thing and ran into my chute which was floating on top of the water. It took us a while, but we finally got the chute and the equipment bag on board the dinghy.

I exchanged introductions with the guy in the dinghy and found out his name was Bill Balfour and he was from San Diego. That's all I needed to know for now. We had a lot of work to do and not much time to get it done.

I remained in the water and hung on to the side of the dinghy while I carefully handed the two packages containing the insulin to him. He, in turn, carefully handed the packages to another guy on the boat. I asked if the patient or anybody else on the boat could give the insulin shot, and they said they could do it. Job one accomplished.

Now for the mechanical part of the operation. I asked Bill to move the dinghy to the stern of the boat and secure it. I then asked him to open the parachute bag and hand me, carefully, a crescent wrench, an allen wrench and a ball peen hammer. Then tie a half-hitch around the propeller and be prepared to lower it to me. He looked at me and his face was a blank. "What is a crescent wrench and I've never heard of a half hitch?"

I think that there should be a law that a guy shouldn't be allowed to own a boat or a car if he can't tell the difference between a crescent wrench and a hammer. He had me scared. If he dropped the propeller, we were back to square one. I pulled myself over the side of the dinghy and pointed out the tools I needed. Then I tied a half hitch around the prop and secured the rope to one of the oar locks. We were ready to go to work.

I bit down on the mouthpiece of the scuba rig and dove under the boat to check the damage. It was considerable, but easily repairable. I don't know what they had collided with, but it must have been fairly large and made of heavy metal. One vane of the propeller was bent at a thirty-degree angle and the others were pretty badly dinged up. I hoped that whoever was steering the boat when they hit shut down the engine right away. If not, there was a good chance that the engine had internal damage: maybe a piston rod was bent, but we would have to wait and see what happens when we try to start it. I resurfaced and then went back under with the tools I needed.

It took me a while to get the prop off the shaft, as it is considerably harder to work underwater than it is to do a job on the surface. But we were finally ready to start the engine.

I moved away from the boat, crossed my fingers and gave the signal to crank the engine. It started right away and idled just fine. The real test would come when he brought it up to full power and engaged the propeller. I signaled the guy to bring the throttle all the way forward and the engine responded without a sign of vibration. Success!

I Drive Yacht Back to Acapulco

I climbed the ladder and dropped into the boat. Time to meet the crew, and if ever there was a bunch of people who had no business being on a crippled boat in the middle of the ocean, this was the group.

Ruthie, the wife of the boat owner, Bill, and the patient, was an executive secretary. Under normal circumstances, she was probably a very attractive woman, but right now, she looked like hell. She was pale, haggard and a very sick woman.

Nancy was one of the other females on board. She was taking care of Ruthie as best she could. She said that she didn't want to go on this trip in the first place and couldn't wait to get off the boat. She was married to George, a mild-mannered man who owned a large new car dealership in San Jose. His idea of roughing it was going to an outdoor movie and he seemed as if he would break down at any time.

Henry and Helen Finch made up the remainder of the crew. They were recently retired and he indicated that this was not his idea of having a good time. Not much of a gang you would like to be with in a dangerous situation.

The Cessna and the AT-6 had been circling and when they saw that I was on board the boat, they were ready to go back to base. But before they did, they were going to give us a fighter pilot's farewell. Manny dropped down on the deck and at full bore he buzzed the boat. He was very closely followed by the pilot of the AT-6 as he barreled along about five feet above Manny and practically blew him away. I had my doubts about these two fighter pilots making it back to Acapulco in one piece, but it was good to work with them. I admired their spirit and guts. Bill gave me a pair of trunks I could get into and I hung my jumpsuit up to dry.

My hopes of a good meal were dashed when we checked the galley. All we could come up with were two apples and a banana and a couple of tea bags. I am really going to be hungry by the time we get back to Acapulco. When they had climbed to altitude, I called the AT-6 and got an updated fix and compass direction to Acapulco. We were on course and should be intercepted by the Coast Guard cutter in about five hours.

The crew and I chatted throughout the afternoon while I soaked up the sun. By the time we saw the cutter knifing through the approaching dusk, I knew all their histories and, all in all, it was a dull period. The cutter slowed to a crawl and pulled along side our boat. They threw us a rope and after they tied us to their side, we transferred Bill and Ruthie to the faster craft. Ruthie was looking much better and gave me a feeble smile. She held my hand and said, "Any time you are in San Diego, Jim, you have a place to stay." We untied the rope and then they were gone, speeding off into the growing darkness.

Twelve hours ago I was getting ready to climb a mountain. Now I am the captain of a boat. Only in Mexico. I am beginning to like this country. I kept the bow of the boat pointed toward Acapulco and we continued on course for another four hours. I turned on as many lights as I could. I didn't know how many other ships there were out there, but it only takes one more for a collision.

I was beginning to get sleepy and I did not trust any of the crew to man the controls, so I threw two sea anchors over the

side, tied down the wheel and cut off the engine. I had found an
air mattress in the captain's quarters and tossed it on the deck
and tried to get some sleep. I drifted in and out of sleep and I
was fully awake as the blazing sun leapt out of the brilliant blue
sea directly in front of me. This was beautiful! I really don't think
I could adequately describe how beautiful it really was. How
great it is to be alive! I guess nobody appreciates how great it is
to be alive and in good health than a guy who plays it close to the
edge. Kind of like me, I guess.

Every now and then I think it would be nice to have a wife to
enjoy moments like this with me, but if I had a wife, I wouldn't
be here to enjoy this. I would probably be just like my six older
brothers, married to some fat—maybe not yet, but sure to be—
Polish girl who lived down the street and have a couple of snotty-
nosed, bare-assed kids running around the house and chasing my
old dog Spot.

Not even my idol, Brother Honus, escaped the marriage trap,
and now he has five kids and is gone and will never enjoy a beautiful sunrise like I am seeing. Well, I am not married and have
no intention of getting married any time soon. So, I'll enjoy the
beautiful sunrise by myself. I looked up and the sunrise was
gone. The sun was above the horizon and it was broad daylight.
I hauled in the sea anchors, untied the wheel, kicked the air
mattress aside and started the engine.

About fifteen minutes later, Nancy and Helen came up from
below deck to brew their morning coffee. Neither one of them
had put on makeup or combed their hair. I did not have to take
a second look to remind myself why I was single. It was a going
to be a beautiful day. A day to be enjoyed by just laying around,
but that was not what I was in the mood for.

There was no food on board, but plenty of booze to drink, so
my crew helped themselves. Every now and then one of them
would stop by to talk. It got to be a pain listening to their nervous
chatter and hearing the same old stories over and over again. The
autopilot was broken, so I manned the wheel without a break. I
felt that I could not trust any one of the "crew" to touch anything
to do with the operation of the boat. I had no idea of what they
could screw up, but I was certain if there was something, they
would find it. We saw several small boats as we neared land and

finally, at last, the coast of Mexico came into view. Then, the port of Acapulco.

The Coast Guard sent out a launch to guide us to a dock where the boat would be inspected for contraband and registered. Usually a sum of money placed in the right spot in the bureaucracy would expedite the process, but this was not my worry as Bill was at the dock to meet us. Ruthie was improved and would be able to go home to San Diego within a week. That was good news! The Finchs, Henry and Helen, and Nancy and George—I never did get their last name—were pretty mellow when we docked and they left without saying goodbye. I could imagine the wild tales they would tell about survival on the high seas when they extended their happy hour tonight.

Manny showed up just as I was hailing a taxi to take me to a hotel and a good meal. Of course he offered to buy me a drink and escort me on a tour of all the night spots. I thanked him and said, "All I want is a steak dinner and a quiet place to lay down." I checked in to a small hotel near the airport. I was traveling light, no baggage and my jump suit. Manny offered to outfit me, but I asked him to take me to any place that would feed me without my having to shave and put on a coat and tie.

Over a couple of beers and an excellent dinner of steak and lobster, Manny and I dissected the operation from start to finish. We were in agreement that the level of cooperation between all the government agencies and the people involved was exceptional. I was nodding off half way through the dinner and after turning down Manny's offer to show me the "real" Acapulco after dark, I went to my room and was asleep very soon after my head hit the pillow.

The next morning, I had been awake about ten minutes when Manny hammered on my door. "The squadron leaves at dawn," he bellowed. He later recalled that he heard that line in a World War I movie he had just seen on television, and it seemed perfect to wake me up. Anyway, his AT-6 was gassed up and waiting to fly as soon as we got to the airport. On the flight back to Zacatecas, Manny demonstrated his full bag of tricks but I disappointed him by not getting sick. I told him he should try the same stuff in the F-86 or the new F-100 Super Sabre and maybe he would get better results.

11
Back in
Zacatecas

F r. Lopez met us at the airport and I filled him in on the ride back to Zacatecas. I asked him about Raquel and he said that she was impressed by my adventures and would like to make a parachute jump. I said, "Great, when my equipment arrives from Albuquerque, I can train both of you at the same time."

Fr. Lopez said that the climbing expedition did not go well. They were going to try it again tomorrow—would I care to go? I said I would and he said," Same time, same place."

We met, as planned, at six o'clock the next morning. It was Saturday but no day off for the poor people. The roads were packed with farmers pushing and pulling all manner of vehicles transporting goods to market and cars and buses carrying people away from the city. There were ten of us; Fr. Lopez took six and I got the remainder. Needless to say, my quota did not include Raquel. The locals were making sure their queen bee was going to be kept out of the reach of the Americano. We spent the day with the group attacking a series of small hills, each effort nothing better than a hard walk. Most of them were not in good shape, having just returned from some sort of school in Spain, France or the States.

Back in Zacatecas, we gathered at an ice cream parlor and splurged on root beer sundaes. Raquel's manner was distant but friendly while outwardly cool. This was Saturday night with a lot going on but nobody asked me to join in, so I left. I walked back to the church with Ramon and as I said good night and turned to go he said "I hope that you don't take this the wrong way, but what are your intentions toward Raquel?"

The question caught me off guard and I had to stop and think before I answered. Here I am, a young, healthy, intelligent, well educated, good looking, at least well above the average, single American male and I see a very attractive, young, single American, or Mexican, girl and I want to get to know her, maybe touch her, maybe hold her, maybe make love to her, or maybe—what the hell—don't know exactly what my intentions are. I guess that I'm not much different than any other normal guy in my position. In my mind, she is a very desirable female and I intend to make a pass at her and see what happens. And it is none of your, or anybody else's damn business what my intentions are! I am Jim Hall, mining engineer, Air Force officer, master parachutist and I don't have to answer to any one—or do I?

I am not in the United States. I am in a foreign country. These people have a culture that is different from ours. There was, for example, the violent reaction caused when a jealous suitor thought that I was stealing the affection of his girlfriend just last week. I thought long and hard for a full minute and said "Padre, I am very attracted to Raquel, and I would like to get to know her."

He looked me the eye and said, "Jim, please be very careful with Raquel. She is a shining star in our community. She is the only child of a very wealthy and traditional family. She is the crown jewel of the top level of Zacatecas society. She is attracted to your daring and adventurous life style. She has never met any one like you before and you could be the one to finally sweep her off her feet. So many have tried and failed."

I shook his outstretched hand and walked slowly back to my hotel. As I looked deeply in to his misty eyes and listened to his emotional voice, I had the strong feeling that this man was giving me advice not only with his heart, but from his soul. Perhaps, this was the first time he had really regretted taking that long, difficult, lonely road to the abstinence of the calling of a religious life.

It is Sunday, and I am reminded by the tolling of the bells that I haven't been to Mass since my last visit to Saint Michael's in Deming. I remembered that I wasn't very well received by the Mexican farm laborers in the States, but I am willing to try again down here in Mexico.

I showered and shaved and made the six o'clock Mass. I got a pleasant surprise when I saw that Luis was one of the altar boys. He was glad to see me and we greeted one another like old buddies who had shared many adventures together. He told me that I should go to the eight o'clock Mass, as Señorita Raquel always attended that one.

"I hear Fr. Lopez say to another priest that he thinks she like you. She do not know me, but she smiles and always say hello. She is a very kind señorita."

I have an idea. "Would you give her a note from me?" "Si, Senor," he replied. "You a good guy." He handed me a church bulletin and I printed my message on it. "Señorita Raquel, would you like to go to the movies with me on Wednesday night? Please answer by note to my friend Luis."

I gave Luis my pen to give her in case she did not have one. The excuse that "I didn't have anything to write with" has thwarted many a promising deal, and I did not want anything as simple as this to stop this one. I gave the note to Luis and he responded with a big smile. It looked like I had an ally. My hopes were dashed when I did not see Luis all of the rest of the day. Oh well; all I could do was wait. The ball was in her court.

Raquel accepted my invitation to go to the seven o'clock movie but, first she would like me to come by her house a half hour early. She would like me to meet her parents.

"Of course," I said. "I will be looking forward to the meeting."

Promptly, at 6:30, my cab dropped me off at an address on a shady side street about a half a mile from my hotel. A high wall, topped by a double row of broken glass, separated the street from the grounds surrounding the house. I had no idea of what was behind the wall, but when a uniformed servant opened the door and invited me in, I was surprised to find myself in a virtual botanic garden. This place must keep a squad of gardeners busy 24/7.

"Please follow me," the maid said, as she led me through the flowers and shrubs to a small waiting room. Raquel was seated in a wicker chair with the late rays of the sun shining on her long, coal-black hair. She was one of the most beautiful women I had ever seen. I realized that this scene was staged, but I was impressed, really impressed. It was imprinted on my mind that this young lady was someone who was to be reckoned with and my gut feeling was to be careful. From what I had seen, this beauty came with a very keen and scheming mind. Off to the side, within sight and hearing, sat a chaperone, who I would come to realize would be a part of any dating plans I might have in the future.

We made small talk for about five minutes and Raquel said, "Come, let me introduce you to my parents. Don't be offended if they seem a little cold. That is the way it is supposed to be in our culture."

We walked down a long hallway and into a study with many shelves holding hundreds of books. Her father, a highly respected medical doctor, sat at a desk doing some paperwork, and her mother, a well dressed and very formal, attractive, middle aged woman who had elite Spanish written all over her was reading at another desk.

The introductions were made and the doctor asked me to tell them what brought me to the city of Zacatecas. I told them I was a mining engineer and I was hired by Señor Hernandez to inspect a mining property in the sierras west of the city. While we were at the mine, Señor Hernandez became ill and I am waiting until he decides what he wants to do before I make future plans. I find their city very beautiful and I am enjoying my stay while I wait for a decision.

I told them I was educated in several learning institutions in the United States and graduated from the University of New Mexico. I served in the United States Air Force during the war with Germany and Japan, I am a paratrooper and I am in the Air Force Reserve. The doctor spoke perfect English and did most of the talking. The mother asked several questions in rapid Spanish, but otherwise listened intently.

After a couple of minutes, Raquel rose and said, "We had better be going. We don't want to miss the beginning of the show." Our taxi was waiting and we didn't miss the beginning of the show. I was left wondering—did I pass or did I fail?

Meeting with the General

At Sunday Mass, Raquel had passed a note to Luis asking me to escort her to the regional commander's annual military ball. This was a big deal. Once a year the commander would throw a large gala for everyone of consequence in the military or political communities in the state. The ball was to be held at the commander's mansion, which also served as the military headquarters. This was the social event of the year and an invitation I couldn't refuse.

"Of course, I would be delighted to be your date," I replied. "When and where should I meet you?"

Wednesday was the day and the time was seven o'clock. I should pick her and Tia Martha up at her house. This called for the canceling of all other plans and appointments. I would have to put off going to El Rey until the week end, but no problem. Fr. Lopez had introduced me to a young man who used his private car as a high-class taxi. As I did not have any idea of what the evening held in store, I hired the young man, Enrique, to be available at any time when we needed him. He was a friend of the servants in the general's mansion, so he could wait for our call in the kitchen.

At ten to seven, Enrique and I picked up Raquel and her chaperone, a little, mean-looking female she introduced to me as Tia Martha, her maiden aunt, and we were dropped off at the general's mansion exactly at seven. I was surprised to see the different uniforms worn by the military guests. They were a mix of Spanish, American, French and British mess dress. It appeared that an officer could wear any combination of uniforms that he wanted and not violate any dress code.

I felt very much out of place in a suit and tie. I was definitely underdressed. I received a lot of hostile looks and at first I thought they were because of my clothes, but later figured out those hostile looks were not because of my dress but because I was escorting the beautiful Raquel and that was not greeted with approval by many of the Mexican officers.

We got into the receiving line to be welcomed by the commanding general, Francisco Garcia, and it wasn't very long before one of the sharp-looking captains circulating in the crowd—I assumed they were aides—took Raquel's arm and we were ushered to the head of the line. As we passed several generals and colonels and officers of lesser rank we received many unpleasant looks and nasty remarks. The general greeted Raquel with great affection and fell all over himself to show how pleased he was to see her. Fr. Lopez told me the general had no children of his own and Raquel was his godchild and she was the light of his life.

Raquel introduced me as her friend from New Mexico, a mining engineer and an officer in the United States Air Force. He fixed me with a cold stare and asked me what I was doing in Mexico. Before I could answer, he said, "I will talk to you later tonight."

The rest of the evening was a series of awkward introductions to her friends and some dancing. Raquel seemed to be enjoying the situation and was amused when some people avoided us. It was the first time in my life that I felt I was snubbed because of being an American. It seemed as though I had chosen the queen bee of the upper level of Zacatecas society and almost everyone we met tried to express their displeasure that their darling seemed to like the Americano very much.

As a military officer, I was especially angry with the attitude of the junior officers, most of whom would not last a day in Airborne basic training. It was obvious that their commissions were based on their social standing and not on any military qualifications.

At about eleven o'clock an aide told Raquel and me that Gen. Garcia wanted to talk with us in his office, immediately! Raquel led the way, as she had been in the mansion before and had some idea of where she was going. After a few twists and turns we came to a huge oak door with a large knocker. We knocked and the general bellowed, "Enter!"

The commander was seated at the head of a massive oak table that had been looted from the Governor's Mansion during the revolution. Its beautiful polished surface had been gouged by the rifles and machetes that were carelessly tossed on it by the revolutionary soldiers over the years. The general—he was the equivalent to an American four-star—was a heavy set, brutish man, five foot ten or eleven weighting two hundred fifty pounds or so, with course features and scars on his neck that appeared to be rope burns. The scars turned red when he was angry, which was, I suspected, most of the time.

He gruffly ordered me to sit down at the table and for Raquel to sit on a chair behind me. I figured that he had been drinking the high-powered tequila from the State of Jalisco and right now he was pretty drunk and in a foul mood. Fr. Lopez said that he was basically a Mexican peon, a campasino, who had worked his way up through the ranks and became an important officer in

Pancho Villa's army. Over the years, he learned enough social skills to be accepted in polite society when he was not drunk, and he was smart enough not to drink when he was away from his home turf. He was the complete master in the states he commanded and he did pretty much as he damned well pleased.

He stood up, removed his coat, pulled a .45 caliber automatic from a holster that was hidden by his coat, and slammed it down on the desk. He got right down to business. "What are you doing in our country and what are your intentions toward my goddaughter?" he demanded to know.

I told him I was a mining engineer and I had been invited to Mexico by a Mexican citizen to inspect a mining property. As for my intentions toward Raquel, they were honorable and I have treated her with respect and I intend to continue to do so. I have work papers that permit me to work legally in Mexico as long as I obey the laws and pay the taxes on the money I earn.

The general looked at me long and hard. "Your permits are issued by bureaucrats who work with words. We soldiers work with people, and some of them are very bad people, and we rule with our guns. Your permits are worthless without my people to protect you and I do not want to waste the time of my men to see that you are not killed. I suggest that you do your work up north, closer to the border. You will leave Zacatecas by tomorrow morning, and do not see my goddaughter again."

He pulled himself to his feet, jammed his .45 into its holster, and said. "This meeting is over."

As if by command, two Mexican soldiers, captain bars on their shoulders, moved in and positioned themselves on either side of me. The general started to walk, or should I say, stagger away, and said "What time is it?"

I pulled up my sleeve, looked at my watch and said, "It is seven minutes past eleven."

"What is that badge you have on your watch?"

"They are parachutist's wings, "I said.

The general asked, "How many parachute jumps do you have? Are you any good?"

I said, "I am the best."

"You talk big, Americano. Can you prove it?"

I was beginning to get angry at being pushed around, and I answered, with some irritation, "Get me an airplane I can jump from, and tomorrow morning I will show you," I replied.

"You will have your airplane and your chance. You had better be able to match your boastful words and not have me waste my time. I have important business in mind," he growled. The general rattled off some rapid Spanish and one of the aides rushed from the room.

Gen. Garcia

"I will see you tomorrow morning at ten o'clock at the airport," Gen. Garcia said as he weaved out of the room. The remaining captain escorted Raquel and me to the door and bid us adios. We picked up the very agitated chaperone—she had spent the evening in the kitchen with the servants—got in the taxi and drove to Raquel's home.

Along the way Raquel said, "Don't mess with the general. If you cross him, he will kill you."

I said, "Thank you, but I already had that figured out."

We arrived at Raquel's house, and with the chaperone at my elbow, I shook Raquel's hand and said "Good night." I rather suspected that Raquel thought she had seen the last of me. And the fact that the general could have me killed with no questions asked caused me to carefully run through my options on the way back to my hotel.

Jump at Airport

I set my alarm for six o'clock but I was up and showered before it had a chance to go off. Should I shave? Of course, I wanted to look as professional as possible.

I was glad now that I had Mrs. Breen send both of my parachute bags. In addition to my basic parachuting gear, they contained extras like smoke grenades and colored streamers and other items that could add to the "show biz" aspects of an exhibition parachute jump. I had inspected and repacked my two main parachutes and the reserves so I knew I was working with the best equipment money could buy and it had been tested by an expert, me. I would wear my tailored, white jumpsuit with the red trim. It would be best I not wear the snazzy red, white and blue jump suit with the large American flag on the back. Better not show my American jingoistic side right now. Later, perhaps.

While I was shaving, I figured out the math of today's jump. A lot was riding on my making a perfect jump for the general. Obviously, his reasons for wanting to see how good I was were very important to him. Our conversation last night convinced me that to him, what you were doing is either right or wrong, and if he thought you were wrong, you could wind up with a .45 slug in the back of your head.

I had no idea how much he knew about parachuting or who he might bring with him that knows, or thinks he knows, about parachuting. As far as practical parachuting is concerned, I don't think there is anyone in the world, certainly not in Mexico, that knew more about parachuting than I did. Maybe Dave Burt in California or a professional exhibition jumper in Alaska named Bob Sinclair or a new guy named Jacques Istel, who is starting a jump school back east, could match my knowledge, but I don't think the general can dig these guys up by this morning. So, his, or his aide's knowledge, would have to had come out of a book or a military manual, so I had better make this jump by the book.

The ground elevation at the airport was seven thousand feet, and I would want to have an open chute at twenty-five hundred feet above that. This means that I wanted to be swinging in the harness at ninety five hundred feet above sea level.

During the past several years, I had read just about everything that had been written about parachuting while I was recovering from sprained ankles or bruised hips and back injuries, and up to that time, there wasn't all that much knowledge available. Most of the information came from the Army or the Navy test parachutists at El Centro, California and I had access to most of this information, but not all.

The military had the instruments and equipment to make measurements of such things as how fast a 180 pound body would fall through the air at a certain altitude and temperature and what the rate of descent of that 180 pound body would be under a 28-foot flat circular parachute canopy, but they didn't share that data with civilians, or for that matter, with one another. So we guessed that the average parachutist would be falling at about 120 miles per hour on a normal day, with normal conditions and would hit the ground at about 120 miles per hour if the jumper failed to pull his ripcord.

But what in the hell did a few miles per hour make, either way? I, of course, intended to open my parachute after freefalling through about ten thousand feet of altitude and that meant that the altitude from which I would exit the jump aircraft would be 19,500 feet above sea level. The air in this space was going to be thinner than the air closer to the ground, so I would be falling faster than normal. I would also be using a maneuver called "tracking" that would permit me to move horizontally at about 170 miles per hour while falling vertically at a speed greater than normal, so my time in freefall would be less than the usual 55 or 60 seconds. But this should be enough time to impress the general, his aides, Raquel, Fr. Lopez or any other people who might be watching.

New stuff about controlling the body in free fall had been recently coming out of France and Russia, but most of the things that they called new were old hat to some of the original barn-stormer exhibition airshow jumpers like Americans Floyd Smith or Spud Manning.

I would be falling with three large plumes of red, green and white smoke trailing behind me, the colors of the Mexican flag, streaming from three sixty second military smoke grenades attached to my jump boots. When I opened my parachute at about 9,500 feet above sea level, the smoke grenades should be just about burned out, so after descending another thousand feet under an open canopy, I would pop another three red, green and white smoke grenades that would trail smoke until I hit the ground. Then I would make a dramatic standup landing.

That's the way it was supposed to work. It remained to be seen if it does. If that doesn't impress the old goat, I don't know what else will. Maybe going all the way into the ground from nineteen five and walking away from the crash landing would. But that scenario would be a little extreme, and I don't think even the world's greatest parachutist could pull it off.

It's not yet seven o'clock and I am all hyped up. I guess having Raquel there has given me an added incentive. I went over to the church and invited Fr. Lopez to come see the jump and asked him if Luis could come along. Ramon said that he sure would like to see the jump and of course Luis could go.

We got to the airport at nine o'clock and one of the captains was already there, as was a Cessna 180 with a brand new engine. That was great! The climb to nineteen five was going to take a while, and I didn't want to keep the VIP's waiting. Of course, the pilot had never dropped a parachutist before, so I went over the procedures very carefully with him several times.

He was a young guy, the son of a pioneer aviator in Mexico, and was eager to learn. His name was Raul Parra and I liked him right off. He wasn't too thrilled about the modifications we had to make to his airplane for a parachute jump, but I convinced him I knew what I was doing. I also convinced him that he should also wear a parachute, just like it said in the regulations. Also, it was going to be a little cold at altitude with the door removed from the aircraft, so we better be dressed for it—like wearing a flight jacket. I had Raul drain all the gasoline from the tanks except what we would need for the flight to make the airplane as light as possible and we were ready to go!

We took off at 9:10 and since Raul was used to flying above the normal altitudes, he had brought along oxygen bottles for both of us. It was three minutes before ten when the control tower called us to report that there was no wind on the ground and the general's Mercedes Benz had arrived. This was a pretty special staff car that was "donated" to the general by a drug dealer—just before the dealer was killed while he was trying to escape from the soldiers who were interrogating him.

Fr. Lopez said that the old man was a stickler for promptness and it was said that he had two men who were part of a firing squad detail shot for being five minutes late for the shoot. After they had taken part in their assigned duty, they helped remove the bodies and took their places against the wall.

He was also, obviously, a stickler for efficiency. For my information, the tower said that Raquel had accompanied her godfather, and there was no other female with them. Well, well, no Tia Martha. I guess her parents thought the general could protect her from the Americano.

The general didn't say hello to anyone as he arrived. Fr. Lopez later said that he looked like his head hurt too much to talk. He pulled out a pocket watch to check the time just as I gave the pilot the signal to cut the engine and bailed out. It was exactly ten o'clock.

I had mounted a small red smoke grenade on the wing strut and ignited it about thirty seconds before I exited the aircraft to mark the flight path of the Cessna. I made a clean getaway and I yanked on the lanyard that pulled the pins on the three smoke grenades as I cleared the wheel. The spot was pretty good—I had planned my exit to be short of the target so I could demonstrate the tracking maneuver that permitted me to move horizontally over the ground while in freefall and before pulling the ripcord and opening the parachute.

It was a perfect day for a jump. Not a cloud in the bright blue sky and the red, green and white path I blazed across almost two miles of vertical space must have looked spectacular from the ground. My opening shock was minimal, as I had just bought a new device called a sleeve before I left the States, and it allowed the canopy to deploy slower that usual. I would be jumping a 28-foot, flat circular parachute canopy, U.S.Army World War II surplus that cost me five bucks and I would make it steerable by cutting four of the rear suspension lines and demonstrate how I could control my direction as I spiraled down and made sharp left and right turns and pulled down the front risers to show a glide capability and then on the rear risers to slow down my forward speed—always trying to keep the smoke behind me. In a no-wind condition, the smoke lingered in the sky even after I had touched down. I made that dramatic standup landing and didn't even get a grass stain on that nice white jump suit.

The general walked over, shook my hand and said, "Be at my office at noon." Raquel had that look in her eyes that I had seen in the eyes of the "Buckle Bunnies," the girls who follow the rodeo cowboys. The "my hero" look. Now was the time to strike, but certainly not the place. Luis helped me pick up the parachute and other gear and we drove back into town. Ramon was enthusiastic and said, "That looks like fun. When do we start?"

I replied, "Let's see what the general has in mind first. Then we can map out the future."

On the way back to town, Ramon gave me the rundown on the general. He was a high-ranking officer on the headquarters staff of the chief of staff of the Mexican Army in Mexico City and was known as a troubleshooter who would be dispatched to any state in the country where there was unrest and crime. Lately, that was the western part of Zacatecas and the neighboring state of Sinaloa and the problem was narcotics growing and trafficking.

He was known as a ruthless, no-nonsense military leader, and ruled with an iron hand any area that was under his command. There had been several attempts on his life and he always carried at least one pistol and had used it several times to take out guys who tried to kill him.

His ties to Zacatecas were thick and complex. He was born to very poor parents on a large ranch in northern Zacatecas, near the Durango border, owned by the father of Raquel's mother. At an early age he joined one of the many rebel groups that were trying to overthrow the government in Mexico City. His insurgent group was ambushed at the ranch and all were killed except the general, who at that time was a young rising star in the revolution. The general was given a fast thoroughbred horse owned by Raquel's mother and he escaped the ambush. He credits the then-young girl with saving his life.

Later, as one of Pancho Villa's commanders, he saved the life of Raquel's grandfather, who was to be executed because he was a wealthy land owner. The general and Raquel's mother developed a relationship but it was doomed because of the vast difference in their social classes. They maintained a friendship and the general never married. When Raquel was born, the general was asked to be her godfather and he has always treated her as his daughter.

He had jurisdiction over several other states and moved his headquarters from state to state, depending on where he was needed most. It was rumored that he is a compulsive gambler

and would wager on almost anything. He bets heavily and is a
very poor loser. He has a very bad temper, and for that reason
only his equals will bet with him.

"It will be interesting to find out what he wants to talk to you
about," Ramon said as I dropped him and Luis off at the church.

I drove my Jeep to the military headquarters and was met at
the gate by one of the general's aides. He directed me to a VIP
parking space and accompanied me into the general's office. It
was the same office where, last night, the general had told me I
should be heading for the northern border this morning. What a
difference a day makes. It was an entirely different atmosphere,
as the general got up from behind his desk, shook my hand and
asked me to sit down. He told his aide, "That will be all," and
asked me if I would like a cup of coffee.

I said "No thanks," and with that formality out of the way, he
said, "I want to make you a proposition. I am a betting man and
lately, things have not been going my way. I have an idea that I
think will get me back some of my money." He paused and
looked me in the eye.

"Your performance this morning at the airport convinced me it
is a very good idea. I have a group of old friends who I have
known for many years and we place wagers on many things. One
of my friends, to whom I owe a considerable amount of money,
is a personal friend of the president, Ruis Cortines. They grew up
together and they both fought on the side of Gen. Venustiano Car-
ranza during the Mexican revolution. The president has placed
him in command of a project that is very dear to the president's
heart and very important to him. He is to train and equip an "off
the books" elite Army unit to be the president's personal honor
guard and who will travel with him as he makes appearances
around the country.

"The budget for funding this unit will come from sources other
than the military. These soldiers will not only be 'spit and polish'
parade troops but will be skilled in all aspects of the military. He
has received several assassination threats because of his support
of equal rights for women and several other unpopular ideas, and
the president would be a lot more comfortable when this unit is
in operation.

"They started out with a pool of five hundred men and are now down to fifty. Of these fifty, a group of twelve men have just returned from special training at the U.S. Army parachute school at Fort Benning, Georgia and their commander, my friend, is bragging that they are the very best in the world and there is nothing they cannot do when it comes to parachuting. He is very, very proud of them.

"Here is my idea. I will bet him that I have a man who can parachute to a spot and hit it closer than any of his men. In fact, he can hit that spot better than any ten of his best men. He will laugh at me, and that makes me very mad, and he will say, "I will take that bet, and I will give you odds."

"We will have a contest and you will win and I will take back from him a lot of my money and my self esteem. Can you do it? Will you do it?"

He got to his feet and he looked like a carnival barker who had spotted a rich rube. "Can you do it? If you do it, I will give you a gun permit and honor your work papers."

I could see that the general was really excited. He sat down and his face was flushed as he poured himself a glass of tequila. I was also a betting man and I knew the thrill of having a case ace (an ace as your down card) in a high stakes game of five card stud and having an ace as one of your showing cards as well as a king, and you knew that there was no way an opponent could beat your hand, will give you an unbelievable feeling of power. And I also knew there was a lot on the line and my future in Mexico was depending on my answer, and my performance.

I said, "You bet I can. When and where are we going to make this parachute jump?"

"Fantastico," he said and ran toward me to shake my hand.

"This weekend, I will bait the hook. Then we will make the rules."

12
Ace

I was back in town for the weekend. Mrs. Martinez, the elderly lady who took care of my apartment at the hotel when I was out of town, had asked me to take an old chair and part of a desk to the city dump. I put the stuff in the back of my Jeep and drove to the city limits. I tossed my cargo and as I drove away, I noticed a group of teenagers pitching rocks and poking sticks at something on the ground. Drawing closer, I could see that it was an animal, a dog, who twisted and jerked each time he was hit. He was a fair-sized dog, white and black, very dirty and covered with blood, both dry and fresh. Every time they knocked the dog down, he would stagger to his feet, assume a four-legged stance and hold his head high.

I got out of my Jeep and ordered the kids to stop tormenting the animal. They were typical wise-ass teens, and told me to shove it. When I threw away the desk, I had saved a leg to be used to hammer stakes into the ground while I was surveying. I picked up the leg and advanced on the group. They scattered and slunk away muttering curses.

I approached the dog and our eyes locked on to each others'— his blazing with hate and fury and mine seeking to let him know I was a friend. He was panting heavily and blood was running from his mouth. One ear was torn and he had cuts on both sides of his head. We stared intently at each other, and after a minute or so, his front legs collapsed, and he rolled over and closed his eyes. He was in really bad shape. I thought of leaving him there, but I admired his fighting spirit and I decided he deserved a chance to live. I had a piece of canvas in my Jeep that I used to place on the ground when I worked on the vehicle and I laid it next to the dog. As I rolled the dog onto the tarp, he tried to bite me, but all he could do was make the effort and growl.

I lifted him up onto the front seat of the Jeep and took him back to my landlady's house. On the way, I stopped at a hardware store, bought a large crate, and some lumber and took the material to Mrs. Martinez's house. I built a sturdy cage for the dog and left him in the care of the housekeeper.

I purchased a large amount of dried food to feed the dog and gave her money to get him anything else needed to help him get well. I knew, or suspected, that if I just gave her cash to buy things to keep the dog alive, she would let the dog die, and keep the cash for herself.

"He is only a perro," she would say. And "muy feo," or "very ugly, at that. Why spend money on a sick dog?"

I left for the mountains that afternoon with the promise that I would pay her extra if the dog was in good health when I returned, but as I left the dog in the care of the old lady, I had an uneasy feeling that she still might let him die and feed the dog food to her family.

As I got into my Jeep, a young girl ran up and said, "Do not worry, I will take care of your dog." I thanked her and offered her ten pesos.

She said, "No señor, I do not want your money. Your ugly dog looks like he needs a friend." As she walked away, I noticed that she had a scarf wrapped tightly around her head, and I wondered why as it was a sunny day. Something told me that maybe she too needed a friend. I called after her, "What is your name?"

"My name is Elena," she answered and kept walking away.

When I got back to town, I was amazed to see the dog looking fit, growling, baring his teeth and smashing into the sides of his cage. He had tremendous recuperative powers and looked as though he was ready to fight. He was still filthy, caked with dirt and dried blood. The landlady was afraid of him and did not attempt to touch him.

I got a hose and soaked him thoroughly, followed by fifteen minutes of rinsing. At first he resisted being pushed around and showed his displeasure and annoyance by snapping at and biting the stream of water. After a while, he just stood still. He even smiled a couple of times before shaking himself dry and rolling on the ground. I finally got a good look at the dog. I am not a good judge of the lineage of dogs, but from pictures and descriptions, I would say, he was about 90 percent pit bull and 10 percent boxer. He weighed about 35 pounds, was short-haired and rock solid.

The guy who was the overseer of the town dump told me that from time to time the people who ran the dog fights would throw the dogs who were killed or badly hurt into the dump to get rid of them and the dog I had rescued was one of them. Dog fighting was a legal sport in some places in Mexico and the overseer had killed many dogs to put them out of their misery.

The dog had to have a name. What should I call him? Something that had a good solid sound. Something American that would not be confused with a Mexican name.

When I was a little kid, I was an avid reader of pulp magazine tales about World War I American fighter pilots who battled the Germans in the skies over France. The best pilots, who shot down at least five enemy airplanes in combat, earned the title of "Ace." They were aggressive, brave and fought to the death. That sounded like my dog. He had surely killed at least five enemy dogs and was brave and willing to fight at any time. So I will call him "Ace."

Ace looked pretty good all shined up and strutting around his cage while baring his teeth and growling. He looked good enough for me to take him back to the mine with me. First, I had to get to know the dog and establish who was boss. I had no experience as a dog trainer, but I did have some ideas. Ace was a big eater. His former owners must have kept him underfed, not knowing where his next meal was coming from. When feeding time came around he would salivate and eagerly await his food to be delivered to him.

I was going to be in town for the next week so I put a plan in place; I was going to be the only one to feed him or give him water. The first two days I was visible and talked to him often. There was plenty of food outside his cage, and he could see it, but he was given none. He became agitated on the second day and began to bark when I came to visit him. I made a great show when I gave him his food and water during the morning on the second day.

I did not feed him again until the fourth day. During that time when I came to visit him, I would throw him a morsel or two. He would rush to the side of the cage and wait for me to throw him a bone or chunk of meat whenever he saw me coming.

After the second feeding, and with his belly full, he came to the side of the cage and let me touch him. Touch him, but not pet him. On the sixth day, he would allow me to pet him once or twice. On the eight day, he was almost begging for his food and water and he allowed me to pet him as much as I wanted to.

Ace was a very smart dog, and I sensed that we were starting to have an understanding. I fed him in the morning and established the fact that this was the time when he could expect to get food and water. Things went fairly smoothly after that and I patted myself on the back. But Ace, although becoming somewhat civilized, was not conquered. He had been made aware that I was a human who had some authority over him, but I was never treated as a boss, more as a partner. We both had our places in the overall scheme of things, but neither one of us had complete control over the other.

I bought Ace a good, strong collar, black and white to match his hide, and a stout leash. He went everywhere with me. He would prove to be more than a partner. He would prove to be a lifesaver.

Maria and Jesus

It was a raw, wet and blustery morning as I drove into Zacatecas from the airport, a very unusual day for this normally clear and sunny high altitude city. As I topped the ridge before the main street and dropped down into the heart of the city, I saw two little children walking hand in hand.

They looked like a boy and a girl, about six or seven years old. Both were dressed in tattered nightgowns. The rain-soaked, thin cloth of the gowns stuck to their skinny backs, and you could easily see their bony shoulder blades peeking through. Each car that bumped by the kids splashed dirty water on them and when a line of burros passed them, they were pushed up against the walls of the buildings that lined the street.

As I drew nearer, I could see that the taller of the two was a girl whose long brown hair was plastered against her head by the rain, and she was holding the hand of a little boy while she was trying to shield his body from the splashing water. Still, with heads bowed against the driving rain, the girl held tightly to the little boy's left hand while the little boy's right hand held tightly to a small, dirty, white stuffed animal.

I pulled up beside the children and stopped. The kids attempted to go around the Jeep, so I stepped into traffic to stop the oncoming cars. Instantly there was a loud blowing of horns and muffled shouts coming from the cars. As I approached the kids, the little girl pulled the boy to her side and gave me a blank stare. I took off my flight jacket and wrapped it around them. I asked them to please get in the Jeep, but the little girl continued to stare straight ahead as if she did not hear me. I could see that talking was not going to do any good, and as traffic was backing up and the horn honking was becoming more insistent, I made a move to pick up the little boy. The girl flew into a rage, biting and kicking me and making strange noises. I lifted the little boy into the back seat, and the little girl threw herself on top of him as if to protect him. I slammed the door shut and raced around to the driver's side and climbed in.

I put the car in gear, and we were now moving down the street and the kids were absolutely quiet. They just stared into space and cowered in the back seat as we drove toward the center of town. Well, I had rescued two little kids, or should I say, I had kidnapped two little kids, and I had no idea of what I was going to do with them.

The name "Fr. Lopez" came to mind. He will know what we should do. I turned to the kids and said, "Iglesia, Iglesia, Church, Church!" Their expressions did not change, but they made no attempt to jump out of the Jeep so I kept on driving. Finally, we were in front of Fr. Lopez's Santo Domingo church. I was uncertain of what I should do now. If I left the kids in the Jeep while I went into the church to get Fr. Lopez, I knew that they were spring-loaded to jump out and run for their lives.

A woman walked by, huddled under her umbrella, and I stopped her and asked if she would watch the kids while I went into the church. She looked at me as if I was crazy, shook her head, and walked off. I offered the little girl my hand to help her out of the Jeep, but she continued starting at me and held the boy tighter. No help here.

At last an altar boy came out of the church, and I tried to stop him. He, too, must have thought I was crazy and kept on walking. I grabbed him by the arm and said, "Listen amigo. I need your help!" He must have seen me around the church before, as he didn't try to run away while I slowly explained to him that I needed to talk to Fr. Lopez.

He went back into the church, and in a few minutes, Fr. Lopez appeared carrying an umbrella. In the rush of things, I had forgotten it was raining and that I was kind of wet myself.

"What's up?" the padre asked. I took him over to the Jeep and pointed to the back seat. His face broke into a smile as he saw the kids, and he exclaimed, "Maria and Jesus, where have you been? Where is your mother?"

The kids' expressions did not change, but they put out their arms to the priest and they made some strange sounds. Fr. Lopez reached inside the Jeep to pick up the girl, but she would not let go of the little boy. Between the priest and me, we got the kids out of the Jeep and on to the sidewalk. Maria grabbed hold of Jesus' left hand, and Jesus still clutched his little dirty white polar bear in his right. I put my jacket around Maria's shoulders, but she took it off and wrapped it around Jesus. We took the children inside Fr. Lopez's office, and the padre told the altar boy to go get Elena. Within minutes, a young girl rushed in and scooped up the kids in her arms.

The girl looked like Elena, the kid that had told me she would take care of Ace the day I left the dog at Mrs. Martinez's house a couple of weeks ago. This girl had a scarf tightly wrapped around her head, and all I could see was her eyes, but they had to be the same person. The girl was crying and scolding the kids at the same time while hugging them and holding them close. I knew that this was going to take some time to figure out, so I told Fr. Lopez I would talk to him later, and I went on to my hotel room.

This was a pleasant interlude. A rainy day in Zacatecas. Just the right atmosphere to get some paperwork accomplished. I finished two reports on mining inspections that I had been putting off, and by late afternoon, I went back to the church to visit with Fr. Lopez.

As we sat down in the padre's office, I felt that for the first time since I had arrived in Mexico I was going to relax and not be thinking what I was going to be doing in the next few weeks.

With the soft rain falling and while I was drinking several cups of hot tea, I was a world apart from jumping out of airplanes, sleeping with one hand on the butt of a rifle or on the grip of a pistol or fighting off snakes or scorpions and occasionally women, who were not always beautiful, but adequate, and in general, leading a pretty exciting life. When I saw those two little kids that morning, alone and getting the hell kicked out of them by the elements, and fate, and other human beings, my heart went out to them. And the complete devotion of that gutsy little girl to her baby brother, that she was going to protect him against all odds with whatever means she had available, both intrigued and inspired me. I wanted to help this family.

Fr. Lopez is in the business of helping people. I am sure that if I ask him, what I can do, he will tell me, a couple of times over.

"I believe this family needs help and deserves it. What can I do to assist them?" I asked the padre.

He smiled and said, "First, let me tell you the story of the Martinez family. It is a very sad one. Mrs. Martinez was born into a poor family in a mining town in the State of Chihuahua. At an early age she married a young, adventurous gold miner who had just arrived in the country from Germany. Very soon, they had a child, Elena.

"When Elena was three, the husband was killed in a tragic mining accident, and suddenly the mother and Elena had absolutely no money or friends. The mother had to go to work in the fields to support herself and her daughter. She married again, also to a poor miner, and they had two more children, Maria and Jesus. They were living a happy life when misfortune once more struck the little family. The father was injured while working in the mines and died several weeks later. Mrs. Martinez had to return to working in the fields, as she did not know any other job and this time she had her daughter by her side.

"Two years ago, she came to the city of Zacatecas to find better work. She left the children behind with Elena, who continued working in the fields to support them. Mrs. Martinez's health began to fail and soon the only work she could find was with the church. Last year she sent for her children to join her in the city in the hopes that they could find work that could better support the family. Disaster struck before they could move to the city when Elena was kicked in the face by a mule while working on a farm. Elena was hurt, bad. Her nose was broken, some facial bones were smashed and a piece of her cheek was gouged out. This is why she wears a hood or a scarf when she is with people.

"Another consequence of the family's troubles is that Maria and Jesus never learned to speak, and Elena can barely read and write. The children live with Mrs. Martinez and Elena in a shack north of the city. Both Mrs. Martinez and Elena had to work late last night, and neither one of them made it home during the storm. The kids had no one to watch over them, so they went looking for the only family they knew."

Fr. Lopez said, "There are two major things for a successful life—love and money. There is plenty of love in this family. You can't supply that. But you can provide money. You are always looking for a good investment. Here is a good investment, but it is not in a gold mine. It is in a family."

Fr. Lopez sat back in his chair, folded his hands in his lap and said, "OK, what are you going to do about it?"

The padre knew that he was about to tap into the do-gooder side of my nature, and he was going to make the most of it.

"What about the house you are going to rent? That would be an ideal place for the family. It has a walled-in area; you could keep your Ace dog in there. He would have plenty of room to play and fight with the birds and not get into any trouble in the street. Mrs. Martinez could plant a big garden and grow special things that she could sell to the local restaurants. Many, many possibilities."

He had certainly hit upon a good place to start. The family had to move out of that one-room shack for many reasons. I was planning to move into the house he was talking about next week, but it was ready to go right now. The house was a three-room bungalow, with a very large yard. It was surrounded by a high wall—and the first thing that I was going to do was get rid of those damned broken glass bottles that were imbedded in the cement on top of the wall.

I could get them a dog for protection and eliminate one thing where the kids might hurt themselves. Of course, Ace would not be happy to have another dog around, but I could talk it over with him and try to convince him that it was for the good of the children. I'm sure he would understand.

Fr. Lopez had a meeting and I had to get back to moving some paperwork so we stood up and shook hands as if it were a done deal. But what about Mrs. Martinez and the kids? What would they think about the move?

Fr. Lopez said, "I'll explain it to her so that she will know that it is something good for her and the children. It will take a while for it to sink in, but this is the best thing that has ever happened to her in her sad life. By the way, the kids are dried off and are wrapped in blankets and are sleeping in the meeting room. They were pretty tired. They had been walking for several hours before you found them. God put you on that road at the right time and place for a reason.

"But, wait a minute. I will get you your jacket. The kids really liked it. It was so soft and warm. They had probably never felt anything like it. And the patches with the eagles and flags, the colors made their faces light up. Elena liked it too. She has been wearing it ever since you left."

"Tell her to keep it for a while," I said. "It has stopped raining and I have another one I can wear," I said and went out the door. As I stepped out in the sunshine, I felt good about myself, and it was a feeling that I rarely get after a meeting in this dog-eat-dog world. It was nice to be able to help some people, especially the little ones.

I remembered when I was growing up and things beyond my control were making things tough on mom and our family. But in the United States, the government doesn't let people starve. This was not so in Mexico. Mrs. Martinez was happy that she would have a new home and that she would have water inside the house and would not have to carry it from a pump outside. I imagined that Elena and the kids were happy too, but it would come to them on a day-by-day basis as the world around them unfolded as a much better place to be.

Ace had a place to work off his excess energy and at the same time be a guard dog, and we were able to remove those broken bottles. Mrs. Martinez planted her garden and was now growing high-end chilies and peppers and selling then to the top restaurants in the city. The church was allowing Elena time off to attend reading and writing classes, and Maria and Jesus were coming out of their shells and sitting in on the classes, along with that dirty, white polar bear. I guess that Fr. Lopez was right when he said that God had put me on that road at that time on that rainy morning in Zacatecas.

13
Ambush

Ruben was still in the hospital. Fr. Lopez and I visited him every other day, and as his condition improved, he said he wanted me to do the things necessary to improve his claim and make sure that all the property boundaries were well marked and his ownership was legal. I hired Luis for a few days and borrowed surveying equipment from one of Fr. Lopez's friends, and we went back to the claim to do the work.

It took us three days to bring the property up to one hundred percent of what the Mexican law required, and it was late afternoon when we saddled up the mules and headed for the trailhead and Zacatecas for what was to be a routine trip.

It would turn out to be anything but. About a half an hour later, while we were climbing a pretty steep slope and entering a grove of pine and scrub oak trees, the trail was blocked by three evil looking men, one with a rifle and two with large caliber pistols, all aimed at me. My .357 revolver rested comfortably under my left arm in its shoulder holster and would stay there until the sleaziest of the three snarled, "Drop that gun and get off that horse! You too, kid."

I didn't need an introduction to figure out these were the three scum from Juarez who were on our trail. I unbuckled my holster and dropped it with the gun. I did not want to damage my weapon, as I had a crazy thought that I could recover it and somehow I might have a chance to use it later. Luis and I got off our mules with our hands held high above our heads. These were probably three of the guys who had killed Miguel, and I was sure that they would do the same to us if given any excuse.

They herded us into the trees, about two hundred yards off the trail and out of sight. They tied each of us very tightly between two trees. This done, they began to interrogate me in rapid fire Spanish. My poor understanding of the language angered them, as my answers came slowly. I surmised that they had been smoking marijuana for the past couple of hours while they were waiting for us, and they were really pumped up. The leader, a scrawny runt whose face was snakelike and featured a thin mustache, hit me square in the face with the barrel of his pistol. Blood and teeth spurted from my mouth. These bastards meant business. The scrawny runt hit me again with the pistol, and the sight ripped open my right cheek. He hit me three more times, and I was hanging on the ropes.

One of the other mutants started asking Luis questions about what we were looking for and what we had found. Luis said that we hadn't found anything. Then both of the bastards started beating Luis as he hung from the ropes. He was crying, his blood had soaked his shirt and he pleaded with them to stop, but they kept on beating him until he fell unconscious. They were enjoying it so much they kept beating him until they got tired.

Then they returned to me. No more questions, but a flurry of blows all over my body. All I could do was curse them with all my might. I would have given a million dollars for a weapon. Finally they stopped beating me and I remembered hearing the snake say, "Let's go and talk to the boss. These guys ain't going anywhere. Have a nice night. I make joke," he laughed.

I drifted in and out of consciousness, and the first thing I clearly remember is waking up as it was getting dark and I hurt, bad, all over. I was covered with blood and the wound on my right cheek was still oozing. I looked over at Luis as he hung from the ropes and he wasn't moving. All was quiet, and I drifted back into unconsciousness. When I awoke again, the moon was shining brightly. I hurt as I had never hurt before. I glanced at Luis. He was motionless. I thought he was dead, and I would probably join him in the morning.

The next time I forced myself back into reality, the sun was shining in my eyes. I thought I heard voices. The bastards were coming back to finish us off. My arms were numb from hanging on the ropes. I had a splitting headache, my eyes were almost completely swollen shut, my ribs hurt, and blood oozed from the deep cut on my cheek. I had swallowed a lot of blood, my stomach churned and I began to puke. God, I wish I had a weapon and I was untied so that I could use it. Give me a penknife, and I would peel that bastard's head like an onion.

The voices became louder and then began to fade. Suddenly, there was a movement in the underbrush and the big black and white mongrel, Dog, bounded out into the clearing. He stopped and looked over the situation. He sniffed me and began to bark. The voices I had heard were faint and becoming fainter.

I figured that the voices probably belonged to the campesinos we had rented the mules from and when the mules returned without Luis and me, they figured that something bad had happened to us. I tried to holler but all that came out was a gurgling sound and a lot of blood. The mongrel was becoming agitated and started running in circles. After a while, he took off and I was left alone and all was quiet. I struggled to slip my bonds, but the bastards had done a good job of tying me to the trees. My arms were numb and I couldn't move my fingers. I soon became exhausted, and all I could do was curse. Then I heard the dog barking, faint at first, and then becoming louder.

About five minutes later, the owner of the mules and his son appeared. A few strokes of his big machete freed me, and we rushed to Luis. As I feared, he was almost dead but he had a very faint pulse. There was hope, if we moved fast. Both of my eyes were swollen shut but when I propped them open with my fingers, I could dimly see. They walked me to the trail where they had left the mules and carried Luis.

I climbed on to the back of the biggest mule, and they tied Luis to the saddle of the other. The son would walk beside the mule to keep Luis upright. We were about two hours from the trailhead and an hour from where they found us when we heard voices and the sound of mules. It had to be the bad guys. We pulled off the trail and held our breath as they passed by. Suddenly my mule brayed, and he was answered by one of the mules ridden by the enemies. It was a scary moment and no one moved or said a word. The bad guys stopped, listened and probably looked around, and then continued on.

A confrontation would have been fatal for us. But it crossed my mind that maybe we could catch them by surprise and kill them with our two machetes. Revenge! I wanted revenge. But all we had were two machetes against their guns. I was almost blind and our two mule drivers were not looking for a fight, nor would they fight; why should they? The thought of the guy I called the snake, his severed head bouncing over the ground like a soccer ball and me planting my polished jump boot between his beady eyes and scoring a winning goal, made me almost laugh, but that would have to wait until later. I would get my pound of flesh, and I would enjoy it.

We let them pass and when we got back on the trail, we increased our pace. We had about an hour's head start on them before they would discover we were gone. Strange, I felt sure that we had heard only two voices as they passed by. Where was the third guy? By the time we reached the trail head, I was about to pass out and Luis was barely breathing. We laid him down in the rear seat of the Jeep and covered him with our sleeping bags that had returned with the mules.

I took stock of the situation, and things were not good. I could only see out of one eye, and then only if I propped it open with my finger. No one else could drive the Jeep and we had to get Luis to a doctor as soon as possible or he would surely die, and I was far from being 100 percent healthy.

After much talking and negotiating with the owners of the mules, the son agreed to ride with me and help me stay on the road. After two hours of hairraising driving and many close calls, we arrived at my hotel in Zacatecas. We did not stop in Fresnillo, as I was afraid we might run into the third man or any of the bad guy's friends. I parked in the underground garage and left Luis in the back seat covered by the sleeping bags.

I was completely wiped out. Fortunately, the hotel gofer, a friend, was on duty, and I gave him a couple of pesos to take a note to Raquel. I went to my room and washed off some of the blood and grime.

Raquel arrived in fifteen minutes, surveyed the scene, and took charge. She called her father's clinic to reserve a room for me and one for Luis and alerted the doctor that he was needed right away. She told the staff that if any one asked about me and Luis, we had been in an automobile accident. Raquel led me to the Jeep, and she drove me and Luis to the rear entrance of the clinic and made sure that everything was taken care of. Her father arrived right away and the nurses scrubbed me up and made ready for anything the doctor ordered. I told them to do absolutely anything necessary to save Luis' life, and I would take care of all doctor's bills.

After an hour or so of the doctor working on me, a physical inspection revealed that I had three broken ribs, a broken arm, three teeth knocked out, a deep cut on my cheek, a large bump on my head and cuts and bruises all over my body. I had lost a lot of blood, but the doctor said that I would replace it in the next few weeks.

I went to sleep, and when I woke up later that night, the general and one of his captains were standing over me. The first words he said to me were, "Are you going to be able to jump at the commander's convention?" I replied, "Hell yes, we paratroopers heal fast. Count on it!"

He smiled broadly and said, "Your wishes will be carried out as long as you are going to jump."

"What can we do to get revenge on the three guys who beat up Luis and me?" I asked.

"Don't worry, we will take care of them in our own way," he said.

My recovery was normal but boring as hell. Raquel came to see me every day and gave me a crash course in Spanish. I had a chance to read everything I could get my hands on, something I had wanted to do for a long while. The swelling on my face was all gone in ten days, and I was discreetly walking several miles a day. I had to be in good shape for the big jump whenever the general said it was scheduled. My ribs were bound tightly and they hurt if I moved the wrong way, but they were getting better.

The general or one of his captains visited me every other day and I became friends with one of the aides, Jorge Villalobos. Jorge was from the state of Jalisco, the Texas of Mexico, where everything is supersized and superior to any other place else in the country. He was very talkative and a gossip. I soon knew who was who and where everybody fit in.

Jorge liked to live the high life, but was limited by lack of money. He went out of his way to visit me when Raquel was around, and she knew it. Raquel considered him a class below her and gave him no indication that he was anything but a servant.

Several days after I entered the clinic, I asked one of the captains if they had ever found the three guys from Juarez. As a matter of fact, he said, the general had sent out an elite squad commanded by a Yaqui Indian sergeant who always got his man and also got any information that was necessary to convict them.

They captured two of those guys pretty quickly, the captain said, as the general had been tailing me at the request of Raquel's mother. They had a good idea of my movements and traced the two to Fresnillo. They took them back out in the country and interrogated them and learned that they had indeed killed Miguel and that their boss, who was a big drug dealer on the border, stole the high-grade sample that Miguel had been showing around. They said they did not know what happened to the gold sample, but Miguel had said that it was given to him by a cousin who had taken it from a museum, and Miguel didn't find the gold sample where he said he did.

The boss did not believe him, as he had changed his story several times while being tortured, and the boss wanted to make sure, so he sent the three guys to Hernandez's claim to beat the information out of us in case Miguel had not been telling the truth. The sergeant had the two guys each dig a hole, roughly six by three feet, and while the squad was taking a siesta, the guys tried to escape and were recaptured. They were tried after the siesta, convicted, and shot. It just so happened that the two holes were available, so they threw them in and covered them up. (I enjoyed this part.) They reported the incident to the general and he decided that it wasn't important enough to bother with, so as far as he, the regional commander was concerned, it had never happened. Case closed. They could not find the third guy, but they would keep looking.

Hire Big John

A couple of weeks went by and I was living a rather dull but enjoyable life. I was catching up on my sleep, getting a good suntan, and trying to gain some command of the Spanish language under the excellent teaching of Raquel.

She came over to the hotel, accompanied by good old Tia Martha every day but the closest Raquel and I ever got to physical contact was a firm handshake every morning. I spent a great deal of my time trying to figure out some way to get Tia Martha out of the way, but, alas, nothing presented itself. I was seriously thinking of taking the relationship to a higher level but on the mornings when Raquel would come over in a foul mood after a screaming match with her mother about the horrors of marrying an Americano adventurer, without makeup and her hair uncombed, I would be yanked back to reality.

I was walking three miles a day and my ribs were healing and they didn't hurt any more when I breathed. I was ready to go back to work. I had one outstanding commitment and that was to Gen. Garcia. After that, my schedule was open. Why not plan to spend at least six more months here in Mexico and form a company? I already had my work papers and I had made some pretty good business connections and I have had some adventures, mostly good, but some I don't think I would care to repeat, but overall, good stuff. If I form a company I am going to have to have a good man I can depend on in an emergency.

From what I have discovered with dealing with the Mexican male, the jealous or macho ones—and that pretty much covers most of the ones I have had run-ins with—I was always going to need someone to cover my back. What better man than Juan Ochoa—Big John—and he should be wrapping up his commitment to the Mexican Army pretty soon. So the next morning I climbed into my Jeep and headed north to Chihuahua City and then west to Military Checkpoint 81.

It was dusk when I arrived at the checkpoint and John was on duty with another soldier. He was very surprised to see me and his stoic features burst into a broad smile as he introduced me to his partner. A new sergeant had taken over the post, but he was in town meeting with some people from a timber company that was beginning operation in the woods north of the checkpoint. I imagined that if this sergeant was like the last one, the price of business would be going up.

John told the other guard that he was going to his shack to let me say hello to his wife, Luz, and their kids, and he should take over. As we walked to his shack I asked him when his service was finished and, when it was, what did he plan to do?

He blurted out, "Cinco dias mas, Señor Jaime. Five more days."

He looked at me expectantly, "I work for you?"

I said, "I sure hope that you will work for me and that's what I want to talk to you about."

"I will work for you."

We shook hands and entered the shack and little Jaime ran to Big John. When he saw me he grabbed John's leg and looked at me with a wary eye.

Luz smiled and said, "Buenas dias, Señor Jaime. Welcome to our home."

John picked up little Jaime and brought him over to me and said, "This man is our friend. He is your godfather."

Little Jaime didn't seem to know what to do, so he chewed on his hand and gave me a little smile. Big John invited me to stay for dinner but I said I had to get back to Chihuahua City. I said good-bye to Luz and the kids and as John and I walked to the guard shack, I gave him 75 pesos and told him, "This is an advance on your pay and we will talk when you get to Zacatecas. When your bus arrives, go to the Church of Santo Domingo and ask for Padre Lopez. I will tell him about you and he will have a place for you to stay."

We shook hands and I was off to Chihuahua City. When I looked back I saw that Big John was wearing a smile that went from ear to ear.

When I got to Chihuahua City, I didn't bother to call Señor Ortega or any of the other people I had met there. I just wanted to go to bed and get an early start in the morning. I pulled into a new American-style motel, registered and hit the sack. I would eat in the morning.

When I got back to Zacatecas, I found a couple of things had happened while I was gone; the chief one was that Gen. Garcia wanted to see me as soon as I returned. After having breakfast with Fr. Lopez and arranging for living quarters for Big John and his family, I had the father drop me off at the military head-quarters.

The general was in his office and he was very glad to see me. "How are you feeling? Are you all healed up?"

I told him I was in top shape and was ready for anything he might have for me to do.

He said, "Muy Bueno. Fine. The generals have decided to have their annual meeting in Acapulco in two weeks. Will you be ready to go?"

"You bet," I answered, "Tell me when and where."

"We will have the contest at the abandoned military airstrip north and west of the city and you will be there at ten o'clock." He was in an uncharacteristically jovial mood when I left and he ordered one of his captains to give me a ride back to the church.

"I don't know how you do it," the captain said, "but if you can keep the old man in good spirits, we want you to stay around."

"Let's see what happens next week," I said, as he dropped me off.

Fr. Lopez asked me, "How are you doing with Raquel?" I told him, "OK, but nothing unusual is happening."

He said, "Friday is her saint's day and that is a big deal for a girl. Do you want to make her happy?"

"Sure," I said. "How do I do that?"

"Well, you tell Tia Martha that you would like to see Raquel at her house at about ten o'clock on Friday night and you would like to talk to her on her balcony. You will have mariachis to serenade her. It is very romantic and a little old fashioned."

I liked the idea but had no idea how to arrange it. So I asked him to do me a big favor and set it up for me. After I had said that, it struck me that if he had the feelings that I thought he did, it was like setting up a date with your best girlfriend with another guy. But I was only guessing about his feelings for Raquel. Anyway, it was too late to call back my request.

Big John, Luz and the kids arrived Friday afternoon and Fr. Lopez had two rooms ready for them at the church. After they settled in, we went to dinner and everybody was happy. It was the beginning of a new life for the Ochoas, and I was glad to be a part of it. That night, my venture into the romantic side of my life in Mexico turned out to be a success, I think. Raquel was impressed with the mariachis and the serenade; her mother was not, I'm sure. As for Tia Martha, she probably enjoyed the music. I could not see the old watchdog, but the clicking of her crocheting needles told me she lurked nearby. I did know, however, that the serenade didn't help my amorous desires at all because all I got for my efforts was the same old firm handshake through the bars on her window when we said good night.

El Rey Company Formed

The next morning while Big John and I were having breakfast with Fr. Lopez, the padre said that Dr. Alvarez was going to release Ruben this afternoon.

"Let's go see how he is doing, and find out what he wants to do about the property," he said.

I thought that was a great idea so I paid the bill, Big John stuffed a couple of tortillas in his pocket and we were out the door and on our way to the clinic. Ruben was up and around, although looking a little the worse for wear after being in bed for the past several weeks. The doctor said that his system had received a severe shock that came at a very bad time, as he had been pushing himself too hard while expanding his business and he was ready to collapse from exhaustion. Dr. Alvarez suggested that he take a few weeks off and lay around on the beach at Acapulco and spend some of the money he is making on himself before it is too late. Ruben agreed and before he left to fly south to meet his family, he wanted to meet with me and Fr. Lopez.

As we relaxed over a few beers, with Fr. Lopez and Big John watching us over their cokes, we discussed the future. Ruben still had faith that his claim could make him some money, and he wanted to keep it—for nothing more than to honor the memory of his father—and what did I, as a mining engineer suggest he do?

I had given some thought to the value of the claim and the possibility that it could produce enough gold to turn a profit and I had developed a theory that if it worked out to be true, it could be a bonanza. It had been proven that there are traces of placer gold on the property and that the gold had to have been deposited there by an ancient river or large stream. If we could find and map the course, or channel of that river, there is the possibility that we could find some rich pockets of placer gold.

But even if we found the gold, there would be some problems with separating it from the dirt. The biggest problem would be water. But from what I had seen, that problem could be solved with research and planning. There was water further up in the foothills above the claim and if nobody owned this land, maybe we could stake claim to the land between us and the water, and maybe we could divert this water and make it flow to our land and maybe we could build a reservoir to store this water and maybe we could run a pipe from this water to our property or maybe we could dig down far enough to tap the ground water during the rainy season or maybe—a whole lot of maybes.

My mind was racing with many possibilities of uncovering a large deposit of placer gold left by a raging river as it eroded and washed down a mountain to make this desert floor. What would I do? First, I would claim the land above the property. Then I would dissect the property into grids and sample and record what was discovered at various depths and locations on the property and plot this on a large map. This wouldn't take much time and when we were set up, I would hire some manual laborers to do the digging and someone to supervise the sampling and record-ing of the values on the map.

I had been very impressed with the progress that Big John had made from his primitive background to his adapting to the mod-ern world and its customs. If we found the gold I think might be there, we would need someone who was not only bright but a good worker, and who was honest and loyal. Big John scored high in all these qualifications and he would be my choice to be su-pervisor.

I guess that a little of the do-gooder side of my nature figured into this decision. Here is a person who deserved a hand up from the lowly environment he was assigned to at birth and I intended to give him that break. I would hire Luis as our recorder and keeper of the map. Luis was another guy who deserved a shot at the brass ring of life. I would oversee the operation and make the big decisions.

Here's how it would work. We would form a company. Ruben would own 40 percent of the stock. I would own 40 percent of the stock. Big John would own 15 percent of the stock and Luis would own 5 percent of the stock. In addition, Big John and Luis would receive a monthly wage in addition to their shares. Ruben would supply the working capital and cover all day-to-day ex-penses. The current property, and all property claimed, would be owned by the company.

I anticipated that we should start showing a profit within six months. If not, Ruben, Big John, Luis and I would have a stockholder's meeting and decide if we should continue operation or liquidate the assets. I laid the proposition on the table and without blinking an eye, Ruben said, "It sounds like a good business venture to me. I will have the papers drawn up and let's get started right away."

"Good," I said. "I will need two thousand dollars, American, in our bank account so I can start buying things today."

Ruben gulped a little, but said, "It will be in the bank by the time that you need it."

We shook hands and I said, "Big John and I will leave first thing in the morning."

As Ruben turned to leave he said, "I'll call my lawyer and have the papers drawn up today. By the way, What shall we call the company?"

"How about the El Rey Mining Company?" I ventured.

"That sounds like a great idea. My dad would have liked that." He smiled and I thought I saw a tear in his eye. Big John had a smile on his broad face that stretched from ear to ear—a very rare show of emotion from this stoic Indian. I'm sure that he didn't understand half of what had taken place this morning, but he knew it was going to be something good for him and his family.

Fr. Lopez slapped me on the back and said, "I think that you put together a very good business deal for all concerned, but how is this going to affect your lifestyle? This is going to tie you down to one location for a while, at least until you get the operation going, but I am sure that you can handle it."

I really hadn't given it much thought before I made the offer, but I saw what seemed to me to be a good deal in the making this morning and jumped at it. Now to get started and I will figure out the details later as we go along.

I asked Fr. Lopez what he thought about the idea to include Luis in the project.

He said, "This is a chance of a lifetime for this young man. It will change the direction of his entire life. He will never get another opportunity like this again."

I asked the padre to explain the job to Luis, what he would be doing and his responsibilities and make sure he understood it.

Also, he should know he can quit anytime that he feels that he can't handle the work.

I asked Big John to make a list of the things he and his wife and kids would need to live out in the wild for a month or so, and I would see him back at the church in an hour. I wanted to see Raquel before I went out of town again so I asked Fr. Lopez to send one of his altar boys to take a note to her, and to wait and bring back an answer.

The young man left at top speed and returned in fifteen minutes. My request to see Raquel had been granted. When I got to her house I was met at the door by the chaperone, Tia Martha, and when she invited me in, I thought I might have seen a faint glimmer of a smile. Nah, that couldn't have been. If Raquel's mother had seen that, poor Martha would have been out on the street.

Raquel greeted me with a firm handshake and asked me when I was going to let her make a parachute jump, as I had promised. This kind of surprised me, as I didn't remember exactly making that promise, but I was beginning to discover that whenever she wanted something, it was a done deal.

I explained to her the agreement I had made with Señor Hernandez and that I would be out of town for a couple of weeks, and maybe we should forget about it for a while. I told her that I had grave misgivings that if anything happened to her during the training or the jump, her mother would have the general shoot me.

She pouted and pleaded, so finally I said that the next time I came back into town I would train both her and Fr. Lopez to make a jump. She perked up and said, "I'll really be looking for your return."

I met Big John at the church and we went on a buying spree that included a squad tent for the family quarters, a two-man tent for me, a generator with wiring, and lots of other things to make our new home livable. We took a sizable bite out of the two thousand bucks Señor Hernandez had put in the bank, but comfortable employees are happy employees.

I picked up Big John and his family at the church and Ace at Mrs. Martinez's house and we were on our way to San Mateo early the next morning. With the Jeep piled high with pots and pans and bits and pieces of furniture, and the kids and the dog looking out the side windows, we must have looked like something out of "Grapes of Wrath"—a family of Okies driven out of their home by the dust storms and heading for California.

It was slower going than usual, but we made it to San Mateo by noon. The first to meet us was Dog and his pack of mangy mutts. I had anticipated that Dog and Ace would go head to head at first sniff so I had put the strong leash on Ace's collar a few miles back and sat him down on Big John's lap. I was right. Dog tried to get at Ace while the Jeep was still rolling to a stop and Big John had his hands full keeping Ace from jumping from the Jeep and taking John with him. Little did Dog realize that if Big John had let Ace loose, it would take the Ace less than ten seconds to tear an ear off Dog and spit it out. Dog was a big man around these mutts, but Ace was a pro and was not likely to cut an opposing dog any slack for just being stupid. John tied Ace to a fence post and one of the old man's sons put a rope around Dog and dragged him into the shack.

The viejo greeted us warmly and looked over our entourage with amusement. I explained to him that we were going to do a lot of work on the claim and we were going to need his help. He immediately got the picture and smiled. This was going to be a big payday for him and he was going to go all out to cater to our wishes. His kids were already dragging the mules in from their resting places in the woods as we were unloading the Jeep.

I told the old man that we would need to buy three strong mules and a burro for our own and I asked him to buy them for us as he was an expert on mules. I could see the wheels turning in his head as he calculated how much he could tack on to the buying price of the animals, but I figured it was better that he make the money than some guy we didn't know. By the time we finished loading up, we had four big mules and three burros loaded to the max with people and gear.

Big John took little Jaime on his saddle, Luz took Rosita and I took Ace, at least until we were out of sight of the other dogs. Ace was determined to take on the whole pack, as they, not knowing how close they were to having their heads torn off, were barking and nipping at the heels of my mule. The viejo sent along two of his sons and before we left, we paid him in hard money.

The property was just as we had left it and after unloading the animals, Big John and I spent the next couple of hours deciding on the best location for the living area and the corrals. We left Ace to guard Luz and the kids—we also left a .30-30 carbine that she was a crack shot with—and we, Big John and the two boys, the four mules and I, went up into the hills above the claim to cut timber for the buildings we were going to build.

After ten 16-hour days, we had a livable camp and corral constructed and we had explored and staked out the land I thought that we were going to need to carry through my plan.

I was ready to go back to the city. I needed a break. We made a trip into Fresnillo to get extra food supplies and gasoline for the generator. Big John took the stuff back to the camp and I took off for Zacatecas, where I had to figure out what to do about Raquel and the parachute training.

Luiz and Big John

14
Buying the Bug

I was beginning to realize that the back country of Mexico was a big and wild place and sometimes it took hours, and even days, to get from point A to point B if you had to cross rough land. I needed an airplane, not the big, powerful machines I was used to bossing around, but a small, light craft that would take me in and out of tight places.

A new aircraft coming into play was called the helicopter, but its cost was way out of my price range and even if I could afford one, I didn't have the time to learn to fly it. What I needed was a small and light craft like some farmers and ranchers in New Mexico and Texas used to keep track of their land and cattle. I remember several years ago, when I was pulling some active duty at Biggs Air Force Base in Texas, a buddy I had flown with in the Pacific gave me a ride in a Piper Cub. I thought it was pretty neat to be able to take off from the long concrete runway at Biggs and then land in a cow pasture at his father's ranch with equal ease. It was just as easy to take off and fly to the far reaches of the ranch in minutes to look for lost cattle, where it used to take days to do this before they had this craft.

If I could find an airplane like that, I would buy it. I knew that I couldn't find one in Zacatecas, so I had better head north. The next morning, I hopped on a Western Airlines flight and was in Juarez by ten o'clock. I rented a car and drove to Biggs Field to see if I could track down Bill Kelley, the guy who gave me the ride in the Piper Cub. When I checked with the charge of quarters, I was not surprised to learn that he had been transferred to another station. I asked the CQ if he had a locator card on file, and sure enough, he did. Bill was now in Osan, Korea, but his card said that his next of kin was living in Van Horn, Texas, about fifty miles south of El Paso.

I called the telephone number listed on the card and his dad answered. I asked him if he still had the Piper Cub I had flown in with his son, and he said, "Yes." When I asked if he wanted to sell it, he said, "No," but he did have a neighbor who had one just like his and who was wanting to sell it because he was getting too old to pass his flight physical. "His name is Clint Johnson, and here is his phone number."

I called Clint, and he said, "Come on down and take a look at it." I asked how much he was asking for it. He said, "I was going to ask a thousand dollars for it, but since you are a friend of Bill's, I'll let you have it for seven fifty, cash, up front."

I got directions from him and I was there in an hour. The airplane looked to be in excellent condition, not a scratch on the skin, but the engine, the original 65 horsepower model, had lots of hours on it. No big deal—I was going to retrofit the craft with a bigger engine, as I would be operating at a much higher altitude in Zacatecas. I asked him about installing a bigger engine, but the FAA had said no. I would have to buy the newer Cub from the manufacturer. It's made for a bigger engine.

This Cub was painted a bright red, which suited me fine. The normal paint job on a J-3 Cub is a shade of yellow called "Lock Haven Yellow" after the small Pennsylvania town where the J-3 was first manufactured.

Clint told me he had another airplane in the barn. It was called a PA-18 Super Cub, and it had a bigger engine, but he wanted four grand, up front, for it. This was far more than my budget could afford, so I didn't bother looking it over. I had three hundred dollars in cash on me, but I knew I could get the other four fifty from my old bank in Deming.

"Would you trust me with the airplane while I fly to Deming to pick up the cash?" I asked him.

"Any friend of the Kelleys is a friend of mine, but you could leave the three hundred for a deposit," he said. He would pump up the tires and hose down the Cub and I could sign and pick up the papers when I came back tomorrow.

As I drove back to Juarez, I was pretty pleased with myself for the ease with which events were going, but I knew the hard part was going to be getting the airplane into Mexico. It was time to call in a marker from my friend, Don Diego. I put in a call to the Don and he was glad to hear from me.

"What brings you to Juarez?" he asked.

I explained to him that I had bought an airplane and I wanted to bring it into Mexico legally, and base it at the airport in Zacatecas.

"Oh yes, I want to remove the engine and replace it with a much bigger engine, and I am sure it will require a special permit."

He said he would call his lawyer, the same one who got me my work papers, and he would clear it through customs. It would take a few well-placed bribes, but he would handle that.

"I still owe you a favor or two," he said. "To make things more simple, why don't you have the engine replaced in the States before you fly the airplane into Mexico?" he asked.

I explained to him that the engine I wanted to put in the airplane was much bigger than the one that was presently in the craft and the cowling, the metal that protects the engine, would have to be removed and the Mexican Aviation Authority would not let us remove it without a fight. It was a matter of safety, they would say, but it was really an unnecessary requirement.

But in Mexico, if we put some money in the right places, the officials would let you hitch a team of horses to the front of the airplane to pull it.

He laughed and said, "You are learning fast, Señor Jaime. I will take care of this piece of business, also."

I thanked him and said, "I will give you more details tomorrow. But I do know that I will need someone to drive my rental car back from Van Horn tomorrow."

I called an engine shop at the El Paso airport that I had worked with before. The owner was another Air Force pilot and a good friend. I asked them what was the biggest engine they could install in a J-3 Cub. He said, "A 150-horsepower Lycoming, but forget it, the FAA will not allow it."

I told them that the engine exchange would take place at the Juarez airport, and the details have been taken care of. They asked me when I wanted to change the engine. I said, "Noon, the day after tomorrow."

We agreed on a price, cash up front, and it was a deal. I asked him if he could buy an aircraft radio and a hand-held unit that had the same frequencies. He said no problem, I could pay for it when they delivered the engine.

I called Fr. Pat and asked him to pick me up tomorrow about noon at the Deming airport, checked into the bachelor officers quarters at Fort Bliss and went to bed early. I had had a busy day and tomorrow was going to be another one.

The next morning we, one of Don Diego's employees and I, drove to Van Horn and I picked up the Cub and the paperwork. The employee returned the car and I flew on to the El Paso airport where I gassed up. I called Don Diego with all the pertinent information and then called Fr. Pat to tell him I was on time. The Cub handled like a dream, except the controls were a little stiff, and it was so damn slow.

I wanted to fly over the badlands of New Mexico between El Paso and Deming, but the airplane had not been flown for a while and I did not want to take a chance of having a forced landing in that wild country if something went wrong. All went well and I landed at the Deming airport in a little over two hours' flight time. Fr. Pat picked me up and we drove into town to the bank. I withdrew eight hundred dollars and the clerk asked me, "What do you want to do with the five dollars and seventy-three cents that you have left in the account?"

I told him, "Let's cash it out. I don't think that I will be retiring in Deming." Things were pretty much the same on the social scene as they were when I left.

The big news was that Frank Wilson was going to marry the daughter of one of the city fathers this weekend and my two-weeks girl friend, Linda, was engaged to some preacher she had met at college. Doggone it! There went my chance for a date tonight.

The next morning I landed at the ranch in Van Horn. The rancher was waiting for me when I touched down in his pasture. I handed him the check for $450, he wished me luck, and my next stop was the Juarez airport. There I was met by the same young man from Don Diego's company who had returned my rental car. He directed me to a hangar where I parked the Cub. At twelve o'clock sharp, the engine crew drove up in a pickup with a brand new 150 horse engine, and a hoist and welding equipment. By three o'clock, they had the engine hung and everything connected. The mechanic said that his boss told him to install a new model propeller he was selling and to let him know how it works with this engine.

I hit the starter and the engine cranked over on the first try. It's a good thing that we had the aircraft well chocked as the engine at idle had almost enough power to skid the wheels. It sounded great. The guy from Don Diego's office handed me the official papers with all the government seals and signatures embossed on heavy paper, ready to be hung on the wall of my hangar in Zacatecas, and I was good to go. It was getting late so I decided to test hop the airplane while I slow-timed the new engine on the way to Chihuahua City.

On takeoff I got a jolt when the Cub suddenly pulled hard to the left when it reached a certain revolutions per minute and a certain airspeed. That bothered me, but I figured I could fix that when I got back to home base in Zacatecas. The flight to Chihuahua was smooth and I was learning that this modification to the airplane was going to require a pilot to pay a lot more attention to what he was doing when he was flying this Cub. You really had to keep ahead of the airplane because of the huge increase in the power of the engine.

On the last leg of the flight, I landed at Torreon just to make sure that all the gauges were working correctly. They were, so the trip ended on a high note. Fr. Lopez met me when I landed and directed me to one of the small maintenance hangars on the flight line. I shut down the engine and we pushed the Cub into a corner, took everything of value and headed downtown.

Test Fly the Bug

Luz invited me for dinner and as we ate, I told them about the trip to Texas and asked Big John if he and Little Jaime would like to go up and fly around the city tomorrow. He eagerly accepted my offer for him and Jaime to enter the 20th century and fly like the birds. He was very excited and tried to demonstrate to everyone how a bird flies by careening around the small room with his arms outstretched. Jaime was puzzled and looked at John like he was nuts.

Early the next morning, I picked up Fr. Lopez, Big John and Little Jaime at the church and drove out to the airport. There was an air of expectation in the group as they looked forward to doing things that they had never done before. The hangar was empty except for the Cub, and the light streaming through the window high on the wall cast dark shadows that gave the scene a weird appearance.

Little Jaime took one look at the airplane and yelled, "Bicho Rojo, Insecto Grande." I had to laugh, but in the dim light and with the cylinders sticking out from the side of the nose of the airplane, it did look like a big red bug. Little Jaime had just named our new airplane. We pushed the "Bug" out of the hangar and over to the gasoline pumps and while Fr. Lopez showed John how to fill the tank, I did a "walk around" inspection of the aircraft. No one had stolen anything from the hangar, or the airplane, last night so we were ready to go flying.

Big John was looking a little nervous so I decided to take Fr. Lopez up for the first flight. The padre and I strapped into the airplane and as I hit the starter switch and the engine roared into life, Little Jaime squealed with delight and Big John put his hands over his ears. We taxied out to the end of the runway and I called the tower for takeoff instructions. It was a pleasant surprise when the tower operator came up on the radio and gave us instructions in very good English. This was a great way to start off the morning. I ran up the engine, pulled onto the runway and poured the coal to the "Bug."

I was still breaking in the engine, so I let it roll and used plenty of runway before getting airborne. The airplane handled beautifully except when we hit that certain airspeed and revolutions per minute, and then it veered sharply to the left for a few seconds before it straightened out. I would have to make some adjustments this afternoon, but as long as I knew what to expect and how to control it, it was OK to fly. After I trimmed the airplane and we flew straight and level for a couple of minutes with two people and a full load of fuel and had no problems, I felt that I had made a good buy. We flew back and forth over the city and although this was the first time that the padre had flown in a small airplane, he seemed to enjoy it.

Our approach was a little faster than normal, but I had to remember that our ground level was seven thousand feet and the air was thinner than that of El Paso.

By the time we landed, I was preparing myself for the request I knew was going to come, "Can you teach me to fly?" I would, of course. It was something I could do to repay him for all the good things he had done for me.

I replied, "You bet. As long as you keep me in your prayers."

We taxied over to where Big John and Little Jaime were waiting and as soon as Fr. Lopez got out, I motioned for the two of them to climb in. John didn't look as confident as he was a short while ago and Jaime looked as if he was going to cry, so I thought it best that I shut down the engine and get out of the plane and help them get on board.

Big John was a very tight fit in the back seat and I thought of flying with Jaime in the front seat with me, but I dismissed that idea in a hurry when Jaime began to snivel and hang on to John. I moved my seat all the way forward, we squeezed Jaime in on John's lap and we were ready to take off. We cranked up the engine and taxied out to the runway and called the tower. I handed the earphones to Jaime and his eyes grew wide as he heard the tower operator's voice. We got clearance to take off and this time I pushed the throttle full forward and we were airborne in a very short distance. We still experienced the same jerk to the left when the tachometer hit about two thousand revolutions per minute, but no big problem. The extra weight in the airplane was noticeable, but the "Bug" handled it well.

I adjusted the rear-view mirror so I could see what was going on in the rear seat and I saw Big John's head twisting from side to side as he tried to look out the windows while Little Jaime looked straight ahead and was smiling bravely while we climbed to altitude.

The passengers couldn't see much as we climbed, but when we reached five thousand feet, I rocked the plane gently from side to side and they got a pretty good look at the ground. John maintained a stoic countenance but Little Jaime's expressions showed wonderment and disbelief at the things he was seeing. I could only imagine what was going through his mind as it processed all these new sensations.

After a couple of minutes, I chopped the throttle and we began to lose altitude as we returned to the airport. I thought that this was enough for their senses to absorb on their first flight. As we approached the runway, I spotted a bunch of cattle peacefully grazing in a field below our flight path and I shouted to Jaime to watch. I gunned the engine and dove on the herd and they scattered like a flock of birds. Jaime shrieked with delight and clapped his hands and squirmed in Big John's lap as he tried to look out of the window. I guess that I didn't make any friends with a local farmer, but Jamie thought that it was very funny.

We had only been in the air for about fifteen minutes when we touched down, but, all in all, it was a successful day—nobody got sick and nobody cried. As we drove back into town, everyone was chattering, mostly with relief. They had conquered the skies and viewed the earth through eyes different than those of their compatriots and their outlook would never be the same. We dropped off the padre at the church and Big John, Jaime and I went to the hardware store to buy lumber and nails to construct our own hangar within a hangar to house and protect the "Insecto Rojo."

Raul Checks Out in the Bug

Big John and I had finished building the mini-hangar for the "Bug" when Raul Parra landed in his new Cessna 180 and taxied up to our Jeep. He had been on a charter flight to Veracruz and had missed my homecoming last night. He was lavish in his praise of the "Bug" and said he couldn't wait to get checked out in it.

"Since you are going to be my backup, we might as well start your training right now," I told him, We pushed the Cub out on to the ramp and did a complete inspection and a control check. It had been several years since Raul had flown an aircraft that had a control stick but he should be able to master it in short order. A unique feature of the J-3 Cub was that when flown solo, it had to be flown from the rear seat to counterbalance the fuel tank mounted in front of the instrument panel. I tried to emphasize to Raul that the most unusual thing about flying this particular airplane was the unexpected power the 150-horsepower engine and special prop had in throwing around an airframe that weighed less than 700 pounds plus 12 gallons of fuel. One thing I failed to emphasize was the airplane's fault of yanking hard left when the RPM reached two thousand, if only for a second. This would prove to be a fatal flaw, and the clock was ticking.

We taxied up and down the ramp and Raul said, "I'm ready to take 'er up." I hopped out of the "Bug" and Raul got clearance from the tower and started his roll down the runway. He was about twenty feet in the air when the tachometer hit two thousand revolutions per minute and the "Bug" darted sharply to the left. It must have caught Raul completely by surprise and, not being used to flying with a stick, he overcompensated and completely lost control. He bounced a couple of times in the dirt beside the runway. The prop dug into the ground, the airframe buckled, the engine tore loose and the "Bug"—and the last of my savings—were squashed in a thick cloud of dirt and dust.

I jumped into the Jeep, not thinking about Big John and Little Jaime, and headed for the wreck. I was engulfed in an instant anger. A million thoughts raced through my mind. How in the hell had I been so stupid as to let that kid take off in my prized airplane? Hold on, it was my responsibility to make sure that he was thoroughly familiar with the operation of the aircraft before I turned it over to him. Suddenly, the thought struck me: I may be responsible for the kid killing himself. Another thought replaced that one, the hell with the kid, what about my special airplane and my last couple of hundred bucks that I had sunk into buying it?

My Jeep skidded to a stop, adding another cloud of dust to the crash scene and I jumped out and yanked on the door handle on the right side of the crashed aircraft. The door came off of its hinges and Raul fell out on the ground. He was unconscious and my first thought was to get him away from the aircraft before it caught on fire. I grabbed him by the feet and dragged him, on his back, about fifty feet from the crash. There was no fire but the air was heavy with the smell of gasoline.

What passed as a fire truck pulled up and two guys leapt from the vehicle and immediately grabbed a hose and advanced toward the wreckage. They were dressed in the most bizarre uniforms I had ever seen, but I knew they were firemen because it said so on about ten signs plastered all over the truck and their clothing.

Fire or no fire, they were determined to hose down the area, including me and my Jeep. They were not happy when I told them to knock it off, as I didn't want the scene to be turned into a sea of mud. Maybe there were some things that could be salvaged and I didn't to want wade through the water to do it.

Raul was beginning to come to and he was bleeding badly from a gash on the right side of his face. I took off my shirt and used it as a compress to stop the bleeding. I shouted to one of the firemen to alert the tower and have them call Dr. Alvarez's clinic and have them send their ambulance right away.

Just then, Big John ran up, breathing heavily after his dash from the hangar. He was carrying Little Jaime and the kid was scared and crying.

"What happened?" he asked. Before I could answer Raul blurted out, "I lost it. It got away from me before I could control it."

He tried to get up and I held him down.

"Stay still," I told him. "We don't know if anything is broken. We'll let the doctor figure that out."

"But I can't let anyone see me talking to a doctor. I am a pilot, I am strong," he said.

"You are also a guy who almost busted his butt and we don't want it to get any worse," I replied.

"I am sorry, Ingeniero. It just got away from me. I have never had anything like that happen to me. It pitched left and before I could control it, I was on the ground. I am so sorry about your airplane." There were tears in his eyes and he hung his head.

"That's OK, kid, it happens to all of us some time or another. It was pilot error. But the error was mine for not checking you out properly. It was my fault. It was a good learning experience for me, too."

I told John to go to the clinic with Raul to see that my backup pilot gets the care deserving of an outstanding aviator. "We need him in our operation."

"Thank you, jefe," Raul said. "I will pay you back some day."

I looked over what had been the "Bug." About the only thing remaining of value was the radio. The special propeller was bent beyond recognition and the internal parts of the zero-time, 150-horsepower, super deluxe engine were smashed into useless junk. I was looking at a total loss and it was back to square one, or less than square one.

The firemen helped me load the carcass of the "Bug" on top of their truck and we took it back to the hangar and dumped it in a corner. Then they gave me a hand as we pushed Raul's 180 into the late "Bug's" hangar and locked it up. It was a disappointing day for the firemen. They didn't have a chance to put out a fire or use their axes, and I was thankful for that. In fact, I had a lot to be thankful for. I didn't think that Raul was hurt too badly, except for his pride, and I had an opportunity to make possible some remarkable new experiences for some of my friends. It had been a busy and exciting day, and I was ready to have it pass into history.

Buying Super Cub

I drove back to my hotel, took off my boots, had Chico bring me a bunch of cold beers, propped my feet up, drank the beers, stared into space and thought deep thoughts about where do I go from here?

I was essentially broke, but I had a lot of things going for me. My "storefront business" was picking up and I had natives coming in from all over Zacatecas and neighboring states with tall tales of lost gold mines, some with samples that assayed out of sight, and it looked like I would have all the business I could handle. My love life was stalled, but I wasn't in any hurry to push that along, considering the conditions.

My most pressing need, if I intended to continue to pursue the remote country exploration, was an airplane just like the "Bug" but with none of its flaws. With it, I could spend less time hiking out of the boondocks and more time doing exploration work. The Texas rancher had that PA-18 Super Cub with the 150-horsepower engine installed at the factory, and that was exactly what I needed. But the rancher wanted four grand, up front, and that was way out of my price range. I had tried to jury rig a regular Cub with the powerful engine I needed and it didn't work. How can I get the four grand, up front? I could try to borrow it from a bank, but I didn't have any collateral and my job history was not too shiny. I had held a lot of good jobs, responsible jobs, but not for long. I was long on experience but short on staying in one place for any length of time.

All in all, I was a good guy, but banks and bankers don't loan money to someone just because they are a good guy. I didn't know any guys with ready collateral, except for Fr. Pat. He has collateral in the form of a disability pension for combat injuries during his time in the South Pacific in World War II. I think that he will have faith in me. We shall see.

Big John woke me at five thirty in the morning to tell me that Raul was all right except for the cut on his head and a lot of bruises, and he was very, very sorry. Big John said that he also was sorry, as he had been looking forward to many more trips up in the sky and, as Little Jamie says, the "Bug" is dead and can no longer fly with the birds. The big Indian really looked dejected but perked up when I told him I am working on a plan that will bring the "Bug's" big brother to work for us.

Fr. Lopez was up and ready for breakfast when John and I stopped by the church. I told him that I had to make some telephone calls to the States and I was afraid I was going to have some trouble making the connections. Could he help me?

"Sure I can," said the father. The manager of the telephone and telegraph office was a friend of his and he would be glad to go to the office with us and I could make my calls from there. That was a great idea, and he didn't know how important those calls would be to his getting to learn to fly an airplane. After breakfast we went to the telephone office and met the manager. If we were friends of Padre Ramon, we were his friends also.

My first call was to Clint Johnston, the rancher in Van Horn. Did he still have the Super Cub, and if he did, was it for sale?

The answers to both of those questions were, "Yes."

"How much?" I asked.

"Still four grand, up front."

I said, "Hold the Cub for me. I will see you at your ranch within two days."

"What happened to the J-3," he asked.

"It crashed," I said.

He didn't pursue the matter further and neither did I.

My next call was to Fr. Pat. Of course he would cosign a loan for me, He said that he thought I had potential, but it might be nice if I made him the beneficiary of my GI insurance, he joked.

"I'll call the bank right now and if the president ever wants to get to heaven while I am his confessor, he had better sign the papers. I am looking forward to seeing you. Drive or fly safely. By the way, what happened to your super airplane?"

"It crashed," I said. He didn't pursue the matter further and neither did I. I was on a roll.

I reached Raul at his home. "How's your head," I asked.

"It hurts," he said, "and I apologize again for what happened yesterday."

"Forget it. I have more important business to discuss with you. I am going to buy a Super Cub in Van Horn and I need transportation. Will you fly me there?"

"I sure will. When do we leave?"

"Tomorrow morning and bring an extra shirt, as we will probably be staying over night in Juarez or El Paso. I'll see you at 0800 mañana at your hangar."

A little after eight the next morning we were in the air heading for Juarez. The 180 had long legs, so we bypassed Torreon and Chihuahua and landed in Juarez a little better than three hours later. Raul had connections of his own at customs on both sides of the border, so there was no need to call on the services of Don Diego. We went through the inspections and paperwork and were in Deming by eleven o'clock. I asked Raul to fly over the badlands of New Mexico on the way to Deming and this time I had no fear of a crash landing out in the wilderness.

Fr. Pat met us at the airport and we stopped at the country club for lunch. Raul remarked, "I have never been in a country club in the States before. This is pretty classy."

I told him, "Get used to it. Change is blowing in the wind in America."

We got a couple of dirty looks but I thought nothing of it. Fr. Pat was wearing his Roman collar and I thought that these people might have been some of the locals who did not like priests, not that they didn't like Mexicans in their country club. The bank president was pleased to see Fr. Pat but was less pleased, I thought, at the prospect of lending $5,000 to an unemployed mining engineer living a thousand miles away in Mexico. I deposited the check in his bank, got a checkbook, and we were on our way back to the airport.

After we had the loan, I called Clint in Van Horn and told him we would see him in about an hour. Sure enough, an hour later we were circling his ranch. I asked Raul, "What do you think? Can you put her down in that pasture?"

"No sweat," he replied. "It's a little tight, but we can make it." I could feel the tension in the air. He knew, and I knew that he was going to show me he was a damn good pilot or die trying. He came in low and slow and touched the wheels down on the edge of the grass. It was a smooth landing and, out of the corner of my eye, I could see a wide smile on his face.

We taxied up to the barn and there was the Super Cub. Clint had washed and polished the airplane and it shown like a jewel. And it was a bright red. I hadn't even bothered to look at the color the last time I was here. It truly was the big brother of the "Bug." I ran up the engine and it checked out fine. I gave Clint the check for four grand, up front, and we shook hands. The deal was done and we were on our way back to Mexico.

Raul locked the brakes on the 180, ran up the engine to full power, released the brakes and the Cessna sped down the pasture and cleared the trees by fifty feet. I followed and was airborne in less than half the distance. We landed at El Paso International 15 minutes later and parked on the transient ramp. We still had plenty of time to get downtown and pick up the list of supplies I needed to make the Cub the airplane that I had always wanted.

We were back at the airport at seven the next morning. During the shopping trip, I bought ten "walk around" oxygen bottles and masks; these I would need when we were flying above 10,000 feet, I also bought two each 100- and 500-pound dummy bomb shells to be used as baggage pods, ten 28-foot parachute canopies, two 32-foot parachute canopies, five smaller cargo chutes and various straps and fittings that weren't available in Mexico. We checked into a good hotel, had an outstanding steak dinner and retired early.

I resisted the temptation to check out the clubs in Juarez. I was carrying what was left of the $5,000 loan and I wanted to make sure that I returned to Zacatecas with all of it and a first-class airplane. Now, let's see how long it takes me to pay for it.

We landed at Juarez International and I followed Raul through the Mexican customs. No money exchanged hands and that was a very good sign that Raul had established a firm business relationship with the officials. Raul's cruise speed on the 180 was 40 miles an hour faster than my Super Cub, so I took off an hour before him. I followed the highway to Chihuahua and things were going well so I proceeded to Torreon. I located the airport with no trouble and was gassing up when Raul landed.

"How did it handle?" he asked.

"Like a charm," I replied as I finished topping off the tank.

Zacatecas was only ninety minutes away so we took off together. About a half hour out, Raul decided that he would like to practice some formation flying. I didn't think that this was a good idea so I waved him off. I wasn't going to take any chances of putting any scratches on this airplane. We landed at the airport and Raul talked one of the guys who worked at the tower into driving us downtown. As we parted I said, "I'll see you tomorrow about eight o'clock and get you checked out."

"Count on me," he said. "And this time I'll do a good job."

15
Fidel

I had been back in Zacatecas for a couple of days when I got a call from Don Diego's lawyer in Mexico City. He said that I had to come his office as soon as possible to sign some important documents concerning my work papers. As usual, there had been the normal glitches and we were in danger of missing some deadlines.

I checked the weather and the forecast was for lousy weather and a call to the airport told me that I had missed the last flight until late tomorrow afternoon. No big deal, I could drive it and by leaving early in the morning I could be at the lawyer's office in plenty of time.

I asked Big John if he would like to go along and he jumped at the chance. He had never been to the big city and this was going to be an adventure for him. After I signed the papers, we did some sightseeing and were heading north to Zacatecas when we passed a motel that was owned by a guy I had met in Acapulco about a month ago.

I had decided to stop before we got too far outside the city, so this was as good a place as any. We did not bother to go out to eat, as Big John had squirreled away a pocketful of tortillas after lunch and I was not hungry. A good night's sleep later, we were up early and had a large breakfast.

While walking back to our Jeep, we were approached by a man—Hispanic, but definitely not Mexican. He walked with a swagger, and a pronounced limp—a rare combination. His clothes were flashy and the heels on his half-boots were two inches high.

Before he opened his mouth, my sixth sense said, "Heads up, this guy is going to hit you up for something."

After he said, "Buenos dias," in a very quavering, high-pitched voice he blurted out, "My boss would like to talk to you, right away." I looked the guy over and I had never seen him before. I told the guy we were heading back to Zacatecas and we didn't have any extra time to talk to anyone.

"But" he insisted, "You will like to talk to my boss. He is a very powerful man."

I said, "That's nice, but some other time," and I started to get into the Jeep. Out of the corner of my eye I caught the glint of gun metal and I was looking into the muzzle of a hand gun.

"You will come with me. It is very important!" His arm was shaking uncontrollably, and I was afraid that the gun might go off if I made a move to take it away from him.

Big John had been standing next to me and he stepped between us. The words of the gunman, "Get away or I will shoot you," were drowned out by the sound of Big John's right fist smashing into the side of his face. The gun flew out of his hand as he was thrown against a lamppost and he fell to the pavement.

John reached down, pulled him to his feet and slammed him against the Jeep. The blood streaming from his nose blended with the yellow color of his shirt. I bent over, picked up a rag we had been using to wipe the dirt from the windshield, and tossed it to him. He held the rag to his face and looked at us with defiance in his eyes.

"Who the hell are you, and what do you want?" I asked him.

"My name is Ernesto Sanchez, and I am a soldier in the revolutionary Army to free Cuba!"

Impatiently I demanded, "What's that got to do with us?"

"Please, señor parachutist, please listen to my story," he pleaded. "It is very important to our revolution and we are running out of time and money. I cannot fail in my mission," he sobbed, as his tears blended with the blood gushing from his nose and mouth.

Summoned by Fidel

"Three months ago, I saw you parachute jump at the fiesta of the daughter of Don Diego Ortega. Of course, I was not a guest there.

I am but a poor man. I drive a limousine at the airport and some rich people hired me to drive them to the house of Don Diego. There I see you parachute jump and I am very impressed, as I am training to be a soldier and we read books about the battles of World War II. I tell my boss with great praise about your parachute jump and he say, 'Go find this man. Bring him to me. I want to talk to him on a very important matter.'

"Of course I say, 'Si, señor,' as no one say no to our leader. But I do not know where to find you. I have a friend at the limousine company who is also a soldier with me, and he give me Don Diego's address in Chihuahua City. I go there and they tell me the parachutist has gone to El Norte, to a village called Deming in Nuevo Mexico. I tell my leader this and he say, bring him back and I say, 'Si, señor, as no one say no to our leader.

"I do not want to cross the border as my English is not good, but no one say no to our leader so I cross the border at El Paso and the immigration hombres pick me up and put me in jail. They say they will let me go back to Mexico if I promise not to come back. I promise, and they give me a ticket to Chihuahua City."

By now the guy is out of breath and exhausted from telling his story in broken English and Spanish, and the rag I had given to him was soaked with his blood. I searched in the back seat of the Jeep and found a towel that Ace had been using and handed that to him. He pressed it against his face and continued.

"I do not have a car, so I bummed a ride to Mexico City and when I went to the limousine company, they tell me I am fired. I see my friend and he tell me that he had just talked to the Ortega family and they say you are now in Zacatecas. I have no job but I am happy again because I may still be able to do my mission and find you. My friend, he lend me money and his car and I go to Zacatecas and I ask about you.

"A priest tell me that you are in Mexico City to see a lawyer and he do not know when you will return. He see that I very much in a hurry to see you and he give me the address of Señor Ortega's lawyer. I am going loco and I rush back to Mexico City. I have to find you as soon as possible as my friend tell me that our army is almost ready to go back to Cuba and I must complete my mission.

"I go there yesterday in the afternoon and ask for you but they say you have just left. I see you, and recognize you and follow you and see you stop at the motor hotel. I park out front and wait for you to come out, but you do not come out. I sleep in my car and wait until you leave this morning. I do not go into the eating place as I have no money so I wait for you outside."

He stopped again to catch his breath and gagged on the towel and threw up. He was really a pitiful human being and I felt sorry for him. I wondered just who was this guy's boss was and that he must be quite a leader to instill such loyalty in this common man.

When he got control of his emotions I asked him, "Who is your boss? Who is this great leader?

"My boss is Fidel Castro. He is the maximum leader of the revolution. He thinks that maybe your parachutes can help us. Will you please come with me? If I don't bring you he will be very mad. He gets mad very easy. Please?"

"Where is your boss," I asked.

"It is not far, it is to the south of here. We live in a ranch with other soldiers."

My interest was piqued. Revolution. That sounds exciting. I haven't heard that word since my history class in junior high, several years ago. I thought it over for a couple of minutes and then said, "We'll go with you."

There was really no big hurry to get back to Zacatecas. What's a couple of hours? We can make it up, if we have too.

"OK, Ernie, let's go see your boss."

Big John walked over and picked up the Cuban's gun from the gutter. He looked at me and I motioned to him to bring the revolver to me. I asked Ernesto, "Do you have a permit for this?"

"We don't need permit. We pay the cops."

I unloaded the gun, put the shells in my pocket and gave the gun back to Ernesto. He stuck the gun in his pocket and swaggered, kinda, and limped up the street to his car, a beat up Volks. He took our rag and the towel with him.

Ernesto pulled out into traffic and we began working our way through Mexico City in a southerly direction. After a while, we were in the outskirts of the city and then in open country. We pretty well kept on Ernesto's tail, but we didn't have to worry about him losing us. If it looked like we were falling behind, he would wait until we caught up. He wasn't going to show up at the ranch without the guy he was supposed to bring back. The "maximum leader" was not going to be mad at him.

At last, we took a dirt road that dead ended at a checkpoint with a guard carrying a submachine gun. This was a definite step-up from the Mexican gate guards with World War II M-1s. The guard greeted Ernesto like an old friend and as they chatted, I heard the guard say, "Fidel has gone in to town again. He is not here."

We passed the gate guard and followed Ernesto to one of the long, low barracks-like buildings. It seemed to be some sort of headquarters and there was another guard at its door, also armed with a submachine gun. We entered an office and sat down as Ernesto told us that we would have to wait a while because the "maximum leader" was not here. This I already knew, but it was good to know that Ernesto did not realize that I could understand some Spanish. His English was well above average and it was much easier to talk in English than for both of us to struggle in the other's language.

Ernesto said, "Make yourselves comfortable and I will find out when the boss will be back."

When Big John took his jacket off, Ernesto saw that he had a .38 pistol in his waist band and became very alarmed. He said we shouldn't have any weapons in camp and that only the leader's bodyguards carried them. But it was too late now, so it was best that we keep them well hidden or it might mean trouble, "and I don't need any trouble" he sighed. I handed him back his cartridges and he shoved them into his pocket.

I Could Have Changed History

About three o'clock the door opened and in rushed a big guy followed by four young men, all armed. Ernesto leapt to his feet and announced, "I have found him for you."

The big guy stopped in front of me, looked me over, stuck out his hand and said, "I'm Fidel Castro."

I shook his hand and said, "Nice to meet you." I motioned to Big John and said "This is my friend Juan Ochoa."

Castro nodded but did not make any attempt to shake Juan's hand.

"Bring your chairs to my desk and sit down," he said. We did as he requested and he sat down on the other side of the desk with the four young men standing behind him. He started to speak in rapid Spanish but when he saw that I was not responding he said in fair English, "Do you understand me?"

I replied, "Not very well, but if we speak in both Spanish and English, and slowly, I'm sure we can communicate."

He said, "Do you know who I am?"

"Ernesto has told us you are the 'maximum leader' of the Revolutionary Army to free Cuba," I answered.

He shook his head in agreement and asked, "What do you know about the country of Cuba?"

I told him I knew very little about Cuba except what I had studied in junior high school, but I was interested in learning more.

His face lit up and he launched into a short history of Cuba, heavy on the bad deeds of the present dictator, a guy named Batista, and what he was going to do to correct these problems. The Cuban people had suffered for many years under this cruel man and his government and he was going to change that.

As he relaxed, so did his four aides and they assumed a kind of "parade rest." I asked a few questions and then the big one, "What do you want from me?"

"You have skills that I and our revolution can use. I need you to train some of my men to parachute into Cuba when we return. Just like your D-Day in World War II. I fear that Batista will find out where we are going to land and if he is there to meet us, I want him to have a surprise.

"I will also have to have the parachutes and other equipment they will need and hire an airplane to carry them. I am told that with your work papers, you can do these things. I will need an answer fast, as the revolution is in a hurry."

I was beginning to feel that he knew a lot more about my background and what I was doing in Mexico than anyone would have picked up by watching an exhibition parachute jump. It would be natural to ask me to sell him equipment that only I could buy with my work papers, but to train his soldiers for a combat jump—that was a whole different area.

As I was mulling this over, the door opened and a well-dressed man entered. Castro motioned him to come to his side and the man quickly approached his desk. He excitedly whispered something in Castro's ear and the "maximum leader's" face clouded.

He got to his feet and said, "I have some important business to take care of. We will continue this conversation later." He hurried out the door and his four aides followed him.

"What was that all about?" I asked Ernesto. He shrugged his shoulders and said, "Who knows, more trouble with the police or the government, I suppose. The leader has to spend much of his time getting money to pay bribes to everyone from the local cops to the big guys in the government. About three months ago the leader and some of our soldiers were arrested and placed in jail and accused of working against Mexico and helping the Communists.

"They kept them in jail for a month until Señor Cardenas—he was once El Presidente—asked them to let the leader go if he would leave the country and go back to Cuba. Wait here. I will go see if I can find out what is happening. It bothers me when the leader looks worried."

I was beginning to see that nothing went on within the operation that Ernesto didn't know about or was not a part of. Big John had said nothing all afternoon, but I could sense that he was wondering when we will be going back to Zacatecas. In my mind I was going over Castro's offer—at least I thought it was an offer—and what I would have to do to put the deal together, starting with the recruits. How many did he want me to train and where would this training take place?

I assumed that these soldiers would be in reasonably good physical condition, but I would still have to run them through the usual Fort Benning stuff. Lots of running, pushups, hours of calisthenics and the usual BS to get them good and angry to put them in the mood for absorbing the elements and basics of learning to become an airborne soldier. Of course, they would not be airborne soldiers for very long, but they would have to know what they were doing while they were acting as if there were.

How about equipment? No big deal here. I would call ahead to one of the two surplus stores in El Paso that stocked this gear and have them assemble the number of parachute rigs, probably fewer than 20, and have them ready to be packed. I would pack each one, as the soldiers would not be wearing reserve parachutes and I would be personally responsible for everyone getting an open chute. A reserve parachute in the hands of a guy who had never even seen one before can be a very dangerous thing.

Of course, their main parachutes would be rigged to be jumped with a static line and it would be pretty hard to screw that up. Jump boots, helmets, uniforms, as well as weapons, would not be my worry. I would buy an extra ten 28-foot parachute canopies and 500 feet of webbing to make cargo chutes if they were required.

The big problem, and it would be a very big problem, would be a jump aircraft. My first order of business would be to contact the crew of the C-122 that I heard was flying in Yucatan and see if it was available. If we could not get them, we could try another rear-ramp aircraft that I understood was flying out of Mexico City. It is roughly the same configuration as the C-122 but it has three engines and a longer range. It is called the C-125 Raider, built by Northrop out of California. Whatever we can get, it will probably be pretty expensive when they find out what we want to use it for. Here is where the connections that Castro and his supporters have will need to be used to the maximum extent.

Another option would be one of the old World War II C-47s that are flying cargo down in South America. Some of these pilots are pretty gutsy guys and the adventure aspect might overshadow the profit motive. But we will have to wait until we continue our conversation and get more specifics.

Ernesto came back about an hour later and he had no news as to where the leader had gone. "He is a man of great secrets. Most of the time, he tells no one where he will be. He is afraid that Batista's men will pay a bigger bribe than he pays and they will try to kidnap or kill him."

Time dragged on and after a while I asked Ernesto, "How did you get mixed up in this operation?"

"It is very simple," he said as he stood up as if to address a group of new recruits. "I worked in a factory in Havana and one night a friend asked me to attend a meeting where a student from the University was going to talk about all the bad things that were happening to the students who were being beaten by the government soldiers for protesting about the increase in bus fares. The speaker, he is now our leader, Fidel Castro, spoke to us and he told us if we joined together and we grew strong and had more people, we could force the government to treat us better and listen to us.

"He was a very powerful speaker and I said I will follow this man. I became a leader in a cell and we were trained in military things by some professors in their classrooms after hours and we waited for orders. When Castro asked for volunteers to help capture a military barracks, and gain weapons to give to the people, I said I will go.

"It was the barracks in Santiago de Cuba called Moncada, and it was very important to the government. We attacked on the night of a carnival and we thought that the soldiers would be drunk and could not fight, but we were wrong. Our leader, Fidel Castro, fought bravely but we were defeated. Many were killed and many were captured. I was one of those captured. The soldiers were very angry and they beat us up and tortured every one. I had been wounded in the arm and I lay down my rifle and raised my hands, but they beat me anyway. One of the soldiers smashed his rifle into my leg and broke it and jumped on me. That is why I do not walk good.

"Fidel escaped from the fighting at the barracks, but was captured on his way into the mountains. The officers told the soldiers to shoot the prisoners, but the archbishop of the church had said on the radio that if Fidel was captured he should be tried in the courts and the judges should decide what the punishment should be. Some of the soldiers had heard that broadcast and they refused to kill Fidel and his men.

"At the trial our leader was allowed to speak, and he made fools out of the government. He is a great speaker and the people believe him when he talks. They are very mad at him and try to poison him while he is in prison but the captain who is supposed to kill him, he liked Fidel and did not do it.

"Poor captain, they put him before the firing squad and shoot him. The judge sentenced Fidel to prison and he, and some of his officers, they are sent to the new prison on the Isle of Pines. Me, I was not killed and they made me stay in jail in Havana for six months and then told me to get out of the country. Some of my companeros had gone to Mexico, so I joined them here."

He sat down as if to say that the lecture was over.

It was an interesting story, but I still didn't know how he got to be in Castro's revolutionary Army here in Mexico when Castro was in prison in Cuba. I asked him, "What happened after your leader was released from prison?"

"That too, is simple, señor," he said as he stood up again. "When Fidel was in prison he started a school to train other prisoners to continue the revolution. The guards tried to break his spirit by putting him in solitary confinement but he continued to lead us revolutionary soldiers, in Cuba and in Mexico, by messages he had smuggled out of jail. The government offered to let him go, but Fidel refused because they wanted him to say that he would not fight for the rights of the people any more.

"Last May, Batista, the dictator, said that all of us who had attacked the barracks at Moncada did not have to stay in jail any longer and Fidel and his companeros, who were in prison on the Isle of Pines, could go back home. Fidel saw that he could not raise an army in Cuba so he decided to come to Mexico, where he had more freedom. When me and my friends heard this, we found him and we will fight with him to free Cuba from that bastard, Batista. I hope you will join us," he said as he sat down.

Ernesto had given me a little better idea of what I might be getting into and I turned it over in my mind as we waited for our interview with the leader to continue. About six o'clock, three men entered the room, said hello to Ernesto and without introducing themselves, began questioning me in broken English and Spanish. They had to have been tipped off to my fluency in Spanish, so they kept it simple. The smallest of the three seemed to be in charge and I noted that his accent was different from the other two guys. He wheezed a lot and seemed to be having trouble breathing. All three of the guys had a hostile and rude manner and I was not impressed by the treatment I was getting, so I answered them in kind. I wasn't in any mood to be bullied around by a couple of second class aides.

They were peppering me with all kinds of questions about what I knew of military training and, every now and then, they would ask a question about how a people should act when they are living under an oppressive dictator. Most of it didn't make much sense, and about the only intelligent questions were asked by the older, stocky, rugged looking one with a short beard. He had a bad eye and he seemed to be having trouble focusing it. After a while, it was evident that conversation was going nowhere, so they simply walked out.

Again I asked Ernesto what this was all about. He said that the three guys were big shots on the leader's staff. One was a guy from South America, another was the leader's little brother, and the guy with the beard was a colonel, or a general—Ernesto didn't know which—who was in charge of the military training. He said they were mad because the leader was talking to me about training some of his soldiers and they didn't think I could be trusted as they didn't know anything about me. "I keep my mouth shut. I do not want to get into trouble," he said.

It was only much later that I learned the guy from South America was Che Guevara, the leader's little brother was Raul Castro, and the guy with the beard was the famous Cuban strategist, Col. Alberto Bayo. I was standing three feet from the trio and I had a .357 Magnum under my shirt. I could have changed history.

We waited a couple more hours and Ernesto finally said we should probably go to bed. He didn't think Fidel would be back tonight. Anyway, it was time for lights out. He took us to another building where there were two empty cots in a corner, and that's all. We slept in our clothes and our boots were our pillows.

At first light, men were milling around and getting ready to grab a cold breakfast and then form up in squads to go out in the field for military exercises. Ernesto told us to stay inside the barracks out of sight until the men moved out. They might wonder what a Yankee and an Indio were doing in camp. I watched the action through a window but I failed to see any of the three guys who had spoken to me last night.

There didn't seem to be more than 35 or 40 men. Some were wearing parts of military uniforms, but most were in civilian clothes. Most seemed to be in fair physical condition, but there were a few who looked as if they could not make it out of camp if they had to run.

When the men left, we used the latrine and washed up, using our shirts as towels. Ernesto left and returned in about ten minutes with some warm tortillas and a pot of really black coffee. The tortillas were OK—we hadn't had anything to eat since yesterday—but I passed on the coffee. Big John took a swig and made a face.

It must have been super bad for him not to like it. Ernest tossed in two apples and an orange, and that was it. I hoped the troops were getting better rations. If not, my recruits were not going to make very good airborne soldiers.

After breakfast, we went back to the headquarters barracks and waited for Fidel. After we arrived, the colonel, or the general, who had grilled me last night came in and without any introduction asked me about the training I was going to give the soldiers. I outlined the physical conditioning I would give them—he nodded his head in agreement with what I proposed—and then I described the basics of getting out of the airplane, handling the parachute in the air and landing—pretty simple stuff.

He was much more reasonable to talk with this morning, but I could see he would be a bastard to work with, let alone for, and would be a thorn in my side if I decided to join this outfit. He smiled and said he was much more comfortable after I told him what I planned to do. He grew angry when he said that Castro never told anybody, including him, the complete plans of any of his operations. Castro did not want his staff to know as much as he did, but it made it much harder to plan ahead.

Castro arrived at nine o'clock and he looked beat. It must have been lack of sleep, as Ernesto said he did not drink. This time, two aides came in first, then Castro, and then the other two.

He picked up the conversation exactly where he had left off yesterday. He wanted me to train some of his soldiers to be parachutists, to obtain parachutes and other necessary equipment, and to hire an airplane to drop them.

"I will need you to start training the men—there will be between 10 and 15 of my best. Training will start right away—as soon as possible. One of my staff will work with you. His name is Col. Aberto Bayo. Perhaps you know of him. He fought in the Spanish revolution, but he is a Cuban. You will train the men here at the ranch and be ready to move out at any time.

"We will be landing somewhere in Cuba—I will not tell you where until we are on our way. But we will have radio communications with all elements of our operation and every one will know what we are doing, as needed.

"How much money do you want, and when can you start?" he practically shouted.

His blunt speech and direct manner told me that he was in a hurry to get started. But I would need time to get my affairs in order, to assemble the parachutes and, most of all, to locate and secure a jump aircraft.

I faced two big problems in planning my part of the operation. The important things—like when we would launch the attack and where we would land—were things that we would probably not know until the last minute. We would just have to play it by ear. The operation was doable.

Col. Bayo could be training the men while I was on my way to El Paso to get the parachutes. Bayo looked like a quick study. I told him what had to be done and I was sure that he could whip these guys into shape by the time I got back. My work papers needed to be renewed, and that always took a couple of hours, but maybe I could do that in Mexico City on my way to the border.

The "where" was going to be the biggest problem. This would determine everything in the selection of the jump aircraft. The number one requirement would have to be whether it had the range to take off from somewhere in Mexico and drop paratroopers somewhere in Cuba and return to somewhere in Mexico, all over water, and without landing. If the somewhere miles were less than 2,000 miles and the weight of the load was less than 4,000 pounds, excluding fuel, my experience in crewing the C-47 in the Pacific said that we could make it without installing extra fuel tanks. Then we would have to take into consideration that the Cuban Air Force might scramble their fighters, the top of the line—their aircraft, not their pilots—courtesy of the United States government and our program of giving advanced military equipment to the Cuban government, and try to shoot us down.

Castro came from behind the desk and stood over me. Two of his aides followed and took places on either side of him. I stood up and Big John stood behind me. Castro was a big guy, and burly. I didn't look to see if he was wearing Cuban heels, but I had to look up to him. I would say he was well over six feet tall, two hundred plus pounds and his breath stank. He grabbed me by the shirt and pulled me close.

"You will be very important to this operation. Can I trust you?" he snarled.

"I haven't said I will work for you," I replied as I jerked loose of his grasp. He certainly had my attention now. We stared at one another until he turned and walked back to his desk.

I thought it over very carefully before I answered and said, slowly, "I am intrigued by the idea of being a part of your revolution. It presents a challenge that I have never had before. But there are many areas that are not clear to me. We need to talk some more and I need time to think through what may happen if I say yes."

"Your revolution is your life. It is the most important thing you will ever do. You have already sacrificed much for it and you still might very well die for it. But I feel nothing for it. Perhaps when I understand more about what you are fighting for, I will think it is worth the chance of dying for it. I am not driven by the opportunity to make a lot of money. I have more than enough money to satisfy my needs and I can make a lot more without risking my life."

"Let's talk some more," I continued. "Do you want me to parachute with them into Cuba and fight with them, or would I just train them and return to Mexico with the airplane, that is if we don't get shot down?"

"I want you to train them and jump with them if you want to fight for freedom," he said. I thought it over for a minute and told him, "If I train these men, I will command them and I will jump with them."

"Good, then you will be one of us. You will have a rank suitable to your command, and I am sure you will earn it."

He got to his feet and said in a voice tinged with irritation, "I have no more time to talk to you. My secretary will answer your questions, but I don't think you will learn anymore about time and place from him. We will start training as soon as you can get the equipment. All I can say is we have no time to waste. I have a meeting, I must go."

With that, he walked out and slammed the door, almost hitting his number one aide. The aide opened the door, and the others followed like ducks in a row.

All was quiet in the room. Ernest looked scared and said, "You have stood up to the leader and made him mad. That was not smart. I will go get his secretary."

About ten minutes later a small, serious looking, middle-aged man appeared. He was carrying a clipboard, a pad of paper and a pencil. He said, "I can tell you nothing further." He closed the door and walked out. I looked at Ernesto and said, "The planning is very difficult when you do not know when and where you are going, but tell the leader that I will start tracking down the aircraft we need and we will start training as soon as I buy the equipment."

We got to the Jeep, checked around and everything seemed to be all right—no bombs under the hood or obvious things out of place. We got in, drove up to the gate, drove past the guard with the sub-machine gun and were on our way back to Zacatecas. I had a lot to think about and I would take the easy stuff first.

Embassy—Mexico City

As we entered the outskirts of Mexico City, the first thing Big John and I looked for was a place to eat. We spotted a taqueria (taco joint) that looked fairly clean and chowed down. Driving up from the rebel's ranch, my mind was racing a mile a minute running through the things I had to do. I had made up my mind to join the revolution, but I did not want to get too excited before I had a chance to nail down a jump aircraft.

I thought that while we were in Mexico City it would be a good idea to run by the International Airport and talk to the people who had the Northrop Tri-Motor. Also, while we were there I could try to track down the owners of any itinerant C-47s that were looking for work. This would save a lot of time, as I was sure that any deal that was to be made had to be done on a face-to-face basis with no paper trail.

Another way to save time was to have my work papers renewed at the American Embassy. They would have a bigger staff and could give me faster service than I could get in Juarez. Ever since I have been in Mexico I have always been professional in my actions and my dress. Although I was not here in an official capacity, I represented the United States as an American citizen. I would be dealing with fellow Americans and Mexican officials when I visited the Embassy and the airport today so I should be properly dressed and looking sharp. Right now, I looked like hell.

The night spent on a cot in the barracks messed up my clothes and I needed a shower and a shave. So we checked into a small hotel near Chapultepec Park and after a shower and shave I was ready to take care of business.

Big John was fascinated with the tempo of the city and I knew he was anxious to look around. I told him not to get too far from the hotel, as I did not know when I would be back. I also told him to leave his pistol in the room, hidden, as I didn't want any problems with the police concerning gun permits. I had a fresh pair of starched khakis in my bag so I had the maid press them and shine my boots and I was ready to step out on the street and hail a cab. After only a short stint of driving in the crazy Mexico City traffic, I was sure that I would get a ticket and wind up having to pay a bribe to get my Jeep back.

I arrived at the American Embassy about a half hour before the afternoon break. The place was packed but it looked like business was being handled quickly and with some sense of urgency. I was glad to see that our government had not succumbed to the Latino slower pace of life and indifference when dealing with its citizens. A pleasant young American girl took my passport and disappeared to check my records. She returned immediately with a scowl on her face and asked me to please sit down over there and wait for Col. Bitner to come and talk with me.

About five minutes later, a short, overweight man in rumpled civilian clothes entered from a door behind the counter. If this was Col. Bitner, the United States had made a big mistake in letting anyone who looked like this guy represent our country and if he was our representative, thank God he wasn't wearing a military uniform.

He had my passport in his hand and barked , "You Hall?"

I said, "My name is James Hall."

"Come with me," he said as he waved me past a line of people. We entered a plush office with "grip and grin" pictures covering the walls of this toad with various civilians in business suits; nothing to indicate he was military.

"Sit down," he demanded as he slid his large body behind a huge desk and tossed me my passport.

We were off to a very bad start, and I sensed that this exchange was not going to have a happy ending. He put his fingers together, elbows on the desk, and peered at me over his horn-rimmed glasses.

"It is really a small world, isn't it?" he said to no one in partic-ular. "A report concerning you just crossed my desk this morning. It seems, Lt. Hall, that you have been keeping company with some very bad characters. What do you have to say for yourself?"

"I don't know what you are talking about. Please enlighten me," I replied with as much dislike in my voice as I could muster.

"You have been seen at the camp of the Cuban revolution-ary, Fidel Castro, and met with him and his staff several times yesterday."

I said nothing, but looked at him as I would a slimy worm.

"You must be dumber than you look to not know his camp is watched day and night and that there are more spies inside that fence than there are members of his so-called army. His invasion of Cuba is the worst-kept secret in all military history. We think he has Communist leanings and the only reason that he has not been thrown out of Mexico is because of the large bribes he is paying."

He leapt to his feet, only the top half of his pudgy body rising above the desk, and screamed, "Do you want to lose your citi-zenship? If you do, then keep associating with these misfits and revolutionaries. Gen. Batista is a friend of the United States. If he mistreats his people, that is his business and we support him. We are starting a file on you, and if we find out you are working with these rebels, we will ask the Mexican government to yank your work papers. What do you have to say?"

I got to my feet, picked up my passport, looked him in the eye and said, "Blank you, you little bastard. It makes me puke to think that you are in our military system. I turned on my heel and walked out of the office and out of the building. If that son of a bitch was the best the United States had to represent our military in Mexico, God help us. One of these days I hope I would have the good fortune to run into Col. Bitner—then, maybe I will kill him and clean up a small part of our system that is out of balance.

So suddenly it is a whole new ball game. Did I want to lose my American citizenship? Hell no, I didn't. That's the most important thing I've got. I've put my body on the line to keep it—although I did not know it or think about it at the time. I am proud to be an American and a military man in spite of the occasional jerk you find in the system like Bitner.

What to do next? Well for starters I would step out into the swirling traffic on the Paso de la Reforma, hail a cab and get back to the only solid ground I had in this hostile Mexico City—Big John and my Jeep. I raised my arm as a signal and a jazzed-up '50 Chevy cut across three lanes of traffic and almost ran over the curb in front of me. I jumped in, sat back and let the cab driver take my life in his hands as he darted in and out of the confusion of rush hour traffic.

I felt a letdown, a sense of failure. I did tell Castro that if I trained his men I would command them and would jump with them and make sure they had the best equipment available. I told him I would get back to him after I saw if I could get a jump air-craft. The more I thought of it, the more I wanted to do it. I was beginning to feel that I was going to become a part of a cause, a vague abstract feeling that I was going to do something that only I could do, and make a difference to a lot of people.

I had never really given the term "revolution" much thought. A bunch of farmers dressed like Indians tossing boxes of tea in a harbor and then kicking the butts of some sissies in red uniforms who had been trying to boss the farmers around. I had always been on the side of the underdog—I think that I got this from Brother Honus—and from what I had heard from Ernesto and Castro, their guys were the underdogs.

I wrote a note to Ernesto and wished him well in his upcoming operation, but I was sorry to have to tell him that I would not be able to go with him. I have been told by the American Embassy that if I have anything more to do with the Cubans, I would lose my American citizenship. Tell the maximum leader that he is being watched closely and he is correct—his enemies will probably know when and where he will arrive in Cuba, and will be waiting for him. Be prepared and good luck.

It was dusk when we retraced our trip to the camp and we were super-cautious and aware of our surroundings. I had my weapon hidden under a jacket between Big John and me and he was sitting on his revolver. I didn't expect any trouble, but I was ready if the unexpected happened. We slowly pulled up to the sentry box and the same guard who was on duty this morning was still there, with the same submachine gun, and he approached the Jeep from my side. We exchanged greetings, friendly, I was happy to see, and I handed him the letter and asked him to give it to Ernesto whenever his had the chance. No big hurry, but important that Ernesto get it. He saluted and returned to his post and we slowly drove away into the night—until we got about a quarter of a mile away, and then, it was the accelerator to the floor. We were streaking, as fast as a Jeep can streak, toward Zacatecas.

16
The Challenge

The officers who were putting together the contest between me and the Mexican honor guard had kept it a very deep secret, even to the extent of not telling the ten elite paratroopers who were going to make the jump exactly what was going to happen until they would arrive at the airstrip. The annual convention of the highranking officers was being held in the resort city of Acapulco and the paratroopers were to receive a weekend pass for taking part in this special military exercise.

They were being bussed down from their base in Mexico City to an airstrip located about ten miles northwest of Acapulco. The strip was used to practice landings and takeoffs for military aircraft during the week, but was deserted on weekends. The rules for the contest had been worked out and agreed to by a committee of five staff officers, none of them with Airborne experience.

When the paratroopers arrived, they were a happy group of soldiers as they milled around the trucks that had brought them and their equipment from the capitol and the transport airplane that would drop them.

It was the aircraft that was on the top of my list when I had considered making the parachute jump into Cuba. It was an old civilian aircraft, a C-122 that had been put into service at the close of World War II and was currently used to haul timber out of the jungles of southern Mexico and Guatemala. The aircraft was essentially a World War II troop glider with two engines hung on it and it was supposed to carry much heavier loads than the standard gliders that carried combat troops. When the war ended the new Air Force was stuck with it in the inventory and it had no mission. So all these old crates ended up in the boneyard in Arizona to be sold to small nations around the world.

What was unique about this C-122 was that it had a rear loading ramp and was ideal for dropping both cargo and paratroopers. It was based in the city of Merida, the capitol of the state of Yucatan, and was also used to supply archaeological expeditions. It sure was a weird-looking bird and after a close inspection, I could see that it was not made for long-distance flying. Now that I had seen the aircraft and knew where I could find it, I would make a special effort to get to know the crew, as I had earlier been approached by a company that wanted to know if I could drop cargo to teams of archaeologists who worked deep in the jungle. For short trips, this was exactly the aircraft I would need if we could make a deal.

The pilot was a guy named Steve Powell. He was a likable North Carolina native who had flown P-47 Thunderbolt fighters with the 4th Fighter Group in the European Theater. During his combat tour he had shot down four German Messerschmitt-109 fighters and had three probable kills of FW-190's. We hit it off well because of our Air Force backgrounds, and he said that he would be glad to work with me.

The copilot was British and had flown with the Royal Air Force during World War II. The flight engineer, who also doubled as the loadmaster, was from Pennsylvania and had been one of the enlisted men chosen to accompany Lt. Col. Jimmie Doolittle on the aircraft carrier USS Hornet when they made the famous air raid on Japan in April 1942. He did not fly that mission but later served a combat tour as an engineer/gunner on B-25s in the Mediterranean Theater. A good group of my kind of combat warriors, and I looked forward to the chance of working with them in the future.

This model of the C-122 was called the Avitruc. It had been working in Mexico since last year, and had seen a lot of hard service. The crew had never dropped paratroopers before, so I gave them a brief orientation and helped the flight engineer rig a short cable where the static lines of the paratroopers could be hooked.

C-122

We then put duct tape over any sharp edges that might snag on equipment or uniforms.

I met with the jumpmaster of the parachute unit, plus three of the general officers who had served on the rules committee, and we reviewed what they had written. They weren't exactly what I would have liked, but I agreed without dissent, as did the jumpmaster, a lieutenant, who was not about to disagree with the higher ups. The ten paratroopers would jump with static lines and I would freefall.

The target was a piece of white canvas, eight feet by eight feet, placed in the dirt on the side of the runway about half way down the strip. The jump altitude was to be 3,000 feet above sea level and I imagined that the infantry officers thought this would give the paratroopers more time to maneuver and a better shot to hit the target. Bad thinking, but they were making the rules. The signal to exit the aircraft was to be a joint decision by one of the committee members and the loadmaster.

The sequence of jumpers was to be five paratroopers on static lines, closely followed by me, then five more paratroopers. Whoever touched down closest to the target was the winner. There was good will all around and we shook hands and the jumpmaster went back to his group and I walked to the Jeep.

The paratroopers were in high spirits. This was going to be a picnic for them. They would be landing at sea level, a far cry from smashing into the ground at more that a mile high at their drop zone in Mexico City, and they would not be burdened down with ninety pounds of equipment, a rifle, or submachine gun and a steel helmet. They had never jumped from 3,000 feet before, but the longer time under the open canopy would give them plenty of time to check out their new equipment, the best in the world as it was made in the United States of America. We would take off in 15 minutes and after Big John helped me suit up, I spent the remaining time chatting with the flight crew.

They said that their boss back in Merida had been contracted to do this job by a member of the committee who was with the customs department, as they would be in Acapulco delivering a load of hardwood. The committee wanted to use a civilian aircraft, as they didn't want to take the chance that this operation would end up on the records of the military. The C-122 crew was curious; they asked why all the excitement? The Army guys were saying they were going to show the generals how real men could use a parachute.

"Do you think you can beat ten to one odds?," Steve the pilot, asked.

"I can if it is a fair fight," I replied, "but there is a lot of money and prestige wagered on this jump, and who knows what can happen?" To emphasize my remarks, we looked over to where the Army paratroopers were gathered and saw that they were now a somber group. A general officer had just finished talking to them and there was no more slapping one another on the shoulders or joking around. They were a serious bunch as we walked out to board the C-122.

"Good luck, jefe," Big John said.

"I'll see you at the target," I said.

There was a pulldown canvas bench along the left side of the aircraft and it would seat all 11 jumpers. The loadmaster and the general who would help him spot the exit point sat in small seats behind the pilot and copilot. The jumpmasters—there were two of them—would have to stand and hang on as best they could. If, at some other time, there had been seat belts, they were gone, probably stolen by the Indian passengers who thought they needed them more than the aircraft did.

We took off into the wind and climbed to altitude over the ocean. I noted that the wind had picked up and was blowing off the ocean directly down the runway. That would be good to know after I got an open chute and I plugged that information in to the equation I was putting together in my brain.

We turned and started our jump run about five miles off the coast. The two spotters moved up into the cockpit and took positions on either side of the pilots. That was a lousy place to gauge an exit point from, but a bad spot could cut both ways. If they had any smarts or experience they would make the jump run straight down the middle of the runway. I had mentioned this in the casual conversation I had with the crew before the flight. I was hoping, real hard, that the flight engineer was listening.

The chief jumpmaster had his two sticks, or groups, of paratroopers stand up and hook their static lines to the overhead cable. I stood between them and braced myself against the side of the airplane to keep from falling. The tension was beginning to build up in the cargo department and the first group of five jumpers did the "airborne shuffle" and inched toward the open door. The flight engineer stuck his head out of the cockpit and yelled "GO!"

The lead jumpmaster slapped the first jumper in the stick on the back of his parachute cover and screamed into the prop blast, "GO!" and something else that was lost in the air rushing by. After the last man in that stick exited the aircraft, I started to run toward the open door. I took one running step forward and the assistant jumpmaster stuck out his foot and tripped me. As I scrambled to my feet the jumpmaster reached over as if to help me, and instead yanked the ripcord on my reserve parachute.

This is the absolute worst thing that can happen to an airplane load of paratroopers. The chute can foul the controls, the airplane goes into a spin and nobody gets out. I had a pilot chute on my reserve parachute so it would open instantaneously, and it worked just as advertised. I was slammed face down on the steel deck of the aircraft and in a second was in the air, hanging upside down with my right leg caught in the suspension lines of the canopy.

Fortunately I was not knocked unconscious, but my world was black for a couple of minutes before I regained my senses. Whenever I am making a parachute jump, I always carry my super-sharp "KA-BAR" knife strapped to my right jump boot and instinctively reached for it. I had to cut something loose to get free from the tangled reserve parachute or I would be a dead man in a couple of minutes.

Thankfully, reason took over from sheer panic, and I said to myself, "Slow down, Bozo, think before you do something stupid, but think quickly, that ground is coming up fast."

I was spinning to the right and that wasn't helping my equilibrium or thinking any. I reached up, grabbed the right riser and cut through it. The canopy collapsed and I was now falling with the parachute canopy streaming behind me. I pulled the other riser to me and sawed through it. The canopy snapped loose and I was in freefall with my back to the ground. I didn't have any idea of how high I was; all I knew was I had to get an open chute just as soon as possible. I assumed the airborne position, feet together tightly, and yanked the ripcord of my main parachute. As it opened, it wrapped around my body, but nothing hung up and after the opening shock, I was swinging free under a beautiful red and white canopy.

As my head cleared, I turned toward the ocean. Then, when I saw how far upwind of the target I was, I made a 180 degree turn and ran with the wind. As my heart slowed down and I could think a little clearer, I realized I still had my knife in my right hand. That was pretty stupid, but this time I got away with it. I reached down and jammed the knife into the sheath tied to my boot.

My basic military parachute canopy had been changed into a modification called a seven-panel TU, a radical design I had learned about in the Embassy reports and the fastest modification you could make on a parachute canopy without causing it to fold on itself and collapse under certain conditions. I estimated my altitude at about 2,000 feet and my distance from the target at about a quarter of a mile. I pulled down on the front risers and I began losing altitude fast, but I was also moving forward fast. The spot when we left the airplane was bad, so I was tacking into the wind, which had increased to about 12 knots since we took off.

Again, the old parachuting adage—anything that can go wrong, will—held true in the case of the wind. The Army people predicted that it would hold at three knots, but they were wrong. Add the current wind velocity to the forward speed of my parachute canopy and I was whistling along at more than 20 miles per hour. I crossed the runway at about a hundred feet going at full speed toward the target. I could have turned into the wind and cut down on my landing speed, but I did not want to take a chance of landing short of the target. I knew I was going to hit like a ton of bricks, but I reasoned that a broken leg or two was a lot better than a bullet in the back of the head if we lost.

I put my feet together tightly and prepared for a crash landing. I was going to try to make a standard PLF (parachute landing fall) but I was only able to make the first part. I landed on my feet, but everything after that went to hell. The next point of contact was the back of my head and then, again, the back of my head. My feet had touched down on the edge of the canvas target and after bouncing a couple of times, I was now being dragged at a rapid rate through the dirt.

The only thing that stopped me from being pretty badly scratched up was Big John running into the parachute canopy and collapsing it. I lay still for a couple of minutes, and then checked for broken bones. Amazingly, no bones protruded through my clothing, but the left side of my face was a mess from the contact with the steel floor of the C-122.

I looked up and saw that the paratroopers and their canopies were still at about a thousand feet and to the right of the target and heading down wind. There wasn't a chance in hell that any one of them was going to land within a quarter of a mile of the target.

I was the clear winner and it would take a colossal piece of skullduggery to overturn that verdict. Gen. Garcia's Jeep skidded to a stop just as I was gathering up my chute. He jumped from the Jeep and embraced me.

"We did it," he yelled. "We did it, and boy will I rub it in tonight. And, my pocketbook is fat again." Of the group who had assembled around the target, the general and Big John were the only ones who came near me. I could predict that there would be hell to pay when this mess was all sorted out. The paratroopers were still landing and they all were being dragged by the wind that was increasing in velocity. There was going to be some injuries from this and there was going to have to be some high-level maneuvering to cover it up.

The general said that I had better have a doctor look at my face and have the cuts cleaned up. Also, it would probably be a good idea if we would get on the road back to Zacatecas and not be here when the crap hit the fan. Not only did some people lose a lot of money, a lot of people lost face. There was plenty of blame to be passed around, and as the general said, it would be best if we were not here to share it.

My face was beginning to sting and I was still bleeding. Also, I could use a couple of aspirins and maybe a cold beer. I thought that I'd earned it. As the general said, "We did it!" We will leave and meet again with the general back in the now more friendly environs of Zacatecas.

I really wanted to confront the two jumpmasters, but I knew that it would be a losing proposition. Their butts were on the line and they were going to do what they thought was necessary to protect themselves. The quick fix was getting rid of me and they took what they thought was their only means available to make sure they did not lose. If some wise-ass gringo got hurt, or even killed, that was all part of surviving in their dog-eat-dog world. But this was one dog who was a little better skilled in the art of parachuting than the dishonest tactics they used to try and stop him.

Later, when I was in a much better position, I would extract my vengeance. For now, it is probably best that Big John and I be on our way. The general had sent a Jeep to bring back my reserve parachute and some Army personnel drove up and tossed it on the ground. We picked it up and we were headed north to Mexico City.

17
Dave

When I got back to Zacetecas, there was a telegram waiting for me. My college roommate, Dave Burt, was going to be in Mexico City. He was the best and closest friend I'd had at the university, and he was probably the best exhibition parachutist in the business. He was going to make a series of parachute jumps for Coca-Cola. That got my attention for several reasons—the chief one was that I had the only parachuting license in Mexico.

Dave was the guy who got me started in parachuting in the hot wasteland of northern Mexico in the late spring of 1949. We were both veterans of World War II and attending college under the GI Bill in Albuquerque. When we applied for low-cost housing our names were placed in a lottery and the luck of the draw made us roommates in a student housing project at Kirkland Air Base.

We didn't have much in common except we were both enrolled in the engineering and geology departments at the "U." In fact we had lots of qualities that were in opposition to one another. He was from Utah, a Mormon, didn't drink, didn't think that women were absolutely essential to have around, was dead serious about studying and getting good grades and was a Democrat. I was a Catholic from Pennsylvania, loved beer, thought women were absolutely essential to have around, a "hands on guy," not a bookworm, and a staunch Republican. We got along just great.

Dave was a veteran of the 82nd Airborne Division, a master parachute rigger and, during the summers, a Forest Service smoke jumper. He had acquired two complete parachuting rigs somewhere along the way and the only thing more important to him than studying on the weekends was making exhibition parachute jumps for money. I was in the Air Force during the war and the last thing I wanted to do was make a parachute jump. It was far too dangerous. My weekend activity, if I couldn't get a date or ran out of money, was to drive into the mountains of New Mexico in an old beat-up Jeep and go rock hunting. Not too exciting for the average university student, but interesting for someone absorbed in geology.

First Jumps

On spring break of our freshman year, Dave had been doing some outside reading and came across an article about a newly-discovered mining area in northern Mexico where you could pan for gold and have a fair chance of finding some. The drawback was that you had to spend several days backpacking into the area, and we did not have that time.

"Let's jump in," Dave said. "It will be a snap."

Finally, our interests had collided. I still was not convinced that I wanted to make a parachute jump to do this, but after a few practice landings jumping from a picnic table, I said, "Let's do it."

Dave had a '40 Mercury convertible, a much better vehicle for over-the-road travel than my old Jeep, so we used it to drive to the little border town of Douglas, Arizona. When we got there, we asked around to see if we could find a pilot who would fly us across the Mexican border and drop us.

An old farmer who owned a Cessna 140, a real dog of an airplane to parachute from, said he would do it for a price. We had the price, so Dave and the farmer took off to the south into the Sonora desert of Mexico in search of a place we had only seen on a map. The farmer and his airplane returned in about an hour and then it was my turn to make my first parachute jump.

I asked the pilot, "At what altitude did Dave make his jump?"

He said, "About 1,500 feet," so I put on my main parachute, hopped into the 140 and said, "Let's go."

He looked at me kind of strange-like and asked, "Ain't you going to take that other parachute?" It was really crowded inside that little airplane, so I said, "Forget it. I won't need it and it is just something more to carry."

That was a dumb mistake that nearly cost me my life, and safety-conscious Dave almost had a heart attack when he found out about it. The old farmer was navigating solely by the ancient compass on his dashboard so we took off and headed into the desert following the little needle. About a hundred miles later, we spotted the smoke from a fire that Dave had built.

This was the moment of truth! I struggled to get out of the small airplane, put my foot on the wheel, and then grabbed the wing strut. I was finally ready to go, but it was obviously taking me longer to accomplish these basic steps than it should have and the pilot was frantically yelling, "Jump, jump!" It seems that my body was causing a lot of drag and we were losing altitude, fast. I imagine that we were down to about 800 feet when I fell free from the airplane. I pulled the ripcord immediately—and dropped it—but that was the last thing on my mind at the time. I was upside down when the parachute opened and it wrapped around one of my legs. Damn, that stretching hurt.

I was now falling head first and, although I had never made a parachute jump before, I knew that this wasn't the way things should be happening. If I had a reserve parachute, this was the time that I should be deploying it. But I didn't have a reserve parachute. It was sitting back in Douglas by the side of the airstrip. As I flailed around, my leg broke free and I was snapped to an upright position. Bang! I hit the desert floor, hard.

That was some experience, but I didn't think I'd like to try it again. I missed the spot where I was supposed to land by about a half a mile and Dave was out of breath when he ran up to me.

"What happened?" he blurted out.

I thought that was a dumb question, and I slowly shook my head. He looked over the scene. "Where is your reserve?" Another brilliant question to someone who evidently hadn't done a very good job at what he was supposed to accomplish. He turned his back, stamped his foot and almost swore.

I never saw Dave lose his cool before or after, but that time he was pretty close to it. I dusted myself off, picked up the parachute and we slowly trudged back to where he had built the fire.

We spent the rest of that day, and all of the next, prospecting, but no gold could be found. We packed out to the nearest road and luckily flagged down an ore truck that was heading north to the border. We made it back to school in time for our first Monday class, but I don't think we learned as much from the lecture as we did in the desert of northern Mexico.

I was, of course, excited at the prospect of seeing Dave, so Big John and I jumped into my jeep and headed to Mexico City. As we drove around, I was in deep thought. My reverie was broken by Big John's shouting, "Look, Jefe, one car jumped on top of his friend." It was John's first glimpse of a double-decker bus.

Dave in Mexico

Dave was waiting for us when we arrived at a rather expensive hotel in the east part of Mexico City. I hadn't seen him for about three years but he looked fit and in good physical condition. He had spent the last five summers at smoke jumper headquarters in Missoula, Montana, as a jumper and rigger. During the fall and the winters he crewed on a fishing boat in the Bering Sea between Alaska and Russia, a very dangerous but high-paying job, which exactly fitted his temperament. He was willing to work in the dangerous occupations, but he expected to be paid accordingly.

We checked in and I remarked, "You're living pretty high on the hog, ain't you buddy?"

He said, "Enjoy it. I've signed a sweet deal with the Coca-Cola Company and this is part of the package for the jumps I will be making."

I asked him how he got permission to jump in Mexico, since I had the only license to make a legal parachute jump in this country—not that I would do anything to try to stop him. He said the Coca-Cola Company has lots of connections here in Mexico and they can pretty much do anything they want to do. A little money here, a little money there, and things get done.

I nodded my head, "Yeah, I know what you mean."

He continued, "Hey, if you want to jump with me tomorrow, I'll split the pot with you. No, wait, I don't want to spoil you in the ways of the business world. Make that sixty-forty," he offered.

"It's a deal. I'll take it. I was going to do it for nothing."

He laughed and said, "You'll never learn. You're probably still jumping for the military for free, and giving the Air Force all the hard-earned improvements we have stumbled upon, or figured out, while busting our asses to make a buck in the civilian world."

I had to admit I was giving the armed services thousands of dollars worth of parachuting experience in lectures and demonstrations that they were not getting from their test jumpers because of unrealistic and just plain stupid rules and regulations.

The Air Force had outstanding test parachutists like Chief Warrant Officers Ed Murray and Mitch Kolowiski and Capt. Joe Kittinger of the test units at El Centro, California and the Systems Command, who were capable of coming up with some of the ideas that we civilian professional parachutists had to work out, but they were never given the freedom to act on their own.

Things like the "buddy system" of freefall parachute training or the four-line cut parachute canopy modification could not be officially taught at Air Force survival schools because the Air Force did not invent them. This cost our flying services untold millions of dollars in injuries and several deaths because the aircrews were denied this training.

"Hey, let me show you some new gear and some of the gimmicks that are on the market since last we jumped together," Dave said. "I had a chance to talk with a couple of new guys who are getting into the parachuting business, not in competition to us in the jumping end, but in sales and in instructing students, like a jump school, but for civilians. They have a lot of good ideas and seem like good businessmen.

"One is a French guy, but a good guy as he served in the Marines in Korea. His name is Jacques Istel. The other is a guy I met with the Seattle Sky Divers, Lew Sanborn.

"They have developed a new device called the deployment sleeve that slides over the parachute canopy, and prevents it from opening until the jumper is in an upright position. It really cuts down on the opening shock," Dave said.

"That should really be something that would help you," he added, in what was meant to be a jab at me. "I still cringe when I remember some of those rugged parachute openings you used to have, particularly the one at the air show in Albuquerque. We thought you broke your neck," Dave added.

Dave Burt and Jim Hall

"I have learned a lot since then, and I intend to show you tomorrow," I said, as I gave him the Italian hand sign for "up yours."

"By the way," he said, changing what he knew was a sore subject, "I met a guy in Alaska last fall that would be an outstanding addition to the company we used to talk about starting when we were at the University of New Mexico. His name is Bob Sinclair and he is by far the best of the jumpers in Alaska, but he scares the hell out of me with some of the stuff he pulls off.

"But he is no dummy. He is a master parachute rigger and a wizard on a sewing machine. He made me a breakaway rig that I will try out when I get back to the States. Stuff like that and a bunch of new, far out ideas. He is also working on a camera that he can use to photograph other jumpers in free fall. Keep this guy in mind when you decide to come back to the States.

"But I wanted to show you some new gear," he said as he pulled a couple of parachute bags from out of a closet. The bags contained six brand new 28-foot flat circular parachute canopies, each with a different modification, from the blank gore to canopies with many panels removed; from the basic design to Derry slots and tails. (I did not tell him that I had not only seen these modifications, I had jumped them.) The one he would jump on any particular day would depend on how much wind was blowing. There were other parachute canopies being developed but he said he would stick to these old tried and true ones that he could depend on.

Then he got serious, which was his nature. Dave was a perfectionist. He would plan everything down to the second. From the takeoff time, to the time over the target, time in freefall, time under the open canopy, where he was going to land and how much time it took to present whatever our sponsor wanted us to present. In the case of tomorrow's jump, it was a trophy to the winner of a very important soccer game. The trophy was provided by the Chamber of Commerce and the jump was paid for by the Coca-Cola Corp.

Pretty simple stuff for us Americans in the mid-fifties, but a big deal for many people who had never seen a parachute jump, especially up close. And the public would have a chance to touch the daring aeronaut, and maybe even get some trinket he would give away! And to have two of the "Sky Kings" jumping on the same day. This was going to be something.

Dave was a good-looking guy, at least above average, and he played the part of "Sky King" to the hilt. He wore a pure white, tailor-made jump suit with a bright red Coca-Cola logo emblazoned on the back and another over the left breast pocket. His main parachute canopy was also pure white, with six-foot red script letters spelling out Coca-Cola sewn inside the open canopy. He could not get away with this modification of his parachute canopy in the states. The Federal Aviation Agency would gasp, clutch their breast and ground him immediately. Why, this might make the canopy malfunction and it would not open properly and the parachutist might fall to his death. Well, this might be what the people came to see and it is also why the parachutist wore a reserve parachute and he had better be trained to use it correctly.

But in Mexico, as Dave had learned fast, you could do almost anything you wanted to do if you had the money and knew where to put it, so he had a local seamstress sew the letters inside the parachute canopy, and the show went on. Dave was going to be the main event and the Coca-Cola people really built him up. He was the "World's Greatest Parachutist;" he had made parachute jumps all over the world, Alaska, Canada, the United States, Mexico, Panama and Korea. It didn't matter that those last two places were troop jumps on maneuvers while he was in the Airborne, they were still in the world. Coke's public relations people were the tops in their profession and I didn't recognize Dave after sitting through the interviews and hearing about all the daring deeds he had done. Big John enjoyed these sessions immensely and drank the free Coke until it was running out his ears. Some of the pretty girls thought he was cute, and he didn't quite know what to do about that.

The next day dawned bright and clear and the weather forecast called for calm all day. Even though there was to be no wind, Dave chose to jump the hottest parachute canopy he had in his inventory. He didn't want to take any chances of missing his target. I chose the old reliable Derry, 1941 vintage, slots and tails. This was the chute we used in the Forest Service smoke jumpers and it always worked. You landed much softer and I felt sure that Dave's expert spotting would put me close enough to find the target with the four mile per hour forward speed of the Derry chute. Anyway, if I missed the target, I could say that I was supposed to land short, as Dave was the main event.

Dave was carrying a small gold trophy that was to be presented to the team's owner. Two very beautiful, scantily clad señoritas would be carrying the big trophy that was to be presented to the team and if Dave missed the target, not many people would notice. However, just in case Dave missed and I hit, I also carried a small gold trophy and we would say that I was supposed to make the presentation. That was show biz.

The Coca Cola distributor had rented a Cessna 180 from a local flying service who had a contract to fly its executives all over the country. Dave had instructed the secretary who had made the arrangements to make sure the pilot was told to remove the right side door and to cover with tape any object that could possibly snag a jump suit or parachute. She assured Dave that the pilot was an old experienced pilot, would be easy to work with, and spoke perfect English. We arrived at the airport fifteen minutes before scheduled takeoff time, and it was a good thing we did.

The right side door was firmly in place and when we told the pilot the door had to be removed, he said, "No speak English." The ruckus attracted the attention of the manager of the flying service and he rushed up to see what was going on. Dave explained to him that the door had to removed and if it was not, they would lose their contract with Coca Cola.

The manager quickly got the picture, and a mechanic magically appeared from out of nowhere and the door was gone. Score one for the Americano Paracadistas. We had won the argument, but now we had a very angry pilot who had lost face in front of his peers, and he had suddenly forgotten how to speak English. Things were not looking promising that the jumpers were going to have a nice day as the 180 staggered down the runway while the old pilot muttered dark thoughts to himself—in Spanish, of course. After all, he "No speak English."

As we were climbing to altitude—we were going to do a thirty-second delay from twelve five, with smoke—I asked Dave to show me the drop zone. He had a hard time locating it from among the jumble of buildings in a suburb of Mexico City, and when I picked it out, my heart skipped a beat. It was a bull ring and to say it was a tight DZ was an understatement. I gulped and turned so that Dave did not see my eyes widen in surprise and, probably, fear. There were a lot of hazards down there that could ruin your whole day and your body.

When we got to jump altitude and the tower at Mexico City International gave us clearance, the pilot pretended that he did not understand the instructions and would not turn on Dave's jump run. Dave was hollering and screaming and I thought that he was going to beat the pilot over the head with the golden trophy he had strapped to his leg. Dave's contract was depending on the success of this jump and the pilot kept flying straight ahead and not paying attention to Dave's instructions.

We always carried a six- or eight-inch hunting knife on the top of our reserve parachute to cut away malfunctions and Dave unleashed his and held it to the pilot's neck. That immediately got the pilot's attention, and he miraculously regained his ability to understand and speak English and turned on Dave's shouted jump run. After what seemed like hours, with Dave looking out the open door and turning back to the pilot to shout corrections to him, Dave yelled 'CUT' and bailed out. I followed on his back

The Bull Ring Target for the Jump

pack and by the time I had stabled out and got my bearings, I could see I was in trouble. I was far upwind from where I should be if I was going to open at twenty-five hundred feet, so I pulled right away. I was swinging in the harness at about ten thousand feet, and as I looked down, I could see Dave still in free fall and trailing red smoke. I had forgotten mine and yanked the lanyard that activated the grenade on my boot and got a face full of red smoke. Oh well, I had about three minutes to figure out what happened before I touched down and faced the crowd.

I turned and pulled down, hard, on the two front risers and ran toward the bull ring. I could see that Dave had landed inside the bull ring, but I was going to have a hard time stretching my glide to make it over the wall. I had planned to pick an open area outside the ring, but I couldn't find one so I held the slip and prayed. I had visions of smashing into the side of the ring, but at the last second I caught a little updraft and cleared the rim by about a foot.

The crowd was rushing toward Dave, and I slammed into the mass of humanity and knocked down a couple of guys, but I walked away from the landing and a few pesos took care of any injuries to my fans. Looking back on my exhibition jumping career, that probably was one of my better jumps. It certainly was exciting.

Dave and I never discussed that jump and I don't know what happened to the knife, so it was our word against the pilot's. Our reputations as the "World's Greatest Paracadistas" were preserved and I'm sure they thought the pilot was nuts when he told them about those two crazy gringo paracadistas.

After the jump, we signed autographs and visited with the huge adoring crowd. I could see where a person could get an exaggerated image of himself if he took this adulation seriously. Of course, it didn't affect me. I remained my old humble self. Some of the gifts and trinkets the fans stuffed in your pockets or tried to shove inside your jump suit were curious. When I got back to my hotel and I was sorting through the junk, there was an envelope with a pair of pink panties inside with a note and a telephone number. The note said, "If you are interested, call — —." That one was too much of a gamble for this country boy, so I passed.

I was getting ready to leave when a well-dressed, professional-looking middle-aged man approached me and asked if I had a few moments to talk to him.

I, of course, said, "sure." He reached out his hand and introduced himself as Dr. Cervantez.

"I will be brief," he said. "I saw the parachute jumps you and your partner made this afternoon, and I was impressed by the reaction of the crowd. I am on the board of directors of an organization that is starting a new clinic that will perform expensive surgeries on poor people who do not have the money to pay for them. We will be a charity organization and we do not have funds to advertise our service to the public. We will be opening our doors shortly after the new year and we are in great need of an event that will announce to the poor people that we are here to help them. A free event that is open to the public is what we need, something exactly like your parachute jump. But we do not have the money to pay for it. Will you help us, for free, and make a parachute jump for our clinic?"

I had always thought this type of payback to the community by high-paid professionals was an excellent idea so I said, "Tell me more about your organization." He did, and it sounded like a worthy cause to me, so I said, "You bet. Please give me a date and tell me where."

"That is wonderful. The date is Jan. 12th, a Sunday, and I will send you all the other information. By the way, do you know of any poor people that would need an operation that will make their life easier to live?

I said, "No, but I will ask my good friend Fr. Lopez. I'm sure he will know someone."

Then the thought struck me, how about Elena? I asked him if his organization had any plastic surgeons on their staff? He proudly said, "We have the absolute best in Mexico, and maybe in the hemisphere."

"Then I have a patient for you," I said. "Fr. Ramon Lopez will contact you and I will see you on the twelfth."

This trip to see Dave was turning out to be very valuable. I asked Dave where he went from here. He replied that his next jump was in Odessa, Texas and instead of his white jump suit and jumping the Coca-Cola parachute canopy, he would be wearing a Santa Claus suit and his parachute canopy would be red and green. That gave me an idea. Next Sunday was Fr. Lopez's church Christmas party for the kids. Why not have Father Christ-

mas arrive from the North Pole by parachute? I made the pitch
to Dave.

At first, he was cool to the idea, as he had another jump scheduled in Albuquerque for the next day. I reminded him that even
good Mormons sometimes needed an extra shove to make it
through the pearly gates and I was sure that Pius the Twelfth
would agree to give him that extra push if he needed it. But only
if he would do this good deed. He laughed and said, "This is the
first time you have ever conned me using religion. Anyway, I
would like to see what you have going in this little Mexican town
that would keep you away from the action in the States. Write
out the complete information for me, in English, and I'll be there.
Oh, one condition. You will jump with me as my elf. Better yet,
as a reindeer. I will need someone to pull my sleigh."

"It's a deal," I said and I wrote out the instructions and gave it
to him before Big John and I hit the road north to Zacatecas.

18
Santa Claus Comes to Zacatecas

When I told Fr. Lopez that there was a good chance that Santa Claus and one of his reindeer would parachute into the children's Christmas party next Sunday, he could hardly hold back his enthusiasm. He said that this was just what they needed to get the volunteers excited. The church had formed a committee to oversee the event and Fr. Lopez asked me to meet with them to tell them about the new addition to the program. They were a lethargic group and none of them had ever seen a parachute jump and my idea seemed strange to them. One by one, they caught on and by the time that the meeting broke up, there were little groups huddled together trying to come up with new ideas to add to this outrageous plan.

What they finally decided was that the children would be told that Santa Claus and his reindeer were flying around the world looking for good little boys and girls who were helping the grownups who were taking care of them. When they found a group of these good kids, Santa and one of his reindeer would parachute down and give these good little boys and girls presents to put under their Christmas trees. And the kids could talk to Santa and pet his reindeer.

The Christmas committee was going to meet in two days but the next afternoon Fr. Lopez called me into his office and told me that word had gotten around to the police department that this parachute jump was going to take place Sunday and the department was worried that they would not have enough police to control the crowd. They asked the padre not to advertise the jump on the radio or in the newspapers and to let the church members know about it through word of mouth. They did not have the money to hire more police to control the crowd that gathers when you have a free event. And, by the way, where was this event going to take place?

Good question. The committee decided to have a meeting right now and look for and find a suitable place. Two members of the committee and I toured the city in my Jeep and by the end of three hours we agreed on a soccer field about a half a mile from the church. It was an easy walk from the church and there were no power lines or telephone poles that Santa might run into. A committee member would obtain permission, and hopefully, no bribe would be necessary. Plans seemed to be going smoothly and Fr. Lopez was pleased at the way the people were working together.

Mrs. Martinez and Elena were part of the team making the suits for me and the two other reindeer. The big problem was that no one had ever seen a reindeer—as a matter of fact, neither had I. They came up with all manner of weird-looking animals and the matter was not settled until the professor at the museum brought several pictures to the sewing circle. Dave had a store-bought Santa Claus suit, so that problem was solved, and a baggage cart from Mexicana Airlines at the airport could be a good double for Santa's sleigh.

By Friday, the committee had nailed down most of the details and we were looking good. One possible glitch was the bureaucrats at the airport. A new aviation chief had just been appointed and at this late date, he was not sure that the necessary permits could be obtained from Mexico City in time to approve the jump. This seemed like a classic situation for a large bribe to be placed in the "right place." However, the committee did not have any money, and if the new chief was looking for his first big score, he had picked the wrong group to put the bite on—the Catholic Church in Mexico. Fr. Lopez and the committee were very angry and they took out their anger on the church members of the official's family and in short order, the necessary permits, approved, and with official stamps all over them, arrived from Mexico City. Santa Claus and Rudolph had been cleared to go, provided that they found any good little boys and girls in Zacatecas.

Dave called from El Paso on Saturday afternoon to say that the jump at Odessa had gone well and that Santa would be waiting to be picked up at the Zacatecas airport that night at nine o'clock. I met him at the airport, and while we were loading his gear into my Jeep, a Mexicana pilot stopped to apologize to Dave. When he left I asked Dave what that was all about and he laughed and said, "I wanted to carry my parachute on the plane with me and not in the baggage compartment. You know the old adage, in parachuting, if anything can go wrong, etc.

"Well, all my Santa Claus stuff is in that bag, and without it, there is no visit from Saint Nick, and the airlines are not famous for having your baggage arrive at the same time and place as the passenger. The stewardess said that they did not allow passengers with parachutes on their flights. I showed her that the parachute was not packed, but she said, no matter. A parachute is a parachute. Anyway, she said, he might have a Santa Claus hat in that bag, but he looks like a bad guy to me.

She wouldn't let me sit down and finally the pilot came back to see what the problem was. He was an ex-Air Force guy and he laughed and said, "I'll make a deal with you. Let me put your ripcord in my pocket—I'll give it back to you when we land—and you can sit down."

I looked at Dave. He needed a shave. He could pass as a bad guy. On the drive back into town he gave me the rundown on the jump in Odessa. Along the line of "in parachuting, if anything can go wrong," the sponsors of the event had contracted for a Cessna 180 to be the jump ship. This morning, the engine of the 180 blew up and couldn't be fixed in time for the jump, so they hired a guy with a low wing monoplane. The area where they wanted Dave to land was going to be tight and to determine the spot to exit the aircraft and land in that small area would be almost impossible to do while jumping from a low wing airplane. They found a guy with a Cessna 172 but he had never dropped a jumper. Dave explained to the pilot how they were going to do it, and he made a successful jump. In fact, Dave almost landed on the convertible that was to be Santa's sleigh.

I assured Dave that we had a first rate and experienced jump pilot in Raul Parra. In fact, I recommended that he use Raul for some of his future jumps while he was in Mexico.

The city of Zacatecas was going to sleep as we drove up to the hotel, and after Dave had a Coke and I had a cold beer, we turned in. Dave had had a tough day and tomorrow, Santa and Rudolph were both going to earn their keep before they laid down to rest. We had breakfast with Fr. Lopez and he and Dave hit it off from the start. Dave was usually uptight around Catholic clergy, but the padre put him at ease.

After we ate, we drove out to the drop zone and showed Dave the area where we would be landing. He remarked that I was getting a pretty good feel of what makes a good DZ in an urban setting as opposed to the boondocks—a rare compliment from a guy who knew both sides of the parachuting business. It was just ten o'clock and already the church members were beginning to gather to get a good place to watch the arrival of Santa. Fr. Lopez, Dave and I greeted the people and I doubted that they realized how closely the two Americanos they were talking to resembled Santa and his sidekick, Rudolph. We were at the airport at 10:30. We met Raul and went over the complete jump plans. Dave was all business and I could see that Raul did not think that all this detail was necessary, but he listened and did not say anything.

After the meeting was over, we packed the chutes and inspected the smoke grenades and other pieces of equipment we would be carrying. Dave had brought one of the new sleeves, designed to slow down the parachute opening, but he wasn't going to let me jump it. He said I could take the opening shock better. What a friend.

Dave's parachute canopy was professionally dyed a bright red and green and mine was a United States Army surplus C-9 red and white canopy that had been thrown in a tub of green dye, and it looked almost as good. But either canopy would look spectacular against the bright blue Zacatecas sky. We suited up in the hangar where we were out of the way and nobody could see us change from two ordinary looking guys into Santa and Rudolph.

Dave's custom-made Santa Claus suit was bulky and was going to cause him some trouble in freefall. He could stuff his full beard and his hat inside his coat, but the pillow that would be his big belly would have to be supplied after the landing. An extra hat and big white beard would be with the support crew on the ground, just in case. Santa wasn't Santa without the big white beard and he might lose that beard in the one hundred-plus mile per hour wind in freefall.

My costume as Rudolph the Red-Nosed Reindeer was well made by Elena and her mother, but was also loose-fitting and would be difficult to handle in freefall. The ladies had fashioned me four hooves. Three I could wear during the jump, but the fourth, on my ripcord hand, had to be attached after I landed. I could stuff it under my fake reindeer hide but there was no way I could jump with the antlers attached to my head. The antlers and the red nose will have to be attached after I landed.

We took off at 11:30 and made a couple of passes over the drop zone to give Dave an idea of the area. A road crew was burning trash about a quarter of a mile from our landing spot, so there was no reason to drop a wind drift indicator. There were some clouds in the sky, but, all in all, it was a perfect December day for a parachute jump.

We had been on pure oxygen from the time we took off, so we were both in good shape. We were now at fourteen thousand feet above sea level and were turning on our jump run at two minutes to high noon. We popped the thirty-second red smoke grenade to give the people on the ground the signal that Santa and his reindeer were about to arrive from the North Pole. I, Rudolph, would free fall for thirty seconds, trailing green smoke, and open my parachute at approximately twenty three hundred feet above the ground. My smoke would last another thirty seconds and I would keep heading into what wind there was to

Jim as Santa Claus

keep the smoke behind me. I would try to land at the far end of
the field where the sleigh was parked.

My fellow reindeer and a couple of elves would gather around
me to shield me from the view of the crowd while I put on my
antlers and my reindeer face and adjusted my red nose, out of
sight of the people. Dave, or Santa, would bail out a few seconds
after me and free fall for twenty seconds, trailing red smoke and
open his parachute at approximately forty one hundred feet
above the crowd. Santa's smoke would last another forty seconds
and he would spiral down and try to land in front of the crowd.
His elves, or support ground crew, would crowd around him
while he stuffs his pillow belly under his suit and puts on his big
white beard and his hat. Rudolph and his reindeers would have
about two minutes to get to Santa, and pick him up and that was
plenty of time to get ready for Santa's big entrance.

Everything went as planned, except Santa got some red smoke
on his suit. I had a pilot-chute hesitation that scared the hell out
of me—imagine Rudolph "streaming" in front of all of those kids.
And Rudolph lost his left front hoof in the 120 mile per hour wind
blast in freefall and it had to be replaced by a veterinarian who
happened to be on the reindeer support crew. Also, Rudolph's red
nose had to be tightened as it kept falling down and the reindeer
mask that covered his face had to be taped in place.

The crowd was huge. Word of mouth is very big in Mexico and
there was no need to advertise in the press. The police did have
their hands full as some of the kids went wild. They had never
seen a parachute jump before and to have Santa and Rudolph fall
out of the sky and give them presents was just overwhelming.

By the time we got back to the church, the three reindeer were
beat and Rudolph, at least, could have used a cold beer. Santa was
having a great time and was spending most of his time looking at
the señoritas instead of the kids. When we got to the church,
Santa ducked into a side room and changed places with another
Santa who looked more authentic and spoke much better Spanish.
Just saying, "Ho, Ho, Ho," got old after a while. I spent some
special time with Maria and Jesus and I am sure that they didn't
catch on to who the reindeer was.

With Little Jamie, it was different. When I slipped up and
spoke in English, he would cock his head and give Rudolph a

strange look. Elena said she was very proud of me and followed me around like a puppy dog. Raquel said, "Do you know how dumb you looked with that red nose and those stupid horns?" I could feel one flame flickering out and another growing stronger.

Dave caught the first plane going north out of Zacatecas that afternoon and before he left he said, "We still make a good team. I hope we can put together that company one of these days." I gave him one of the reindeer suits and he said he would try to use it in one of his upcoming jumps. But he said, "That would mean I would have to train another jumper and I don't know if I want the extra competition."

Could there be something blowing in the wind?

Elena Gets a Break

I had a hard time holding back from telling Fr. Lopez about my good news concerning talking to Dr. Cervantez in Mexico City. While the party was going on, I told him that we had to talk about a very important matter after the kids had calmed down, Santa and Rudolph had left and the kids were in bed. Over his cup of hot cocoa and my cold beer, I briefed him on my conversation with Dr. Cervantez and the doctor's promise to help us in any way he could. The padre was so excited that he jumped up and down.

"How great is God. He works in mysterious ways and he uses strange people to carry out his good works. We must tell Elena right away," he enthusiastically exclaimed.

I reminded him that it was after ten o'clock and we had better wait until tomorrow morning when Elena and her mother arrived for work. Fr. Lopez and I met the two women when they walked in the front door of the church. Before they could take their coats off, the padre began telling them what we had planned for Elena. Neither one of them seemed to comprehend what Fr. Lopez was trying to tell them, so he went over it again. The women talked rapidly back and forth and Elena pulled her hood more tightly around her head in what seemed like a defensive maneuver. Could it be that Elena did not want to come out from behind her head coverings and face the world, or could it be that she enjoyed hiding and not wanting people to talk to her?

Fr. Lopez sensed the confusion and said, "Why don't we talk about this after lunch this afternoon?" This was not the reaction I had expected. Was this another time when I had thought that I was doing a good deed and had stumbled into some Mexican custom that I didn't understand? Oh well, I will let Fr. Lopez work it out with the family and tell me what we should do. I would still honor my promise to make the exhibition parachute jump for the clinic in January.

At the meeting of the Christmas committee that evening, Fr. Lopez told me the hesitation and confusion with Elena and her mother was because that neither one of them had ever been to a big city like the capitol and they were frightened. Fr. Lopez calmed them down and they were now excited. He had called a wealthy cousin who lived in Mexico City, and she volunteered to meet Elena and be her chaperone for the entire time she was in the city. Fr. Lopez would drive them to and from the clinic and would stay at his cousin's house. He would be at their side throughout the entire operation.

I was very glad that was settled. Now the Martinez family not only could look forward to a happy Christmas but a New Year filled with promise. The holidays were a festive time at the Santo Domingo church.

Fr. Lopez was really into helping the poor, especially the kids, and I helped out when I could. I even played Santa a few times. If a kid was especially good, or needed a little special lift, I would take him or her up in the "Bug" and fly over the city. Most of the time, I could strap two of them in the back seat and I had them lined up outside the hangar. After the flights, some of the kids acted as if they had circled the moon and I sometimes wonder what that little airplane ride did to change their future lives.

My business more or less stopped the weeks before and after Christmas, so I kind of kicked back and enjoyed the parties and the socializing. But Christmas in Mexico just wasn't the same as Christmas back home. To fill in the time I had between the holidays and my scheduled jump in Mexico City, I ran down a few leads that Mario had uncovered, but the samples the natives brought in did not match the geology of the areas they were supposed to come from. Dr. Cervantez sent me the information I would need for the jump and included a picture of the area near the hospital where he wanted me to land. It was an open field with no high tension wires, at least that I could see, so I would not have to get there early to check it out.

Dave was back in the states and would not return for a couple of weeks, so the "World's Greatest Parachutist" would not be jumping with me. However, through the PR the Coca-Cola people had put out about him, a lot of people probably though I was the "Sky King" so we didn't need much advertising. Raul had agreed to fly me down in his 180 so that took care of a lot of problems. The jump was scheduled for twelve o'clock on Sunday so Raul and I flew down to Mexico City the night before.

Our quarters were at the clinic. It hadn't opened yet, but the nurses were on hand, and with nothing to do, they wanted to party. Raul and I were kind of held hostage, and we had nowhere to go, so what could we do but join them? During an exhibition jump the pilot is as important as the jumper, or almost as important, so tonight I would have a chance to keep my eye on my pilot to make sure he was in good shape to fly tomorrow. It was a good party, and we got to bed early.

The next morning I walked the drop zone with Dr. Cervantez and he told me what he would like to see, starting at noon. Essentially, I would jump from 14,000 feet above sea level, do a 30-second freefall, trailing red smoke, open my blue and red parachute canopy at 2,300 feet, land and present the keys of the new clinic to the president of the doctor's association.

Oh yes, I would be wearing a doctor's white starched smock over a blue jump suit, which were the colors of the hospital. Also, after landing, I would put on that silver reflector thing that the operating doctors wear on their heads and hang a stethoscope around my neck and carry a clipboard. When I presented the key to the clinic to the president, I looked just like one of the staff.

The jump went as advertised. There was very little wind and I was jumping a Derry slots and tails whose four mile per hour forward speed handled the wind nicely. However, I did have a little trouble on the landing. There was only one policeman to control the crowd and as I turned to make my final approach I saw the crowd surge forward, run over the cop and what was once an open field was now a sea of humanity—mostly little kids and I was going to wipe out a couple of them if I continued on

course. At the last moment I pulled down hard on the right front
riser and crashed into a Taco stand that was on the edge of the
parking lot. It was not a very dignified entry for a member of the
doctor's staff. I twisted my bad left ankle but that was the least of
my problems. Part of the mob was trampling my beautiful new
blue and red parachute canopy into the dirt and the rest of them
were trying to lift me on their shoulders. I managed to dump the
canopy by releasing the capewells before my public dislocated my
arms but I knew that I would never see my main again. I shouted
to the Taco guy that I would see him later as I was triumphantly
carried from the drop zone by screaming admirers.

At the reception that followed, I was introduced to Dr. Mendas,
the plastic surgeon who would be performing the surgery on Elena
this coming Wednesday. When he introduced us, Dr. Cervantes
said, "He is the absolutely the best plastic surgeon in the country,
and probably in the hemisphere. I told him I thought he would do
a good job and this operation was very important to me.

Dr. Mendas had a little boy with him, probably about eight or
nine, and he was standing there with his mouth open admiring
my uniform. I took my paratrooper jump wings off my chest and
pinned them on his sweater. He looked at the wings and touched
them as if they were the Holy Grail. I wanted the doctor to think
of me and Elena when he saw the kid wearing the wings around
the house. Anyway, last night I didn't have an opportunity to give
my very first pair of jump wings to one of the very pretty young
nurses and tell her that I never thought that I could give the
wings to anyone until I met her. And ask her if she would like to
"get away from this crowd" and come up to my room where I
could pin the wings on her uniform in a more appropriate setting.
Too bad. It looks like I will have to carry my extra set of wings
in my pocket tonight if the nurses have another party.

Raul arrived about an hour after the reception started and he
was wearing the extra blue jumpsuit I had dyed with the rest of
the stuff. He looked sharp, and was a hit with the girls. He said
that he would have to use this gimmick the next time he flew me
for a jump.

Fr. Lopez had driven Elena and her mother down from Zacatecas
on Saturday, and they were staying with his wealthy cousin. This
morning they were at the clinic and I had a chance to talk to them

both before and after the jump. The padre had brought some of his wealthy relatives with him and he proudly announced to them that he was going to do that parachuting thing as soon as we got back to Zacatecas.

After the excitement quieted down, I had some time with Elena. I took her hand and told her that I was really looking forward to seeing her after she got rid of that hood.

"I am living for that day," she said.

Raul scored a date that night with a nurse and I curled up with a good book. We had a late takeoff the next day and landed back in Zacatecas a little after one o'clock. It had been a good weekend.

Fr. Lopez returned from Mexico City on Saturday with Elena and her mother. Dr. Mendas said that he was very pleased with the operation and all the bandages should be removed within six weeks. During that time, Dr. Alvarez would be in charge of her recovery but the surgeon would be checking on her daily. Incidentally, Fr. Lopez said, the kid was wearing my jump wings on his sweater, a different sweater, when the doctor made his rounds to see Elena. I would say that gift of the wings to this young man was more valuable to us than having some pretty nurse wearing my "first jump wings" on her pajamas.

19
Ace
Makes a Jump

One day I received a copy of the 82nd Airborne Division's magazine from a friend I had served with when I was in the smoke jumpers. His name was Sgt. Charlie Viviano, and in addition to being the hardest worker on our firefighter crew, this guy would read any piece of paper that had anything written on it. He had the answer to any question you would care to ask him, and he was usually right. He was now living in California, and in a letter I wrote him, I wanted to know if a dog could make a parachute jump and he said, "Hell yes." In fact, their outfit had a jumping dog, and he sent me a picture of the dog, all suited up and surrounded by a bunch of paratroopers from the 508 Parachute Infantry Regiment. They were ready to board a C-46 troop carrier aircraft, and the dog didn't look too happy.

Ace had made several flights with me on the "Bug." He seemed as though he really enjoyed it, and when we were at the airport he never hesitated to jump in when I asked him if he wanted to go flying. Once we got airborne, he would stick his head out the window and snap at the wind rushing by. So I looked at Ace and said, "Partner, if that mutt in the 508 can be a parachutist, so can you. Lace up your boots, and let's go out to the airport."

I went to the canvas shop that had made my rig for the para-scuba jump and had them build a good, solid parachute harness for Ace. It was essentially a canvas sling with four two-inch wide lengths of 500-pound webbing that served as risers to connect the sling to a 16-foot cargo chute. To cut down the inherent oscillations

in this type of cargo chute, I cut four long slits in the canopy. Two
of these slits were closer to the rear of the canopy than the other
two in order to give the canopy a little forward speed.

While I was having Ace make practice jumps from a three
foot high platform, I noticed that his short legs had a tendency to
collapse as he hit the ground when he was coming straight down
so I figured that a little forward speed would make him roll and
take some of the shock on his shoulders. I don't think that the
Ace realized that he was going to be the subject of some experimental procedures, as we were going to be writing the book on
parachuting dogs. I also made a series of dummy drops with a 35-
pound sack of sand, and it looked like the rate of descent of the
16-foot parachute canopy was something that Ace could handle.

With this test work done, we were ready to "hit the silk." Ace
was going to be the test subject for what was probably going to
be the first parachute jump for a Mexican dog.

We decided to make the jump at a small airstrip about twenty
five miles from Zacatecas, because the ground elevation was
a thousand feet lower and also so that we would not have any
problems with the government air control people at the big airport at Zacatecas. Fr. Lopez and Raquel and the mountaineering
club had volunteered to be our ground support, so we were all set
to go. Our jump altitude was going to be 3,000 feet, as I didn't
want the Ace to have too much time to look around while he was
floating down on his first jump.

Ace's first jump, like all military paratroopers' first jumps,
was going to be a static line jump. His static line was going to
be hooked to a secure part of the aircraft, in this case, the pilot's
seat, and its job was to rip the cover off Ace's parachute container
when he was ten feet below the airplane. This would start a
series of events that would end with Ace having an open parachute canopy about two seconds after jumping out the door of the
airplane.

I would sit in the open door of the 180 with my back facing the
sky, and I would hold the Paradog in my arms. At the signal from
the pilot, I would push backwards from the airplane and fall free
with the Paradog until the static line opened Ace's parachute. If
all went as it was supposed to, Ace dog would be snatched from
my arms, his chute would be opened, and he would be floating

in the air 2,900 feet above the Zacatecas countryside. All this in two seconds.

He was going where no other Mexican dog had ever gone before, and he should be earning a place in the annals of Mexican aviation history. For the record book, I guess his name would have to be listed as Ace Hall, as I never did find out the name of his dog dad.

Everything went as it should have and after I saw that Ace had an open canopy, I pulled my ripcord at about 2,000 feet. All was calm and peaceful, but I was descending much faster than Ace, and I knew I was going to have trouble judging the point where he was to touch down. But, no big deal as there was very little wind so he wouldn't be dragged too far if his chute didn't collapse after he landed.

I looked down and saw that the members of my support group were all running toward the spot where they thought Ace would land. Raquel was in the lead by about a hundred yards. I made a stand-up landing and as Raquel ran up to me, she stumbled and something metallic dropped to the ground. I rushed over to help her to her feet, but she quickly crawled over and picked up the object she had dropped. I could see that

Ace on Target

it was a stiletto knife, probably eight inches long and gleaming in the sunlight. She quickly tried to hide it and put it down the front of her blouse.

Before I had a chance to ask her about it, she defensively blurted out, "I carry it with me at all times. I call it my avenger. If I am ever in a position where a man takes my virginity without my whole-hearted permission, I will take his life, and I will be cleansed by his warm blood." I didn't say a word, but I vowed to remember the words she had spoken with such sincerity and conviction.

Ace was still floating down and landed about fifty yards in front of us. From what I could see, he hit on all four feet, his momentum carried him forward, his shoulder dug into the ground and he did a complete somersault. Good dog! Exactly the steps the field manual said one had to make to execute a perfect PLF (parachute landing fall.) And he did it on four legs. That's twice as good as the most experienced paratrooper. When we ran up to him, he was on his feet and shaking the dust from his hide. His tongue was hanging out and he looked at me as if to say, "Well, how did I do, Jefe?"

I poured him a drink of water in my cupped hand, and he drank it, then licked my face, kind of a kiss. He had never done that before.

Studies by some behavioral scientists said that after a parachute jump, females are more inclined to want to make love—something having to do with experiencing fear without getting hurt. I didn't have any idea that it had the same effect on canines. We learn some things in strange ways.

Fr. Lopez and Raquel's group were impressed by the jump and several of them expressed a desire to make a parachute jump, but I did not make any offers that I would teach them. Right now, I was wondering just what I was going to do about the promise I had made to Fr. Lopez and Raquel. Since everything went so well, I thought we should repeat the jump and give Ace more practice.

The support group was interested in how I was going to repack the parachutes out here in the field. Everything they had heard about the care of parachutes was that they had to be treated with the utmost care, so they were surprised when I stretched out the canopies on the ground, and after removing some sticks and small rocks, I proceeded to fold the nylon panels. Raquel helped me with the packing. She did a pretty good job of pretending she knew what she was doing and that increased her standing with her peers.

The results of the next jump were much the same as the first, except that Ace landed a little harder, but he was not hurt. All in all, the operations for the day were a success and my being accepted by this elite group got a boost. Raul did not land after the last drop and flew back to Zacatecas. He had a charter flight to Mexico City and was running late. Ace and I packed up our gear and caught a ride with a car load of mountain climbers who were in a festive mood.

About ten miles out of town we stopped at a gas station to fill up and get a coke. I offered to pump the gas and just as I had finished topping off the tank, four motorcyclists roared up to the pumps. They were dressed in leather, wore bandana headbands, were bearded and dirty and looked rather intimidating. One of the bikers skidded to a stop and almost ran over my foot. He dismounted, approached me, grabbed the hose from my hand, then pushed it back and ordered, "Fill up my tank."

I yanked the hose away from him, placed it back in its holder and told him, "Fill it up yourself."

"Ain't you a gas attendant or some sort of military guy who is supposed to serve people like me?" he demanded to know.

I was still dressed in my white jump suit with the military patches on it, so I could see that some ignorant jerk like this guy might mistake a renowned exhibition parachute jumper like me for a gas station attendant. Frankly, after the stellar performance I had just put on, my ego was crushed. I said, "Screw you, you ugly bastard," and repeated, "Do it yourself."

He snatched the hose from the pump and thrust it at me and yelled, "Fill up the tank, gringo, or I will make you eat this hose." It didn't take me long to see where this conversation was going, so I checked my options. My mountaineering companions were cowering against their cars and ready to flee, I did not have my .25 or .357 automatics with me, I did not have a club, and these scruffy bozos were about to give my elite friends and me a lesson in real life on the streets or the highways. My only asset was Ace, the newly-minted paratrooper who would certainly welcome a fight to uphold the Airborne tradition.

Ace, who was on his leash, was being held by one of the girls and his ears were straight up and his body was shaking. He knew that something was going down, and he was ready for a fight. The biker who had been holding the hose dropped it and advanced toward me. The chain that had been wrapped around his waist was now swinging above his head, and he was slobbering and grinning. I grabbed Ace's leash and yelled, "Get him!" Ace made a giant leap and hit the biker at belt level and knocked him to the ground. I pulled Ace up tight before he could get to the biker's throat and yanked him away from the guy who was now desperately crawling away. My mountaineering buddies were scrambling all over themselves to get into the cars, and that included Fr. Lopez. I guessed that he sensed his backwards collar wasn't going to prove to be a deterrent to a pair of brass knuckles. The bikers were uncovering all kinds of weapons, and they were ready to do battle.

Things were happening fast, so fast that it was almost a blur. Our side just wanted to get the hell out of there as soon as we could and the bikers really didn't know what they wanted to do, but, of course, they wanted to fight. It was amazing how quickly the cars filled up, and the car Ace and I piled into was already rolling when we jumped in.

We were traveling down the highway when everybody started talking at once. "Did we leave anybody behind?" It was agreed that all our people had been accounted for and everything became quiet. No one spoke for the remainder of the trip into town. I did not know anyone in the car, so when we reached the church, I just got out and said, "See you later."

Fr. Lopez and Raquel were not around, so Ace and I went to our room, where Elena was cleaning up. When we entered, she pulled the scarf tightly around her face before greeting us. I asked about the kids and her mother. She said they were fine, and she quickly left. I tossed our parachuting gear on the floor, took off my boots and laid down on the bed. Ace pulled up his sleeping mat and put his head down. Elena magically reappeared with a cold beer for me and a pan of water for Ace, and all was right with our world. We had done good.

20
Get Good Lead—
Send In Mario

The weekend was peaceful and I had decided it was time to form a new mining company and make its headquarters in Zacatecas. Fr. Lopez directed me to a lawyer friend of his and the guy drew up the papers in no time. He suggested that the name of the company should be The National Exploradora y Explotadora de Minas, S.A. When I said that that was a pretty impressive name for a company that only had one person, the lawyer replied, "The padre said that you had big plans and that you would grow into the company."

Ever since I had arrived in Zacatecas, I had operated a "storefront" business managed by a retired professor who worked part time at the Museo Rafael Colonel. He was a sharp guy and he knew a lot about minerals and geology. We would encourage campesinos and peons who had lived in the sierras, or who still had family who lived many days away from the city in the boondocks, to bring in samples of what they thought were valuable minerals. The professor would listen to their stories and if a sample looked like it might contain something of value, I would have it assayed and tested. When I received the results back from the tests that were performed on some samples, I was, on occasion, amazed at the results. If the assays were a true representation of the property that they were supposed to originate from, the properties were worth thousands of dollars.

When I would check the locations against the geologic maps printed by the Mexican Government, the two usually did not jibe. I had no idea where the samples may have come from, or where the campesinos got them. I surmised that they were stolen from a museum or a private collection. In the rare case when the sample looked like it may have come from a certain geologic formation, we interviewed the owner and filed it for further action.

Every now and then, we would come across an opportunity that could turn into a real treasure. One such opportunity presented itself about three months after we had opened the storefront. The rumor had been on the street that I was going to open the office and I was looking for mining properties in the sierras. One day, a young laborer, a tough-looking guy who had just come into town from working on a ranch north of the city and was now working on a construction project near Fr. Lopez's church, came into the business and told a story about a very old gold mine that had been operated by the Spanish Conquistadors many years ago. If this were true, it had to be in the fifteen hundreds and that was a long time ago, like 400 years ago.

The mine was located near a small village where he was born and his father used to tell the family about how the Spaniards made the Indians work in the mines like slaves until the Indians rebelled and killed all of the Spaniards. No one in the village knew how to dig for the gold so the timbers that held up the mine workings rotted and the mines caved in and nobody bothered with the mine any more.

The man left home when he was a teenager but he was sure that he could find his way back to his village. He had come to Zacatecas with an older brother, but the brother was killed in an automobile accident the first year they were here and he never had a chance to go back to his village.

The professor told him that we couldn't do anything about looking at the mine until we had a sample of the ore from the mine. The laborer, seeing a chance to get back to his village and having somebody else pay for the trip, said he would go back to the mine and bring back dirt that could be tested if he had some money to live on. He was a poor man and didn't have any money. The professor asked him to come back tomorrow morning after he talked to the boss and maybe the boss will pay him to go to the mine and bring back samples of the dirt.

The professor told me about the interview and I was interested, as I had never worked on a mine that was this old. I was at the business the next morning when the man came in. I heard his story and he sounded like an honest guy. I showed him a map and he looked at it closely. I could see that he didn't quite understand all the symbols and marks but after a while we came up with a rough idea of where he wanted to go and how to get there.

I asked him how many days did he think it would take him to get there and back to Zacatecas? He said, judging the time it took him and his brother to cross some mountains and go around some mountains, on foot, and then second class bus to the city, he could probably make it there and back in two weeks. He would need bus fare and money to live on.

"You look like and talk like an honest man," I told him. "I will give you five hundred pesos. I will see you when you return.

"What is your name, my friend," I asked him.

"Mario," he said and walked out the door.

He returned several weeks later with a couple of samples that looked promising and I had them assayed. They tested positive for gold, silver, lead, and a trace of uranium, which was much more valuable than the gold and silver. This find looked like it might be a possible winner, so I took the next step up in the chain that would qualify a prospect to advance to the top of the "must do" list. That step was to send Mario back to the prospect, with a trustworthy employee of my company, to take more samples and bring them back to be assayed.

Who should we send? The only person available was the professor's nephew. He was a young, scholarly kid hired to do interviews with the campesinos who came into the business to tell us their stories. The professor told me that the kid had studied mineralogy and some geology at the Universidad Nacional Autonoma de Mexico and that he was fully qualified to take samples and tell us, when he returned, something about the geology of the region. I hired him, as I didn't have any other candidate.

This project looked as if it had some merit, so from now on, my company was going to pick up the tab for any more exploration. I gave Mario a thousand pesos for bus fare and other expenses. I also gave them my camera and two rolls of film. The property was really way out in the boondocks and it was going to be very difficult to get there from the city. It was located in rough country near the borders of the states of Durango and Nayerit, but still in the state of Zacatecas. The Rio Bolanos ran near the area that Mario had pointed out and I was hoping that there was a sand bar big enough and long enough to get the "Bug" in for a pickup. But we would have to wait and see until I had a first hand look at the area.

Mario had gotten into the property by crossing mountain trails from the east side of the sierras but we thought that this time it might be easier and faster to take the bus to Tepic, the capitol city of Nayerit and approach the property from the west side of the sierras. That meant taking the overnight bus to Guadalajara and another bus 220 kilometers to Tepic before they could start using local transportation into the sierras. It could take them as long as a week to get into the property and another week to get back to Zacatecas. This would be a long trip. The kid said he was looking for excitement and adventure, but little did he suspect how much he would get before he got back.

Mario Returns—Assay

Mario and the kid were back. Mario was excited but a little worse for the wear, while the kid was haggard and subdued. I had the feeling that the kid had seen about all the adventure that he cared to see and was glad to be back home. The thousand pesos I had given them were gone so I gave another 200 to Mario and 50 to the kid. I dropped the samples off at the chemist's office and asked him to get me some answers as soon as possible, even if he had to work over the weekend.

The next morning we met at the storefront business. There was me, Mario, the professor, and the kid, and I had asked Fr. Lopez to sit in on the debriefing to sort out any difficulties in the language and the terms that were sure to come up. From looking at the two guys who had just made it, I guessed it had been a very difficult trip and they probably had many obstacles to overcome before they made it back to Zacatecas. Mario did the talking and the kid kind of hung his head and closed his eyes and listened.

They made the trip to Guadalajara without problems, but they missed the bus to Tepic and had to sleep in the bus station that night. When they got to Tepic they couldn't find anyone who could give them anything that resembled a bus schedule to any of the villages they would have to pass through on their way to the sierras. By hit or miss they arrived at the point where they could go no further by vehicle so they had to rent two mules to continue. The owner asked for a deposit of 700 pesos to guarantee the mules would be returned in good shape, but Mario got him to accept 500 pesos and his watch for security.

Using the maps I had given them, they headed into the foothills, not knowing exactly where they were going. It was tough going and the fact that Mario had been raised with mules and the people who owned them, was responsible for the two of them finally reaching the village where his father had lived. I asked the kid about the geological formations he saw and where the Spaniards had been digging. He was vague in his answers and said that what he saw were caved in holes in the side of the hills and rounded mounds of soft dirt.

"How about veins of hard rock? Did you see any quartz crystals or metamorphic rocks?" I asked. He mumbled that he was very tired and that they "didn't spend much time digging in the dirt." He looked like he would have liked to be anywhere but here, answering questions. I realized that for whatever reason I wasn't going to get much out of him. Later, maybe he would be more willing to talk.

I asked Mario if there was anyplace near the mine where we could land a small airplane. It was a useless question to ask, as I would have to make the final decision when I was on the ground. It wasn't so much a matter of having enough space to land as having enough space to take off.

The meeting broke up and I gave Mario another 500 pesos and the kid 50. We would meet at the same place when the assay reports came back.

Two days later, I had the results, and they were better than I had expected. Overall the samples showed more gold, but not the "maravilloso" amount the kid had predicted for a dark rock he had picked up and carried back in his pocket.

"Look!" he said. "You don't have to be an engineer to plainly see the specks of gold in my rock."

I sadly had to tell him those specks of gold were iron pyrite, better known as "Fool's Gold" and worth exactly nothing.

The time the professor said that the kid had spent in the mineralogy class at the University in Mexico City, was probably spent day dreaming about the girl he was going to meet after class—a common fault among young geology students and mining engineers.

The most promising result from the assays was the greater amount of uranium present. If it was found in any sizable amount it would be worth much more that the gold found with it. This alone could make the entire venture worthwhile.

One thing that bothered me was that they didn't find any veins of hard rock material. However, it might have been that as they were inexperienced in sampling and didn't want to do the extra work required of digging in the solid material, they didn't get a good sample of the hard rock.

Oh yes, my camera was stolen the first day they passed through a village on the way into the sierras. But Mario said, "Señor Jaime, I still have your two rolls of film."

This looked like a lead that could pay off. I was sold. My trip to the mine of the Spanish Conquistadors was a go.

21
To the Mine

The long-range weather report called for clear, crisp conditions for the next two weeks, so I cleared my schedule and prepared to devote my complete attention to a full-scale demonstration of my ideas about how a geologist and mining engineer could successfully explore for gold or other valuable minerals in the remote regions of Mexico. I had carefully, and slowly, checked Raul out on how I wanted him to fly the Super

Jim, Raul and the Bug

"Bug," including many short field takeoffs and landings. Finally, to my satisfaction, he was well qualified to be my back-up pilot.

I would call the operation "Conquistador" in honor of the brave, but not necessarily kind and gentle, Spanish warriors who pushed over the mountains and up the canyons to the place where they thought they might find what they were searching for—gold. This place, where Mario had said they had dug dirt samples from the old Spanish mine workings, and had tested for gold and an even more valuable mineral, pitchblende, was such a place, but what had caused the Conquistadors to dig here?

I was beginning to get excited at the chance to walk in the footsteps of these Spaniards whose boots kicked up this dirt more than four centuries ago. What were the relationships between these men, who only a year or so before had trod the streets of Madrid or the farms on the plains of Spain, and the Indians whose ancestors had lived free in these mountains from the beginning of time? Did they live in peace until the Conquistador's relentless drive to find more gold pushed the Indians to rebel and rise up and murder the intruders who treated them as slaves and worked them to death?

Ever since he had returned from his village, I had employed Mario at the storefront. Although he lacked any formal education, he was a fast learner and an eager student for the professor. He worked well with the campesinos and he had a very good memory, so he was able to relay the information he was getting from the interviews to the professor. He had become a valuable member of my team and ready to take part in "Operation Conquistador." I gave myself a week to dry run the operation and that week would start when we took off from the Zacatecas Airport at 0600 next Monday morning. Until then, we would practice short field landings and takeoffs with Raul and I would spend several hours working with Mario on how to operate the hand-held radio and how to recognize and fix the normal problems that could, and probably would, arise.

We would duplicate the conditions we thought we would encounter during the actual operation and by the time we were finished, I would be sure that we could handle the job. Our seamstress made a carrying case for the radio that included a pouch for two spare batteries, and we were good to go. Mario left for his village on D-Day minus seven with instructions to be ready for the Super "Bug" to appear over the drop zone he had chosen for me to parachute into at about 8 o'clock on the next Monday morning.

As soon as he saw or heard our airplane, he was to set fire to a pile of brush and make a lot of smoke. He would then contact us with the hand-held radio. When he contacted us, we would make several low passes and then drop our cargo container with my supplies. After Mario retrieved the container and examined the contents and determined if anything was broken, he would notify us. We would then fly over the surrounding area and pick out a place where Raul could land and pick me up after the inspection. A pretty simple plan, on paper. It remained to be seen how well it would work in real life.

Cargo Drop

The introduction of the air-dropped equipment container, or pod, was going to make my life a whole lot easier. On earlier jumps into remote regions, I had to live off the local economy—that means eating the same food and drink as the natives. I had gotten very sick from eating rotten meat that had been preserved in very strong chili sauce and drinking contaminated stream water. I quickly learned that having severe diarrhea while walking and climbing mountains for several days or riding a mule for that time takes all the glamour out of being an exploration geologist or mining engineer. I also quickly learned to go hungry and thirsty for a couple of days. In addition to food and water, I packed a hammock—it is also not glamorous to sleep with bedbugs, mites, cockroaches, fleas, spiders, and lice, and these things are always found in the huts of the natives. Toss in snakes and scorpions on the ground, and you should be sure to pack a hammock if you want to get a good night's sleep. Also to be included should be a lightweight waterproof tarp, heavy socks, medical supplies, halazone tablets and geologic tools.

Knowing that these things were going to be available to me after I landed by parachute was a great relief. On several previous expeditions, before I developed the cargo container, not all my cargo drops were on the mark. Bad spots due to misjudging the ground wind strength or dropping from too high an altitude were big mistakes, but the chief reasons for losing my supplies were that the locals got to them before I did. I soon learned that the back-country people would steal absolutely anything they could get their hands on, and my supplies were like gifts from heaven to them. At first I was mad as hell at the people, but when I saw how desperately poor they were, I always packed extra food and left whatever supplies or gear I had not used to whoever appeared to be the head man and hoped that he would share the stuff with his people. I also usually left my parachutes and, to this day, I am sure you can find 28-foot U.S. Army surplus parachute canopies covering baby cribs or acting as mosquito netting in huts in remote regions of the sierras of Mexico.

Lately at night when I would sit down and drink a few beers and think deep thoughts, I was beginning to realize that I had been pretty damn lucky not to have been killed and my body left along the side of some mountain trail in Chihuahua, or Durango or Zacatecas for the vultures to feed on, or buried in a shallow grave without even a pile of rocks to mark my passing. Let's face it, I wasn't liked by the natives, except for the ones who thought that they might gain something if I found that their "lost gold mine" was of some value. You didn't have to scratch too deeply to guess that they figured this outsider was a danger to their way of life and it might be a good thing to kill him.

And this was just in the back country. Sometimes in the city, it was worse, particularly among the guys who thought that I was trying to make out with their girls. I had been doing this mine exploration as a lone wolf. From now on I was going to be taking a partner with me. Right now, the only one I had available was old Ace. He was somebody I could trust and all it took to keep his loyalty was an occasional hamburger and a juicy soup bone, and maybe a gentle kick now and then. Ace and I had a relationship, and we understood each other. Now that I had taught Ace to parachute, or at least I had taught him to overcome whatever fears he had of making a parachute jump, I would put him to work. This upcoming jump would tell if it would work.

It was early Monday morning and the Super "Bug" is rolling down the runway at Zacatecas airport at 0600. I am flying from the front seat and Raul is in the back. We are carrying the cargo container with about sixty pounds of gear and food in it and the plane is acting a little strange. I take note that I had better have Raul practice taking off with a loaded cargo container a couple of times to avoid a future potential screw up. It is a beautiful day and about two hours later we are circling the sierras above the canyons where I think our target is located. I gun the engine a couple of times but no sign of a signal fire. I have the radio turned on and the volume is at full power. We are picking up a lot of static, mostly from the engine, a problem that we have not been able to solve, but I am hoping we can work through that glitch. We are picking up a faint voice and as we circle, it fades in and out. The voice is getting stronger and, of course, it is Mario. He must be pointing the antenna toward our airplane but he fades out.

I tell him to follow the "Bug" and his signal grows strong again. I tell him to light the fire and he replies, "I have lit it."

"I can't see it," I tell him. Suddenly, off to my right I see a faint, white wisp of smoke. We are at 11,000 feet above ground level so I drop down to 9,000 and circle the smoke.

Mario's voice is coming in a lot clearer and I can see the flames. Mario has built his fire on a level piece of ground about 200 feet square and about 500 feet west of what could be called a river during the height of the rainy season but now was no more than a stream of flowing water about five feet wide.

From the maps I had, I would say this is the Rio Balonos. It would be very important if the property we are going to inspect would prove to have ore worth developing. It looked like the ground surrounding the river was about 6,000 feet and the mesa about the river where Mario had built his fire was probably 6,500. We flew an up and down search pattern over the area and located several prominent landmarks that would help us pinpoint the area tomorrow morning and then dropped lower to plan what would be the best jump run. At this part of the canyon, the river ran pretty much north and south, so we could use the river as a reference and make our jump run from the north to the south, depending on the wind.

We practiced the jump run five times, and I had Raul fly the last three using the landmarks as aiming points. After I was satisfied that there were no questions about how we were going to do this tomorrow, we flew a couple of practice runs for the cargo drop at various altitudes. The ground winds seemed to be light so we decided to drop from an altitude of 500 feet. I radioed Mario that he and his people should stay away from the center of the mesa, as cargo chutes sometimes failed and 60 pounds of gear falling at 60 miles an hour could wipe out a person.

I made a long pass, and I had to pull up once to clear a small hill before releasing the cargo container about two hundred feet north of the mesa. The chute deployed cleanly and the cargo landed in the middle of the drop zone. This method of cargo dropping was the way to go! I looked back over my shoulder and saw the group, dogs and all, running toward the cargo. When I talked to Mario, I told him to be sure that tomorrow they leave the dogs in the village and tied up good and tight. With Ace jumping, there was sure to be one helluva dog fight if the dogs were there when he landed.

Raul pulled in the static line that had been attached to the cargo, and we climbed to altitude to look over the area for possible pickup sites. We selected a likely mesa about ten miles down the river and about a quarter of a mile up a steep embankment on the west side. After I finished my inspection, I could follow the river to where it made a sharp bend to the left and then climb the embankment to the top of what looked like a level area about 600 feet long. From the air, it appeared that there was a lot of brush to make a fire, and to help the smoke show up better, I had packed a pint can of motor oil in the cargo. I had also brought along a bag containing a couple of pounds of lime and as we crossed over the end of the mesa, Raul played the role of a bombardier and tossed it over the side of the airplane. I had intended the lime to splatter and spread over a large area where it would be easily seen, not only from the air, but from ground level so I would be sure I had the correct mesa. The package must have impacted a small bush, as it failed to scatter, but this marker would have to do. We climbed to 1,000 feet above the ground and made a final pass over the village.

Everybody from miles around was standing around and looking to the sky as I gunned the engine and waggled the wings of the Super "Bug." A large group of dogs and men were clustered around the cargo chute—I hoped Mario was one of them—and I imagined that there was some pretty heavy thinking going on as to how they could steal the contents of that container.

I said goodbye to Mario on the radio and told him we would see him tomorrow morning and we headed back to Zacatecas. It was a little after 11:30 when we called the tower for clearance to land at Zacatecas. I got permission to make a touch and go and after taxing up to my hangar, I got out and changed seats with Raul and he took the "Bug" up for several practice short field takeoffs and landings.

Before we called it a day, we shut down the engine, put approximately 60 pounds of dirt in the spare cargo container and Raul practiced takeoffs and landing with this added weight and configuration. Experience with airplanes had shown us that it is a good idea to practice doing the things that you haven't done before, before they sneak up and bite you in the butt. We were back, everything was a go for tomorrow and I was on time for the late Mass.

Jump Day—Conquistador

I was awake before the alarm went off and waiting at the door of the hotel when Raul drove up in his old Ford. He was ten minutes late, but no big deal, as we would be flying his Cessna 180, and we could make up that time with no problem. When we picked up Ace, he looked at me as if to say, "What's up, jefe? Don't I get any breakfast?" My answer would have been. "No, nobody in this airborne outfit eats before they jump." The Cessna was gassed up and after a thorough pre-flight, we loaded up.

Before I had gone to sleep last night, I had carefully checked our parachutes. In addition to me and Ace, Raul would be wearing a parachute. This was a requirement when I made a jump. I had learned the hard way that when a pilot is dropping jumpers, he should be wearing a parachute. One time I was on a load of military jumpers and one of the team accidentally deployed his reserve parachute inside the aircraft. It yanked him out the open door and his reserve chute became ensnared in the controls of the tail surfaces. Three of us jumpers got out of the plane before it went into a spin and crashed killing the jumper and the pilot, who, against regulations, was not wearing a parachute.

Before our preflight, we had removed the right side door and the passenger seats of the Cessna, and all we had to do was hook up Ace's static line and we were ready to go. We spotted the signal fire about twenty miles out from the target, and it was not quite eight o'clock. It seems that Mario was not going to take any chances that we could not see the signal, and he had a good fire going with lots of smoke. We had been flying at 9,000 feet, and we had been sucking on the oxygen bottles ever since taking off. I had rigged a mask and bottle for Ace, and although he didn't like it, he was getting enough oxygen to keep him alert. Raul dropped down to about 1,000 feet and made a low-level practice run to wake up the people. Mario was coming through on the Cessna's radio a lot clearer than he was on the "Bug's" receiver and that told me that we had better get a new radio for the "Bug." We will take care of that when we get back home.

After the pass, Raul climbed to our jump altitude of 2,500 feet above the ground. Although the smoke from the fire told me that the ground winds were light, I would drop a wind drift indicator from our jump altitude to give me a much better idea of the winds all the way to the ground.

My parachute, a four-line cut modification, could fight a slight wind, but the chute Ace was jumping was used for cargo, and even though I had removed almost four panels to eliminate the oscillations, he would be drifting at the mercy of the wind, just like our wind drift indicator. The indicator told me that the winds aloft were coming from the south, and we should exit the aircraft over the river and let the wind blow us back over our target.

Using the landmarks we had picked out yesterday, Raul started a long jump run and I moved into my jump position sitting with my back facing the open door. Raul would keep the aircraft straight and level and give me the signal to jump when we were over the exit point. Ace had been dozing on the floor, but sensing the rising tension in the cockpit, he shook off his oxygen mask and waited for orders. I turned Ace's back toward me and grabbed the front and back of his parachute harness while keeping his weight on the cabin floor.

My eyes were riveted on Raul. He lifted his right arm, the signal to stand by to bail out, then he cut the power to the engine to reduce the prop blast, and three seconds later, slammed his fist down on the instrument panel. I yelled "go" to Ace, pushed back with all my might, and ducked my head as we entered the slipstream and disappeared under the tail of the airplane. The static line on Ace's parachute stretched taut as it ripped the parachute canopy from the pack. In a split second the opening canopy snatched Ace from my arms, and he was gone. I was on my back when I saw Ace's parachute snap open, momentarily collapse and then blossom full open into a beautiful white umbrella. I turned over on my stomach and fell another 500 feet to make sure I was falling fast enough to get a good positive parachute opening.

When my chute cracked open, I was almost at terminal velocity, about 120 miles per hour, and I was in a head-down position. When my head cleared—I had been seeing all kinds of stars and flashes of light—I looked up to check my parachute canopy to see that it was fully open and I did not have any malfunctions. I breathed a sigh of relief; there were no rips, no tears, or no lines over the top of the canopy. I made the 4 line cut and rocked my canopy back and forth in order to get a clear look above me to see where the Ace was and how he was doing. He was coming straight down; the modification I had made to his canopy was preventing his canopy from oscillating, but the wind was blowing him to the north faster than my larger canopy was moving. I made a 180-degree turn and ran with the wind until I was sure that I would land at a place where I was in front of him. When he touched down, I wanted to be able to deflate his canopy if it looked like he was being dragged.

I made a fairly soft landing on the north end of the intended drop zone, and Ace touched down about 25 feet in front of me. He landed on all four feet, his legs collapsed, and he took most of the shock on his belly. The wind was knocked out of him; he was dazed, but other than that, he was up and flashing his special grin. I could just imagine the jump story he was going to tell his grandpups about this jump.

Mario and about ten natives arrived shortly after we landed and, yes, they had a couple of mangy dogs with them. As soon as we landed, I snapped the short, strong leash on Ace's collar and I now had him reined in tight. As the crowd skidded to a stop, the dogs went wild.

What was this? A short-haired, tough-looking dog that fell out of the sky. They did not know what to make of it, but if they were looking for a fight, Ace was willing to give them one. His teeth were bared, his eyes flashed, he was in his fourlegged stance, and he was ready to rumble. I told Mario to get rid of the dogs, and after a great deal of kicking and beatings with clubs, the mutts scattered. The dogs looked like they were accustomed to harsh treatment and when the yelling started, they were gone.

Mario greeted me with a handshake and introduced me to some of the elders. They kept their heads down and did not make eye contact. These guys looked like they had led a very rough life. I would have a hard time estimating their ages—even the kids looked old, and most of them were skin and bones. In this culture, a well-fed person would be hard to find. I called Mario over and reintroduced him to Ace. The Ace made a slight indication that he knew Mario and gave me a funny look when I handed Mario his leash.

I field-packed my parachute and bundled Ace's gear around it. One of the younger kids made a tentative attempt to feel the parachute cloth, but an elder knocked his hand away. I indicated that it was OK to touch the strange material that permitted a man to float down from the sky. I intended to leave both parachutes with the natives. I wondered how they would divide the cloth and cords and hardware among the people, but I was sure that they would figure out something that I had never thought of before.

Just then, Raul made a pass at about 500 feet and gunned his engine a couple of times. I had temporarily forgotten how I got here. Mario was carrying the radio in its case around his neck and when Raul's voice crackled from the device, he rushed over and handed me the mike. The reception here on the ground was much worse that it was in the air and I could barely make out what Raul was saying. I told him both Ace and I were unhurt and everything was OK down here. He waggled the wings of the Cessna, gunned the engine, and said, "I'll talk to you tomorrow afternoon around three o'clock." I told him I understood, and he flew off to the east.

I took Ace's leash from Mario and the group, without direction, walked toward the village about 500 yards away. We stopped at one of the huts that seemed a little better maintained than the others and Mario said, "This is where my father lives. He is very sick, but he would really like to meet you."

"It would be an honor to meet your father," I said. I waited outside the hut as Mario entered and in a few minutes, he asked me to follow him. The old man was laying on a mat on the dirt floor and he raised his hand to greet me. He was, indeed, very sick, and he, too, looked like he had led a very hard life. The viejo tried to speak but we could barely hear him. Mario put his ear to the old man's lips and listened intently. He was speaking in a dialect I could not understand and I am sure that Mario did not understand it either, but he faked it and said that his father was very happy to meet me and that he welcomed me to his village. The old man tried to get up, but the effort was too much for him and he fell back and passed out. Mario said that we would come back later and we all filed out into the bright sunlight.

Ace didn't quite understand what was going on and he stayed very close to me. The black gnats and flies were really chewing on him and they were having a field day with the opportunity of feeding on some new American blood, mine. I asked Mario to bring me the cargo container and without a word from him, one young man bolted from the pack of natives surrounding us and disappeared behind the huts. He returned in a few minutes with the silver bomb and Mario proudly produced a key.

With a flourish, he opened the nose of the container and the group pushed forward to see what I took from it. I sorted through the contents and came up with some insect repellent and a quart of water. I closed the container, Mario put the lock back on it and the young man returned it from wherever he had found it. Mario asked if I wanted to go into another hut to discuss our plans.

"I would rather stay out here in the sunshine," I replied. Out here I could at least see what was biting me. The natives didn't seem to be bothered by the creatures that filled the air, but Ace and I were spending a lot of our energy swatting the black ones we could see and the pale, almost invisible ones that we could feel. The locals laughed when I started rubbing the repellent on Ace and pointed to some mud on the ground and indicated that I should smear it on the dog.

A kid brought me a gourd of water and poured it on the ground and then mixed it with the dirt to make a thick paste. One of the men made a move to put some of the mixture on Ace. The dog growled his disapproval and lunged for the man's arm. I yanked Ace up short and the guy jumped back in alarm, lucky to still have his arm in one piece. If Ace was going to get a mud bath, I would have to give it to him.

Ace looked me in the eye as if to say, "Do we really want to do this, Jefe?" I picked up a handful of mud and carefully, very carefully, patted some on his back. His lower lip dropped, but he stood still until I had pretty well covered him. Then I smeared the repellent all over my face and hands and used parachute suspension line to tie my shirtsleeves and pants tightly to my arms and legs to keep the little bastards out. It seemed to me that they could drill through a solid cement wall to get to human flesh.

I asked Mario where I could go to relieve myself and he spread his arms wide and said, "Anyplace out there." Ace and I walked about a hundred yards from the village. We found a pine tree and both peed on it. It was a male bonding thing. It also gave me a chance to give Ace his breakfast, a hamburger I had been carrying in my pants side pocket. I could imagine the natives surprise at seeing a dog wolf down what they would consider a full meal.

I also gave Ace a drink of the pure water we had brought from Zacatecas. We were careful not to spill any. It was going to be valuable stuff, probably the last drink of water he would get that was not treated with halazone purifying tablets. If he got sick, that would be almost as bad as my getting the runs or throwing up.

We walked back to the village and I told Mario that we were ready to go to work. He had the cargo container brought back and I took out my geologic tools, including sampling bags, and we walked down toward the river. We passed through the corn, or maize, fields farmed by the villagers, and Mario explained that this was their main source of food. If this crop failed, there was a good chance that some of the villagers could starve.

This village was luckier than most others in this area, as it had the river near by. The villagers also grew squash and other climbing plants and I saw a few fruit trees, but that was all they had to eat. Agriculture was a foreign science to me but it seemed as if they could learn to grow several more crops, they would not be in so much danger of starving.

I did not see any sign of small animals, such as rabbits or squirrels, or any birds or rats, so I imagined that the natives had hunted down any of the creatures that had lived here. But the one animal I did see was goats, lots and lots of goats.

Half way down the embankment on the way to the river, I saw what we had made this trip for—an outcropping of weathered, decaying rock and signs that someone had dug into that rock, but not recently. The panoramic view of the area was something out of a basic geology textbook. The small stream now flowing at the base of this embankment had at one time, probably centuries ago, been a raging river and had exposed and worn down this vein of hard rock. Any person with even a limited knowledge of where gold should be found, such as a priest traveling with a band of Conquistadors, would have known enough to pan the sands at the base of this outcropping and he probably found traces of gold. That would be the answer to the question of why the Conquistadors stopped at this place to mine for gold.

The answer to the other big question—why did they abandon the gold mine—was probably for the reason the natives told Mario. After who knows how many years, the Indians could not bear the cruelties of their Spanish conquerors, revolted, overwhelmed their masters and massacred them. The Indians, seeing that the Spaniard's quest for the beautiful yellow medal had only brought them pain and suffering, destroyed all traces of the conquerors' mining operations and went back to living their peaceful way of life.

Mario had brought two men with shovels with him and I directed them to dig into the soft, weathered material until they encountered solid rock. Meanwhile, I took two other men with me and spent several hours getting an overall view of the area. I had planned to stake a mining claim and using my Brunton compass and two 10-foot poles as measuring sticks, I had the men erect stone markers, or monuments, to establish the boundaries of my claim. Then I took pictures of the markers and the landmarks to make a record of what I had done.

I had bought a new camera, a simple one, so all one had to do was point and shoot. My last two expensive cameras were stolen and I didn't want this one to look too attractive to the people I came in contact with.

I also wanted a camera that did not attract too much attention. Mario had told me to be very careful of taking the pictures of some of the natives, especially the older ones. They had a super-stition that you are stealing their spirit. The spirit goes into the front of the camera and comes out the back on a piece of paper and it is gone from their body. This was another one of those in-tangibles that could sneak up and bite you on the butt if you were not careful.

I never understood or tried to figure out the Indians' thinking on this, or many other beliefs, so that is one reason why I always carry a gun, a knife and Ace when I am in the back country, and most of the time when I am in town. I intend to leave Mexico alive.

Mario and Jim

By late afternoon, I was at the river's edge walking up and down and analyz-ing how the river and its water could be used if the ore deposit should turn out to be economically fea-sible, first to develop the gold and second for the uranium. I had made some inquiries, discreetly, about the value of a uranium find without raising the hopes of the people who were very much interested in anything dealing with the nuclear program, but I had received no guidance as to the interest of the Mexican government. I did know that with the nuclear arms race heating up between the United States and Russia, a discovery of any significance would be of great importance to all three governments.

I had brought a gold pan with me and I picked out a place that would be a likely area for gold to be trapped, and started pan-ning. Mario looked on with interest and asked if he could try it. I told him, "OK," but said he should wait until we see if I found any gold.

On the very first pan full of sand and gravel, I found some, but not much. A few flakes of gold and some black residue that was obviously heavier than the host rock. Maybe uranium, pitchblende? I tried several other spots, but with no better luck. Each time I panned a shovel full of sand, I demonstrated the technique to Mario and after about ten minutes, I thought he was ready to try it.

Gold panning is a skill that is only acquired by lots of practice, so I left Mario and crossed the river to the east side. I was hoping to pick up some sign of the outcropping on the west side, but nothing matched up.

While crossing the river to the west side I encountered some human waste floating down from up river. Mario had not mentioned any other villages, but it would be natural that other people would be living along the river. Ace had been wanting to take a drink from the river and, fortunately, I had stopped him. I didn't need a sick partner this early in the game. I would slip him a drink of the good water we had brought with us when we were out of sight of the natives.

When I got to the west side of the river, Mario was still panning but he had failed to turn up any more gold. It was disappointing, but my main interest was the hard rock vein. The two men who had been digging in the outcropping had reached solid rock and I would have liked to start examining the quartz, but it was getting late and I wanted to make very sure that we were ready for the night. When we returned to the village, there were small groups of men standing around jabbering to one another in a very strange dialect. I couldn't tell if they were hostile or friendly so I held Ace with a tight grip. As we approached, they would drift back into their huts and reappear after we had passed.

So far, I had not seen one woman and very few small children. Very strange, or was it? I knew nothing of their culture and I guessed they knew nothing of mine. Smoke from cooking fires drifted out the doors, there were no windows in the huts, and it was probably a good way to get some relief from the millions of bugs.

Mario directed me and Ace to a small hut at the end of the village street. This looked like this was going to be our headquarters for our stay here. There was a place where a cooking fire could be built and I asked Mario to bring us some tinder so I could build a small fire to heat our cans of stew. I was glad that I would have a place to feed Ace out of sight of the Indians as I was sure that they would not have liked to see a dog eating and drinking better than they. Mario returned with a small amount of firewood, but, luckily we didn't need much and I had a small fire going in no time. I asked Mario if he would like to eat with us and he readily accepted. During the years he had spent away from his village, I am sure that he had acquired a taste for city food and the stuff his neighbors were eating was as foreign to him as it was to me and Ace. In fact, I remember that I had seen him slip a couple of cans of beans into his pack before he got on the bus to leave Zacatecas.

It was going to be OK to eat in the hut, but I wasn't about to sleep inside. I saw that Mario's face and arms were covered with ugly red welts, the mark of the ravenous one-eighth-inch long and razor-thin bedbugs that lived in the huts and came out at night to prey on the human blood banks. I imagine that the local bedbugs have been spreading the word that a tasty Americano is going to spend the night with us and he has even brought along a delicious, short haired, plump perro for us to feast upon.

This is where a hammock and a place to hang it is worth its weight in gold. As yet, I haven't taught Ace to sleep in a hammock but I could fluff up his chute and he could burrow into it and get away from some of the gnats, flies and fleas. I was going to hang my hammock between one of the poles that helped hold up my hut and the corner pole of the hut next to mine. I didn't consult with my neighbor, but I assumed that it would be OK as long as it didn't pull his hut over. I had to improvise to make two lengths of rope to string the hammock, as I had failed to include the half-inch nylon rope that belonged with the hammock and served as its anchors. I wouldn't make that mistake again.

Eating was a problem. The flies and gnats would fight you for every bite of food and the only way to beat them to the food was to stick your head in the smoke from the fire. Ace was having a tough time and the volume of his food intake was increased about 100 percent with the addition of black gnats. We finally gave up, put the food aside and hoped that things would be better tomorrow. We had a spectacular sunset and as soon as the sun dropped below the high sierras to the west, it was as if a switch had been thrown and it was dark. Things suddenly became quiet and the night settled in.

Unusual Drop Zone Inhabitants

Scorpion (Alacrans)

Rattlesnake

Mite

Deer Fly

Flea

Bedbug

Tick

Gnat

This lasted for about ten minutes and then the quiet was replaced by the pounding of a thousand hoofs. The goats that must have been grazing on the other side of the village had returned and they took over every available square inch of outside territory in the village, including under my hammock and Ace's sleeping space. Ace didn't like that one bit and as hair and parts of goat flew every where, Ace regained his space, and then some. No one seemed concerned, the social life continued, cooking fires still smoldered in some huts and finally things stopped moving around and it was quiet again. There was a slight chill in the air and I pulled my parachute canopy tighter around me and one by one, the cooking fires went out. I was tired so it didn't take me long to drop into a deep sleep.

Some time later, I was awakened by a drumming sound, a steady rhythmic beat, Bang, bang, bang, bang. As I sat up and rubbed the sleep from my eyes, my surroundings assumed bizarre proportions, an almost surreal effect. I had stayed up late the night before reading about the Spanish Conquistadors and their brutal life and death battles with the Aztec Indians among the pyramids in what is now Mexico City, and some of the graphic images remained imprinted on my mind. The rays of the full moon filtering through the smoke from the cooking fires could have been very much like what the Spaniards viewed as they saw in the distance the Indians sacrificing their comrades on the stone altars of the terraced steps of a temple. The soldiers would watch with fear as they saw the Indian priest lift his curved obsidian knife and cut open the soldier's chest and pull out his beating heart and offer it to his gods. He could have been thinking, "There but for the grace of God, go I."

The drumming continued and I remembered that the sound of the snakeskincovered drum was the last thing the captives heard before they died a horrible death among these heathens in a godforsaken land far from home. After this ritual, the bodies of the Spaniards were kicked down the high steps of the pyramid. There, the Indian butchers waiting below, cut off the arms and feet and flayed the skin off the faces. The tender parts were kept to be eaten and the rest was thrown to the animal pit. The Spaniards' flayed faces, with the beards still on, were later dressed "like a glove" and kept for ceremonies. This was sometimes the price the Conquistadors paid for their quest for Mexican gold.

My gruesome and grisly thoughts were shattered by the snarling of Ace and the squealing of the scattering goats as the dog took a chunk out of the goat that had been causing the banging. This goat had been banging his head against the shack my hammock was tied to in an attempt to get at some food on the other side of the wall, and all he got for his troubles was a bite on the ass by an angry foreign dog. I was wide awake now and I was wondering—if it were 400 years earlier on this exact location, who would I have been more afraid of, Mario and his Spanish ancestors or the Indians and their Aztec ancestors? They both would have been brutal and savage enemies. The goats had calmed down and the village slept quietly, but I could not join them. I was left to spend the next hours thinking about what might have been.

I was happy to see the eastern sky change from black darkness to gray to a faint yellow, and at last, a brilliant gold. It was going to be a pretty day. The goats were on their feet and inching toward the eastern edge of the village. Someone opened the gate and they streamed out at a gallop to search for some tasty grass for breakfast.

As soon as the goats were gone, two women appeared from out of nowhere, and with rake-like brooms, cleaned up the streets and the spaces between the shacks. Next came men with basins of dirty water to throw into the street, and the cycle of village life started all over again for another day. Ace got to his feet, growled a couple of times and looked at me as if to ask, "What's for breakfast, boss?" He remembered where he had gone to relieve himself last night, crawled through the fence, found the old tree stump, and returned. I followed him, and we were ready for whatever the day was to bring. I started a small fire in the cook stove and heated some water for tea and warmed up a can of stew. I shared the stew and some tortillas with Ace and met Mario as he was coming from his father's shack. I asked him how his father was doing and he said he was still sleeping. I offered him some hot water and instant coffee, and he eagerly accepted. I had found that instant coffee was always a good way to start the day with rural people.

I told Mario that I wanted to uncover any other veins of potential ore on both sides of the river, so I would need the two guys with the shovels. We spent the rest of the morning digging and sampling and by noon, I was ready to wrap up the inspection. Mario had explained to me the hierarchy of the village, and following his suggestion, I distributed my parachute canopy, its pack and assorted hardware, and any food I had left over to the village headman and left it up to him to hand it out. I kept Ace's chute and harness, the cargo container and my geology tools, and we were ready to bid farewell to the townspeople. Most of the natives stayed inside their shacks, and the only one to say goodbye was the headman.

There wasn't much more Mario could do here to help in the inspection of the property, so we decided that he could go back to Zacatecas by airplane. He could walk with Ace and me to the landing zone we had picked out from the air and carry the samples we had dug up from the property. Ace and I would be picked up first by Raul, then I would return to pick up Mario. That would save him another week of walking and bus riding. I imagined that this back and forth was getting old, as this would be his third trip in a month.

We made pretty good time while we were walking down the canyon bottom along the river. Recent flood water had left a lot of rocks stirred up along the water's edge so it would have not been feasible to land the "Bug" down there. It was a good call to choose the land above the cliffs as a landing zone. Ace had been running in and out of the water and jumping from rock to rock. We were passing through an area of sharp slate and flint rocks, and I noticed that there was blood in the water and that Ace was limping badly. I called him out of the water and inspected his paws. He had cut the pads on his two front paws on the sharp rocks, and it was painful for him to walk.

This was a problem that we did not need. The cuts were deep, and they were bleeding badly. We had almost reached the bend in the river that I had calculated was the place where we should begin to climb up the cliffs. We stopped and I used my KA-BAR to cut strips from Ace's parachute to make bandages to wrap his cut paws. I tied the bandages tightly, but they just slowed the bleeding and it was apparent that there was no way that the dog was going to be able to climb this steep slope.

I was carrying the radio, Ace's parachute, the cargo container, the geologic tools and my weapon. Mario was carrying a sack containing about fifty pounds of rock and dirt samples that we were taking back to Zacatecas to be assayed. We found a place where we could hide the rock samples, the parachute, the container and the tools. Mario could come back for these things later, but we had to have the radio. Now, Mario would carry the radio, and I would carry Ace as far up the slope as I could and then we would switch loads.

As we were sorting this out, we heard shouting from up the river and two young men from Mario's village came running up to us. "Your father. He is dying. You come quick," one kid shouted.

Mario was stunned, and so was I. What in the hell could happen next, I wondered.

Lots, I was to find out.

Mario looked dazed. He stammered, "I must go, jefe."

Before I could think, I blurted out, "No, we must get to the top of the hill!"

Mario stood there in a state of confusion. I shoved the radio into his arms and shouted, "Let's go!" I bent over and picked up Ace and resting the side of his body on my back, and his legs on either side of my neck, I started to climb, clawing hand over hand up the slope.

I came to a small ledge and was pausing to get my breath when I saw a sudden, rapid movement in the shadows. It was a snake, a really big snake. I instantly reached for the .25 automatic in my shoulder holster and as my right arm crossed over in front of my face, I felt a sharp pain in my forearm and a blow that knocked me backwards. As I fell, I dropped Ace and tumbled down the slope. The snake fell with me, and on top of me, and as I hit, its fangs ripped a chunk of meat out of my arm. I was panic-stricken and laying face down in the dirt as I tried to get my gun out of its holster. The snake's body thrashed back and forth and, I guess, tried to bite me a couple more times as I tried to get away from him. Finally he was no longer looking me in the eye and had slithered under the rocks. The adrenaline was surging through my body and by the time I had freed my weapon, the bastard was gone. I was shaking badly as I frantically looked around for Ace. He was under my body, not saying anything, and I was sure he was wondering what was going on.

I shouted to Mario, "Quick, help me get the dog up the hill!" To one of the kids, I yelled, "You, take the radio!"

Mario and I pushed and pulled Ace about half way up the slope. When I saw this wasn't the way to do it, I yelled to Mario, "Help me get the dog on my back!" I was still running on adrenaline and when I topped the hill, I kept on moving for another ten yards before I stopped. I glanced from side to side in the hopes I could recognize a landmark or anything else to tell me whether we were on the correct mesa and pickup point. I didn't see a thing that looked familiar. Damn, I hoped we had guessed right when we made the turn down at the river. I dropped to my knees and Ace slid off my back. I looked at my arm and the blood was pumping out at the same rate as my labored breathing and something in my past training said this is good. I had my KA-BAR and it was good and sharp, but something in my past training said, we don't cut snake bites and suck out the poison anymore. So I just looked at it and let it bleed.

I glanced up and Mario and his two friends were standing there waiting for instructions. I didn't know for sure we were on the correct mesa, but I did know that we were going to need some firewood. I told the men to quickly get some brush and small branches and pile them out in the clearing so they were ready to be set on fire.

I was beginning to calm down and think more clearly so I told Mario: "Go to your father. Thank you for helping me. I will return to pick you up in two days, in this spot."

Mario said, "Adios, jefe," and he and his two friends ran down the hill.

It was two o'clock. Raul was supposed to be here at three. Ace had been taking all the action in and he just lay there and stayed quiet. This animal was amazing. He could read my mind, at least sense my moods, and act accordingly. I was sure that his paw pads hurt and he wanted to tell me that as he tried to pull the bandages off and lick the cuts. My arm was beginning to throb and swell and the bleeding had stopped, but was still oozing, and small patches of blue and purple began to appear at the edges of the wound. I had never been bitten by a rattlesnake before, but I would guess that if the poison didn't kill you, the fright sure could. I knew that my life was in some kind of danger and I should see a doctor as soon as possible, but I also knew that getting excited was also bad, so I told myself, "Calm down."

About a quarter to three, I heard the sound of an aircraft engine. I got up to light the signal fire, but he was overhead before I got to the pile of brush. It was a red airplane and it had to be Raul and the "Bug." The radio was on standby, so I pressed the mike button and requested Raul to come in. He did, right away. I asked him to circle the pickup point and he was right over us. He radioed that there was a tree about half way down the clearing where he wanted to land and requested that I knock it down. I told him, "Negative, we have an emergency down here and get that damned airplane on the ground just as soon as possible."

He must have sensed the lingering fear in my voice and said, "Roger that. I'm on my way down. I'll let you take it off."

There was no wind but he made a low pass over the area he would duplicate on landing and pulled up and went around. After a long final approach, he put the "Bug" down and stood on the brakes. He didn't roll a hundred feet. I picked up Ace and we fast walked to the plane to meet him. He saw the blood all over my arm and pants so he didn't offer to shake my hand.

"What's up,?" he asked.

"Snake bite," I replied.

"Can you fly it with that arm?" he anxiously asked. My arm was hurting but I knew that was going to be a risky takeoff, so if we busted our asses, it was going to be my fault.

"No sweat," I said. He set the brakes, idled down the engine and jumped out. He climbed into the back seat, strapped in and I handed Ace to him. Ace sniffed him a time or two, recognized him and gave his little smile that everything was OK. Raul snapped the short leash on Ace and they were all set.

I climbed in the front seat, strapped in and looked the cockpit over. Everything looked good, so I spun the plane around and taxied back as far as I could go and still remain on solid ground. I turned her around, put the brakes full on, set the flaps and ran up the engine to max power. I said a silent prayer and released the brakes. The 150-horse engine and the new prop bit into the air and we were rolling down the clearing. It was then that I saw the tree Raul had mentioned but it was too late to stop now. I held the nose down and pulled back on the stick at the last minute. No sweat. We cleared the tree by a good foot, or maybe a few more. I set a course for Zacatecas and Raul said, "What about Culiacan or Mazatlan?"

"I can get better treatment in Zacatecas and they won't give me any lip about treating Ace as a person," I replied.

I kept the throttle at full power and we climbed toward Zacatecas. We declared an emergency at Zacatecas airport and made a straight-in approach. I landed on the taxiway and drove up to my hangar. I jumped out and Raul handed Ace to me. I put him down and he knew enough to stay put until Raul got out to pick him up. I got back into the airplane and after Raul opened the door, taxied the "Bug" in to the hangar. We got in Raul's truck and we were on our way to the hospital.

We went into the emergency room and I showed the doctor my arm. He said, "No problem." He commended me on opening the wound to let it bleed and help wash out the poison. I said that he would have to give the credit to that bastard snake. If I ever see him again, I will tell him that the doctor paid him a compliment, before I blow his head off.

The doctor cleaned the wound, gave me a shot of something and said that I had better stay overnight. I agreed. I had taken enough chances for today.

The doctor took the parachute cloth off Ace's wounds, cleaned the cuts, put some salve on the pads, bandaged them and told him, "Stay off of your paws for the next couple of days." Ace and I shared a room. We didn't take a bath and were both asleep in less than ten minutes.

22
The German

Felix Mendoza had several pilots working for him at his flying service and one was a German national named Heinrich Muller from Hamburg, Germany, who was now a Mexican citizen. From the top of his blonde, brush haircut to the soles of his Luftwaffe flying boots, his very being screamed "Nazi storm trooper."

I hated him from the very moment we were being introduced and he spat out with contempt, "So you are the big, bad American super parachutist. You know, we Germans are the ones who invented the 'lightning war' using paratroopers. We are the best in the world."

I answered with, "Perhaps you have never heard of the 82nd Airborne Division at Normandy or the 101st Airborne at the Battle of the Bulge or Bastogne?" I looked him square in the eyes and withdrew my hand. He turned on his heel and walked away. Any relationship with this thick-headed jerk was doomed from the start. I told Felix that I did not want to fly with this guy and if I must, it had to be an extraordinary emergency before he should send him to pick me up.

I would see him from time to time at the airport, or at a small cantina where I would stop to have a beer after being picked up by one of Felix's pilots after a jump into the sierras. We never exchanged greetings or, if we did, it was under our breath and it would begin with "That son of a bitch..."

When he was flying, he always carried a beautiful German Army pistol called the Luger. This was a collector's weapon,

much-prized by American infantrymen and paratroopers during
World War II. When he wasn't flying, he carried a .32 caliber
automatic in a shoulder holster, concealed, but worn so that
everybody knew he was armed and dangerous. I don't know
where he got the gun permits, but I was guessing that he was
paying some hefty bribes to hang on to them.

When he wanted to be particularly obnoxious, which was
often, he wore a German flying jacket with the Nazi flag sewn
inside the rear lining and a six inch black swastika on a white
background on the right shoulder. My blood would boil when I
saw this jacket, and I wished I could jam the whole damn thing
down his throat. He wasn't much of a pilot and was considered
ham-handed, at best. He flew the airplane as if he was driving a
truck and his landings were one bounce after another, even at
sea level. He treated the ground personnel and mechanics with
complete disrespect and, I'm sure, that if Felix was not so well
liked, Muller's aircraft would find its tanks filled with a mixture
of water and sugar with every fill-up of aviation gas.

Felix kept him on as a pilot because it was difficult to find someone who was willing to work part time. Felix would not let him
fly passengers, even on sightseeing flights, because of his attitude
and disposition. Muller would hang out at the terminal in hopes
of picking off a female tourist or two, but if he did, it was usually
some ugly old maid from the midwest. He was relegated to flying
cargo in and out of small airstrips on coffee plantations and he
was assigned an old Cessna 170 that had its doors removed to
make it easier to load and unload the cargo.

Late one afternoon, I stopped in to have a beer at the "Blue
Moon" cantina after returning from a jump in the "tierra caliente"
of southern Michoacan. As one of the waitresses behind the bar
slid the cool bottle of beer down the counter, I noticed a large,
black shiner on her eye.

"How did you get that?" I asked. She scowled and nodded
toward a table where Muller, wearing his Nazi flying jacket, was
regaling a group of British tourists about his exploits during World
War II, in Mexico, no less. He saw me at the bar and noticeably
raised his voice so I would be sure to hear. The tale he was telling
was when he had worked for an old and distinguished shipping

firm in Vera Cruz during the height of the war. His main job was to receive and decode secret messages giving the departure times of cargo ships and oil tankers from Mexican and South American seaports. After work, he would drive up into the foothills behind Vera Cruz and, using a high-powered radio transmitter, feed this information to German submarines lurking in the Gulf of Mexico and the Atlantic Ocean.

He laughed about being decorated by the German government for his contributions to the German war effort. He was proud of being responsible for the large tonnage of shipping sunk by the U-boats and the allied sailors who drowned in the shark-infested waters of the Gulf and in the Ocean. "The Germans would have won the war if it wasn't for the help the international Jew bankers gave to the United States during the war," he told them.

He looked at me and laughed. I felt like slitting his damn throat with my "KABAR" knife, but Mexico has a law against killing snakes in a bar. I left my beer untouched and walked out. I would not remain in a place that would have that bastard as a customer. One of these days....

My day would come, and it did. One day in late June, while I was working out of the airport in Acapulco, I received a call from a wealthy businessman, a friend of Don Diego. He had a son in college who was writing a report when he found a story about a group of Mexican miners working a gold claim in the mountains above Acapulco. During a period of unrest the miners were forced to abandon the claim when they were attacked by Indians. They never went back, but they did make a map and the young man found a copy of this map hidden away in the research book he was working with in the library. He was excited and asked me, "Can you find the location of this claim from the air and then jump in and do a survey?"

I told him anything is possible and I would be willing to see if it could be accomplished. The first thing would be to look at the map and determine if it were authentic. We ended the conversation with the promise that he would take care of the authentication process and get back to me if he thought it was worth the investment.

The next week he called and said he was satisfied that the map was made in the 1870s and asked how I suggest they proceed. I said I thought that the best thing to do was hire an aircraft and fly over the target area and see if we could locate any of the landmarks marked on the map.

That sounded like a good idea to him. Could I meet him and his son at the Acapulco airport on Saturday at 10 o'clock? I could, and I would have an aircraft ready to go. After we made the inspection flight, we could determine where we go from here.

We all met on time at the airport and piled into Felix's Cessna 180 and headed north and east. The target area was about 100 miles from Acapulco and in some very rugged country. We were on site in less than a hour and we began the search at 3,000 feet above the ground so that we would have a broad overview of the countryside. Felix held the aircraft straight and level as the three passengers hunched over their copies of the map.

My clients, the father, Señor Rivera, and his son Humberto, were products of the upper class who ran a large business in Mexico City, and I could see that this was going to be an adventure for them, although a vicarious one. We were making a grid search and as we completed our first north-south pass Humberto shouted out, "Look," and he pointed excitedly to a large spire of rock that had a small rounded pile of rocks on either side of it.

Sure enough, it was on the map, and using that point as a reference, we soon saw, or thought we saw, two other outcroppings that appeared on our maps. I asked Felix to drop down so that we could get a closer look at what was on the ground. Felix said, "Make sure your safety belts are tight," and nosed over the 180 in a fairly steep dive. Both Humberto and his dad blanched, or more exactly, they turned a light green, and clutched at anything they could hold on to. The air was smooth at 3,000 feet, but down on the deck it was turbulent at this time of the day. I pointed out various features that indicated that some mining activity had taken place here, but my clients were too busy trying to keep their breakfasts down to look, or even to care, about the things on the ground that were racing by at a dizzying pace.

Felix pulled the Cessna up in a steep climb and asked if we wanted to take a closer look. Señor Rivera swallowed a couple of times and in a squeaky voice said, "This is it, I am sure of it." Humberto nodded in agreement, as we climbed to smoother air.

I had seen what appeared to be many prospect holes and some drifts that ran into the sides of some of the rock formations.

It was clear that someone had spent a lot of time trying to discover something, but what?

"What now?" I asked as we circled above the target.

"I say, we go for it. I think this is what we are looking for. Let's go back to Acapulco, please," said Señor Rivera.

We landed at the airport, and our passengers were still a little shaky on their feet as they walked to the passenger terminal.

"I'll call you when I get back to my office," Señor Rivera said. Humberto indicated that he didn't feel so hot, and waved as he headed for the bathroom. It looked like we had a deal, but I would have to wait until I got a call from Señor Rivera.

The call came on Monday morning and Señor Rivera asked if I could meet with his lawyer that afternoon to iron out the details of having me parachute into the sierras to explore for gold at a site we had decided to be the prospect he was interested in. I figured that I could leave tomorrow morning, make the jump, spend two days inspecting the property, take ore samples, spend one day walking out to a deserted airstrip, be airlifted back to Acapulco, have the sample assayed, write a report with my recommendations and submit it to Señor Rivera within a week.

I gave them a price, they gave me a check for 50 percent of it, they signed some worthless legal documents that gave them the rights to anything I discovered (it was up to them to determine who owned the property we were exploring) and we had a deal.

I talked to Felix to see if he was available to drop me in the morning and the first of several things that were to go wrong with this adventure popped up. Felix was having personal problems and he had to be in Chilpancingo tonight and would not be back until late tomorrow. I did not want to train another jump pilot on such short notice, so I would wait for Felix. The extra day gave me some time to catch up on some paperwork and do a little reading, and I was well rested by the time Wednesday rolled around.

We took off at first light and were over the target in about an hour. We circled a couple of times at about 300 feet and I dropped my digging tools, without a parachute, and we climbed to jump altitude. I dropped a wind drift indicator and it told me that wind was not going to be a problem at this early hour of the morning. My drop zone was going to be a spot in the center of what appeared to be the remains of a group of ancient adobe buildings.

I exited at three thousand feet and pulled the ripcord when I reached terminal. I had maintained a solid stable position in free fall and I waited for the canopy to unpack. Nothing happened. Damn it. Another pilot chute hesitation. Either the pilot chute spring is getting worn out or my body position was perfect and I had a low pressure over my back—a rare occasion for me. I dropped one shoulder to change the air flow and I was starting to tumble as the canopy deployed. I had a wicked opening shock than left my head full of shooting stars and my body aching. I had not packed my chute with the new invention, the sleeve, as it was just some thing more to pack out. I don't think I will make that mistake again. I had made the 4 line cut and my rate of descent was normal but I made a turn close to the ground to miss a large rock and I landed on an oscillation and slammed into the ground. Something told me, this was going to be a rough day.

I checked myself for broken bones, waved to Felix to tell him I was OK, picked up my tools and I was ready to go to work. I did a thorough walkaround and by late afternoon, I was ready to start sampling and mapping the property. There were a couple of quartz veins mixed in with metamorphic rock, but nothing jumped out at me to shout these diggings were something special. The prospect holes could have been eighty or ninety years old but the weathering had caused them to cave in and the quartz veins that the miners had followed into the formations did not show me any indications that they had led to anything unusual. This was going to be pretty boring work, but I was getting well paid for doing this exploration work, so I did it and enjoyed it as much as possible.

The night fell, and it started to rain. Not hard, but hard enough to make it uncomfortable if you were out in it. I wasn't. I found an outcropping of rock and I made a fairly soft bed in the loose dirt with my parachute. The next day was the same as the first and by then I had accumulated about two hundred pounds of dirt and rock that I had sampled. I sorted that down to about fifty pounds of high grade and marked the locations on my map. I was going over the final report in my head and unless the samples revealed something that I could not see or sense, this trip was going to be chalked up to experience.

It rained again that evening and I spent a peaceful night. I was up at dawn, packed my parachutes, my pick and shovel and put all the samples in a white collection bag and started down the hill. I followed a dry stream bed for a while and the going was pretty good, but I had to leave it when I started a series of up and down climbs to keep on course to the airstrip. That night I spent in a natural cave and again had a restful sleep.

I was up again at dawn and managed to follow several streams downhill until I had the airstrip in sight. From then on, it was cross country and the going was a little slower but I still made my destination about a half hour early. Felix was due to pick me up in about a half hour. The hard part of the job was over, and I could start to unwind. How wrong I was.

Crash

One o'clock came and went and no Felix. At two o'clock, I was beginning to get worried and at three o'clock, I was mad. This was very unlike Felix. In my business, you put a lot of trust in the people who support you. It can be a matter of life and death if you are injured or you are stranded out in the jungle or the high sierras by a pilot who pledged to pick you up at a certain time and fails to do so.

I was having dark thoughts, when I heard the drone of an engine and then saw an aircraft coming down the canyon at the far end of the runway. "That's a pretty stupid approach," I thought. Felix should know better than that.

As he was over the end of the runway, I could see it was a Cessna 170. No, it couldn't be, I thought. As the aircraft bounced to a landing, I knew my worst fears were realized. It was Muller. He rolled out and spun the airplane around in a sloppy circle and when I approached, he snarled, "Get your ass in here, Yankee. I don't have all day to wait on any prima donna."

He kept the engine running at a high speed and while he stood on the brakes, he still had a hard time keeping it under control. I had field-packed my main parachute in the container and I slipped into the harness so I could use the parachute canopy as a buffer against the rear wall of the passenger compartment. I tossed in my sack of samples, my reserve parachute and then my tools and we were rolling down the dirt airstrip for take off.

Muller used all of the runway to get the plane into the air and instead of turning to get out of the canyon, continued flying straight ahead. The walls of the canyon were closing in on us and if Muller did not make a turn while we had the airspeed, we were going to be in real trouble. We were climbing slowly, but we were not gaining altitude above the canyon floor. I was beginning to worry so I tossed out the sack of rock samples to lighten the load, but that fifty pounds didn't do a damn thing to help us. Pretty soon we were going to be at the point of no return and we were going to smash against the face of the cliff at the end of the canyon.

I snapped my reserve parachute onto the D-rings of my parachute harness and grabbed Muller by the shoulder and yelled in his ear, "You dumb square-headed son of a bitch. You had better turn this thing around or you're not going to make it." Sweat was running down his thick neck and he had a death grip on the controls. I noticed that I had a hold on his shoulder where he wore that damned black and white swastika patch and I had a wild thought. I could reach down to my right boot, grab my "KA-BAR" knife and cut that hated patch off his jacket like an Apache scalping an enemy or, better yet, sink the blade into his back.

"Pull up, you bastard," I screamed, and he screamed back at me, "If you don't like it Yankee, get the hell out." And I did.

As I left the airplane, it was beginning to shake and fall off on one wing. I knew it was about to stall. My weight dropping away gave the Cessna a few more moments of life, but it was doomed. I was on my back as I saw the plane drop off to the right as the "square headed son of a bitch" tried to make a right turn and stalled out when he lost what little lift he had and fell out of the sky. I yanked hard on the ripcord of the reserve and got a wicked opening shock and the canopy hit me in the face as it streamed by my head. The chute opened immediately, and it was a good thing that it did. I slammed into the top of a tree and it barely broke my fall before my feet touched the canyon floor.

I did not see the Cessna hit, but I heard a muffled thud and then a secondary explosion. I hoped Felix had insurance on the aircraft. I didn't think twice about the pilot.

I had landed in a side canyon among a big jumble of rocks. I laid there for about ten minutes and breathed in the clear mountain air. It was great to be alive. I got to my feet, field-packed my reserve with my main and sat down again. Should I spend a couple of hours trying to find the wreckage in the hope that bastard was still alive, or should I walk on down the canyon to the airstrip and see what happens next? No contest. I started walking downhill.

It was rough going at first, but got easier as I lost elevation and the canyon widened. About five hundred yards down the canyon, I found my sack of rock samples. Things were beginning to go my way. Now I could finish the report and I would not have to go back in to collect more samples. Dusk was just beginning to darken the sky when I reached the end of the airstrip. It was sheer pleasure to walk on that thousand feet of dirt runway. I got to the end and threw my parachutes and samples on the ground. After a while, I made a bed with my parachutes and stretched out to get a good night's sleep. It rained again that night. I had no protection from the elements and I got soaked. I was wet, but I was alive.

The next morning at about 6:30, I heard the beautiful sound of an aircraft engine. As the aircraft made a sharp turn over the end of the runway for the final approach, I knew it was Felix.

His first words after he landed, turned the plane around and cut the engine were, "What in the hell happened?" Mine were, "Where in the hell have you been?" We shook hands and we both laughed. We loaded my gear into the 180 and took off. After the wheels cleared the ground, Felix gained airspeed and made a gentle turn to the left and we were out of the canyon, Now, that wasn't too hard, was it? We gained altitude and made a couple of passes over the crash site, but we could not see any sign of the 170.

On the flight back to Acapulco, Felix explained that his personal problems—a pending divorce from a wife who hated the flying business—required him to be in court in Chilpancingo early yesterday morning and he couldn't get back in time to fly in and get me. He asked his on-duty pilot to do the job but Muller had insisted that he be given the honor of picking up the Yankee parachutist. He wanted to give him "the ride of his life"—and he did. Thank you Heinrich, you made my day.

When we got back to Acapulco, Felix organized a search team and flew them into the airstrip the next morning. When the team got to the crash site, they were a day late. Local Indians had been there earlier and had taken anything of value. All that was left was a skeleton of the airplane, no instruments, no seat, no engine, no nothing. Muller had been killed in the crash and the Indians buried him in a shallow grave, stripped bare, down to his skivvies.

Now, when I am sitting alone in front of my fireplace and I think about my time in Mexico, a picture comes back to me. The sun is setting and somewhere, in the Sierra Madre del Sur, an Indian is sitting at his camp fire dressed in a leather flying jacket, with the white and black swastika sewn on the right shoulder sleeve, while his companion admires a shiny pair of Luftwaffe boots that are keeping his feet toasty warm and his brother polishes a beautiful German Army Luger pistol. And, somewhere, in the depths of the cold waters of the Atlantic Ocean and the Gulf of Mexico, groups of American and British Merchant Marine sailors, condemned to sleep forever in a watery grave far from home by the treachery of Heinrich Muller, smile and give a "thumbs up."

23
What Happened to Fidel— What If?

D ave had an exhibition jump lined up for Coca-Cola in Acapulco but had to cancel out, so I gladly agreed to fill in for him. After the jump, who should show up but Ernesto Sanchez of the Revolutionary Army to Free Cuba. He was one of the throng of autograph seekers waiting for me at the Coca-Cola booth on the beach when I dropped my parachute on the sand and accepted their applause.

He greeted me like an old friend, and I was actually glad to see him. I was more than a little interested in what had happened to him and Castro's army after I had last seen them at the rebel's training camp. We agreed to meet at a hotel down the beach about an hour after I had fulfilled Dave's contractual commitments of talking to members of the press and signing autographs.

After the crowd faded away, I met Ernesto at the appointed time and place. I ordered two beers for each of us and paid for them before Ernesto had a chance to reach for the bill, just in case he had intended to. I didn't want to embarrass him on the chance he did not have the cost of the drinks. He looked like he had the same clothes on as when I first met him, so I played it safe.

I felt kind of sorry for him, as I figured when he showed Castro the letter I had left for him at the guard gate, the "maximum leader" would blow his stack and chew on him as the bearer of bad news. I broke the ice by asking him what he had been doing since we had last talked. I had followed the news in Time magazine about Castro's landing in Cuba, but the coverage was spotty and I had no idea how the revolution was going. He seemed hesitant to talk and clearing his throat he said, "The leader and his army landed in Cuba early last December."

I stopped him and said, "I am very interested, so please start your story on the night I left the letter for you. If you have the time, I would really like to hear the story in detail to see what might have happened to me."

He relaxed a little and continued, "When I take your letter to the leader, he is very mad and throw it on the ground and say bad things. At the time, things are not going good for us and the immigration people are saying that we are going to have to go back to Cuba or pay more money. We continue training and gathering more men and, suddenly, about three weeks after you leave, the leader tells us we are leaving, but not all at once so the officials do not know we are going. We go, one by one, in our cars to a little town on the coast north of Mexico City. There is a small boat there. I am surprised when they say this is the boat we are going to sail back to Cuba.

"More men show up than can fit on the boat, so the leader he have to choose who can go. He make speech and thank us for being patriotic and wanting to free Cuba but he can take only so many men, and the rest of us can join him in Cuba on our own. I was very sad that I was not chosen to go on the boat, but I have no special skills. I am now working construction in Mexico City, and I will go to Cuba this summer and join my companeros in the sierras when I make the money for transportation."

He looked like he really meant it when he said he was sad. He paused and finished his first beer. I asked him a very important question that had bothered me ever since I left the letter for him at the camp.

"From the information you have, would it have made any difference in the success or failure of the landing if I and my parachutists had jumped in front of the landing?" He took a long drag on his beer and looked off in the distance before he answered.

"You and your squad would have been killed or captured and then killed, as the government commander had said no rebels should be left alive to go back to the cities and form new groups to again attack the dictator Batista.

"If you would have parachuted on the date when the leader and his men were to have landed in Cuba, you would have faced the full force of the government troops, and your eleven brave companeros and you would have a place in the history books of Cuba as the first to give your lives for the freedom of Cuba.

"Those of us who were left here in Mexico did not know what happened to our men until about six weeks after they left on the boat. We tried to call our friends in Cuba, but all they could tell us was that the Army had said that the leader and his army were all killed or captured or were being hunted down

Castro with His Favorite Rifle, 1958

like animals in the mountains. One day, a member of our exile group received a call from one of the men who had left on the boat. It was Faustino Perez, one of our commanders and a man we could trust. He said that the leader had sent him back to Havana to tell us, and all who would listen, what had happened to Fidel and his army.

"He told us that many things went wrong as soon as they left Mexico. They had much trouble with the engine, and the water was very rough and stormy, and many men got sick. The boat was overloaded, and there was very little room for the men. They were going much slower than they had wanted to go and they fell behind the schedule. They were supposed to land at a small dock where they could unload what heavy equipment they had on the shore of Oriente Province north of Niquero."

He smiled and said, "I remember that you were very interested and wanted to know where we would be landing. Do you have a pen?"

I handed him my favorite pen—the one I used to autograph pictures and other things for my admiring fans—and he took a paper napkin and drew a pretty good map of the island of Cuba, pinpointing the cities of Havana, Santiago de Cuba, Guantanamo Bay and Niquero.

"You and your parachutists would have landed on a rise above the highway and protected our men from the dictator's troops coming from the military base at Manzanillo." He jabbed his pen into the napkin at a place that looked like it was about fifty miles north and west of the landing site and said, "That is Manzanillo."

Fidel Castro's Landing Sites in Cuba

My thoughts jumped back to the time when I was running the stats on what aircraft had the range and the load capacity to take us to and return from what now would have been a suicide mission to Cuba. The C-122 from Yucatan would not have made it, for sure. The Northrop Raider would have been, at best, a poor choice and that left the old, reliable C-47, the same ancient bird that dropped our troops at Normandy.

I'm sure I could have found a C-47 in South America and a crew that was willing to do the job, so it would have been a go. But the thought of being a footnote in the Cuban history books did not particularly appeal to me as I sat here drinking a cold beer on the beach at Acapulco, having just signed a bunch of autographs for adoring señoritas.

I grabbed my pen from Ernesto just as he was slipping it into his pocket. Ernesto continued, "The boat, it was called Granma, missed the place where the city people who were supporting us had a Jeep and two trucks and about fifty men, plus supplies, waiting to take the leader and our companeros into the sierras. Instead, the boat landed about twenty-five miles south of Niquero, in a swamp, and all the equipment and a big radio were lost. Faustino said that eight men were also lost. He thinks they drowned..

"When they got to dry land, they were shot at by two patrol boats and an airplane. The leader, he cursed and said that the government people were tipped off about where they were going to land. They tried to hide in the low bushes as they worked their way toward the sierras. They had no food or water, but they had to keep going or the soldiers would catch them. On the third day they came upon an area of sugar cane and the men were able to chew the cane and get something in their bellies. They paused to rest, but the soldiers found them and set the cane field on fire and shot the companeros as they run away. Everyone scattered and Faustino, my cousin, Universo—he was a bodyguard of the leader—and the leader were the only ones left in their group. Everyone else was killed or captured. They could hear the soldiers shooting the prisoners, and they were afraid so they remained hidden under the cane.

"They hid from the soldiers for two days and kept moving forward. Then they came upon a farm where the owner was a friend of the revolution, and he gave them shelter. Faustino thinks the soldiers thought they had killed all the rebels and went back to their barracks and quit looking for them. The leader and his two companeros wait at the farm for any men who might have escaped the soldiers and finally several more men show up, including the leader's little brother and the South American, and they move on toward the sierras.

"The leader gave Faustino orders to make his way through the lines and return to Havana to help the city people and to tell the members of the M-26-7 movement that he and his army were in the sierras and continuing the fight.

"It take several days, but Faustino he make it back to Havana and the leader and twelve men, all that was left of the army that had departed Mexico, sneak into the sierras. They did not have rifles for everyone but the leader he make a strong speech and say, now he is sure they are going to win."

Ernesto paused to down the rest of his beer, and I ordered two more for each of us.

I said, "What's going to happen to you now? What can you do to help the M-26- 7 group from Mexico, and when will you leave for Cuba?"

"I will try to raise money and recruit new members from the exiles here in Mexico, and I will leave just as soon as I earn the money for my transportation back to Cuba. I have been told that the first thing I should do when I get back home is to contact the M-26-7 group in Santiago de Cuba in the Oriente province. They will know how to get in contact with the leader and, although they suffered many losses, they have strong leadership and will continue the fight.

"Their commander is a young man named Frank Pais, I met him here in Mexico when he came to coordinate the uprising with the leader's landing in Cuba, and I was very impressed. He was with another revolutionary group. The leader convinced him to join with us, and he made him part of his top staff. I will probably have enough money to leave here by the first of June and go straight to Santiago. I will not stop to see my mother in Havana. I will wait until we take over the capitol. Then I will be a hero, and my mother will be proud."

The sun was beginning to set as we left the hotel and walked to the parking lot. We shook hands, and I slipped him a twenty. "Have a beer on me when you get to Havana. Lots of luck, companero." He smiled as he slid behind the wheel of his beat-up Volks and drove off into who knows what or where. I often wonder what happened to him.

So, if I had gone on that mission, I would probably be in an unmarked grave, along with eleven Cuban companeros, overlooking a little town called Niquero in Cuba. What an end to the career of a bright young parachuting mining engineer who still had a helluva lot more to accomplish before he died.

It was going to be a beautiful tropical night, far too nice to spend back in my hotel room, so I decided to take a walk along the beach. I was a little shook up at Ernesto's frank account about what would have probably been my fate if I had led that jump into Cuba. I pondered about how life has some strange twists and turns, and sometimes a higher power has to step in and yank you back from making some terrible mistakes. From the start, my sixth sense warned me that this was a Mickey Mouse operation, but it was adventure, high adventure, and I was too damn bull-headed to let it pass.

It sickens me to think that Col. Bitner, that no-good son of a bitch, might have had a large part in saving my life. I was spring-loaded to hate a guy like him in his position when I followed him into his office that day in Mexico City. I had had it up to my eye-balls dealing with worthless slobs like Bitner in the military system who had blocked my efforts to do what I thought was best for my career.

Right now, I am torn between being a full time military officer and leading the carefree life of a parachuting mining engineer. He was the typical glad-handing, ass-kisser who fawned over king-making politicians, who advanced jerks' careers over grunts like me. I convinced myself that it was an act of God, and Bitner did not have a damn thing to do with my not going on that mission.

I was deep in thought when I almost stumbled over a little kid who was playing in the sand. I said, "Sorry bud. How are you doing?"

He looked at me and did a double take and yelled, "Sister, sister, it's the sky man." A beautiful buxom blonde, about 17 or 18, appeared out of the dusk and exclaimed, "It's the parachutist. We saw your parachute jump and, man, that was groovy. Come and meet my dad."

She dragged me over to a family group just picking up their blankets before returning to their hotel. They were a family from Milwaukee and were in Acapulco on a company vacation. We introduced ourselves and after some small talk about what an exciting and carefree life I must lead, the mother said, "You must tell us more about it," and asked if I would like to have dinner with them.

The little kid jumped up and down and squealed, "Yea, Yea!" and the buxom daughter flashed me an enticing smile that said, "I would really like to get to know you, maybe we can get together after dinner." I looked at her and wondered why the Good Lord made young girls so beautiful and desirable.

"Sorry, but I have to leave for Zacatecas right away," I lied. "Maybe another time. It's nice to have met you all." I turned and walked back to my hotel room.

24
Hank

It was a beautiful Sunday morning in Zacatecas, but it wasn't just any Sunday. Today was the day that the bandages were to be removed from Elena's face. This was a festive occasion. Her surgeon, Dr. Mendas, had flown in from Mexico City and he would have the honor of presenting the "new" Elena to the world.

There was bedlam in the room. Maria and Jesus were uncontrollable and Mrs. Martinez was trying to stay calm, but she was shaking like a leaf.

Dr. Mendas asked everyone to close their eyes while he unwound the bandages and then open them on his command.

Not everyone did, of course, and the room erupted with squeals of delight when the last roll of white cloth fell away from her beautiful face.

This was the Elena that we knew was hiding behind those bandages. A beautiful swan, not an ugly duckling. The scene was one of complete happiness and joy, but everyone was crying except Elena. The family and Fr. Lopez were thanking me for making this possible, and it got to be embarrassing, so I told the padre that I had to do some important work on the "Bug" out at the airport.

I was doing some maintenance on the engine when Fr. Lopez drove up in his pickup. As he walked up, I could see that he was holding an envelope in his one hand and a cold beer in the other. I greeted him and said that I was glad to see him, especially on this hot day.

"The telegraph office just delivered this telegram for you and I thought that it might be something of importance," he said.

I thanked him, tore open the envelope, read it and liked what I saw. It was a message that said, "Will be in Chihuahua City Sept. three. Staying Plaza Hotel. Meet me. Will take trip Barranca de Cobre, signed Hank Henderson."

This was great news! Hank Henderson was an old and dear friend of mine from World War II. He was a redneck from Ponca City, Oklahoma, and the first of his kind that I had ever met. He amused me, he amazed me and he surprised me with his outageous way of expressing himself, his off-the-wall actions and his carefree attitude toward life. Everybody called him "Hammering Hank" because of his ability to hit the long ball in baseball and softball, and he was also a pretty good shortstop. Not as good as I was, a fact that was hotly contested by Hank and his fellow crew members, but if not as good, at least a close second.

I met Hank on Tinian Island in the Mariana Islands when a new B-29 crew was assigned to our tent to replace Lt. Mason's crew that had been shot down the day before. He was a tall guy, over six feet, weighed about 190, and rough looking. A tech sergeant, he was the senior enlisted man on the crew and the central fire control gunner. At 23, he was several years older than most of us and when you talked to him, you knew who was in charge.

As he entered our crew's tent, he growled, "Is this bunk taken?"

"You ain't no Yankee, are you?," he asked me.

"Half and half," I replied. "My dad was from Pennsylvania and my mom from the Old Dominion, that's Virginia to you."

He stuck his hand out, and said, "Close enough for government work," and tossed his parachute bag on the cot next to mine.

"How about a drink?" he asked as he pulled a bottle of whiskey from the bag.

"No thanks, I'm a beer drinker."

"That's OK, that just leaves more booze for the grownups," he laughed as he unscrewed the cap from the bottle and threw it on the dirt floor. I gave him a puzzled look and he said, "Back in Oklahoma, when we open a jug, we mean business and we are going to drink it all."

In the weeks that followed, I learned to like Hank a lot, even more so after I had flown several combat missions with him and his crew. In the air, he was a no-nonsense leader and took control of the defensive armament of the bomber when the airplane was under attack. And that included admonishing the crew's over-eager second lieutenant bombardier to "Keep your damn hands off those forward turrets until I tell you to fire, sir."

In late July, 1945, our squadron was pretty badly mauled on a night bombing raid over the heavily-defended Japanese city of Osaka. Among the B-29s that limped back to our airfield on Tinian was Hank's bomber. They had been hit hard by the radar-controlled anti-aircraft guns the Japs had just acquired from Germany and they had flown all the way back from Japan on three engines with most of the crew dead or wounded. A 37-millimeter shell had exploded in the gunner's compartment, killing both waist gunners and badly wounding Hank.

I went to see Hank in the hospital that night, and he was in critical condition. As I left, I told him "Hang in there, and everything is going to be all right."

He looked me in the eye and said, "Jim-Bo, I have about as much chance of getting out of this mess as a one-legged man in an ass-kicking contest."

After we landed from the next mission, I went back to the hospital to see how he was doing, and he was gone—not dead, but on his way back to the States. "It looked real bad for your friend," the nurse said.

So I was surprised to receive a much-forwarded letter from Hank in 1951 saying that he was alive and well and had seen a newspaper clipping about me making a parachute jump in Albuquerque and he was going to track me down to see what made me so damn dumb to make a parachute jump on purpose out of a perfectly good airplane.

Bus Trip

He did not die, as predicted on Tinian Island. He recovered after a year or so in a V.A. hospital in Oklahoma, attended college at the Colorado School of Mines, and was now a geologist working for a large mining company in Tulsa. We exchanged letters for five years, but our paths never crossed. Now his company was sending him to Mexico to inspect two mining properties and this would be a great chance to get together.

The third of September was just two days from now, so I was going to have to hustle to take care of all my obligations here in town. His reference to the Barranca de Cobre was interesting, as we had discussed visiting this rugged canyon region in our letters, but nothing was specific. Just in case, maybe I should take some hiking gear along. Hank met me in the lobby of the Palace Hotel in Chihuahua City and it was great to see him.

I usually don't get too excited over reunions, but this one was something special. Hank and I had seen a lot of action together and he was one of the true friends I had made during the war. We laughed, and joked and in general had a good time.

"You sure beat the odds on that ass-kicking contest, didn't you?" I said.

He gave me a strange look and said, "What are you talking about?" I reminded him of his parting words before he left Tinian and refreshed his memory. He grinned and said, "I was feeling kinda low about that time."

We talked about what had brought him to Mexico and he said that when his company was looking for someone to go down to Mexico, he jumped at the chance. Things were getting dull in Tulsa and he was looking for excitement. The assignment was going to another geologist, but when Hank learned that the mining properties were in and near the legendary Barranca de Cobre, he got the job by telling his boss that he could do it in less time than the other geologist.

His company was interested in two mining properties, one near the town of Urique located in the deepest of the five canyons that form the mystical Barranca country and the other in the canyon carved in the Sierra Tarahumara by the Rio Batopilas.

The next morning we got to the bus station at 6:30 to catch the first-class bus that was to leave at 7 o'clock. The dispatcher said that the bus wasn't going to leave until 8 because the driver had overslept and he couldn't make it until then. A second- class bus was getting ready to leave and maybe we could get a seat on it.

Before I could answer, Hank said, "We'll take it. It will give me a chance to absorb some of the Mexican culture."

I tried to explain to him how the second-class bus system operates, but he had already thrown our backpacks on the top outside rack and they were rapidly being covered with all manner of furniture, pots and pans, bedding and just about anything imaginable. When the bus driver shouted, "Let's go!" we were, fortunately, standing near the door and we were caught in the mad rush and were pushed into the bus.

We ended up with a seat in the middle of the bus and by the time that the driver fought his way to the steering wheel, the bodies were packed so tightly you couldn't see more than six inches in any direction. The stench was overpowering and it promised to get worse as the temperature rose. I tried to open the window on my side, but it was jammed shut.

The campesino in the seat in front of us got his window half way open before the glass shattered. He calmly removed the broken glass and tossed it on the floor. The fresh air felt good and by this time other passengers had managed to open their windows and the movement of the vehicle got the foul air circulating.

I glanced at Hank and gave him a weak smile. The town of Creel, the end of the line for this bus, is about three hundred kilometers west of Chihuahua; this should give Hank ample time to absorb the Mexican culture. "This is Hank's adventure," I thought. "Let's see how far we can go before he's assimilated enough of the culture and says 'I have had sufficient indoctrination'."

We stopped every mile or two to pick up and drop off passengers and soon we had people hanging on the sides and riding on the top of the bus. I was sure that by now the load-carrying ability of this vehicle far exceeded the capacity it was designed to transport.

Our first scheduled stop was at a town called Cuauhtemoc, about 130 kilometers from Chihuahua City. From what I could see from my window, it seemed to be a fair-sized town. But what really surprised me, and caused Hank to get very excited, was a group of girls dressed in typical Mexican clothes. But every one of them was as fair-skinned and as blonde as my first true love, sweet Elaine, whose mother and father were both born in Germany.

There was no way we could get off the bus to check this out, so we just enjoyed the view. I later found out that these strange apparitions were the daughters of Mennonite farmers who settled here in the early nineteen twenties. I made a note to visit this town at a later date.

I thought that the bus was as full as it could get, but I was wrong. The driver's helper lowered a platform at the rear and opened a door, and we had a new annex. Several natives got on board, carrying chickens and leading two goats. A short while after we resumed our journey, two of the chickens got loose and flew into the bus. One landed on Hank's shoulder and relieved herself, much to the amusement of our fellow passengers.

Meanwhile, one of the goats was making its way up the center aisle and using her nose as a pointed prod, was vigorously pushing the people aside. This caused a great deal of squealing and jumping around by the women, who made up most of the standees, as all the seats were taken by men, me and Hank included. This commotion was a great source of amusement to the passengers and brought smiles to the faces of the normally taciturn farmers.

In time, the chickens were collected, the goat was tied down and the passengers settled back into a lethargic state that would help get them through the next 51 kilometers to the junction point of La Junta where the rivers start to flow to the drainage that will take them to the Pacific Ocean.

When the bus pulled into the station at La Junta, both Hank and I had decided that traveling by second-class bus was not the way to make the best use of our limited time. We filed out with the passengers getting off the bus and were almost trampled by the people who rushed to take our seats. After the assistant driver had dug our backpacks out from under the mass of junk that covered them, we went into the station and asked the ticket agent if there was a private contractor for hire who operated between here and Creel. He reluctantly pointed out a garage across the street and we followed his pointed finger.

The owner of the garage owned a World War II Dodge weapons carrier that was the ideal vehicle to travel this road, and we were in luck. A couple had rented the carrier and they were going to Bahuichivo, the place where we would have to start backpacking to get to the Urique River and they would be glad to split the cost of the trip with us. It was a deal and we were to leave in a half an hour.

We chatted with the man and wife—they were from England, and they promised to be good company for the next 200-plus kilometers. There was a cantina next to the garage and, of course, we decided to stop in and have a cold beer while we waited. We sat down, ordered a beer and were relaxing over the good fortune we had to have found a ride so quickly when three rough-looking men appeared from a dark corner where they had been sitting.

They came right over to our table and the biggest of the three said, in broken English, or I think he said in broken English, "We thought we smelled some rotten Texans in our bar and we are going to throw them out in the street."

Damn it! This is the same scenario I had run into a couple of times before in the back country of Mexico. A Mexican laborer who had gone to the United States as an illegal alien had been mistreated or cheated out of his earnings or wages by the American who had employed him, usually a farmer or a rancher in Texas, and the laborer returns to Mexico and he has a grudge that sometimes turns into a hatred for Americans, especially Texans, and to a Mexican who has had too much to drink, all Americans look like Texans. When this laborer encounters an American, a lone American, in the country, away from the law, he takes out this hatred on this American, sometimes with unpleasant results. We were now in such a situation.

The group stepped back from our table and one of them broke a long-necked beer bottle over a chair. Things had turned ugly in a hell of a hurry. Under my jacket I was carrying my .25 automatic in its shoulder holster. Under Mexican law, the gun permit I had been given by Gen. Garcia in Zacatecas was invalid, but Hank and I were about to have the crap beat out of us, or worse, and I knew that groveling and pleading that we were not responsible for the sins of some Texan wasn't going to get us out of this jam. Our backs were to the wall and there was no chance of running.

As the big guy stepped forward, I pulled back my jacket, unsnapped the restrainer flap on the holster, yanked out the weapon and fired. The bullet slammed into the dirt floor, ricocheted with a high-pitched whine and buried itself in the bar. I had intended to fire a warning shot near the big guy, but I came within an inch of hitting him in the crotch. He must have felt the breeze of the slug going by as he reached for his testicles and gasped. "No se permite..., You are not permitted to have..."

The three guys just stood there with their mouths hanging open and the guy with the broken bottle let it fall to the floor. I took a deep breath and said, in a voice I hoped was not high tenor, "Get the hell out of our way!"

We picked up our backpacks and headed for the door just as the garage owner burst in. "What the hell happened?" he demanded to know.

He got the picture right away and said, "We better leave, pronto, right now!"

West to Bahuichivo

The driver of the weapons carrier already had the engine running as Hank and I tossed our backpacks in the rear and piled in after them. I was still shaking from our encounter with the three locals and it was a big relief to sit down.

"Where in the hell did you get that gun?" Hank asked.

"It's a long story. I'll tell you about it later," I replied as I took stock of the situation.

"Man, we almost attended an Oklahoma lynching party, and we were fixing to be the guests of honor," Hank laughed as he slapped me on the back.

We were barely outside the town when the road changed from gravel to deep ruts in the mud made by the tires of many logging vehicles. Our driver shifted down to second gear, then low and finally, into four-wheel drive as we climbed a steep incline. "Soon it will be mucho better," he shouted over the noise created by the grinding of the gears. And it did get better after a mile or so of heavy traffic that diminished as the trucks turned off to other timber-cutting areas.

Our two traveling companions were Albert and Betty Baxter from Manchester, England. He was a professor of mathematics at a university and she was a retired elementary school teacher. They had been in Mexico for three weeks and this was their first trip outside of the big cities. Al sat up front with the driver and he had a map and a guide book on the seat beside him. It was going to be his job to point out all the points of interest and landmarks along the way. A canvas cover enclosed the rear of the weapons carrier and the driver asked it we would like to have it removed so we could enjoy the scenery. We said "Yes," and the driver pulled over to the side of the road and we helped him remove the cover.

The road had been one bump after another so we decided to remove our sleeping bags from the back packs and use them as seat cushions. My sleeping bag had concealed a short-barreled M-2, fully-automatic military carbine. When Hank saw that he remarked, "Jesus, you are a one-man army. Are you looking to start a war?"

I replied, "I hope not, but have you noticed lately things can happen pretty damn quick in the back country of Mexico, and as I am sure they say in Oklahoma, you never want to take a knife to a gun fight."

"Well, praise the Lord," Hank said, "I don't think that I will need a gun down here. I can sweet-talk my way out of most any situation. I'm a lover, not a fighter."

I was sure he would live to regret those words. He seemed to have forgotten our earlier encounter.

We were traveling through some big pine groves and Al, who was also a bird watcher, was busily trying to spot and catalog the different kinds of bird life. I told him he was wasting his time. Any birds or small animals that lived close to the road were hunted down and killed a long time ago by the natives. He huffed and said, "Pretty uncivilized of these chaps."

"You ain't seen nothing yet," I remarked.

Al kept up a running commentary on the sights and sounds that we encountered along the road, and Betty faithfully recorded all his observations in a large black notebook. I asked him if he was going to write a book about his adventures in the new world, and he said maybe. But things had been dreadfully boring up to now, "except for your dustup with those blokes back at the bar."

We bumped along, mile after mile, as Al called out the places of interest. When we reached the town of San Juanito, about 20 miles outside of Creel, he announced that the altitude was eight thousand feet and this is the coldest town in all of Mexico. Betty thought this was an important fact and dutifully recorded it in her notebook, but to me it meant that we were about a half an hour from a warm meal at the rest stop in Creel. Not necessarily a good meal, but at least some warm tortillas smeared with honey or butter.

The town of Creel was somewhat of a surprise. About 5,000 people lived here, and, as Al told us, it was the center of the lumber operations in the surrounding mountains and a place where the Tarahumara Indians come to trade. We stopped at a small restaurant on the main street and I had a couple of tortillas, and that was all. I suggested to Hank that was something that was safe to eat and he should not touch the other food. We were going to have a tough time for the next few days and we sure didn't need one of us to come down with a case of dysentery or the runs while we were on the trail.

We left Creel refreshed and in less than twenty minutes we passed El Lazo, the highest point on the road between Chihuahua City and the Gulf of California, and the scenery was beginning to get interesting. We could catch occasional glimpses of the rugged topography off to our left, and Al suddenly announced that we had arrived at Divisadero, the first place you could get a view of the fabulous Urique river that had carved the Barranca de Cobre in the volcanic soil of the Sierra Tamahumara. The driver pulled over and as we walked out of the pines we were treated to an incredible panoramic view of the canyon country. This was the end of the rainy season and the lush green vegetation and the turquoise blue of the sky made for a scene that was almost impossible to describe.

We kept moving forward and passed many areas where the company that was building the railroad between the Gulf of California and Chihuahua was boring tunnels through the steep canyon walls and building bridges above the canyon floors. It is an enormous and ambitious project and I looked forward to riding this railroad when it was to be finished in 1961.

But right now, we are stuck at a river crossing where a temporary bridge is being built to replace one washed away last November. A D-8 caterpillar bulldozer is towing vehicles through the shallow, but swift-running river, and although this is a Mexican government

Canyon Country Overlook, Baranca de Cobre

job, if a driver is willing to give the Caterpillar operator a tip, your
vehicle magically gets moved up to the head of the line.

Our driver indicated, with elaborate gestures, that he left his
wallet back in La Junta, but if the passengers were willing to chip
in, we would be able to get across the river much faster. We, of
course, contributed, and we left the river behind and continued
on and the government tractor driver had supplemented his personal income. This was Mexican free enterprise at work in the
back country.

We finally arrived at Bahuichivo, where we parted company
with Al and Betty. They were met by a guy who was to pick them
up to take them to a trading post that had been converted into a
hotel from a Jesuit mission. He said we were in luck as he had an
extra room he could rent to us for a good rate. We told him we
would have to decline his offer as we were in a hurry and we
had to get on the trail to Urique. He said that was OK, too. He
had a cousin who was a guide and he would give us a good rate
to lead us over the mountain, and we better have a guide as some
of the trail had been washed out and he would hate to see us get
lost in such a wild place. This guy was going to get some of our

money, one way or the other. But he had a good argument; we
could not afford to get lost in this country.

Over the Mountains to Urique

So, following his cousin, we were on our way to Urique. If the
first part of the trail was any indication of what lay ahead, we
were in for a tough time. As soon as we left the road, we made
an almost vertical climb for about a mile. Just as the sun was dipping below the trees, the trail leveled off and it was much easier
going. It was getting dark fast, so we decided to make camp while
we could still see. The trail was bad enough during daylight. We
didn't want to take the chance of falling over the side and into a
canyon in the dark.

As we spread our sleeping bags out at the base of a large pine tree,
our guide announced that he knew some people in the area and
would see us in the morning about sunup, and abruptly took off.

This seemed a little strange. Were we being set up? There was-
n't much we could do but be alert and pull that old carbine out
of the sleeping bag and slip that 30-round clip into the great
equalizer. We built a small fire and heated one of our cans of
thick stew and enjoyed supper. I gave my shoulder holster and
automatic to Hank and we were ready for the night.

Without discussion, I said, "I'll take the first watch and I'll wake
you at ten." Hank nodded his agreement, but he wasn't ready to
go to sleep. We had pretty well talked ourselves out last night, but
we rehashed some old adventures from the "big war" until Hank
dozed off. We had not seen any animals, big or small, all day, but
now that things were quiet, I noticed all kinds of sounds. The
wind rustling the leaves on the oak trees and caressing the boughs
of the pines, a jackass braying somewhere in the distance, the cry
of a coyote, or was it a hungry wolf? I reached down to feel the
reassurance of the cold steel of the M-2, and all was well.

I was wide awake at ten and Hank was sleeping so I let him
sleep until the first rays of the sun caused the tops of the tall
pines to come alive with a glorious golden glow. Hank awoke
with a start. "Why the hell didn't you wake me?" he said rubbing
the sleep from his eyes.

"I wasn't tired and there is no use for two of us being a pain in the ass all day long," I answered. We built a fire to heat the water for the tea for both of us. A surprise—Hank was a tea drinker. We tossed the tortillas we had saved from our lunch yesterday into the fire, and that was breakfast.

As we finished, we heard a large commotion in the underbrush and our guide appeared. I suspected he had figured out that we had a weapon and he did not want to take the chance of spooking these two Americanos. That was a very wise decision, as an M-2 carbine on full automatic in the hands of a frightened Americano could ruin the night or day of anything that might be prowling out in the bush. We put out the fire, picked up our packs—I carried the M-2 out in the open and Hank put the automatic under his jacket— and we hit the trail. We were going to have to push it to make it to Urique before dark, but I didn't want to spend another night on the trail. I needed some sleep.

It was a good tough walk and we were slowed by some steep climbs and a few fast flowing streams, but we arrived in Urique about 4 o'clock in the afternoon. The guide did know the correct trails and he was worth the 100 pesos we paid him. We had no trouble locating Hank's contact and quickly arranged to meet him the first thing in the morning. He didn't seem too glad to see us and he gave us no help in finding a place to stay or to eat. It was obvious we were not welcome in his world.

We found both a place to stay and a place to eat at a boarding house near the center of town. After a light meal—we were very careful to stay away from anything that might make us sick—we took a stroll downtown. It didn't take us too long to walk the entire length of the main street and take in all the social activities. What houses there were hugged the banks of the river or clung to the steep sides of the hills.

We sat down on a bench in the town plaza, a small patch of level ground carved out of the side of the steep canyon wall, and relaxed. There was no twilight here in the canyon, and darkness arrived as soon as the sun disappeared behind the rugged mountains to the west. No one else seemed to be moving as we walked back to the boarding house. An occasional dog barked at us, but outside of that, no one seemed to notice that we had arrived in town. It was easy to lie down on the rather hard bed and be asleep in a couple of minutes.

We were up at dawn and had several cups of hot tea—we had brought our own—and the hot water was on the stove in the kitchen. As we dressed to leave for the mine, Hank pointed to my automatic, "Should we take this?" he asked.

"You bet your butt," I said as I strapped on the shoulder holster, inserted the gun and pulled my jacket over it.

"Boy, you are a slow learner," I chided him. "Did you happen to see any cops helping little old ladies across the street since we have been here?" He laughed, and I think he got my point.

The property was within walking distance of the boarding house and we were standing on the tailings dump below the mine in ten minutes. Hank shot a roll of film to show the mine's location in reference to the town and the river and we waited for the care-taker. He arrived a couple of minutes later and said he was late because he had to borrow two battery-operated headlamps from a friend. He was still his surly self and never volunteered any information except when asked a direct question.

The mine had not been worked for many years, and looked like it. Even at the entrance, the timbers were decayed; one side had caved in and only a small opening remained to provide an entryway. A few lengths of iron rail tracks were stacked to the side as were three ore cars and the cast-off odds and ends of the mining business. Outside of that, the area looked like any other hole dug into the side of the canyon.

I hadn't discussed with Hank exactly what his company wanted him to do on this inspection, but I imagined they wanted to give a junior geologist some field experience, verify that the property actually existed and find out if he thought that there was any chance it could turn a profit.

When the caretaker handed us the headlamps, I asked him if he was going with us. He said, "No, señor." Hank gave him a dirty look and I imagined that the first line of his inspection report would say, "Number one, fire this no-good bozo who is supposed to be taking care of your property."

Hank said, "Let's go," and without thinking, I followed him. A few seconds later, I was greatly relieved to see that a cave-in had

Jim Hall and Hank Henderson

completely blocked the drift and we could go no farther than 20 feet. It looked like someone had tossed a couple of sticks of dynamite in the drift and deliberately blocked the entrance.

Well, so much for the mine inspection. I could see the anger building up in Hank's face. What could he do? Did the caretaker know about this? He had to know that someone had sabotaged the property he was supposed to be watching if he was doing his job. Why? These and other questions had to be answered by someone other than Hank.

As for me, I was happy that I would not be poking around in what was obviously a very unsafe and dangerous hole in the ground. I remembered that not so long ago, I had said that I would not go underground again, but here I was following a friend like a sheep. I was ashamed of myself and vowed to not get put into this position again. I had dodged another bullet, but only I knew it.

Hank was furious, but held his rage in check. We walked out of the mine into the beautiful sunshine. Hank handed his head-lamp to the caretaker and said nothing to him. I followed suit and we walked back to the boarding house without a word being spoken.

"Damn it," was all Hank had to say.

Over the Mountains to Batopilas

Breakfast was still being served, and as we ate, we had a chance to talk to the owner. He asked us where we were going from here and I told him, "A town named Batopilas," and showed him a map and pointed out the town.

He said, "I know the town and you have quite a trip ahead of you. What are your plans?" We told him that we had not made any plans and the people in Hank's company had told him to go to Urique first, and see what the "weather" has been like.

The owner said, "One thing is for sure; it is going to be a rough trip and you will end up riding horses or mules before it is over. And you will have to have a very good guide, and one who has recent knowledge of the trails and you will have to pay him, or them, well."

Hank had the money, but we were concerned what the term "well" meant. The owner, like most everyone we had dealt with in Mexico, had a cousin in whatever business we needed, who was just the guy for the job, and he would give us a good deal. He recommended a stable on the west side of town, very near the mine we had just "inspected." He even offered to send one of his employees with us so that we wouldn't get lost.

The cousin was a likable fellow named Guillermo Rivas and he would certainly give us a good deal. Guillermo is the Spanish name for William and we asked if we could call him Bill? He flashed a big grin and said, "OK, it is Beell." We told him we wanted to go to Batopilas, and we were in a hurry.

"Have you ever been there?" I asked him.

He said, "Yes, several times. It is going to take three days, maybe less, depending on the condition of the trail."

"Where is Batopilas from here?"

He pointed across the river toward the high mountains to the southwest. I looked at Hank and I was sure he was wondering, as I was, what we were getting ourselves into.

"Is there any other way?" I asked.

"We go by the rio. But it is 'muy dificil,' very hard and many days."

That didn't give us much of a choice and we both said, "over the mountain."

"How much will the trip cost?" I asked Bill. He smoothed out a patch of dirt with his shoe, and picking up a stick, started to scratch some numbers in the sand. I stopped him, tore a page out of a notebook I carried, and gave it to him with my pencil. A little embarrassed, he said, "I no write good." He flashed a grin and continued to scratch in the dirt. I was beginning to like this guy.

"How many mules?" I asked.

"Three and a burro," he said and "mules are 20 pesos per day and the burro is 15, and that includes the saddle. Food is free, mules eat on the trail.

"How much for your guide service?"

"Thirty five pesos per day." I showed him the paper as I added up the total and handed it to him. He said, "Momento," and went inside the stable.

He returned without the paper and said, "Deal—330 pesos to get to Batopilas, but I have to get back home and...?"

I said, "Of course, that is another 330 pesos more." He smiled broadly and shook my hand.

"And maybe a little extra for a good trip. OK?"

He said OK.

"Here is 300 pesos in advance," I said. "Para la casa, For your house in case the wife needs something while you are gone."

He was a happy man and I was sure that we were going to get along just fine on this trip.

"You are in a hurry? We go now?" he asked.

I said yes, and he was already putting a saddle on a good-looking mule.

"These are my best mules. They will travel fast. I have a cousin who lives along the trail and if we hurry, we can be there before it gets dark."

In less than a half hour we were crossing the river and heading into the mountains. They loomed large and menacing in the distance, and I had my fingers crossed, hoping our new friend and guide knew where he was going and how to get there.

About an hour later it became clear that we were not going to attack the mountains head-on but would be following a crease between two of the peaks that was not visible from the valley. The animals were fresh, and we made good time until we encountered a recent rock slide and had to dismount and pick our way through some huge boulders. The thought struck me that I would not like to be in the way of some of these boulders if something caused them to come crashing down the mountain.

As it started to get dark, the animals picked up the pace as if they had a goal to reach before we lost the daylight. Sure enough, as we topped the next rise, there was the cousin's house, nestled in a little field surrounded by lush grass. These guys had been here before. There was plenty of feed for the animals. They would not stray and would be ready to go first thing in the morning. And there was a place where we could put down our sleeping bags and be able to go to sleep without worry—well, at least not much worry—of being bushwhacked by unknown enemies.

In the dark, we built a small fire beside the cousin's shack, broke out the tortillas we had saved from this morning's breakfast, heated up our next to last can of stew, brewed some tea and thoroughly enjoyed our supper. We declined the cousin's offer to sleep inside his shack and instead spread our sleeping bags outside his living area. We didn't want to take a chance of bedbugs and other critters sharing our bags, and with a slight breeze blowing, the flying insects would be grounded, so it should be a nice night. We went to sleep under a beautiful, almost full moon, but I still slept with my right hand on my carbine and I'm sure Hank also had my automatic close at hand.

Morning came far too soon and we were saddled up and ready to ride as the sun came up over the eastern mountains. We left 100 pesos for the cousin and his family for the grass and water for the animals and for his hospitality to us.

By noon we were at the top of the trail and it was awesome to look down, way down, on a steep canyon that we were going to have to descend and then climb out of. I had expected that the canyon we had just climbed out of was the last one we would have to climb and when I realized that we had at least one more to go, my morale took a hit. It dawned on me that I really didn't know exactly where we were in this jumble of peaks and valleys, and things could get a lot worse.

I hoped my disappointment didn't show on my face and be transmitted to Hank and Smiling Bill. I considered myself the leader of the group and it was important that I maintain a brave front. Smiling Bill gave the animals a chance to catch their breath before we started down a trail that seemed to become narrower and narrower and closer and closer to the edge of some deep drop-offs.

Bill sensed our growing apprehension and yelled to me, "Don't try to guide the mules. They are smarter than we are. They know what to do." As we descended lower and lower and the mules retained their balance time after time after stumbling and sliding down the terraced trail, I was beginning to think that the mules were a cross between a mountain goat and a flying squirrel. My grip on the reins was getting tighter and my legs were stiff and sore from squeezing the sides of the mule.

I was beginning to see things. At least, I thought I was seeing things. Small, dark men ran and jumped behind rocks as if to hide from us. The going was slow and to keep from looking down, I looked up and around and, sure enough, there were small, dark people looking at us from behind rocks and what appeared to be caves in the sides of the canyon. On a place where the trail became wide enough to be called a ledge, Bill stopped to rest the animals and I asked him if he had seen these little dark men.

"Si, señor. They are very dangerous hombres. They are called Tarahumara Indians and they live in caves and sometimes come down from the mountains and kill Mexican ranchers and farmers. They can run up and down these mountains like our mules and they never get tired."

"Can we speak with them," I asked.

"No, señor, I am afraid of them and you had better keep your rifle ready."

We rested for about a half hour and then started back down again. What trees there were changed from pines to oak and then to scrub oak as we descended. We had spotted what seemed, when we were several thousand feet higher, to be a meadow, and we reached it in late afternoon. What a relief to be on fairly level ground and not hanging on the edge of a cliff.

Even though it was several hours until sundown, Bill said we should spend the night here, as the animals were hungry and there was food and water. If mules can get stressed out, these guys should be near the breaking point.

I knew that I was getting close, and I suspected Hank was also. My legs hurt, my head ached and I was willing to call it a day. I didn't get an argument from Hank, who was already taking the saddle from his mule. I dismounted from my mule and I could hardly stand up. The mule shook himself and looked at me as if to say, "Well, get this damn saddle off me and let me eat or I will dump you over the next cliff we come to." Strange, I hadn't thought of a name for mule, but at this instant, he looked just like my old mine foreman, Mike Scharnhorst, so I will call him Mike.

The little meadow seemed like one of the most beautiful places I had ever been. I don't know if it really was or that I was so happy to be off that mule and off that trail that anywhere else would have seemed to me like heaven. We took the saddles off the mules, unloaded the long-suffering burro, hobbled them and walked around in circles to loosen up our muscles and joints. There were a couple of small oak trees in the meadow so we spread our bed rolls under them and just lay there and looked at the sky.

Looking up at the walls of the canyon, I could still see dark forms darting from rock to rock. I wondered if they might come down here tonight, and if they did, what then?

Hank and I had our usual hot meal of stew and tortillas and tea and lazed around until the sun dipped behind the mountains to the west. Smiling Bill ate by himself because that's the way he wanted it. He didn't seem to want to talk much and neither did Hank and I, so it became quiet and we went to sleep. But we still kept the weapons close at hand. What about those little dark men up in the caves?

My watch said 4 a.m. when I awoke and glanced over at Hank. He was wide awake. I guessed that we were both hoping the next mountaintop would be the last before we reached our goal of the canyon that contained the richest silver deposit in all of Mexico and maybe the world. But probably there was a little bit of fear of what these last few thousand feet of narrow trails hugging the canyon walls would bring. It couldn't be worse than yesterday, or could it?

Smiling Bill was already up, and it could have been he was the reason that we woke up so early. Whatever the reason, we were all ready to face the new day. As the sun rose we were climbing up the fairly steep side of the depression that formed the meadow and begrudging every foot we gained in elevation knowing that we would have to climb down that distance on the other side. We reached the top of the hill that formed the south side of the meadow at about nine in the morning and were greeted by an absolutely spectacular view of the steep rocky canyon that dropped probably three thousand feet vertically and three or four miles horizontally to the sparkling water of the Rio Batopilas.

We pulled off to the side of the trail and dismounted as Smiling Bill tightened the various straps and buckles that held our saddles to the heaving sides of the mules. We could see Bill's facial muscles tighten as he looked down and said, "Slowly we go. Slowly."

The narrow trail was noticeably steeper and rougher than the one we had just climbed and there seemed to be more loose stones that could cause the mules to slip and stumble. The morning was crystal clear and you could see for miles across the canyon and up and down its length. On the other side of the canyon the greens and browns blended together and made some of the slopes look perfectly smooth. In my mind, the rugged beauty of the canyon country far surpassed that of the Grand Canyon or Yellowstone Park. The trail zigzagged down the mountainside, sometimes like the steps of a staircase and sometimes in a long back and forth incline.

My mule, Mike, and I were leading the procession and Hank and his mule were on the tier about four feet above us and Bill was on the tier above him. I noticed that Mike was a little more nervous and jumpy today than he had been, and he was easily distracted. Mike and I were inching our way along a narrow ledge with a sheer drop of about eight or nine hundred feet on the right side when somehow he got all four feet planted together in a space of about twelve inches. He froze and as his mule mind was processing the situation, Hank's mule dislodged a small boulder and it bounced down the mountain side right in front of us.

Mike was spooked and he shifted his feet, which caused him to lose his balance. It looked as if we were going over the side. I pulled hard on the reins and jerked his head back and gripped his sides as hard as I could with my knees. His big ears stood straight up and I could feel the electricity surge through his body as he made a tremendous leap forward.

I was looking at the sky and I thought I could see eternity through the two ears of that mule when I landed on my back with a bone-jarring thud on the trail. I hit my head, and everything was a blur as it moved in slow motion. My mule's big, brown body filled my vision and I saw him land on the tier below us, stumble and almost regain his balance, and jump again and land with all four feet on the next tier. I didn't dare to look down again and I tried to embrace the canyon wall with my arms.

I crawled very slowly along the ledge until I reached the place where the trail reversed itself and continued crawling for about ten more yards into the rock slide and then I just collapsed. When I looked down, I saw Mike the mule standing on the trail about eight feet below me with his ears laid back. His whole body was shaking. He did not dump on the trail and I did not dump in my pants, but I'm sure we both came close. We had both almost bought the farm and in that instant, I vowed that I would never get back on a mule, or a horse, or a burro unless it was standing on level ground, or near-level ground. My mountain-climbing days on the back of a beast of burden were over.

Smiling Bill had pulled off the trail and was sliding down the slope toward me. He was no longer smiling and breathlessly asked, "Que pasa?"

"What the hell do you think happened?" I replied, "That damn mule and I almost fell off the mountain and busted our asses."

Hank had also pulled off to the side of the trail, dismounted, and slid down the mountain to ask, "What happened?" I replied, "What the hell do you think happened? That damn mule and I almost fell off the mountain and busted our asses." No one knew what else to say, so we just stood there and stared down the mountain still to be traveled.

Mike the mule was still standing on the trail with his reins hanging down to the ground. He hadn't moved and he was still shaking. It did my ego a little bit of good to know that even mountain mules can have the crap scared out of them, just like a brave Americano. Bill inched out on the trail to Mike, grabbed his reins and led him back to join the group. My saddle was hanging to one side, pushed there by the mule's violent gyrations, but no straps were broken. We stood around for about 15 minutes more and Bill said, "Let's go."

"You go," I said. "I am going to slide down the rest of the way on my ass. No more tightrope walking along the edge of a cliff for me."

"Me too," echoed Hank. "My mama didn't raise any idiots that would get on a mule after that display. I can slide down a hill better than I can fly."

Bill was looking at a couple of scared Americanos. All signs of machismo were gone. We were kind of like the rat caught in the trap. He didn't want the cheese, he just wanted out.

"But señor, the mules know the way," Bill pleaded.

"That's fine. Let them go ahead and we will follow," I said.

So we did. The mules stayed on the narrow trail, and I am sure that they were much happier without the Americanos on their backs, and the Americanos slipped and slid and stumbled down the mountain side and picked up cuts and bruises on their back sides, and rips and tears on their clothes, but they didn't have to look over a precipice to see the canyon a thousand feet below.

After about two hours of this, we were past the worst of the steep drop-offs and an hour later the trail was such that we could get back on the mules without being in danger for our lives. We breathed a sigh of relief when the mules began to move faster and cheered when they could dip their heads in the swift flowing Rio Batopilas. We had made it. We were off the mountain and the town of Batopilas was only three miles away.

Batopilas

The mules seemed to sense that their journey was over and now that they were on level ground, they literally pranced into Batopilas. I guess they hadn't thought far enough ahead to realize that they had to climb and descend those mountains once more to get back home again.

It was hot in the bottom of the canyon, it was siesta time in the city, and not much was moving. The relaxed mood of the town and the fact that all the adrenaline had been drained out of my body on the mountainside, combined with the clip-clop of the mule's hooves on the cobblestones, made me want to go to sleep.

For a moment, I thought if I glanced around I would see Mexican peons with serapes draped over one shoulder and large sombreros pulled down over their eyes, and if I looked up, I would see banditos on top of the adobe buildings. But in reality, all that greeted the three weary travelers were a few stray dogs and the shimmering heat waves bouncing from the street. And we certainly didn't look like John Wayne and his gun fighters riding into town to have a shootout with the bad guys. We were riding old beat-up mules covered with trail dust and our clothes were torn into rags by the mesquite and cactus.

Smiling Bill pulled up along side me and asked, "Where will you stay?"

I replied, "I don't know. I have never been here before."

"I have a cousin that has a room he will rent to you. It is a good deal," he said.

"That's OK with me. I am ready to get off this mule, but I need a place to take a bath."

"My cousin can get you a bath, and he is just up the street."

I turned to Hank and said, "What do you think?"

"Hell, yes. My company will spring for the President's Suite," he said.

With that, Bill put his heels into the sides of his mule and galloped down the street. He had disappeared into a side street so we stopped when we got to that intersection and waited. He was back in ten minutes and with a big smile on his face said, "You are very lucky. He has the room available. Follow me."

We did and we were pleased when we saw the room. It was simple but clean and had two beds and a wash basin. "What about a bath?" I asked him.

"There is one next door, but it is yours when you ask."

We unloaded our packs from the burro. I gave Mike the mule an affectionate whack on the rump and shook Bill's hand. I had learned to like and trust him as a friend, and I was genuinely sorry to see him leave. Hank paid him the remainder of what we owed him and gave him a 200 peso tip. I added another 300 pesos and wished him luck on his trip back to Urique. I knew we spoiled him for the next American, but we had been through a lot together and he was a friend, and we geologists and engineers take care of our friends, especially when we are spending a big company's money.

We spread our sleeping bags over the beds, stripped down to our shorts and collapsed. I was just about to doze off when there was a timid knock on the door. I opened it and there was a smiling young señorita with a tray and on that tray was six cold beers.

"Señor Bill, he send this to his friends," she said. I thanked her, almost kissed her, and gave her 20 pesos. Two of the beers were open and Hank and I had downed them before she had walked ten feet. My body was covered with cuts and bruises and I hurt all over. I was still keyed up, and sleep would not come. Hank was about the same, but we both knew that we had to make contact with the guy who represented Hank's company, so we did not sleep and just laid there and enjoyed the moment.

The bath was a washtub with a pail of cold water. I asked the young lady if she would warm some water and she said, "Right away." She had anticipated my request and returned with another bucket of warm water. With a wash cloth, I removed most of the blood that covered my body, but it sure hurt. It was not a bath to remember, but in the long run, it felt good.

Hank followed suit and after a change of clothes, we went out to find Hank's contact. A few inquiries led us to the man we were looking for. His name was Hector Rincon, an old miner who was well liked by all the people we talked to. He lived in a little shack on a back street on the edge of town. He was, I guessed, about 65 or 70 years old, was bent over and dragged a leg. His appearance said that he had led a hard life, but his attitude was good. Unlike the caretaker at the property in Urique, he was eager to help Hank.

As it was getting dark, Hector suggested that we go to a place where there was light, as he had some things to show Hank. As luck would have it, there was a cantina on the main street and it was on the list of the businesses that were hooked to electricity. Hector had some assay reports from the mine—it was named "El Caballo"—that he was going to show us, but first, he would give us a history of the mine.

Hector asked Hank if he understood Spanish. Hank said, "Hell, no. Even English is taught as a second language in Oklahoma." Hector looked at me. "Do you understand Spanish?" I said, "Yes, but speak slowly."

The old man launched into a narrative about how the mine was discovered many years ago in the 1500s, 400 years ago, by the "adelantados," or Spanish conquerors, better know as the conquistadors, and how the mines became the most famous silver mines in the world. Somewhere along the line, a horse figured into the history of the mine and that is where it got its name, "El Caballo." The Mexican Revolution caused most of the mines to close in 1810 and then, during the American Civil War, the Wells Fargo Company bought this mine.

The "El Caballo" mine was a major producer of high-grade silver ore until it was shut down after World War II. Hector had worked as a miner and a mine foreman until 1948. After that, he was hired to keep people from entering the mine and stealing any of the high-grade silver ore that they might find. He checks the mine almost every day and has been almost trapped several times by cave-ins, but he says Dios protects him and he will never die inside the mine.

I tried to explain to Hank what Hector had told us, but between Hector's explanation and my translation, Hank probably missed a lot. The bottom line was that we would meet Hector at 7 o'clock tomorrow morning at his shack and he would take us to the mine. We asked him about transportation to El Fuerte, the next big town to the west, and he said he thought a second-class bus took passengers and left in the afternoon, but he was not sure of the time. Everything was closed now. We could ask in the morning.

"How about another beer?" We had several more and although people were beginning to come out to walk the street, we decided that we had better get some sleep and returned to our room. The girl at our "hotel" said that we could eat breakfast next door at 5 o'clock and she would wake us up, if that was OK. It was OK with us, and we turned in.

A light, insistent tapping at our door told us that it was 5 o'clock in the morning and time to get up. The breakfast was eggs, beans and tortillas—we supplied the tea bags—and it was pretty good. We met Hector at his shack on time and walked to the mine. The mine entrance was about a mile from Hector's house and there was little to distinguish it from the several other mine entrances that were bored into the cliff that paralleled the road.

At first glance, I immediately saw a major problem. How do you not cross over into your neighbor's property when working your mine? The first person to be hired would have to be a first-class underground surveyor and the next would have to be a first-class lawyer, but that was not Hank's problem. Hank took the required photographs of the mine and its location with respect to the town, and he was ready to go to work. Hector had brought with him three battery-operated head lamps, three flashlights and three hard hats.

Hank asked if I would like to join them in their inspection of the mine and I said, "No, it will be a rare occasion when I go underground, and this isn't one of those times."

Hank said, "I kind of figured that you had gotten enough of the life underground, but who needs an assistant when you are the world's greatest geologist! You can hold down the fort, and we will see you when we get back."

After they entered the mine, I checked out the surrounding countryside and tried to determine what would cause the ancients to think that they would find silver or gold or any other metal here. I walked around for about two hours, and I didn't see anything that would lead me to believe that this was part of the richest silver discovery in the world. I didn't think that the conquistadors, or the padres, were any better geologists than I, so I would have to chalk it up to pure luck, or maybe divine intervention.

When Hank and Hector hadn't returned in almost three hours, I began to worry. Hank wasn't going to take any samples so that couldn't be a reason to take so long. When they finally did reappear, I asked the world's greatest geologist what took them so long. Hank said that Hector took him to all the places he had worked, and he sure had some interesting stories to tell.

I reminded Hank that he didn't speak Spanish and he said, "Hector acted out all the things he had done and you know, a good geologist can understand these things."

I asked him what he thought of the property, and he said, "Very interesting. I will tell you more about it when we have the time." I noticed he was carrying two baseball-sized rocks crisscrossed with native silver. Pure silver! The vein that produced these rocks would be worth thousands of dollars a ton.

I was skeptical that maybe Hector had pulled a switch, but no chance, not on the "world's greatest geologist." I was looking forward to our session when he was going to tell me what was "very interesting" about his mine inspection. Both Hank and Hector were in high spirits as we walked back into town.

When we arrived at Hector's shack, there were two men waiting for him, and they didn't look at all like Mexicans. They were dressed in weird-looking clothes. Instead of pants, they wore bright colored loincloths and what looked like a bedsheet draped over their shoulders. On top of this was what reminded me of a GI poncho, only it was white cloth. Both men wore bright red headbands with a tail about two feet long hanging off to one side. Their skin was very dark, a reddish brown, almost a mahogany and they wore sandals, or what looked like sandals, but I could swear that I saw a tire tread on the bottom of one sandal. Hector greeted them warmly and they seemed happy to see him, but they made no effort to shake hands or embrace him.

Hector spoke to them in a tongue that was harsh, maybe Germanic. Hector said to me, in Spanish, "I would like for you to meet two very good friends of mine. They worked for me at the El Caballo mine about five years ago.

He spoke to them in their language and told me to kind of bow and not try to shake hands with them. He said, "They are Tarahumara Indians and they have come down from the mountains to buy presents for the first-born son of their chief, or leader."

So these were the savage Tarahumara Indians who were so feared by Smiling Bill. I looked them over and they didn't look so savage to me. They were of medium height, about five foot seven inches, and weighed about 140 pounds. But they didn't look like they were aggressive at all, in fact, they seemed almost shy and withdrawn.

Hector and the Indians talked for a few minutes and then they turned and walked away without saying goodbye. After the Indians left, Hector said, "How would you like to go to a party? The Tarahumaras are having a celebration to honor the birth of the leader's new son, and they have invited me and my friends to attend. I'll bet you will never have a chance like this back in your country. And they have the best corn beer you have ever tasted. Do you want to go?"

I said, "Hank has to inspect another mine several days from here. This sounds exciting, but first we have to find out when we can leave here."

"I will take you to the place where the buses are. Then we will see when you can leave. It is right next door to a cantina where we can have some beer; good deal, huh?"

We walked up a slight grade to the main street, then several blocks to a nondescript building where someone had set a table near the front door and placed an awning over it. There sat a man—I would call him a city slicker by the cut of the clothes he wore—reading what appeared to be a newspaper. A sign on the table said, "BILLETES."

We stood before his table for several minutes before he put down the newspaper and asked us what we wanted. I said, "We want two tickets to El Fuerte."

He asked if we had the money. I told him, "Yes." He waited until I pulled my money from my pocket before he said, "That will be 20 pesos each, one way." I handed him the money and he gave me two tickets from a roll he had hidden under the table and went back to reading the newspaper.

I asked him, "When does the bus leave?"

"Manana."

"When?"

"Mas o menos, twelve." "More or less, twelve." Hector looked at me and said, "Then it's a deal. Let's have a beer. OK, you go with me tonight."

I looked at Hank and said, "We have been in a hurry this entire trip, and now we have a whole day to kill. We started out to do some sightseeing, so how about we take in this beer party?"

Hank said, "Why not?" We stopped at the cantina and ordered a beer while Hector explained how we were going to get to this party. He had a cousin who had a Jeep, and he was sure that his cousin would take us up the river about five miles where we could rent some horses to take us to the Tarahumara's camp. He did not say how far away the camp was and, regrettably, we did not ask.

We made plans to meet Hector at his shack at 6 o'clock, and then walked back to our room. The town was having siesta time, so we joined them. Then about 4 o'clock we came out to explore the town of Batopilas. The town was larger than Urique and there was some evidence of the splendor that had once made this remote village a glittering gem in the wilderness, but all in all, there wasn't much to see.

Anyway, both Hank and I were having stomach pains. The eggs and beans we had for breakfast weren't sitting well, and we decided it was best to go back to our room. When 6 o'clock came, we thought of canceling out on our agreement with Hector, but we decided to go through with it so as not to make Hector lose face with the Indians. As we were walking to meet him, Hector and his cousin pulled up in a Jeep, and we were committed. We passed the place where the trail we took over the mountains intersected the road and then continued traveling several miles farther east until we arrived at a stable where a young boy was dozing in the setting sun.

Hector jarred him awake by kicking the chair out from under him. "We want to rent some horses. Where are they?" Hector demanded to know.

The frightened kid stammered, "I must bring them from the pasture."

"Quickly," Hector shouted, and the boy scurried off in the direction of the woods.

While we waited for the kid to bring the horses, Hector told us more about the Indians. Most of the year these Indians live in caves high on the canyon wall. They don't dig these caves; they are naturally formed when parts of the canyon wall flake off due to the change in the climate and other geologic functions.

The Tarahumara Indians are roughly divided into two classes. The ones who live in the caves and avoid all contact with the outside world are called the uncivilized Tarahumaras, and they are feared. The other ones, like the ones we were going to visit, are called civilized Tarahumaras; some of them live in caves, and some of them live in shacks made of logs and sod and dirt.

The Jesuit missionaries tried to convert them to Christianity starting in the sixteenth century, and although some Jesuit religious teachings still exist, the Tarahumara are pagans. They believe that the soul works at night while the body sleeps. For the moon, night is day and during the day the dead spirits and the soul do their mischief. This sounded a little spooky to me, and Hector was still trying to explain it to us when the boy returned with the animals, two large mules and two small mules.

Hector assured me that we would not be riding near any drop-offs, but Hank and I took the large mules as our mounts, just in case. It took us about an hour to saddle up as Hector and his cousin weren't much help, and the kid was not a skilled ranch hand. When we were ready to go, Hector asked the kid, "Where are the Indians?" and the kid said, "Follow the trail."

We did just that. It was easy at first but soon became complicated. Finally, everyone admitted, we were lost. While we were milling around in the dark, trying to figure out which way to go, we heard in the distance whooping and hollering and what might be singing. We were found, and we headed for the noise, breaking new trails as we went.

Beer Bust

About an hour later, we had arrived at the rancho, and the party was going strong. The full moon was low in the sky and its light distorted everything and cast long shadows over the cleared areas between the shacks. We tied our animals to a small group of trees outside the rancho and walked into the area illuminated by the moon and many campfires. Nobody seemed to notice us until one of the men who had been walking in a circle with a group of men—I guessed they were dancing—approached us and greeted Hector. He motioned us to come and join the group standing around a large black pot.

Each of the men held a hollowed-out shell of a squash plant, a gourd, that they dipped in the pot. The ground surrounding the pot was churned into mud by the spilled liquid and the bare feet of the men who crowded around the pot. We were at a tesguinada, essentially a Tarahumara beer bust.

Tesguino is a fermented drink made year-round from sprouted corn. Like the bathtub gin made in the United States by amateurs during prohibition, almost anything can wind up in tesguino, including grass and baby fecal matter. (I didn't find out about the latter ingredient until after the party.) It takes about ten days to prepare the drink, and once it is ready, it has to be drunk within 12 to 24 hours. If a hundred gallons were made, it all had to be drunk. Hank said, "That sounds like back home in Oklahoma."

These beer parties happen several times a year and the people eagerly look forward to them. If a man has a large project to do and the only way to get it accomplished is with the help of his neighbors, he will invite the surrounding community to a big beer bust. Everybody gets drunk and has a good time, the project gets done and everyone is happy. It is not unlike what our ancestors did on the western frontier while we were winning the west.

Both men and women take part in the tesguinada and the children are usually left at home. Under normal conditions the Tarahumara people are reserved and shy, but after drinking this fairly strong liquor, they seemed to lose these distinguishing characteristics, and when the opportunity presents itself, they engage in sex, often extramarital sex, and it can be with anyone in the rancho. It has been said by people who study the Tarahumara people that because they are shy and reserved, the unusual things they do during the tesguinadas is one of the main reasons the race is kept alive. These beer busts usually take place at community projects and that is where the sexual promiscuity happens. As I looked around, I saw there were many couples outside of the glare of the campfires doing their part to preserve the race. It reminded me of the fraternity parties we used to have back in college, but a little less discreet.

These beer parties also presented the opportunities for the Tarahumaras to settle old scores with others who have wronged them. Fights are rare but they do happen and sometimes people are killed.

The party was getting louder and louder and more and more people were coming to our circle to meet the Americanos. I guessed that we looked as strange to them as they did to us. There was one young girl that seemed to be particularly interested in Hank. She was not very attractive, at least by the standards that we Westerners judge women, and Hank whispered to me, "Wow! That girl is coyote ugly." I asked him what he meant by that remark and he said, "Son, I'll explain it to you later."

As the night wore on and the people got drunker, a small group of young Tarahumara men were giving the Americanos and their Mexican friends nasty looks. I noticed that Hector was getting nervous, so I asked him what was going on. He said that two of the young men had been in town last night, and the police had stopped them and wanted to know what they were doing in town after dark. They did not give the cops the answer they wanted, so the police arrested them and put them in jail. While they were in jail, a group of Mexican prisoners beat them up, and now they wanted revenge and they didn't like the idea of these Mexicans—we were included—being at a Tarahumara party.

A Tarahumara man came over to Hector and after they had a conversation, Hector looked unhappy and frightened and said that we had better leave. This was a strange twist. The other day, the Mexicans were going to beat me and Hank up for the wrongs done to Mexicans by Americans we did not know; now the Indians were going to beat up me and Hank for the wrongs done to Indians by Mexicans we did not know. For a couple of peaceful guys, trouble seemed to find us no matter where we were.

Without a word to each other, we put down our gourds and started to walk back to where we had left the mules. It got real quiet and the dancing stopped. I didn't see any weapons, but there were plenty of rocks laying around and they could do damage to you if one of them bounced off your head. An elder stepped between us and our animals and he held up his hand. Here we go again, I thought, and the odds against us were much worse than the last time. The Tarahumaras, in my mind, had grown from five feet seven to six foot four and there were a bunch of them and they were drunk to boot. The .25 automatic in my holster felt as if it weighed a hundred pounds, my mind was racing, and I was thinking, what if?

Hector was talking a mile a minute, both in Spanish and in Tarahumara, and I didn't need an interpreter to tell me that he was explaining to the elder that we were good guys, and we loved the Tarahumara Indians. The elder listened intently, nodded and stepped aside. The crowd surged forward but stopped when the elder help up his hand and let loose a tirade of gibberish that we scarcely heard above the breaking of the tree limbs as we untied our mules. We were in the saddle and on the trail in record time.

Later Hank exclaimed, "It has been some time since the Indians have chased an Oklahoman from their territory."

We had no problem following the trail downhill to the stable where we had left the Jeep and no trouble finding the way back to Batopilas. It was 2 o'clock when we got to bed, and we slept

well. That was, until 7 o'clock, when there was a loud knock on
the door. It was Hector. Since our bus did not leave until 12, and
the bus was always late, how would we like to see a very old,
very beautiful church that very few people get a chance to see,
and it was located just a couple of miles down the river from
Batopilas? His cousin was one of the few people who knew
where this church was located because it is in a side canyon
where people never visit. No one knows who built this church or
when they built it. We would never have this chance again. His
cousin knew exactly where it was and if we walked fast, we
could return by noon.

I would like to see this beautiful church, but I just couldn't put
my faith in Hector's, or his cousin's, idea of time and place, so I
answered for both Hank and me, "No, thanks, we would like to
visit the church, but just not this time."

I went back to bed, but I could not sleep. Hank was still asleep
when I got up at eight. I did not want to wake him so I slipped
out without washing up. I had been thinking that it would be a
shame to completely miss seeing a town that I had read so much
about in my geology text books, so I decided to do it while Hank
slept. To my surprise, I found a small restaurant in one of the
downtown buildings that at one time must have housed a mining
company's headquarters. It had seen better days, and I guessed
that you could call it quaint, or at least unusual.

The waitress was young and pretty but did not seem to be
impressed with the handsome young American so he just ordered
eggs and beans and tortillas. I thought I would give this combination another try. It was a lazy morning, people were strolling by
and a burro train loaded with bags of feed and fire wood stopped
beside the chair were I was sitting and the animals relieved themselves on the cobblestones. There went my appetite and as I got up
to leave, two strikingly beautiful young Mexican girls came out of
the back room and waltzed by me and out the door to the street.
They were dressed in crisp print dresses and high heels and they
left a faint scent of Estee Lauder perfume in the air.

I just stood there with my mouth open. I was ashamed of the
way I looked. My clothes were torn, I needed a bath, and I hadn't
shaved for a couple of days. I muttered, "Buenos dias," as they
glided past and they smiled sweetly and hid behind their parasols.

I could hear them giggle as the door closed. Suddenly, in that instant, I was homesick.

I had never been homesick before. Not in the South Pacific islands, not at school in Albuquerque, not in Montana, but here in a little town in the Sierra Madres of Mexico, in a town that was in the heart of the richest silver mines in the world, where I was having a beer for breakfast along with eggs, beans and tortillas.

What caused this epiphany, I will never know, but I decided to stay, asked the waitress for another table, sat there feeling sorry for myself, ate the eggs, beans, and tortillas, left a big tip and walked back to my room.

Hank's feet were just hitting the floor when I entered the room. He rubbed his eyes and said, "What's happening in the outside world? If there is anybody out there looking for a fight, I'm not interested," he laughed. "I make Mexican joke."

Hank splashed cold water on his face, we put our backpacks together and we were ready to face the day. We stopped in the kitchen next door, got some warm tortillas, filled a canteen with hot tea and headed downtown.

Up ahead we saw a bus loading passengers and Hank said, "Can that be our bus?"

"Naw, that can't be. We've got three hours before we take off," I said.

As we got closer, we could see the little city slicker guy taking tickets and packing people and things on the bus. When we reached the bus, I asked the slicker, "Is this the bus for El Fuerte?"

He said, "Si."

"I was not understanding something here," I said to him, "This bus is not supposed to leave for three hours..."

"I have sold all my tickets. There is no reason to stay here. We get head start," he said, in a matter of fact way.

I started to say, "But what about our tickets?" but I knew it would be wasting my breath. I felt like pushing his head through the side of the bus. He took our tickets, we got on the bus, he sat down in a reserved seat behind the driver, and I stood with my back against the driver and my chest against Hank. Hank stood with his chest against some other peon all the way to El Fuerte. All in all, I guess we should have been glad we didn't miss the bus.

Our luck changed when we got to El Fuerte. We got a seat on a first-class/second-class bus to Los Mochis and then a first-class bus to Culiacan. It said first class on the sign but was definitely second class in mechanical condition. I was concerned because the driver had a lead foot, and we passed everything on the road while we drifted from one side of the road to the other. But before we knew it, we were in Culiacan, the capitol of the State of Sinaloa.

This is the place where Hank and I would part ways. He would catch a second-class bus going east into the foothills, and I would continue south to Mazatlan. We didn't have much of a chance to talk on the bus as Hank was having stomach troubles, and he wanted to try to sleep.

As we shook hands and said goodbye, we did agree that we had a very "interesting" trip and we would make sure to get together again soon. We joked about Hank's next mine inspection being in hostile country, but he said he would be OK; he could talk himself out of any bad situation. "I am getting to know these Mexicans real good."

I asked him if he wanted to borrow my automatic and he said, "Hell no, if I can't talk, I can run."

After the last few days, my trip back to Zacatecas was going to be downhill all the way. After stops in Mazatlan, Tepic, and Guadalajara, finally I was back in Zacatecas just as dawn was breaking. I was soon walking into my hotel room, badly in need of a bath, a shave, a change of clothes and a few hours of sleep, lying down and not sitting up.

25
Dave Injured

There were several messages waiting for me but none seemed to be very important, so I took a long hot bath, shaved and sacked out. I was awakened about noon by a knock on my door.

It was Fr. Lopez, and he looked concerned. We exchanged greetings and I invited him in. He was nervous and said, "We must call Mexico City right away. Your friend, Dave Burt, the paracaidista, has been injured. He is in the hospital and the doctor wants to talk to you as soon as possible.

It took a while for this message to sink in. Dave hurt on a jump? When a guy jumps out of an airplane for a living, there is always a chance of his getting hurt, but Dave Burt? Not likely. Dave, without question, was the best exhibition parachutist in the business, and something had to have gone drastically wrong for him to be hurt. He did everything by the book. He was a much better parachutist than I ever hoped to be. My mind had a tough time processing this news.

"Come with me," Fr. Lopez said. "We will go to the telephone office and they will get you through right away."

We put the call in, but we did not get through right away. We got bounced around from doctor to doctor and from ward to ward until finally we found a doctor who said that he was one of the medics who had operated on the Americano paracaidista. The doctor said, "This man had a very bad wound. It was a compound fracture to the femur of the right leg and gangrene took over before he reached our hospital. Their medicine in the hospital in

Sonora was not good. Your friend is in very bad condition. That is all I can tell you."

Mexico City was about three hundred miles south of Zacatecas and a rough drive. Air was the only way to go. I called Raul, but he was out on a charter. The best that the airlines could do was get me on a local flight at 10 o'clock tonight. That had to be it, so I waited.

After landing at Mexico City International, and a cab ride, I was at the hospital at 12:30. Dave was asleep but I had a chance to talk to a doctor who had some knowledge of Dave's condition. He was more optimistic than the guy I had talked to this morning, but we would have to wait until Dave was awake tomorrow to get something definite.

I found a chair in the waiting room and dozed on and off until about 6 o'clock, when things got busy. I got to see Dave at 8 o'clock and he was very happy to see a friendly face. He said that there weren't too many of them around here.

The main concern was "Who is going to pay the bills for this Americano who is without friends here in Mexico City?"

Naturally, my first question to Dave was, "How in the hell did this happen?" The long and the short of the jump story was that after making a paid parachute jump for Coca-Cola, he was approached by a charitable organization that was having a fair the next day and they asked Dave if he would please make a parachute jump for them, for free. His do-gooder gene must have been working that day so he said OK.

The next day dawned clear but windy, so Dave elected to use a seven-panel TU, the best canopy to compensate for the high wind. The target was in an open field, good luck here. But the jump was to take place in the late afternoon. Bad luck there as the winds will be their strongest. He was going to make a 30-second delayed jump using smoke. Dave always did everything by the book, so he would jump from 10,200 feet. He would freefall for 30 seconds or 4,700 feet, his parachute opening altitude would be 2,500 feet, the ground elevation was 3,000 feet—add them all up and he would get the jump altitude of 10,200 feet above sea level. So far, so good.

Dave said, "My exit point was a little short because I had a raw pilot who was slow to react to my commands and I got out early.

No sweat there, as I could make up the distance after the canopy opened by running downwind. I came over the target at a high rate of speed and I turned into the wind at about 300 feet to slow my forward speed.

"I noticed that a TV camera truck was on the drop zone, a no-no, and he was trying to chase me down. I tried to miss the truck by turning downwind, but the jackass drove right under me and I hit the truck going about 25 miles an hour. That wasn't so bad, but the truck had a loudspeaker horn welded to a jagged piece of angle iron on top of the cab, and that jagged piece of angle iron tore into my leg and busted the femur and ripped a chunk out of the leg about a foot wide. It hurt like hell and I bled all over the place.

"Talk about a Chinese fire drill! They damn near strangled me trying to stop the bleeding. The last thing I remember was going to the hospital in the back of a pickup truck."

Dave was in the hospital about five days before they discovered the gangrene and airlifted him to this hospital in Mexico City. This bill was the main reason why they were worried about who was going to pay for this.

Dave looked awful and said he felt worse than he looked but wanted to know when he was going to get out of this place? The doctors consulted and said, "Not for some time," and "who is going to pay for this? And who will have the power of attorney to authorize any further procedures, like removing the leg?"

I said, "How about we talk about this after things calm down?" When the doctors and the hospital administrators left, Dave and I had a chance to talk.

First things first. I asked him if his parents knew what had happened to him and where he was. He said that the hospital had finally reached his dad and that he was on his way to Mexico and would arrive here this evening. Dave said his dad is a take-charge guy and will handle all the details about what they can or cannot do. This was a great relief to me, as I did not want to make the decision, if it had to be made, to cut off his leg. For an adventurous guy like Dave to lose a leg would be a tragedy, and I didn't want to have to make that call.

As for the parachute jumps in Acapulco he had contracted for, I could make them. Not as well as Dave, but close enough that the public couldn't tell the difference. The public relations people should be able to pass me off as Dave for this weekend without too much trouble. After that, they would have to figure out something else.

Dave was really down, and it looked like the plans we had dreamed about forming a parachute company back in the States were going to have to be put on hold and maybe forgotten. We talked about a lot of things but the conversations always came back to "Who ever heard of a one-legged exhibition parachute jumper who could lead an expedition into darkest Africa or the Lost World in South America?"

After a couple of hours of this kind of talk, Dave was getting tired and the nurse said I should go away and let him get some sleep. The administration staff had been in touch with Dave's parents and they told me that Mr. Burt would arrive in Mexico City at 4 o'clock. Good. That would give me some time to be by myself and think this thing through.

As I left the hospital, an administrator asked me who was going to pay all these hospital expenses. I wrote them a check for $300, about all I had in my account and I was sure that I could cover, told them that this was a "good faith deposit" and we would talk about the rest of the bill when I returned.

I was waiting at the airport when Mr. Burt's flight arrived from Los Angeles. I scanned the passengers as they got off the plane and I spotted him right away—at least I spotted a man I thought Mr. Burt would look like. He was tall, thin, dressed in a dark suit and had a very serious look on his face. I could see where Dave inherited his professional manner. I introduced myself to the man and, sure enough, I was right.

As we waited for his bags—there were several, and it looked like he intended to stay for a while if needed—I updated him on Dave's condition. While we were being driven to the hospital, I tried to make small talk, but everything I said was met with an awkward pause and I finally shut up and we continued on in silence.

I rather suspected that he and his wife did not fully approve of the lifestyle Dave was leading and, as I was a part of that lifestyle, I was not held in very high regard. We were two intelligent young men, both with hard-earned technical college degrees, sacrificing our careers jumping out of airplanes looking for who knows what? It could be seen as a waste of higher education dollars.

When we reached the hospital and entered his room, Dave was asleep. The nurse said we should wake him and we did. The father/son greetings were formal. The father seemed like he was proud of the son, but perhaps a little angry about the situation. The son was very happy to see the father, but cautious. Mr. Burt told me he had business friends in Mexico City and he would be staying with them. They would take care of his needs while he was here.

I excused myself after asking Dave if there were any other instructions for me in my dealings with the public relations people at Coke. He said no, but since I was representing the "world's greatest parachutist," I had better abide by all the safety rules and during the autograph sessions, I shouldn't take too seriously some of the things the fans might say. He gave a wistful smile and said, "I would like to be going with you."

I picked up my bag and left. I caught a cab to downtown and got a room at one of the big hotels. All I wanted was a place to stay, a place to take a shower and a place to go to sleep. I was emotionally exhausted.

Plans for Jump

I put in a call to the public relations people at the Coca-Cola office at eight o'clock the next morning. I asked to talk to the boss, and the secretary said, "You have got to be kidding. Try around 10 or so, and you might catch him."

At 10:20, I didn't get the boss but I did get a guy who said he was Boss Segundo, or the second boss. The head of the department was in New York City, but Boss two could answer all my questions. His name was Francisco Bravo and he was a funny guy.

But at this stage of the game, I wasn't looking for a funny guy, I needed answers. Answers like, what was going to happen this weekend and what part was Dave going to have to play in it.

"Let's do lunch and I will tell you all about it," Francisco replied and I met him at noon at one of the better restaurants in Mexico City. He was, as I expected, a short, rather overweight young man, who I was sure would be the life of any party. One of the first things he asked me was, "Do you like girls?"

I guardedly said, "Yes."

"Well then you must stay over tonight and I will show you some of Mexico's finest."

I told him, "Some other time. I have to get back to Zacatecas to take care of business and pick up my parachute gear."

He looked perplexed and said, "Are all you American paracaidistas so damn serious. Señor Dave is always business, business."

The food was good and by the end of the lunch I had found out that the contract called for a Saturday morning parachute jump into a beachfront hotel to present a trophy to the winner of a beauty contest and an afternoon jump on Sunday to land on the beach, just to show the Coca-Cola logo on the parachute canopy. Francisco would be my contact and he told me to make sure that I arrived on Friday evening.

I thought this bozo was going to be a little hard to work with, but he must be pretty good at what he does to be employed by this large company. I stopped by the hospital to see Dave on my way to the airport and his condition was still very serious, but on hold. I assured him that everything was on track concerning the jumps and I could see that he was relieved.

Dave was a guy who did not want to leave the details to anyone else and I was a guy who didn't "sweat the small stuff." But I was learning that in parachuting, you do "sweat the small stuff" because that is the stuff that sneaks up and bites you on the butt.

I remarked that one had to have a lot of patience to deal with these advertising people.

He said, "Some of us have the necessary skills to get the job done. When we form a company, let me handle that end of the business, OK?"

"That will be fine with me," I told him. "I am much better talking with the campesinos and the mules than I am with the city slickers."

Yesterday when I visited Dave, I had not noticed a stack of parachute bags piled in a corner of the room. They had been forwarded to him from Hermosillo and, amazingly, nothing had been stolen, as far as Dave could see. One bag contained all the gear he was wearing the day of the accident, and it was not a pretty sight. The whole mess was covered with blood. He must have lost a couple of pints of blood before they stopped the bleeding. I was going to have to take all this stuff back to Zacatecas and have it cleaned up as good as new if I was going to pass myself off as "Dave Burt, the World's Greatest Parachutist."

One thing that couldn't be salvaged was his white jumpsuit. What hadn't been ripped apart by that hunk of iron on the sound truck was sliced into pieces by the rescue medic's sharp scissors. But—a stroke of luck. He wasn't wearing his shiny new Coca-Cola jump suit for this charity jump. It, along with his white scarf, was still packed in another bag. When I unpacked the parachute bag that contained the bloody equipment that Dave was wearing, I had to laugh.

"What's so damn funny?" Dave asked.

"Look at this parachute canopy." I showed him the blood-stained mess and grinned. "Remember, back in jump school at Fort Benning, how the instructors used to tell us recruits about the terrible things that could happen on a parachute jump. And every night before a jump, we would gather at the enlisted men's club, drink, beer, lots of beer, to bolster our courage for the jump the next morning, and sing battle songs about the gory things that might happen if our parachute didn't open? Songs like "Beautiful Streamer," and "Blood on the Risers," and "He Ain't Gonna Jump No More."

I laughed again as I held up the bloody parachute canopy. There was a silence, a heavy silence. There was no need to say I was sorry. I was making a joke that in this situation was not very funny.

I made sure that I had Dave's Coca-Cola parachute canopy and harness, as well as his white jump suit and white scarf that were packed in his best parachute bag and I stuffed the other parachute gear in one of the remaining bags. I also took the bloody canopy with me. No use leaving that here as a reminder for Dave. We shook hands and he said, "Do good."

I looked him in the eye and said, "I'll not do anything that will spoil the image of the "World's Greatest Parachutist."

"You better not, you bastard," he grinned. This was the first time I had seen him relax since I had been here.

"And I'm going to show you and everybody else who is going to jump again. I know you didn't mean to be a jerk, it just comes natural for you every now and then. Do good for the Company."

On the way to the airport, I began to give some serious thoughts to forming the company Dave was talking about. Between us, we had shown that there was money to be made by using parachutes in specific areas. I was making very good money by using the parachute to get into places that were difficult to reach. The relatively new machine, the helicopter, could replace me, but it would be years before they could do the job as cheaply as me and the "Bug." And there will always be a market for the exhibition parachute jumper and the new sport of recreational parachuting looks like it is going to be big business.

With smart guys like Istel and Lew Sanborn opening up jump schools for civilians back east, what about us opening up a school in California where there are just as many adventurous kids and the weather is much nicer?

The big question right now is what's going to happen to Dave. A company like this would have to have a guy with a good business head to run it, and I'm not the guy. Dave is.

I have skills, but business is not one of them. I also have a deep feeling for the military service and that is sure to get in the way of our company selling any advancements we will surely make in the science of parachuting. I owe a lot of who I am and what I am to my military experience, and I will always be a part of it. These thoughts were racing through my mind as the old DC-6 bored holes in the sky on its way to Zacatecas.

Beach Jump in Acapulco

When I arrived back at my hotel room in Zacatecas, I found a message from Fr. Lopez to call him when I returned. He was very concerned about Dave's condition, and for some reason, he wanted to talk philosophy and how it was God's will that things happen the way that they do.

For a young guy, he had wisdom far beyond his years, I thought, and since he was in the mood to talk, I settled in to hear some Religion 101, kind of like the stuff I suffered through when I was a novice in the seminary back in Pennsylvania. I would have rather been drinking a cold beer instead of the hot tea in my cup, but I was a captive audience and, if Ramon wanted to bare his soul, I could at least listen. Anyway, I might learn something.

He sensed that I was having some second thoughts about my life and asked if he could be of any help. I said, "No. I'll have to work it through myself. But thanks, anyway."

The next two days were busy ones. I gave Mrs. Martinez the task of washing and scrubbing the blood and the grime out of Dave's equipment while I took a flight up to Durango to look at a gold property that hadn't been worked since the nineteen twenties. I had seen the place before and I was not impressed, but a client was willing to pay me for my official opinion and I had the feeling that I better take the job, as I was going to need some extra cash.

By Friday morning I had all my gear cleaned up and I was ready to go. As I walked out the door on my way to the airport, I received a telephone call from Tulsa. It was Hank's boss from the engineering company he worked for.

"Where in the hell is that guy?" he wanted to know. The last they heard from him was when he arrived in Chihuahua and was going to inspect the Urique mine. Would I please contact him and tell him to call his office, immediately? I told him I would start tracking Hank down as soon as I got to Acapulco.

After we landed in Acapulco, I rented a car and checked in with Felix. I wanted to make sure I had a jump aircraft for tomorrow morning. He said that everything was ready and he would see me in the morning. I crossed to the other side of the airport to see if Maj. Morales was around and bumped into him as he was coming out of the briefing room. He was all suited up and was ready to walk to his AT-6, so I fell in step with him and another guy who was lugging a parachute.

Manny was glad to see me and after the greetings, he introduced me to the man who was going to be his rear seat passenger and had attended the briefing with him. The guy was short, stocky, mean-looking and was very quiet. His name was Joe, nothing more, just Joe. He was on loan from the United States drug agency and had been working with Manny for about six months. They were going to fly north to the State of Sinaloa, do some low-level searching for a new crop of marijuana plants along the Verde River north of Mazatlan, land at Culiacan and attend a meeting there all day Saturday. They would return Sunday night.

"Stick around and I'll give you that tour that I have been planning for you, and it always gets postponed," Manny said.

"I would really like to take that tour, but let's see what happens over the weekend," I replied. As we walked to his aircraft I remarked. "It's a small world. I have a very good friend, he is a mining engineer who has gone missing in the area you will be flying over. His name is Hank Henderson. If you should hear anything about him, please, let me know.

He said, "Will do," and completed his walk-around inspection of the AT-6. He strapped his passenger, Joe, into the rear seat and growled as he climbed in the front, "Where in the hell is that lazy fire guard?"

Just then a young enlisted man ran up pulling a fire extinguisher. "It's about time," Manny muttered as he shrugged into his parachute harness, pulled his white scarf from the map case, carefully tied it around his neck, put on a World War II leather helmet, saluted and mashed the starter button on the instrument panel. The big engine roared into life with a cloud of blue-black smoke and the Mexican version of the Red Baron was ready to fly.

I drove to the hotel where I would be staying and where the jump would take place tomorrow, and walked the area. For a drop zone, they had about 300 yards of sand with many beach umbrellas and other obstacles scattered around. I had no idea of what they were going to do about that, but that wasn't my worry. I would deal with that tomorrow.

Francisco met me at the registration desk, surrounded by a large group of young, good-looking girls. Most of them looked like they were from Latin countries, but there was a stray blonde here and there. Francisco must have had something to do with the judging of the contest, and the girls knew it, because the little guy would not rate a second look from any of them if they didn't think he could help their careers.

"The airline said that your flight arrived an hour ago. Where have you been?" he demanded to know.

"Taking care of business," I replied.

"Well, I too have been taking care of business," he said with a silly grin. The girls giggled at his little joke, and it was obvious that he was going to play this to the hilt. I didn't have any idea of what part I would play in this scenario, so I would just have to wait and see what evolved.

It was a beautiful morning in Acapulco and it was great to be alive and breathing in the crisp, salty air. I was up at 5 o'clock this morning and decided that I would start the day off right with a three or four mile run on the beach. I wanted to get ready for what was surely going to be an interesting day.

As I trotted along the beach, I thought about all the things that had happened to me since I came to Mexico and about all the things I have been a part of. I have had a lot of excitement and I have had the hell scared out of me more times than I care to remember, but all in all, I have survived without too much brain damage.

The parachute jump with the crown was supposed to take place around 11 o'clock. I got out to the airport about 9 o'clock and got all my gear laid out and inspected and was ready to go when Felix arrived at 10. The organization running the beauty contest had sent an armed guard to accompany the crown and if he was any indication of the value of the crown, it couldn't be worth more than a couple of hundred bucks. He was a short, fat Indian who looked like he wanted to go to sleep. I didn't think he could have put up much of a fight if someone wanted to steal this symbol of the highest beauty in the land.

It came to my mind that the company could get more publicity from someone trying to steal the crown than it was going to get from my bringing the crown into the contest by parachute, but I— I mean Dave—was getting paid to jump and not to make policy.

Francisco had sent one of his gofers to stay on the telephone with the hotel to give me a pretty accurate time to get airborne for the jump. Everything went as planned. I jumped with smoke from 12,500 feet—a full minute in freefall—and opened my parachute at 2,500 feet. Dave would have been very proud of me, as I obeyed every rule of safety in the book. I ignited two red and green smoke grenades as I descended and landed dead center in front of a small wooden platform that had been erected for the presentation. A good show!

I carried the crown in the front of my jump suit above my reserve parachute and the thing that I remember most about the presentation was that when the queen bent over to accept the award, I saw that she was wearing falsies. There went my illusions that there was nothing fake about these perfect girls.

Also, up close, she wasn't very good looking. I guess that it paid off to be cooperative with guys like Francisco and other judges.

After the presentation, the cops let the crowd swarm toward the platform and they raised me on their shoulders just like they did in Mexico City with some kind of futbol player. They trampled my parachute canopy into the sand and yanked me in several different directions all the while shouting like some primitive tribesmen worshiping their gods. By the time I got my parachute risers disconnected from my harness, I thought they were going to pull my shoulders from their sockets. No one was thinking except me and I was thinking that I was never going to jump into a crowd of these idiots again. By the time they had carried me away from the platform, I had kicked enough of the people in the head with my jump boots that they dropped me.

After that mob scene, I didn't look much like a "Sky King" and I was mad as hell. However, thinking that there may be reporters around, and remembering the promise I had made to Dave about not doing anything that would hurt the image of the "World's Greatest Parachutist," I kept my mouth shut, picked up my badly-mauled canopy, excused myself and, with the help of one of the cops who had been hired for security, retreated back to my room via the rear door of the hotel dragging my equipment behind me.

This wasn't what I had visualized as being the end of a successful exhibition parachute jump. In addition to the parachute canopy being damaged, and the jumpsuit being messed up, I was sore all over.

I took stock of the situation and decided that I could wash the jumpsuit in the bath tub and it would be dry by the morning. It wouldn't be as sharp as something the "Sky King" should be wearing, but I had made up my mind that I wasn't going to get close enough to these bunch of morons to let them see if it was wrinkled or not. I am going to land in the water, and if any of them get close to me, I will drown them.

The contract called for the parachute canopy to display the Coca-Cola logo and I would fulfill that part of the contract by giving the audience a good look at the canopy as it descended and disappeared under the water. I had three smoke grenades left, red, green and white, and after a short freefall, and I had an open canopy, I would ignite them. This would draw attention to the descending parachutist and the logo on the canopy.

But all these plans wouldn't do us any good if we could not salvage the parachute canopy, and right now, as I looked at the mangled mess on the bathroom floor, I had my doubts that it could be safely jumped. I filled the bathtub to the brim and tossed in the canopy. This place was going to be a mess by the time I was finished, but so be it. The contract was on the line and this jump had to be made with this one and only Coca-Cola canopy. I filled and emptied the tub several times, shaking and soaking the sand from the nylon, each time scooping the sand from the tub before draining so the maintenance people would have less work to do on the plumbing after I was finished. It was all part of the plan to protect the image of the "World's Greatest Parachutist."

With each rinsing, the parachute canopy was looking better. The nylon cloth was not ripped, though it was badly battered, and there were no lines broken, but many were dangerously frayed. At the end of two hours, I had washed most of the loose sand and grit out of the canopy. When I spread it out over the bed and furniture, it didn't look very airworthy. Oh well, on this jump I will gladly wear a reserve parachute. After this exercise, I took a break and lay down. Nobody seemed to miss me, and no one knocked on the door.

Later that afternoon I had a good lunch and walked the beach and girl watched. I met two very attractive school teachers from Denver but they did not want to be split up and realizing that it wasn't going to be too much fun watching an absolutely gorgeous sunset with both of these very attractive girls, I went back to my hotel room.

When I walked in the door I saw that the red light on my phone was blinking, so I called the desk right away. The clerk said that Major Morales wanted me to call him as soon as possible, and here was the number. I dialed the number and the operator patched me into a remote unit and they brought Manny to the phone.

He got right to the point. He said, "We may have some information about your missing friend. The drug agency Manny has been working with in Sinaloa made a bust last night and they had information that an American had been seen with these scum during the past week. We are interrogating the leaders right now, and will be all night, and the guy you met yesterday, Joe, is the best in the business and if they know anything, he will get it out of them. I'll call you as soon as we are finished."

Hank mixed up with drug dealers? How could that happen? That rotgut booze he drank back in the islands during World War II was the strongest stuff I had ever know him to touch. But drugs. No way.

Crap. Now I have one more thing to worry about. I did not feel like going to sleep so I looked around for a magazine or a newspaper to read, but I didn't find one. There was a beat-up bible on the table so I stumbled through the first 25 or 30 pages in Spanish and that was enough to help put me to sleep. Back in the seminary, I had pretty well memorized the first part of the Bible and my memory told me that the Spanish version of the Bible pretty well followed what I had learned in Pennsylvania, so all was right with the world. Right now, my world was pretty much screwed up, but I knew that it could all be worked out. I closed the book and went to sleep.

Meet Hollywood Types

I was up early again and I was excited with the prospect that Manny and his agents might have some good news about Hank's whereabouts. But my hopes were brought crashing down when the telephone rang and Manny's voice on the other end of the line said, "He is dead. Your friend, Hank, has been murdered. I'm sorry, companero, the drug dealers killed him."

"But why would they kill an American engineer?" I asked.

"He stumbled onto a drug deal going down and they thought that he was a narcotics agent. He spoke very poor Spanish and he had a strange accent, not like any other American they had dealt with. He laughed with them and he showed no fear. So they shot him, many times."

"Thanks, amigo," was all I could say.

Manny took a deep breath and said, "Señor Jaime, if it is any help to you, the man who confessed to shooting your friend tried to escape right after the interrogation, and he was killed. Joe had to shoot him many times. Joe thought you would like to know that."

So Hank is dead. He finally got himself into a situation he could not talk himself out of. So much for that Oklahoma confidence, good old boy baloney. Could my automatic have helped him? I doubt it, as he probably would have never tried to use it.

He was a lover, not a fighter. What a helluva way to end a promising career. What a helluva way to start a beautiful Sunday morning. I went for a long run on the beach to clear my head, but it was no use. All the memories of the good times and the bad times I had shared with the "hick" from Oklahoma raced through my mind. He will always be a part of my past.

Felix was going to be my pilot for today's jump, so I decided to wait until I got to his hangar before I would pack my parachute. I wasn't looking forward to this, as I knew that what I was doing was not too smart. It would take a miracle for this chute to work 100 percent, and today I had a feeling that I was all out of miracles.

I stretched the parachute canopy out on the hangar floor, making sure not to get any grease or oil on it—as if this would make any difference at this stage of the game—and very carefully inspected it. I did this out of habit and I went through the motions, even though I knew that I was going to jump this canopy no matter what I found wrong with it.

I had to do it. It was the only one like it on the face of the planet and we, Dave and I, had a contract we had to honor. I stuffed the canopy into the container and it bothered me that the pack was almost impossible to close. Even through it was made of nylon, the abuse and washings that it had gone through had caused it to fluff up and stretch all out of shape. It gave me a very bad feeling.

The news of Hank's death hung heavy on my mind, but I tried to put that aside and concentrate on the mission at hand—the jump this afternoon. Felix cleared the airspace for 2 o'clock with Acapulco Control and also the jump altitude of 5,000 feet. I was going to make a jump and pull—that is, I would exit the aircraft and pull my ripcord right away—and not wait to gain extra speed by going into freefall. This way, I would not be

Coca-Cola Canopy

putting the additional strain on the fabric of the canopy that it would have to take if I opened the chute at the terminal velocity of 120 miles an hour here at sea level. There was much less chance of it being blown apart or ripping to pieces.

By the time 2 o'clock rolled around, the wind was gusting up to 15 miles per hour and sometimes more, but I felt that I could handle it. I just had to crank in enough slack to make up for a bad spot or a change in the wind velocity that would prevent me from landing in the water. We took off early in the 180 and Felix circled Acapulco Bay several times to do a little sightseeing.

The view from one mile up was really spectacular. To our west we could see far out into the blue Pacific Ocean and to the east, the blue and green mountain tops of the Sierra Madres del Sur. Below me, the bay was crowded with hundreds of floating objects from surf boards, to rafts, to yachts. What a nice way to spend a sunny Sunday afternoon.

The Acapulco tower cleared us right on time and we started a long jump run. I had briefed Felix to cut the power and to slow down the plane to just above stalling speed before I jumped. I was still worrying about the canopy being able to withstand the opening shock, and the less strain on the canopy, the better. When it came time for me to exit the aircraft, Felix misjudged my instructions and cut the power far too early and we began to lose altitude before we reached the exit point. I was faced with the decision of continuing to lose altitude or increasing the power to maintain our jump altitude. I yelled at Felix to push up the power to increase the speed and maintain the altitude.

Was this a wise decision? I would find out in a couple of minutes. When we reached what I figured should be my exit point, I slapped Felix on the shoulder, gave him the thumbs up, and bailed out. When I got into the slipstream, I did not want to take a chance that I might hit the tail, so I delayed pulling the ripcord for an extra second. I held my breath as the canopy unpacked from the parachute container and I didn't have to wait long to know that this was going to be a rough day for the American. After much flopping and flapping around, I looked up to see a tangled mess.

My brain told me, "You are going to have to have more parachute than this to work with or you are not going to have a successful afternoon." I was in a tight turn to the right and as I looked up again to check the canopy, I saw a couple of broken suspension lines trailing in the wind. I also sensed that I was falling much faster than I should be, but I couldn't be sure, as I had nothing to compare it with. I could see that I had at least two suspension lines stretched over the top of the canopy, creating a perfect "Mae West," or brassiere effect. This would cause a jumper to descend faster and seriously impede his ability to steer his canopy.

Fortunately, I had altitude to work with before I hit the ground, or if I was lucky, the water, to take action. But what action to take that would not make matters worse? I could see some lines flapping around, but how many? I knew that two lines were running over the top of the canopy, and before I had a chance to steer this mess, I would have to cut these lines. I couldn't see any major rips or tears in the canopy as yet but I didn't know what kind of stresses or strains I might put on this failed piece of fabric when I started to modify its configuration, and putting stress on one part of the canopy, could cause another side to fail.

I knew that I could cut at least four suspension lines without causing the canopy to collapse in on itself if all four were in a row, next to each other. But what if they were scattered among the twenty-eight? I was getting a little dizzy from the spinning, so I told myself, you had better get busy and move and start acting. I carefully reached down and pulled my "KA-BAR" from its sheath.

I had to go slowly. If I dropped the knife, I was really going to be up the creek. Before I started to swing that knife around, I took stock of my options. What about dumping the reserve parachute? My training and experience told me that this would be about the last thing to do in this situation. I had seen several parachutists streamer into the ground when, in a panic, they pulled their reserve and it tangled with the main parachute and collapsed both the chutes.

I reached up and pulled down the riser that held the two lines and held them in front of my face so I could be sure of what I was cutting. I sliced the lines, one at a time. They snapped loose and that stopped the spinning and now I had a chance to look down. Damn it! I was still over land. In fact I was over a hotel and a parking lot with wall-to-wall cars packed in tight. Not a good place to try to land. I looked up at the canopy again and I could see suspension lines flapping all around, but how many? I knew I was smoking along and if I hit the pavement at this speed, I was going to dig a hole.

Instinctively, I pulled down on the front risers and—a glimmer of hope—I was getting some forward speed. At last, luck was beginning to shine on me. The lines I had cut and the damaged ones that were broken were giving my parachute canopy the four-line effect and I was moving downwind at a pretty good clip. But I knew that I had more than four lines cut or broken, because when I pulled down too hard on the front risers the canopy would collapse and my heart would stop until it caught air once more.

I was getting a crash course in canopy management and every time I looked down I was getting lower and the cars and telephone poles and the trees were getting bigger and the concrete and asphalt pavement looked more solid and unforgiving.

At last, I had the canopy in a glide mode where the lift over drag ratio was where I wanted and prayed, for it to be. The wind had picked up and I crossed the beach at about 40 miles an hour and suddenly below me were all those pretty floating objects I had seen from five thousand feet above and I was on a collision course with the biggest object of them all. I pulled hard on the right risers to avoid slamming into the deck of the yacht and my canopy collapsed, putting me into free fall from about thirty feet above the ocean. I plunged into the water at a high rate of speed and, with a great deal of relief, missed everything that was solid.

As I hit, my reserve parachute flew up and smacked me under the chin and drove a couple of teeth through my lip and cheek. I popped to the surface spewing blood and oily sea water from my mouth and nose, but there were no broken bones that I could feel.

I heard a lot of noise and I looked up to see a bunch of faces of beautiful people hanging over the railing of the yacht, and every one of them had a glass or a bottle of beer in their hand.

"Come join us for a drink," was among the shouts I heard, and that sounded like a great idea to me.

A small rowboat was tied to the anchor chain, so I crawled in, unhooked the risers and pulled the worthless, but life-saving parachute canopy in after me.

They lowered a ladder and I climbed up to the deck, where I was greeted by about thirty drunken men and women. I immediately noticed that all the women were damn near naked. This was quite a shock to my system. From a near-death experience to, maybe, a near-heaven experience. One of the beautiful girls thrust a beer in my hand and another equally beautiful angel took off her bra and wiped the blood from my face before she hugged and kissed me. I had been through a wild and intense roller coaster of emotions for the past ten minutes and my circuits were overloaded. I just stood there with the blood dripping out of my nose and mouth and stared.

"Great performance, super job. Man, you are the greatest. Tell us about it," were just a few of the comments I heard from the people who crowded around me and pushed and pawed. I wanted to get away from all this attention so I worked my way to the side of the deck and sat down. I now had a beer in both hands and the girl with the bra, or better still, without the bra, had followed me.

"What the hell is this all about," I asked her.

It was a "wrap up, or going away party for Marvin Greenberg, the Hollywood producer. He had just finished shooting a motion picture film on the 'rich and famous' people in Acapulco.

"Were you in the film," I asked her. "You sure are a beautiful woman."

She smiled and said, "No, not me. I'm just a simple gal from Cedar Rapids, Iowa, but a damn good hairdresser to the stars. It pays well and I don't have to entertain all the bigwigs."

The party kept on going and I was soon forgotten. But the girl stayed with me and kept wiping the blood off of my face until it stopped bleeding. She wanted to know what I was doing in Mexico and said that it all sounded very exciting. She was a good listener and after I got used to talking to an almost naked woman, we talked for about an hour. I was unwinding and I soon began to forget the jump and all the things that had happened recently, but I could not forget that Hank had been killed and Dave may lose his leg.

The party got wilder and she said "What are you doing tonight? I need some close companionship with a guy like you. Since I have been down here, I haven't met anything but a bunch of slick-haired lovers who need to keep reminding me how fortunate I am to be with them."

This question brought me back to reality with a jolt. It was now 4 o'clock. I had reservations to catch a flight back to Mexico City at 6 to join Mr. Burt in a meeting with the hospital administrators and Dave's doctors to see what the plans were for Dave's recovery. Then I had reservations to catch the 10 o'clock flight back to Zacatecas to meet Luis at noon tomorrow to take some important new equipment to the El Rey mine.

I looked at this lovely young thing and my lower lip must have dropped a foot when I said, "I have to attend a meeting in Mexico City in four hours."

Damn it. Duty calls. The girl—I never did know her name—was obviously not happy, but I'm sure a lot less than I was. She smiled and said "let's not let this be a complete bust. Come, I'll introduce you to Marvin. He is a great guy and he likes to talk with people who are achievers and who might give him story ideas he can later claim as his own."

We worked our way through the crowd on the deck until we were in the presence of Marvin. There was no question as to who was the boss of this group of ass-kissers and who signed the paychecks of the people on this yacht. Everybody treated Marv as if he was the king and his wish was their command.

He was a likable fellow, about 60 years old and had been in the movie-making business for a long time. He was an independent producer and was now working out of Twentieth Century Fox Studios in Hollywood. The girl introduced us and said, "Marv, this guy has some real interesting stories, and he is worth listening to. He sure snowed me in a hurry, and you know that is no easy job."

Marvin shook my hand and said, "That was a real impressive show you put on this afternoon. Do you do this kind of stuff for a living?

I replied, "Sometimes, but I am a mining engineer on a day-to-day basis." I told him some jump stories and his face broke into a smile.

"Hey, this is extremely interesting to me," said Marv. "I am looking to produce a new television series based on the adventures of two guys like you, who travel all over the world and jump into dangerous places, and meet pretty girls—he paused and winked at the girl—and who are just all-American boys. I would really like to talk with you about this idea at length, but I have pressing business on my mind right now."

A young very scantily-dressed female moved closer to him as he called over a hanger-on who moved at the speed of light when Marv motioned to him. "Sam, take this parachutist's information and make very sure it gets to my secretary when we get back to Hollywood."

To me he said, "I'll be back in my office in about a week or ten days and I expect to see you at Fox Studios then. He gave me his card and said, "Show this to the guard at the gate and if there is any problem, tell him to call me personally."

I took Marv's card, Sam took my information, and the girl wiped my face one last time with her bra. She took my hand and held it for a long time, looked into my eyes and said, "Too bad, all-American boy. Maybe we will meet again."

I walked to the ladder, almost fell overboard when I missed the first step while looking back, got in the boat, and headed for the shore.

I Talk to Dave at Hospital

We landed on time in Mexico City and I hailed the first cab I saw. I was mulling over what happened on the yacht and Marvin's offer to come see him in Hollywood. A television series based on my life—well, based on the life that someone like me could possibility live if you compressed the time and eliminated the dull day-to-day stuff between jumps.

Imagine living and associating every day and night with people like I had just left on the yacht. Being a movie star, even a minor one. What an incredible way to live. I'm sure that it had its down side, but still, it would be nice to give it a try.

I was still turning the thought over in my mind when we arrived at the hospital. Dave was wide awake and anxious to start the meeting to find out what was going to be his treatment schedule. I asked him how he felt and he said OK, but the staff was sure stingy with the pain killers. The staff told him that they had to cut back on the medicine, as a new group of people had taken over the management of the hospital and they were working hard to bring down expenses.

Dave wanted to know how the jumps went in Acapulco and I covered them point by point, but I wanted to get through the technical debriefing and the business stuff so I could tell him about Marvin and his offer to have me come to Hollywood and discuss the possibility of doing a television series based on what we were doing here in Mexico.

Right now, Dave was more interested in getting his leg operated on and knowing what kind of a life he was going to be able to live after the operation. Part of the glory of being a free-wheeling parachutist had been dimmed by the reality of his injury. He was more concerned by what happened to his prized Coca-Cola parachute canopy than he was about the possibility of going to Hollywood. I was still talking about Marv when the door opened and in walked the chief of hospital administration and the two doctors who had been working on Dave's case. It was 8 o'clock on the dot, and our meeting was about to start.

I asked Dave where his Dad was and he said that last night they had received a call from home and there had been an emergency and his Dad had to fly back to Utah to straighten out the problem. He would be back down here just as soon as he fixed the trouble. So, I was once again the one who would represent Dave's interests until his father returned.

The three men were all business and started the meeting right away. No small talk, let's get down to the facts. The lead doctor said that Dave was in a holding pattern. He didn't mince words. If there were no setbacks, there was a good chance that they would not have to amputate Dave's leg and all they would have to do was open the wound and clean out the dead tissue. The staff would have to monitor his condition closely. It will be touch and go for the next few days.

"Any questions?" he asked.

I knew that Dave wanted to know just how much damage had been done to his leg, so I inquired. The doctor said that if there are no complications, Dave will be able to walk, but with a bad limp for the rest of his life. Not a good forecast for a guy whose life had been one adventure after another, but it could have been a lot worse.

As the group stood up to leave, the administrator addressed me, "The hospital management has grave concerns that your friend, Mr. Burt, will not be able to pay us for his medical care, both past and future. During the last year, the hospital has been losing money because of the increasing number of patients who have not been able to pay their bills. Many of them are Americans who are here on visitor's visas and have no means of support.

"This hospital has been taken over by new management and we intend to restore this hospital to the status it once held as one of the premier medical facilities in Mexico. To do that we have to fill the beds with people who can afford this expensive care. Therefore, unless Mr. Burt can prove to us that he will be able to pay for this care, we will have to transfer him immediately to a charity facility. We realize that there is considerable risk here in Mr. Burt's case, but I hope that you understand that is not our problem. We hope that the doctors at the charity hospital are able to take over his care, but you have to realize that they do not have the advanced equipment and skilled surgeons we have."

This was not a conversation I thought we should be having in front of someone who was facing the prospect of having his leg amputated while under the care of the best available doctors in the country and these same doctors were saying that they were going to place him in the hands of less-experienced surgeons at an inferior hospital.

I said, "Let's talk about this back in your office." Before the administrator could reply, Dave said, "No, let's settle this right now. My family will get the money to pay for this, but it might take a couple of days. They are not going to let me die in Mexico because I am broke."

"But," the administrator blurted out, "We need the money right away. I have two people who are willing to pay cash for this room, in advance, and I am going to move one of them into this room the first thing tomorrow morning."

"How much money do you want?" I shouted.

"We will have to be covered to the extent of at least $4,000," he shouted back.

I pulled out my check book and started to write a check, although I knew that I didn't have anywhere near $4,000 in the account.

"How do I know there is the money in your bank account to cover this bill?"

"Give me until noon tomorrow, and if the money is not in your hands, the deal is off," I shouted back at him.

Things were getting real tense. The two doctors had been standing by and had made no attempt to enter the conversation. The lead doctor spoke up and said, "I am terribly ashamed and embarrassed that we are putting our patient's life in danger over his ability to pay for his care, but we are in a severe financial bind. I will give you my word that no action will be taken on your friend's case until after noon tomorrow."

He gave me his card and said, "Call me tomorrow morning and we will resolve this." With that, the three of them walked out; the two doctors arguing with each other and the administrator with my hot check in his hand.

I told Dave that I had to make a couple of collect calls to his Dad and to Fr. Lopez and I would be back before he went to sleep. He looked very mad and he looked very worried. I grabbed a cab and went to the first big hotel on the way to downtown. I asked for the manager and told him I had an emergency and that I had to make some out of the country telephone calls. He didn't ask me if I was a guest at his hotel, but I assumed that he thought I was, and he showed me to an unused office.

My first call was collect to Fr. Lopez in Zacatecas. A novice answered the telephone and he said that he could not accept collect calls. I told him he would take the call or I would make sure that he burned in hell if he did not. He must have thought that I was crazy, but I got his attention. He said Fr. Lopez was teaching a class and he could not disturb him. I told him that Fr. Lopez would be praying over his dead body if he didn't call him to the phone. There was a silence and then I heard the sound of rapidly retreating footsteps.

A short time later, Fr. Lopez was on the phone and I explained to him all that had happened at the hospital. He understood the urgency of the situation and would get on it immediately. The padre was out of his league stuck in a place like Zacatecas, but I was sure that he would get promoted later on in his career. The problem, right now, was that we needed $4,000 immediately. Those guys at the hospital were serious. The fact that Dave could very well lose his leg if he was moved and placed in another facility that was not equipped to give him the care that was necessary didn't seem to be important to them. Their bottom line was what counted.

My bank account was low, but I did have some assets that a friendly banker could accept as collateral for a quick loan. I asked Fr. Lopez to call my bank—it was also his bank—use his connections and have the paperwork drawn up to place $5,000 in my account tomorrow morning, and co-sign if necessary. Also, call his religious connections in Mexico City and have them call the hospital and plead with them not to move Dave until he was operated on to repair his leg. I would be back in Zacatecas by midnight and I would see him at 7 o'clock tomorrow morning.

My next telephone call was to Mr. Burt, but I had no luck here. The operator could not get through to Salt Lake City, and I had to give up if I wanted to catch the airplane on time. I stopped by the hospital and brought Dave up to date on what was happening and told him that I would keep trying to reach his dad and tell him we needed him back here as soon as possible. I told Dave that under no circumstances should he let them move him anywhere. We had people working on his case and it would be squared away by noon tomorrow.

He said, "You bet your life. This airborne trooper ain't going anywhere."

I tried to catch a nap on the plane back to Zacatecas, but it was a waste of time. Zacatecas was quiet when I rolled in about midnight and it was good to be back in my own bed. Elena had placed a note on my pillow welcoming me home.

I was up, showered and shaved and at the church when Fr. Lopez finished his six o'clock Mass the next morning. Over breakfast, I told him everything, well, almost everything, that had happened on the trip to Acapulco, what I knew about the murder of Hank by the drug dealers and most of all about my great concern that the hospital in Mexico City was going to remove Dave from this top-of-the-line hospital before their surgeons operated on him and move him to a charity hospital.

Fr. Lopez said that I had a right to be concerned about the treatment Dave would receive in a charity hospital. He said that he had visited many of these hospitals and in some, in fact in a high percentage of these hospitals, the conditions were deplorable and they did not have experienced doctors or skilled surgeons. It is not their fault but they have to exist on very small budgets and they cannot pay their doctors and nurses very well. Of course, the doctors have many bills for schooling and office expenses, so they go to work for the big hospitals.

I asked him, "What about the doctor's oath, the creed they are supposed to live by?"

"You mean the Hippocratic oath they take when they graduate from medical school?"

"Yes," I said,

He explained that it is their ethical code and they swear to abide by it when they start practicing medicine, but in Mexico, as in many other countries, when they get out in the real world and start to have families and have monthly bills to pay, they go to work in the hospitals that can pay them more. "Money talks, and you were very wise to recognize this fact early on and told them you are going to pay whatever they asked," he commented.

Fr. Lopez had called the bank president last night and the president said that he would have a secretary come in early and the papers would be ready by the time the bank opened at 10. Luis checked in with me at the hotel to make sure that we were still going to leave for the El Rey mine at noon and I told him we had to keep that schedule. However, it would be a good idea if he picked up most of the supplies before that and he could practice driving the Jeep around town and if he didn't run over anybody, he could drive the Jeep all the way to San Mateo. This made his day and I was glad that someone was happy this Monday morning.

I met Fr. Lopez at the bank and we signed the papers and the required money, $4,000, was wired to Mexico City within 15 minutes and the other thousand was credited to my account, just in case. This was probably a record for a speedy transfer of funds for a bank transaction from Zacatecas. Even though the bank president was an old friend of the padre's, he had Fr. Lopez co-sign the note and guarantee that I would turn over the keys to my hangar at the airport that held the "Bug."

Friends are friends, but business is business. We would work out the terms under which I would be able to fly the "Bug" when I got back from my trip to the El Rey mine. This arrangement was going to be a real pain, but I would have signed almost any agreement to get that nerd at the hospital finance office the money to keep Dave in his hospital until after his operation. Something kept telling me that I just couldn't trust that bastard and I should rush back to Mexico City and camp out in front of Dave's room to make sure they kept their word. But that was not possible, so I would have to put my trust in their word. I again asked Fr. Lopez to use what influence he had in the religious community in Mexico City, and he assured me he would do his best.

Him, I trusted. I had seen that sometimes religious connections were far better than political connections when doing business in Mexico. But Dave was an American, and a Mormon, and neither one carried much weight south of the border. Fr. Lopez took me to the telephone office, an area where his connections had been very valuable to me in getting my long distance calls through to the States, and on the first try, they connected me to Salt Lake City. Dave's father hit the roof when I told him what the hospital administrators wanted to do with Dave. He couldn't wait to get off the phone and make reservations to Mexico City.

The problems at home had not been solved, but they were now much less important than Dave's situation. I felt much better when I hung up the phone. I could envision the old man burning up the telephone wires and calling in all the markers he had in Mexico City.

Luis picked me at noon sharp. One thing I was trying to teach him was that when you say you were going to be some place at a certain time, you be there on the dot, or have a damn good reason why you were late. This was kind of contrary to the Mexican system. Mas o menos, more or less, just didn't get it in my book. Luis had made all the stops to pick up the supplies and gear we needed to take to the mine, except the most important one. It was a mechanical gold pan that I had ordered from Denver, and it was essential to our increasing the gold production at El Rey.

As we started to drive out of town, Luis asked me if we could stop by the taco shop where his new girlfriend was working. We were running late, but I had sensed that this would be a big deal for us to drive up, him in the driver's seat, and introduce his girl to the big boss.

And it was. The shop was in the market district downtown and Luis cautiously wove the Jeep around and in and out and between all manner of vehicles and livestock until we got to his girlfriend's work place. He stopped and blew the horn. That was a signal for four or five young, giggling girls to come running to the door. As a group, they weren't much to look at, and Luis's girlfriend was the homeliest of them all. But she, I was to find out later, had a good disposition. She shyly put out her hand and touched the hood of the Jeep and said "Hi."

After the introduction, Luis lowered his voice, and in a tone of authority, said it was getting late and we had better be on our way to the mine. He put the Jeep in gear and slowly pulled away. But he wasn't looking where he was going and banged into a burro that was being offloaded. I gave the owner a five peso note, and the girls tittered, but all in all, Luis had made a big impression.

26
The Flight to Merida, Yucatan

I had finished breakfast and I was writing a report on a gold property I had inspected last month for a Mexican mining company when there was a knock on my door.

It was a young man, a runner from the telegraph office and he had an urgent message for me. The telegram was from Tuxtla Gutierrez in the southern Mexican State of Chiapas. The telegram said, "Need your services immediately. Have special urgent cargo dropping job. Call as soon as possible to 998-0909." Signed, Steve Powell.

The name didn't ring a bell right away, until I remembered Steve Powell; he was the pilot of the old World War II transport that dropped me and the Mexican paratroopers in Acapulco last year. His outfit was located in Merida, Yucatan, and he was a long way from home. I had never followed up on my desire to work with him in dropping cargo in Central America after that jump, but it sounded like something that I would still be interested in.

I walked to the telegraph/telephone office where the manager, as usual, assisted me in getting a line to Gutierrez. It turned out to be a little more difficult than usual, as a series of fierce tropical storms was hammering the southern part of Mexico and Central America. When we did get connected, Steve told me that they have been working with several archaeological expeditions in Central America and the reason they were in Chiapas is that bad weather had grounded them and they couldn't get back to their headquarters in the Yucatan.

They had two routine cargo deliveries to make, one in Guatemala and the other in Honduras, but yesterday when they tried to land at the locations they found that the roads and their landing areas had been washed way by the storms. These developments turned a routine situation into an urgent one, especially the delivery in Guatemala. Steve and his crew were caught unprepared and the only option they had left was a cargo drop. But they needed someone who was an expert and who had the necessary equipment. "Can you do it?" he asked.

While working with Dave Burt in the States on several of his far-out projects, I had picked up a lot of experience in cargo dropping and while I was in the smoke jumpers in Montana and I had a sprained ankle, I worked in the parachute loft, where I had learned quite a bit about heavy equipment cargo drops. I considered myself an expert, at least the only guy who could qualify as an expert in this part of Mexico. In addition, I was the only one who had the equipment to do the job.

"Of course I can do it," I said. "What kind of stuff will we be dropping?"

Steve said, "A thousand pounds of food and medical supplies, all packaged up in bundles of a hundred pounds or less, just waiting to have a parachute canopy attached to them."

This was going to be easier than I thought. My 28-foot personnel parachute canopies would be ideal for these loads. Then I asked, "Is there anything else?"

Steve said, "Yes, and this is going to be the tough one. It is a piece of equipment that is absolutely essential that we deliver tomorrow. Our most important customer is an archaeological expedition in northern Guatemala. At great expense, they have drilled a deep water well that has been a life-saver for hundreds and hundreds of Indians in the region. It supplies all their drinking and cooking water. They are absolutely dependent upon this water for their existence.

"Two days ago, the Indian in charge of operating a gasoline engine that drives a generator that provides the power to run the pump screwed up and allowed the motor to run out of oil, and it burned up. The storms have churned up and polluted every stream for miles around and this is the only source of uncontaminated water for the Indians, as well as the archaeological expedition. The expedition is from Harvard University, no less, and they have discovered an important site at a nearby village and they are ready to reveal this to the world.

"This is really an emergency situation for all concerned. The University has shelled out a large amount of money to buy a state-of-the-art, German-made motor to replace the ruined one. Our future contracts are on the line and depend on our delivering it in one piece."

I held my breath and asked how much it weighed. His answer would be very important. I didn't want to have to use more than one canopy on an individual load, as there was always a chance for the chutes to tangle and the cargo to be demolished when it hit the ground.

"About 160 pounds, without gas and oil, and they have plenty of that in the camp," he said. I ran the numbers through my head and thought that 160 is too much for a delicate load such as this to be dropped on a 28-foot canopy. But the last time I was in El Paso I had bought a couple of 32-foot parachute canopies to use when I trained Raquel and Fr. Lopez to jump, and one of them could probably do the job.

"I can do it, even if I have to carry it down in my arms," I boasted. "Anything else?" I asked.

"That's it," Steve said. "When can you meet me at my hangar in Merida? This storm has passed and we are taking off for home right away."

"It will be pushing it, but I will be there before nightfall," I told him, and hung up the phone.

Hot dog! This was just what I was looking for. A chance to make some extra money and right now I needed it. The "Bug" was in hock to the bank and a payment was coming due. I had enough to cover next month's rent at the hotel but I did not have the cash for the mortgage on the house that Mrs. Martinez and the kids and Ace were living in. My credit was A-1 all over town and I didn't want to let anybody know that I was short on cash. That would be the kiss of death.

I had two due bills on mine inspections pending, but I couldn't count on them to bail me out in time. The El Rey mine was doing well, but the board meeting was not until six weeks from now, so that cash would be too late.

I had been invited to attend a mining convention in El Paso the next Monday and meet with the big wheels in two mining companies hungry to invest in gold properties that were long shots and off the beaten track. If I could show them some, they were willing to pay me to investigate and if they panned out, they would cut me in on the profits.

The future looked good, but I needed to create some cash flow right now. To do it, I've got to take chances. I could get some up-front money for the cargo drop and be back in time to make the convention in El Paso.

Before going back to my room, I sat down and ran through the steps I would have to take to make this a successful project. First thing, how was I going to get me and my equipment to Merida? I put in a call to Raul and I got his mechanic on the phone.

"Raul, he no here. He go to Mexico City. Be back mañana."

"Damn that guy!" I thought. "He is never around when I need him. Well, not always, maybe fifty percent of the time."

The airlines are out of the question, as was driving. That leaves the "Bug." Ugh! About nine hundred miles of stick and rudder time at less than one hundred miles an hour. Also a couple of re-fueling stops as well as the various state airport officials with their hands out and probably bad weather at the end of the journey. But I had better get on with it. Nobody said that this life was going to be easy.

I called Fr. Lopez and told him what I was going to do and he agreed to handle everything while I was gone. My next stop was the bank, where I picked up the keys to the hangar. The secretary wanted to know when I would be back and I told her three or four days.

"When are you going to give me a ride in your air machine, Ingeniero?" she teased as she dangled the keys in front of me.

"Whenever you agree to take a walk with me in the moonlight," I answered as I snatched the keys from her hand. I might have something going here, but I didn't want to take a chance of messing it up while Raquel was still in the picture. Later, perhaps.

When I got to the airport, I had the kid who works there help me push the "Bug" out on the ramp and he filled up the gas tank and checked the oil while I reviewed my parachute canopy inventory. I tossed the 32-foot canopy in the back seat and added ten 28-footers, and all the necessary associated hardware and webbing. I had considered taking Ace's parachute, but I thought better of it. I intended to get these canopies back someday, but I didn't want to take the chance of his chute ending up as the wedding dress for some Indian in Central America.

I took along one of my personnel parachutes, because in the cargo-dropping business, you are always working near open doors at five hundred or so feet above the ground and anything can happen. I double-checked the gofer's work and made sure he had filled the tank to its thirty-six gallon capacity. I planned to cruise at five thousand feet at about one hundred plus miles per hour and a full tank would get me well beyond Mexico City before I had to refuel. I had grabbed two large sandwiches from the hotel kitchen and a bottle of Coke and that was going to be my lunch on the way to Merida. I kind of felt like Charles Lindbergh, but instead of the Atlantic Ocean under me, I would have the rugged terrain of Mexico.

I passed Mexico City on its east side and the "Bug" was chewing up the miles like one of its big brothers. My right arm was getting tired from keeping the airplane on course and I tried my left arm, my knees and even my feet to keep it straight and level and relieve the boredom, but I kept nodding off. I had gotten a good night's sleep last night, but I was having trouble staying awake.

I turned the oxygen to full on and that helped a little, but the thing that got my attention was when a jetliner crossed in front of me, at my exact altitude, maybe a little higher, and I went through its jet wash. I caught a glimpse of a silver streak, probably a new 707, as my head whipped around. What a wake-up call. From then on, I kept my head on a swivel.

Three hours and ten minutes after the "Bug's" wheels left the runway at Zacatecas, I touched down at Orizaba, Vera Cruz. I refueled the "Bug" myself and was in the air before the airport officials had a chance to question me on my papers and tell me it might be a couple of hours before they can get clearance for me to leave. However, if I was willing to help them pay for the use of a private line to Mexico City they could probably speed up the process. I didn't bother to get a weather report on the situation in the Yucatan peninsula because I was going to press on no matter what the forecasters said. I needed this job.

Everything was going great and I planned to refuel at Villa-hermosa, two hundred miles to the south, when the engine started to run rough. I went through all the standard procedures but things got worse and suddenly the engine just quit. I had been following the highway and my first thought was to put her down while I still had a paved surface. I nixed that first panic reaction when I realized that I might need a mechanic to help me fix the engine.

I hadn't flown over anything that looked like an airport, but then, I wasn't looking for one. But now I was. I rocked the air-plane back and forth and scanned the countryside. Up ahead, but in the distance, I saw what looked like a city. As I got closer, I saw that it was actually two cities, about three miles apart. I turned the "Bug" toward the one to the east because it was bordered by a large body of water and if they didn't have an airport, maybe I could dead stick the plane on the beach.

I was now at four thousand feet so I put the "Bug" in a max glide position and hoped for the best. As I got closer to the city, I saw an open space on its outskirts and headed for it. I was on the edge of the seat as I was coaxing the "Bug" on toward the clearing; it was an airport. I heaved a sigh of relief when I knew that I was going to make it. In fact, I had enough altitude to make a 360 degree turn as I lined up for my final approach. I touched down long so I could roll out as close to one of the hangars as possible but my plane still stopped in the middle of the runway. Good job, Jim!

My palms were sweaty and my legs were shaking as I crawled out of the "Bug" and I thought of kissing the ground, but I didn't. I was surprised that nobody rushed out to meet me, as this was obviously an emergency. Then I realized that it was siesta time. I walked over to the hangar and rousted a mechanic who was sleeping under the wing of an old Stinson aircraft.

"What do you want?" he growled, very much annoyed that I had disturbed his sleep. I told him I wasn't sure what was wrong with my airplane, but I did need his help to push it off the run-way. He was not a happy mechanic, but he did help me push the "Bug" into the shade of the hangar.

I was expecting the worst when I raised the cowling on the engine, but I was vastly relieved when the first check I made revealed the problem. When I first bought the "Bug" I had installed a filter in the gas line and it had a glass bowl. That glass bowl was now completely packed with sediment from a rusty gas storage tank. Damn it! I had made another dumb mistake. In my haste to get away from the airfield at Orizaba, I had neglected to check the fuel line. I unscrewed the bowl, flushed out the line and cranked up the engine. It ran fine. Chalk up one more to experience.

While I was working on the engine, the mechanic had topped off the gas tank and had gone back into the hangar. When I went into the hangar to pay him, I noticed that he had just hung up a telephone. I paid for the gas and gave him ten pesos as a tip, rather generous, I thought. He tried to stop me at the door and said, "What do you have in your airplane? My friend the customs inspector will want to know."

I said, "None of your business, and get the hell out of my way."

He did, and I taxied out to the runway and lined up for my take off. As I started down the runway, I noticed a pickup truck coming down the runway from the opposite direction toward me at high speed. I had not put down my flaps because with all this runway, I didn't need them. I was rolling and the truck was rolling and we were on a collision course. The outcome for either of us wasn't looking too good so I dumped the flaps and the "Bug" leapt into the air and cleared the truck.

Well, almost cleared the truck. My right landing gear hit the emergency lights on the top of the truck and blew the tire, and maybe bent the gear. But, we were flying and I would worry about the gear when I had to land. I was back on schedule and my next stop was Villahermosa.

Checking my map, and doing the rough math in my head, I figured that now that I had a full load of fuel, and with a little bit of luck, I could make Merida without having to land to refuel. I was going to go for it! It was a relief to be back in the air and I relaxed and looked forward to another three hours of boring holes in the Mexican sky. When I overflew Villahermosa, I ran out of the highway that had been acting as my compass so I turned toward the east and the Bay of Campeche so I could use the coastline to guide me. The countryside was turning very green and I was flying over a lot of swamp land. Not a good place to have to land if the engine quit again. Midway between the cities of Campeche and Merida, I began to run into some rough weather and by the time I had the runway at Merida in sight, it was raining and the "Bug" was being bounced all over the sky.

During the flight, I hadn't spent much time thinking about the problems I might have in landing, but now it was top on my list of worries. I called the tower and they gave me permission to land on the ramp close to the big hangar where Steve said his airplane was located. Luckily, the considerable wind was on my nose and using full flaps, I dropped the "Bug" on the ramp. I had very little roll and the blown tire pulled me to the right, but no ground loop. A little bit of luck, and some good airmanship resulted in a happy outcome.

The tower had called Steve and he and the flight engineer, Bud, were waiting for me on the ramp. "Pretty good flying for a bomber guy," Steve said as he rushed up to the airplane. I said, "A piece of cake."

Steve and Bud seemed genuinely glad to see me and we took up our good relationship where it had left off last year. They put a rolling jack under the right wheel and we pushed the "Bug" into the hangar. It was good to be inside the hangar, and things get even better when we got to the office and they broke out an ice chest full of cold beer.

After we sat down, their first question was, "What in the hell happened on that parachute jump back in Acapulco?" Bud said the two jumpmasters and the Mexican general were jabbering back and forth and seemed to be very happy about the way things had gone, but we couldn't understand them.

"Bud, here, had seen the one guy trip you and the other one pull the ripcord on your reserve parachute and you being dragged out the rear of the airplane, and he didn't know what to think. After the rest of the paratroopers jumped, we flew back to the international airport at Acapulco and dropped the three guys off and then flew back to our base. No one ever told us who had won the bet, but it sure didn't look too good for you."

I took a slug of the Corona beer and told them the rest of the story, at least what I knew of it. Steve said, "Hey, that explains a few things that seemed strange to us. That afternoon our boss got a frantic call from the general who had hired us and the general asked the boss to destroy all evidence that we had ever been in, or near, Acapulco on that day and for the crew to forget anything that happened. Our cooperation would assure that the customs people would look kindly upon us in the future if we helped them. Case closed."

After we finished another beer, we walked out into the hangar and there was the big, ugly C-122 and the bundles of cargo piled beside it. Bud helped me unload the cargo chutes and the rest of my gear from the "Bug" and I began packing the chutes. Steve brought me some hot beans and rice and we spent the next several hours shooting the breeze while I readied the cargo for the drop to-morrow. They had many interesting stories about their adventures while flying in the jungles of Central America and about their in-teraction with the Mayan Indians, the revolutionaries in Nicaragua and El Salvador and the "grave diggers," as they called the archae-ologists who spend their time unearthing ancient Mayan ruins.

As usual, I took these "war stories" with a grain of salt, but even if only some of these stories were true, Steve and Bud were lead-ing a very exciting life. It was after midnight when I secured the final bundle and made a last-minute check. The all-important motor was going to be dropped after I had made several success-ful passes over the drop zone and was sure I had the exact exit point to guarantee the cargo was going to land where it must.

Bud broke out a collapsible cot and I went to sleep in front of the loading ramp of the C-122. I was going to make sure that no-body went near the cargo. The success of this operation was now my responsibility and I wasn't going to take a chance that any-thing that I could control was going to screw it up. As I dropped off to sleep, I was happy to hear that the wind was dying down.

The hangar was bustling with activity at six o'clock the next morning. I helped the crew pre-flight the airplane and I met the new co-pilot, Russ Hagen. He seemed like a nice guy and had certainly paid his dues during the war. He had flown a com-bat tour in B-24 Liberators as a pilot. His first mission was the famous low-level raid on the oil fields in Romania and he later flew another combat tour in B-17s with the "Bloody Hundredth Bomb Group."

The co-pilot who had flown with us on the Acapulco jump, the ex-RAF pilot, was killed last month while trying to land in a thunderstorm in Panama. Steve was lucky to get this new guy and he fit right into this bunch of battle-hardened combat veterans.

It had stopped raining but the wind was still blowing at about ten miles per hour, which meant that more wet weather was on the way. I was surprised that the Mexican custom officials were not on hand to inspect us before we took off but Steve said they were still giving him some slack when they flew humanitarian missions, and anyway they had paid their dues for this month.

The archaeological dig in Guatemala would be our first target. It was located about two hundred miles south of Merida very near the border of Guatemala and the country of Belize. It was east of Lake Yaxha and was called Talco. Steve said that the Guatemalan government was very strict about people having a passport, but no sweat, we didn't plan to land there. The expedition had been digging there for about a year and it was a very important part of the Harvard University's operation in Central America.

The Harvards were a stuffy lot, not very friendly. He guessed that they looked down on guys like him and his crew but they seemed like good people and did many helpful things for the natives, like drilling the deep water well. The boss is a female named Sarah something. She is a good looker, built like a brick outhouse and getting up in years—about 43 or so, and rules the operation with an iron hand. If we screw up she lets our boss know it, so we don't cross her.

The old C-122 shook and rattled and looked like a hard bird to fly, but Steve didn't seem to mind and kept a tight grip on the wheel. Russ established contact with the camp when we were about thirty miles north of the lake and they came in loud and clear. The speaker had a very pleasant southern drawl with a touch of high-class British in her voice and Steve said, "That's the hammer in the velvet glove. That's Sarah."

The lady gave very clear and concise information as to the wind direction and where we should drop the cargo and added, "We were counting on you guys showing up, and you're damn lucky you did. We are really hurting. I know you chaps are pros and we need to see you prove it."

Steve, like most ex-military pilots—especially fighter pilots—had a "hotdog" streak in him, so he went into a steep bank as we lost altitude and came over the camp at full bore at less than a hundred feet. I am sure that the people on the ground were off the spark plug in the motor and we can't back it out—it is jammed in tight. Even if we could, it wouldn't do us any good because we do not have another spark plug," she said.

With steel in her voice she continued, "Listen up. We need the tools to work on the German motor, we need an instruction manual and we need a spark plug. We have an extremely grave problem here and I am now giving that problem to your company. I am no longer telling you what to do, I am pleading for you to help us."

There was complete silence in the cockpit, and the only thing you could hear in the background was the laboring of the old engines. All eyes were on Steve. After a moment's thought, he turned to Russ and said, "Tell Talco that we understand the situation and we will get back to them."

At this time we had all the problems we needed. We still had a good couple of hours flying time over a very hostile jungle in an old crate that was kept in the air by a pair of worn-out engines, one of which was likely to catch on fire at any moment. If that happened, we all had parachutes and we could bail out and that would take care of the immediate problem for us, but without us, the Talco people and the natives that depended on them were in for some tragic times. Hopefully, that wasn't going to happen, so we had better start thinking about how we were going to get the tools and parts to Talco and get that pump working.

Steve turned around to me and said, "Jim, I'm having all I can do flying this damn thing and watching the gauges, so I'll turn the discussion over to you."

My mind was going a mile a minute and I answered, "Thanks a lot, buddy."

The bottom line was simple. We needed a simple spark plug and a German wrench that fits it. And we needed to screw that simple spark plug into a motor that will drive a generator that will power a machine that will pump fresh clean water that hundreds of people will drink and stay alive.

There were a few problems here. First, getting that simple spark plug and second, delivering that simple spark plug to Talco. I grabbed Russ by the shoulder and shouted to him, "Call ahead to company headquarters and tell them to go to the place where the Harvards bought the motor and buy a spark plug, no, buy several spark plugs, and deliver them to the hangar. Also, buy all the German metric tools that are needed to work on the motor and, this is very important, buy a tool called an "easy out" in American. I don't know what the Germans call it, but it is a drill bit that has reverse threads that will back out the part of the plug that is still jammed in the cylinder head. Make sure it is the right size. Also, pick up an operating manual for the motor, preferably in English."

If all goes well, we will get the part to the airport. How are we going to get it to Talco? My flight engineer experience tells me that by the time we get back to the hangar at Merida, the number two engine on the C-122 will be totaled and have to be changed. But we have no choice but to keep it running with low oil pressure if we will have any chance of making it back to our base and this is going to burn up its insides. What can replace our present airplane? We do not need a big plane for a cargo drop, but we do need one big enough to battle the rough weather we are having, and will continue to have, for the foreseeable future.

Steve took the mike from Russ and put the radio on the speaker and told the operator to put the boss on the phone. I gave my thoughts to Steve and he repeated my demands to the boss back at company headquarters and added, "We need this stuff as soon as possible."

About ten minutes later, the boss called back and he said, "We have a problem here. The distributor said that they do not stock any spare parts and the only thing that they have in their inventory is another motor just like the one he sold to the people from Harvard. The conversation was coming over the speaker and I asked the boss to offer to buy the spark plug from that motor and we would pay to have the replacement air freighted to him.

The store manager was now on the phone and the boss asked him if he would sell the plug to us. His answer was "Hell no. What if a customer came in and wanted to look at a motor? We might miss the chance to make a sale." My anxiety was growing as well as my frustration and I asked the boss to ask him if he knew that this was an emergency and people's lives depended on our getting this part. The manager told the boss that he was aware that this was an emergency but that our problems were not his problems and he was not going to help us.

It was four o'clock before we got airborne and it was now raining very hard. Bud tried to climb up through this mess, but he had to level out at five thousand feet and we flew on using the compass as our guide. We passed through one weather cell after another and sometimes when we were in the clear, Bud could check our location by using landmarks he had seen since he first started flying this route several years ago. Bud was a very good pilot and he was especially careful in using the correct power settings and in avoiding any violent changes in altitude when flying through the rough weather.

I had been monitoring the radio and making transmissions every now and then and suddenly, Sarah came up on the net. In her most pleasing voice she said, "I knew you Yanks would not desert me and my people. What is your ETA?"

I replied, "We will be over your camp in about fifteen minutes. How is the weather down there?"

"It is bloody erratic. Sometimes blowing like the dickens, and sometimes very little wind. We will be praying for calm when you drop the cargo.

"By the way, there has been another change in our situation here and it makes things even more critical. The Mayan Indian mechanic who takes care of all our things mechanical has disappeared, along with his family. My advisors say he has lost face with his people and he will not ever be seen again in the area. We have several PhD's in our group, but no one who knows how to use the most common of tools. Do you happen to have a 'handyman' with you?"

The "Iron Hammer's" last request was delivered with a smile and a desperate plea in her soft southern drawl.

After a pause, Bud looked at me and said, with a kind of sneer, "With all your big bomber B-29 experience, that mechanic's job should be a piece of cake for you. And I know that you are a pretty fair parachute jumper. How about it?"

I gulped a little, and to gain some time to think I said, "Let's take a look at it from twenty five hundred feet or lower."

Bud started to let down from our altitude of five thousand feet. We passed through several cloud layers and the wind seemed to be blowing from several different directions at the same time.

When we had dropped down to twenty five hundred feet, I asked Bud to make a pass over the clearing so I could check the wind sock. Through a break in the clouds, I caught a glimpse of the sock, and I didn't like what I saw. It was swinging back and forth and sometimes standing straight out from the pole. But considering what was at stake, I decided that I would make the jump and take my chances. Damn it! This is going to screw up my chances of getting to that mining convention in El Paso, but I'll worry about that later. The cargo drop would probably be successful, but who in that group would be able to put the system in working order and not completely mess up the entire system while trying?

I asked Bud to continuing flying at this altitude to give me a chance to take the stuff from the cargo box and jam it inside my flight suit and when I was ready, he should drop down to a thousand feet and I would make a jump and pull and forget the delayed free fall from the higher altitude. I worked my way into the parachute harness and pulled the straps up tight.

He said "stand by" and I started to crawl toward the door. He turned and yelled, "You know, you are out of your mind. You don't owe any of these people down there a damn thing."

I yelled back at him, "You are probably right but as we used to say in my Army Air Corps, it is just another chance to excel."

The wind was bouncing the airplane all over the sky at this altitude so I asked Bud to slow the airplane down as much as he could.

Bud said, "OK, but I still have to keep plenty of power on in case we run into any sudden downdrafts." A short time later he yelled, "Ready," and as he skidded the aircraft, I popped the door open and squeezed out into what seemed like a hurricane. I dropped away from the airplane and immediately pulled the ripcord. Out of the corner of my eye I saw the parachute canopy explode from the container on my back but I never felt an opening shock. I glanced down and I realized that my body was parallel to the ground. Then I oscillated up and down and up the other side. I sensed that I was moving pretty fast and the ground, or anything else I could see, was a blur.

When I passed from the clearing into the dense green jungle, I saw I was traveling downwind at a high rate of speed and I didn't want to hit that wall of trees with my face so I pulled down on the right rear riser with all my might so I could turn and land with my back toward the trees.

My last thoughts before touchdown were, "Damn, this is going to hurt real bad." I smashed into the foliage and braced myself for a sudden stop against a tree or a large rock. To my surprise, the closely-packed plants and small trees slowed my body to a smooth stop and I ended up wrapped in my parachute canopy. Boy, was I lucky to have missed the clearing and land in the small trees!

The fabric of the canopy was flapping wildly and the rain was beating me down into the mass of tropical plants, but I didn't mind. I could hardly believe it. I was alive and I was a very happy parachutist. I was going to walk away from what was a very difficult parachute jump with nothing worse than a wet flight suit. I had been hurt more on an exhibition jump landing on two inches of Kentucky bluegrass in a football stadium. I looked around and there was no body fluid gushing out of my body and no bones sticking out of my clothes. I moved my arms and legs and swiveled my head and everything worked just fine.

I struggled out of my parachute harness and didn't even try to pick up the canopy. The natives can have it. Give it to the chief's daughter to make a wedding dress. I unzipped my flight suit and removed the bag containing the undamaged spark plug, the tools and the operating manual. This was the prize. This was what it was all about!

As I was walking out of the jungle, two young Americans rushed up. They were breathing hard.

"Are you hurt? Can we help you?" they gasped. One of them, a girl with buck teeth wearing pigtails and dressed in khaki shorts, a sweat shirt that said "Vassar" and a pith helmet, almost collapsed from exhaustion and I caught her by the arm.

It was getting dark and they steered me to a building where a kerosene lamp was burning. We walked through the screen door and there was only one person in the room, a woman wearing tight khaki shorts. She was bending over a table looking at a map. She looked great from the rear, a fantastic pair of muscular legs and a tight bottom. She looked even better from the front. She had on a man's shirt and it was unbuttoned to the middle of her chest. My eyes bugged out, her eyes locked onto mine and there was silence in the room.

The buck-toothed girl said, "This is Professor Mason. She is the boss of this dig."

So this is Sarah. The iron hand in the velvet glove. The woman who is getting up there in years but is built like a brick outhouse, according to Steve. She had her dark red hair tied in a bun and she was wearing a ridiculous pith helmet. Her face was beautiful but in that get-up, she looked like an explorer out of darkest Africa. I put out my hand, and so did she, and her eyes never left mine.

"Dr. Livingstone, I presume," I blurted out and handed her the bag of stuff.

Whatever caused me to say that stupid line, I'll never know and I just stood there with a dumb look on my face.

She took the bag, opened it, looked inside and flashed a smile that lit up the entire room. In a very seductive voice she said, "So, we have a 'handyman' here with a sense of humor. I knew you Yanks would come through. You are my kind of men and I haven't seen too many like you in a long time."

She hugged me, long and real close and I felt a jolt go through my body, something that I hadn't felt since my college days, when I had been lucky enough to have lured a co-ed into the back seat of the Green Hornet.

There was an awkward silence and I asked her, "Where is the pump. We had better get started while we still have some light."

"Follow me," she said as she picked up the lamp and started for the door. The girl with the teeth said, "Professor, it's raining outside. Don't you think we need a flashlight?"

The Iron Lady's ears turned the color of her hair and she stammered, "I guess I got excited about having the pump fixed." The girl produced a large flashlight and we walked out on the porch. I asked the professor if she had an umbrella. She said, "Are you kidding? But I do have a poncho. How about you?" I told her "I can't get any wetter, so let's go."

We walked about fifty yards to a small building at the edge of the clearing, and here was the cause of all the trouble. The last time I had seen the motor it was brand new. Now it was scratched and scarred and the fittings to the carburetor were rounded as if they had been worked on with a pair of pliers. I didn't know if the Indian mechanic or one of the PhD's had done the damage, but whoever had brutalized this motor had most surely flunked basic mechanic's school.

The generator seemed to be in good working condition, but the pulleys and the belts needed to be changed as soon as possible. Steve or his boss will need to talk to the Harvards when they renew their contract and make a deal to replace this junk with American-made products, and include spares.

Using the special tool, the easy-out, I backed out the broken spark plug and using the metric wrench I carefully replaced the spark plug. I checked and cleaned the carburetor, hooked the motor up to the generator, and replaced the gas tank that came with the new motor with the larger one that had been part of the old one. We were ready for business.

The motor started right away, the generator started generating electricity, the pump began to pump and the storage tank began to fill up.

The operation was a success but I would have to carefully check out at least two of the PhD's on the care and operation of this equipment before I left.

But right now, it was dark and I was tired and I would sure like to have a beer. On the off chance that she might have a cold beer, I asked her.

She said, "No, but I have something much better than that. We make our own home brew for special occasions, and I decree this to be a special occasion."

Sarah had been my helper for the past hour and it was very close and very hot inside the pump house and we were having more body contact than if we were wrestling. My nostrils were filled with the smell of one hundred percent girl, plus a latent fragrance of some exotic perfume. I had taken off my flight suit and Sarah had unfastened another button. I wiped the sweat from my face and said, "Let's go," and she said the magic words, "OK, let's go back to my quarters and have a drink, or maybe a couple of drinks."

It was still raining and Sarah put on her poncho and asked me if I wanted to share it with her. I declined, as I was still wet and there was no reason both of us should be miserable—although the thought of being close to her under any circumstances tempted me.

On the way to Sarah's quarters, we ran into an old Mayan Indian man with a lantern in his hand. We stopped and she introduced me to Jose, the night watchman. She told him to be sure and check every now and then to make sure everything was all right with the water pump.

I asked her, "Why do you need a watchman?"

"Well, you know, a crocodile might wander into camp. Anyway, it helps the economy to employ some of the older people who have no way of making a living."

We passed a hut that probably served as a recreation room and through the window screen we saw two guys playing chess and two others reading by the light from a single hundred-watt bulb. Sarah said, "Let's stop here. Two of the guys in there are potential conscripts to work on the pump system, but of course they will never rise to the level of my personal "handyman.""

As were entered the room the two readers greeted the boss but the other two never stirred or removed their eyes from the chess board. We stood over them for a full two minutes before guy "A" finally moved a piece. As a chess player, I saw that it was a stupid move and I thought to myself, that guy couldn't be too bright. He was wearing horn-rimmed glasses and when he looked up, the pupils of his eyes were magnified and he looked like a frog. He said, "Thanks a lot for getting the lights fixed. How did you do that?"

Sarah put her arm around my shoulder and said, "This is our savior from the sky. His name is, she paused, shook her head and asked me, say, what is your name?" I replied, "My name is Jim, I think. I usually wear a name tag so I don't forget."

Nobody's expression changed and I knew that my attempt at humor had failed again. I could see that I could never make a living with this group as a stand-up comic.

Sarah continued, "This is Fredrick Burton. He has a doctorate from Yale and one from Harvard—both in economics." He had a smug look on his face and didn't bother to look me in the eye or shake my outstretched hand.

I didn't like him at all and I said, "You don't play much chess do you? That was a really dumb move you just made."

He said, "Huh," and gave me a blank stare.

Sarah turned to guy "B" and introduced him as Anderson Hildabrand. He has his doctorate from Oxford in Philosophy and will be teaching next year. He also didn't make any effort to shake hands or acknowledge that I was a person.

I thought, "What a pair of nerds." After a pause, Sarah said, "These are the two guys I was talking to you about training to operate the motor and generator, but let's talk about it in the morning."

After we got outside in the rain, Sarah yelled, "Well, what did you think of them?" I yelled back, "What's the chance of getting the Indian to come back?"

Sarah's quarters here in the jungles of Guatemala were a slice of a teenage girl's room back home. It was divided into two sections. The first section, the one I was most interested in, was the living quarters. It had a small single bed, several pieces of furniture made of mahogany by the Indians, a straight-back chair and a wash stand. The other section was where she kept her "grave diggers" clothes and other tools of the archaeologist's trade.

She pulled back a heavy curtain and removed a collapsible Army cot and smiled and said, "This is for you." I helped her set it up and she said, "I don't have a pair of pants for you to wear, but I do have a large beach towel that should fill the bill. She returned to the closet and tossed me the towel and a sweat shirt—the sweat shirt seemed to be a standard part of the uniform worn by the diggers—and said, "I'll turn my back until you get changed, and then we can hang your clothes in the work room. If it quits raining, they will be dry by the morning."

I took off my soggy boots, my iron pants and shirt and pulled the sweatshirt over my head. The sweatshirt wasn't exactly what I would have chosen to wear in public. It was pink and had the letters "WESLEYAN" written across the front, but it fit.

When Sarah turned around and looked, she flashed that million dollar-smile and said, "Jim, you sure look cute."

I said, "Thanks. Now where is that home brew you raved about?"

She went into the archaeologist's side and returned with a jug and two green squash gourds with pink "Ws" drawn on the side with a magic marker.

"I still have the old school spirit. The 'W's are for Wesleyan College where I was 'brung up' in Macon, Georgia. I'm sure they would be proud of me if they could see me now."

She lifted the jug to her shoulder like a redneck moonshiner and poured me a cup full of the brew. I took a drink like it was beer; that was a big mistake. That stuff was stronger that the shine my old man used to make in our cellar back in Pennsylvania.

I coughed a couple of times and Sarah gave me that radiant smile and said, "Take it easy, 'handyman,' the night is still young."

I could no longer hear the rain bouncing off the corrugated iron roof and I assumed that the rain had stopped. This was confirmed when I looked out the window and I could see an occasional shaft of moonlight break through the swiftmoving clouds.

As Sarah was hanging up my wet clothes in the work room, there was a timid knock on the door. She opened the door and there stood a young Mayan man with an anguished look on his face. "Dr. Sarah, you must help me. My wife, she says she is having a baby and she is in much pain. Please help me. This is our first baby and we don't know what to do. We need you."

Sarah was halfway out the door when she turned and said, "Make yourself at home. I'll be back as soon as I can." And she was gone.

When she returned, she was out of breath. She sat down on her bed and said, "These poor people, they have so little and their lives are so difficult. I keep asking the University for more money to help them, but they say, that is not the school's business. You are down here to dig up their past. It is their responsibility to take care of their future."

She went into her work room and when she came back, I sensed that she wanted to talk. She sat cross-legged on her bed and she had a very serious look on her face. Sarah was a very beautiful woman. She had exchanged her work shirt for a Wesleyan sweat shirt, another pink one, but it sure looked good on her, and her hair had been liberated from the severe bun and now hung down to her shoulders. The color was a rich, dark auburn and the flickering lamp light caused a few streaks of gray to stand out. It reminded me of my mother's beautiful long hair.

My mom was light years away from being a vain person, but one luxury she did allow herself was to wash and comb her hair every night after all the kids were in bed. As mom gazed in the mirror, I imagined that it brought back many fond memories of when she was a southern belle growing up in Virginia.

It had been a long day since I had climbed into that old transport at six o'clock this morning and now, with a cup of home brew in my hand and my boots off, I was beginning to unwind. Sarah sat cross-legged on the bed and she sure didn't look any thing like a forty-three or forty-four year old woman, as Steve had said. Steve was a damn good pilot, but I decided that he didn't know much about beautiful women, and Sarah got more beautiful with each swallow of the strong drink.

"Tell me about yourself, Jim. You are a gutsy guy and you take a lot of chances for someone with an education. I don't mean to be an elitist, but you are an engineer. Couldn't you make a good living without jumping out of airplanes?" she said out of the blue.

She caught me off guard and I shot back, "How about you, Sarah? You have 'Doctor' in front of your name and here you are digging in the dirt like a little kid looking for bones and pieces of cooking pots and playing wet nurse to a bunch of spoiled, over-educated brats."

I must have hit a raw nerve and she got a wounded look on her face. I hit her again with, "You are a beautiful and very desirable woman and you are wasting your life away in this rotten jungle in a third-world country."

The room was silent and I thought, now is the time to make my move. I got to my feet and as I was walking toward the bed, there was another knock on the door. Sarah jumped to her feet and yelled, "Who is it?"

"It is me, Jose," a voice said.

"What do you want," Sarah answered, in what I thought was an annoyed voice.

"The pump. She no working," Jose said.

"I'll be right there to look at it," Sarah replied.

Sarah looked at me and gave me a weak smile, I guess it was more of a relieved grin as if to say, "Your timing is lousy."

As I was putting on my boots, she tossed me my flight suit. "You are going to need this. I hope you can fix this in a hurry, 'handyman,'" and smiled that milliondollar smile.

The camp was quiet as we trudged toward the pump shed. As we got closer, I could hear the motor running. That was a good sign, but what in the hell could be wrong with the pump? Several things, many things, and all of them bad.

Jose was waiting for us and as he opened the door, I brushed him aside. I was not a happy worker. The gasoline motor was chugging

away, fine. The pulleys and the belt that were driving the generator were OK, but there was the problem laying on the floor. The
belt that connected the generator and the pump was broken!

"Damn you," I said as I kicked the pump. "You bastard, you
screwed us before! But not this time." There was a spare belt that
had been with the pump unit for some time and all I had to do
was install it. This was going to be a minor repair. I didn't want
to make it look too easy, but I also didn't want to waste any time.
I had other things on my mind. I double checked the set-up, filled
the gas tank, and patted Jose on the shoulder to show him I was-
n't mad at him. We were in and out in ten minutes and as we
left, the water was flowing into the storage tank.

As we walked back to Sarah's quarters, I felt like skipping, but
I had forgotten how to do that 25 years ago and, anyway, it would
spoil my image of a gutsy guy. I was ready to take up where I
had left off, and I was in a hurry.

But my world came crashing down when we got back to the
quarters. The girl with the teeth was waiting for us and she said
in her whining, spoiled brat voice, "Professor Mason. We need
you over at our dorm. One of the girls has problems. Won't you
please come?"

Sarah gave me a "what can I do" look, and followed the buck-
toothed, skinny, stringy-haired, pigtail-wearing, ugly girl into the
beautiful tropic night with the moon shining down and me ready
for love.

Oh, how I wished an Anaconda would slither out of the jungle and grab the buck-tooted one or maybe a crocodile would
emerge from the nearby stream and crush her in its massive jaws.
She sure had thrown a bucket of cold water on all my plans.

I sat down on the cot and thought, what am I to do? I could slit
my throat, but that wasn't a very good idea so I looked around
the room. Not much of interest but I did see a couple of magazines. I was let down when I discovered that they were old copies
of National Geographic. I guessed that was the latest in reading
for archaeologists. I hadn't read one of these magazines, or rather
looked at the pictures in one of these magazines since I was a
little kid.

When I was in sixth or seventh grade, one of my buddies and I
got separated from our classmates on a trip to the library and we

went exploring. We came upon a stack of National Geographic magazines and while we were thumbing through one of them, we discovered a woman from Africa standing in an open field and she did not have a shirt on, or anything else. Nothing.

We thought, so that's what a girl looks like. My buddy remarked, "They sure are different from us." I thought, they sure are. We couldn't wait to get back to school to tell the rest of the gang what we had seen. After that, we always looked forward to these trips to the library. We would fake an excuse to go to the bathroom so we could sneak off to the room where they had the magazines and look at the pictures.

The pictures were always of black women in Africa and it wasn't until I was fifteen that I discovered that white girls had the same things. The magazines I had found were pretty much the same as those in the library, but the thrill was gone so I read some of the articles. I already knew about all I wanted to know about Africa, so I put the National Geographic aside and just waited for Sarah to return.

After what seemed like hours, Sarah glided in and she said, "Sorry, but it is part of my job. I hope you had a chance to improve your mind and learned something new." I said, "I only learned how much I missed you and how beautiful you are." She said, "I guess we had better turn off the lights and get some sleep." She tried to blow out the flame in the lamp, realized that wasn't going to work, and turned down the wick. We both anxiously watched the flame die.

The room was pitch dark except for one ray of moonlight streaming through the window and she was standing in that ray. She crossed her arms and lifted the pink sweatshirt up and off to reveal a body that would put the Venus de Milo to shame. I had seen many beautiful bodies since I was fifteen, but this one had no equal. The moonbeams bounced off her firm, rock-hard breasts and if I wasn't in love before, I sure was now.

Not a word was spoken and she lay down on her bed. I sat up on my cot, reached down to take off my boots, and passed out.

When I woke up, it was morning. The light hurt my eyes and my head was pounding. When I sat up, I saw that I was on the floor. There was a pillow beside me and I was wrapped in a woman's bathrobe. As my eyes focused and my mind began to function, I noted that my boots were still on my feet and my damp flight suit remained zipped up.

What had happened last night? Obviously, nothing. I heard a sound from behind me and I turned around to see my angel, just as beautiful as she was when I last saw her. But this morning, boy did she look different. She was wearing an old gray sweatshirt, khaki shorts, and clodhopper shoes. Her hair was tied up in a severe bun and it was all topped off with that dumb-looking pith helmet. But she still was beautiful. She had a gourd of steaming black coffee cupped in her hands.

I hate coffee, especially black coffee, but I would have drunk hemlock if she had offered it to me. I had never felt this way before toward another person. At this particular moment, I would have probably bailed out of an airplane flying at twenty thousand feet without a parachute if she asked me to do it.

She smiled and said, "Sorry about last night, 'handyman,' but you looked like you needed the sleep. I have to go now to put the diggers to work, but I will be back in about an hour and then maybe you can start training a couple of the students." She touched my cheek, smiled that irresistible smile and said, "Here are a couple of aspirins to take the bite out of that Georgia moonshine. See you in a little while."

There was a canteen of water on the table so I downed the aspirins and got to my feet. I passed on drinking the coffee and sat down again on the cot. To sit on her bed would have been sacrilegious.

I noticed that my lower back was beginning to hurt. I suspected that you don't walk away from a jump like the one I made yesterday without a few aches and pains. I lay down on the cot, and about an hour later I felt better.

A little while later, Sarah returned with some warm rice and beans. I have had better breakfasts, but not with such charming company. It was raining again, and Sarah was eager to have some of her people checked out on the motor, the generator and the water pump. I asked her if she had any other students who might be trainable and she said she was expecting me to ask her that question. She had figured out that I was not impressed with the chess players we had met yesterday.

She replied that she had two students in mind, but one of them was a woman. I told her that was all right with me; I was an equal opportunity trainer. "Women can do more than just sit around and look pretty, and you are a good example."

"Flattery will get you almost anything," she said with a suggestive smile. "Your trainees will be waiting for us at the pump house."

Sarah had brought an extra poncho with her and I put it over my head and we walked toward the shed. The two new recruits she had selected looked a lot better than the chess players. One was a young man from England. His name was Chester Wilkes. He graduated from a college in London with a master's degree in literature. The other student was a girl named Joyce and she was from New York. She had graduated from Columbia with a masters in, of all things, archaeology. I liked them both and they were eager to learn.

In about two hours, we had covered just about anything that could go wrong with the equipment and I promised them that I would ask Steve to include instruction manuals for all the machines in his next cargo delivery.

Sarah showed me around the camp and I made suggestions about how they could do things that would make life easier for the "diggers." But my thoughts were really on how soon night would fall.

As we made our inspection tour of the camp, we passed many of the natives. They stepped out of our way and removed their hats and said, "Good morning, Señorita Doctor." I expected to see them genuflect and cross themselves. Saint Sarah—what a pretty name.

We had just sat down to eat lunch when one of the students approached and said, "Prof. Mason, there is a native who has to talk to you. I think he is the village chief."

We went outside to talk to the man and he was, indeed, the chief of all the villages surrounding the camp. Behind him waited a pack train of sleepy burros. He spoke in a Mayan dialect language and she surprised me, again, as she answered him in fluent Mayan. He showed great respect for Sarah and she returned the courtesy by inviting him to have lunch with us.

This woman had it all. Along with the beauty, she had diplomatic skills. The chief regretted that he could not join us as he was in a hurry. The surrounding villages had a council meeting this morning and decided that, on the advice of the elders who are predicting that these storms are going to last several more weeks, that an emergency trip to a highland town must be made to bring back supplies to feed the villagers, as the rain had destroyed some of the crops. He was embarrassed to have to ask for a loan of three hundred quetzals—this was about fifty dollars, American—against future delivery of local goods to the camp.

Sarah said "no problem" and produced the money from a belt she wore around her waist. This gal was a walking bank and she had an answer for everything. The chief thanked her and asked if he could buy anything for the camp. She said, "Thanks, but we didn't need anything at this time, only your continued friendship." The chief bowed and said, "Señorita, you will always have that."

I had been listening to the conversation and although I did not speak the language, I got the drift of what they were talking about.

The thought struck me that this might be a way for me to get to a town in the highlands where I could hook up with transportation that could get me back to Merida, get the "Bug," fly to Zacatecas and then get to El Paso in time to attend the meeting on Monday. I looked at Sarah, paused, swallowed a couple of times and before I could think this thing through, I said to Sarah, "Ask him if I could go with his pack train."

Sarah looked at me in disbelief. "Are you sure?" she asked.

I nodded my head and said, "It will give me a fighting chance to make a very important meeting in El Paso on Monday morning. If I miss this meeting when I have an opportunity to be there, I will be kicking myself for a long time to come." Sarah relayed my request to the chief and he asked, "Can he ride a burro without a saddle?" I said, "Yes." He said, "OK."

On the off-chance I had heard wrong, and maybe they could delay the departure until early tomorrow morning, I asked, "When are you going to leave?"

"Immediately, right now," he replied. The chief turned and walked back toward the burros and their ears picked up and they started to trot out of the camp. I was wearing the same clothes I had on when I arrived, so I guess I was packed, but not necessarily ready to go. I had not recovered my parachute, so I was leaving something.

I told Sarah, "The parachute is yours. Do with it what you want to, but save a couple of pieces for a scarf. You will be in fashion when you get back to the States." I took her hands and looked into her eyes—they were deep blue—another remarkable thing about a remarkable lady that I had not noticed before.

I said, simply, "I will be seeing you again." I wanted very much to kiss her full on the lips, but I didn't. For her, the whole world was watching, the students—her world at this time—was watching and I didn't want to confuse that world.

I fell in line behind the last burro and we were on our way to the high ground. There would be many streams and many rivers to cross and a couple of mountains to climb, but I hoped I could reach El Paso by Monday morning. I was leaving behind something that I had never known before, but things can be tough when you need a job, and, right now, I did. I needed it badly.

27
Return to Merida

I hadn't even been introduced to the chief, but I was now a member of the party. We had a total of eighteen burros, and as burros go, these were a pretty good-looking bunch. They had been well fed and they didn't look as if they had been overworked.

In addition to the chief, there were five helpers, all young men. They weren't as tough and raw looking as the guys from Chihuahua or Zacatecas, and they acted as if they were on vacation. I imagined that it would be a different-acting group when they were returning with fully loaded, balky, tired beasts. The pack train moved at a fairly rapid clip, as the trail was well-maintained and well-traveled.

About an hour out of camp, we ran into our first obstacle. What was probably usually a slow flowing stream was now a racing river of water. I thought this was going to be a problem, but some enterprising Guatemalan had spanned the flood with two stout ropes, and for a fee, a traveler could use his ropes. The chief paid the man, and I, being a member of the train, got to cross for free. This was all right with me, as I knew that I would need all the money I had to get back to Merida.

The rest of the afternoon was spent crossing smaller streams and wading through puddles. We were always wet and my back was hurting, but no one mentioned riding the burros, so I kept on walking. The chief must have known where we were going, because when we entered a small village, there was a large pot of thick something cooking over a fire and a basket of something that passed as bread waiting for us.

It was every man for himself and we all dipped the bread into the pot and slopped the thick something all over the pot, the ground and ourselves as we crowded around the fire. After a minute or so, I decided that I wasn't hungry anyway.

The chief indicated that we were all going to be sleeping in a small hut and after dinner we all crowded into that hut and found a place to lie down. The Indians all had a combination poncho and serape that was carried on the backs of the burros and that made a good ground cover for them. My only covering was my flight suit. Fortunately, I had taken it off when we left the camp and had carried it over my head when we crossed the streams and, although it was still damp, I had managed to keep it fairly dry.

It was kind of cozy inside the hut, and in short order the chief and his helpers were fast asleep and the place sounded like a bunch of braying donkeys. It was warm enough, but my back hurt like hell and I was miserable. What made it worse was that I had a fleeting thought that I could be back in the digger's camp and maybe, just maybe, I could be sharing Sarah's single bed. I tried to put that out of my mind, but that was impossible, especially when it began to rain—a soft, gentle rain that reminded me so much of that soft, gentle lady. Sometime during the night but well before dawn, the chief got up and yelled something in Mayan and the helpers leapt to their feet and hurried out the door. I quickly followed them, as anything was better than lying on that hard ground.

It was still dark when we ran into the next river. It was the same drill with the ropes, and the water was just as wet. After we crossed the river, the ground began to rise and we were climbing. The brush became less sodden with water and the trail less muddy and the rain stopped. We crossed a road and I was relieved when the pack train turned and followed it. It had to mean that we were near a village. About a mile later, the road was dry and up ahead there was a cluster of huts, and a truck parked in front of them.

This was the end of the line for the pack train and the beginning of another leg of the journey that, for me, I hoped, would end in El Paso on Monday at noon. I said goodbye to the chief and he muttered something in Mayan. I was tempted to ask him why he had asked Sarah if I could ride a burro without a saddle when he never gave me a chance to get near one of the animals.

The truck was going to the next village, for a price. I paid the price and I was on my way with a much better feeling that I had a chance to arrive at my destination. I hitched a ride with several other trucks and vehicles that passed as taxicabs, until we reached a town called Teculutan, where I caught a second-class bus. I tried to get some sleep on the bus, but the road was rutted and the bus bounced up and down so I didn't have much luck.

When the bus pulled into the station at Guatemala City, I wasn't interested in seeing the sights of this old historic town; all I wanted to do was get out of here and head for the Mexican border. I took the next bus north to Mexico and as we neared the border, it dawned on me that I didn't have a single piece of identification. But I did have something that solved all problems at the border, and that was money. I usually carry a small amount of money in my right side pocket to pay for small stuff. The bigger bills I carry in my left pocket, with a safety pin to keep the cash from falling out, or to keep someone from helping themselves to it.

When the customs officer got to me and asked for my papers, I handed him everything I had in my right side pocket. He took it and said, "Is this all?" I turned my pocket inside out and showed him it was empty. He looked at me with disgust and walked away.

Damn, that was a close call. If he had taken me off the bus, I could have spent who knows how long at this outpost, and I would have had to do some dumb thing like knock him on the head and steal his bicycle and continue on my very important journey to El Paso.

I reached Tuxtla Gutierrez late Friday night and tried in vain to sleep on a bench at the bus station with the rest of the peons. The next morning, Saturday, I was flying toward Merida and we landed there at noon.

As soon as the airplane stopped, I went into the terminal and checked the flight schedule to see if they had anything going north that would take me to Zacatecas. There was nothing. I had toyed with the idea of leaving the "Bug" at Steve's hangar here in Merida, and flying commercial to El Paso, attending the meeting, and flying back to Merida and, somehow, going back to Guatemala to see Sarah. After I thought it through, I could see that it was impractical. I hadn't had a bath in a couple of days, I smelled like a goat, and looked worse, and I hadn't slept in two days. But I guess that's what you do when you are young and in love.

I called Steve and was he surprised to hear from me. "I'll be right over to pick you up," he said. From the time I opened the door to his pick up, he couldn't stop talking. For a calm, cool fighter pilot, he sure was excited.

"Bud thought you were a goner when you bailed out in a hell of a rainstorm. He also thought you were nuts. He didn't stick around as he was getting low on fuel, and there was nothing he could do to help you, anyway."

We drove into the big hangar and Steve said, "I know it's early, but I believe that this reunion deserves a couple of beers. How about it?"

"Is the Pope a Catholic?" I replied and we piled out of his truck and walked into the office.

As we were having our first beer, Bud walked in. He greeted me warmly and said, "For a pretty fair engineer, you ain't too bright, but I sure am glad to see your ignorant butt back here." He had been working on the C-122, stripping the accessory parts from the engine and getting it ready to be removed. The company reluctantly decided to buy a rebuilt engine to hang on the airplane and it looked like the crew was going to be back in business in another week.

We spent the next couple of hours getting caught up on what had happened the last few days and we drank all the beer in the cooler.

"Did you meet that tough, sweet-talking gal that runs the outfit?" Steve asked.

"I sure did," I said, "and she is the girl of my dreams. And I don't want any of you common aviators getting any ideas when you get back down there. She is mine and I intend to get back here just as soon as I can, hopefully, as soon as you get this wreck back in flying shape."

They laughed, and Steve said, "I'll be damned if I don't think you are serious. Have you lost your mind? It's in the genes of guys like us to love 'em and leave ' em. I thought you were smarter than that."

I answered, "I guess I'm not that smart. I have really fallen for the girl."

Steve sensed that he was beginning to tread on sensitive ground and he changed the subject. "Buddy, you look like hell. Why don't you take a shower and wash some of that crud off of you and sack out for a while? We have a cot that we keep in the storeroom that we rent out to visiting airmen, and although it is not as plush as the officer's quarters at Andrews in Washington, we'll let you use it at half price. You can pay us when you come back."

I said, "Thanks, I'll take you up on your offer. But first, I've got to get my bird ready to leap out of here at first light tomorrow morning." I looked over the "Bug" and it was just as I had left it, except they had fixed the tire. Bud said that the landing gear was not damaged, and it was safe to fly. I checked the oil, topped off the gas tank and we were ready to head north.

I would be flying light, as all my parachutes were somewhere in Guatemala and Honduras and I didn't even have a personnel chute. I took a shower, shaved and laid down. The old Army cot seemed like a feather bed, at least for a while until my back began to hurt, and I discovered a few other bruises, but I went to sleep anyway.

The next morning, I was ready to go as soon as the ground crew opened the hangar doors. I strapped on the old Super Cub and taxied out on the ramp. I didn't bother to go to the runway and just as the sun sprang up from the jungle, I jammed the throttle full forward and the 150-horsepower engine kicked in and the old Super Cub leapt into the air like a thoroughbred horse and we were outbound for Zacatecas. It was a beautiful day and it was great to be flying again.

I was glad to be gone from the memories of the wet jungle but the one memory I couldn't get rid of was the memory of Sarah. That was going to be hard to do. It was a clear day and there was no significant wind from any direction. I followed the coast line and I landed to refuel at Villahermosa. I would like to extend the range of the "Bug," but I didn't want to land at Coatzacoalcos where I had had the encounter with the customs officer's pickup, as I was sure that the officer would still like to extract some tribute from the Americano airman. I overflew Orizaba and landed at the airport in Puebla.

I had always wanted to visit this town where the Mexican Army defeated the French and gave us Americans the "Cinco de

Mayo" holiday, but I had much more important things to do, so I just gassed up. The custom's officer came out to inspect my plane but since I was not carrying any cargo, he could not think of any reasonable excuse to detain me. So I took off without paying a bribe—a good thing, as I had used my last bit of cash to buy gas.

Three hours later, I was back at home base. I drove into town and when I got to the hotel, Elena was waiting for me. "You are late, mi Ingeniero. I have been worried for you."

I said, "You had no need to worry about me. All in all, it was a dull trip. How are your mother and the ninos?"

"They are fine," she said. "Everything here is still the same."

Maybe everything is the same for you, I thought, but not for me. Since I had left, the world had changed. I now had Sarah on my mind.

El Paso and the Sonora Jump

My flight touched down in Juarez at ten o'clock on Monday morning. I caught a cab and cleared customs at the border without any trouble. No money changed hands, and I was at the mining convention just in time to sit in on a discussion concerning the possibility of finding any gold or diamonds in the "Lost World" area of southern Venezuela. This was a happy coincidence, as this was an area of the world in which I had been interested since I first studied geology.

At noon I met the officers of both companies that were interested in the "long shot" gold mines in Mexico and I was surprised that there appeared to be no animosity between them. I got the feeling that both companies had exploration money to spend as they wished, and may the best man win.

They decided that we would skip the convention-sponsored luncheon and eat out. This we did, at the most expensive restaurant in El Paso.

It was obvious that they were on expense accounts and that the home office was going to pay for them having the best while they were away from home. The booze and the BS flowed freely, and it was hard to keep the conversation on the subject of gold mines in Mexico.

At the end of a two-hour drinking lunch, I managed to get an invitation to visit the headquarters of one company, all expenses paid, to talk to their chief engineer. Their headquarters were in Albuquerque, and they would be available to talk on Wednesday morning at ten o'clock. I hadn't been in Albuquerque since I graduated from UNM four years earlier, so I jumped at the chance to visit my old stomping grounds on their dime.

These highly-paid officials decided to ditch the afternoon sessions of the conference and go see the "girls" across the border. I had been in Mexico before, so I opted out and went back to catch some of the discussions and see the exhibits. I stayed in El Paso overnight and flew up to Albuquerque the next morning and stayed at the Sigma Chi Fraternity house. Although the rent was free, it was a mistake to stay there. I didn't get much sleep, as a few of the "brothers" stayed up all night partying instead of hitting the books. When I was a poor boy and the house manager— a job that paid my room and board—I did not put up with that crap. Needless to say. I was not voted the "Most Popular Sig of the Year" award those semesters.

At ten o'clock I was downtown at the headquarters of the mining company. The offices were plush and the secretaries were young and beautiful—quite unlike the environment I was used to since I had been working out in the field. The chief engineer was a man in his middle fifties, overweight and out of shape. He was a stuffy guy and I had a hard time imagining him wading through the wet muck at the bottom of a mine shaft or tramping up and down the rugged slopes of a mountain. But he was the guy who was going to make the decisions as to where the company's exploration money was going to be spent, and I wanted to get a chunk of that money, so I listened to him and smiled at his jokes and indicated that I thought that he knew what he was talking about.

His most interesting story was about when he was a young engineer in Mexico. While his crew was on the way to a prospect, they passed an outcropping that he thought might contain gold. He wanted to stop and take a sample, but the leader of the crew said that they did not have the time to waste on his inexperienced hunches and some bad guys were on their trail, so they moved on. He did make a sketch in his notebook and vowed that he would return to take another look, but he never did. Now, he was the boss, and by damn, he was going to check it out, or rather, he was going to send me in to check it out.

I told him that I thought that this was an excellent idea and it was a wise move and, even as a young engineer, he was probably smarter than his boss. The price of gold had increased many times from what it was back in the "good old days;" it was now $35 per ounce, and it was certainly worth the chance to take another look at the property.

I asked him if he could show me where this gold was located.

"I sure can," he said. "I remember it as if it was yesterday." He buzzed for his secretary—she was a looker—and told her to bring him the latest topographic map of a certain area of the State of Sonora in Mexico. He must had been impressing her with his "war stories" about when he was a young and handsome mining engineer fighting off Pancho Villa's revolutionaries in Old Mexico, as she knew right where to go to find his maps and returned in less than two minutes with a well-worn topographic map of Sonora. He spread out the map on his conference table and plunged his pudgy forefinger down on the map in an area of eastern Sonora.

"This is it, right here," he exclaimed.

As he removed his finger, I saw a region of closely-spaced squiggled black elevation lines that indicated that this was very rugged country.

I asked him, "How did you get into such inaccessible country?"

He proudly said, "We waited until the rainy season and floated down the river, but we had a helluva time getting out."

In mock admiration I replied, "Boy, you old timers really were tough."

The pretty secretary agreed and said, "They sure were."

I asked him to tell me more about the outcropping. He went into great detail and even pulled out his old hand-drawn map He must have been thinking that someday he would have a chance to go back and prove that he was right.

To be specific, the property was located beside a small tributary of the Rio San Bernardino, about three miles east of the village of Huachinera and about twenty-five miles south of another small village named Bavispe. The outcropping was in a canyon that entered the tributary from the northeast about a half a mile from where the small stream intersected with the San Bernardino.

This location was going to be very easy to find. The big problem would be getting into it and getting out, and my parachute was the answer. I could probably get in there and make the inspection in a day. The stuff was either there or it wasn't. Cut and dried.

Getting the samples out was another story. In this rugged terrain, it looked like a good fifty-mile walk to find a place where we could safely land the "Bug." The river would hold the answer to a quick return, and we wouldn't know that answer until we saw the course that the river had carved through the mountains.

The engineer asked me to give him a price and a time frame to complete the job. I came up with a ballpark figure and doubled it. I knew that the results of this inspection were going to be very important to him so, if he was going to pay me too much to get personal information he wanted, he would make up the difference when doing another project.

He said OK, be back here in ten days, and we've got a deal. I walked out of his office with a check for $3,500, half of the total of $7,000.

As we walked out to the reception desk, the good-looking secretary said, "Are you staying in Albuquerque overnight? I like engineers, and young engineers are hard to find around here. I could show you around and I know that you are on an expense account so it wouldn't cost you anything."

Any other time, I would have jumped at the opportunity, but I had Sarah on my mind. I said, "Sorry, I have to get right back to El Paso. Maybe when I come back."

I was whistling as I boarded the United flight to El Paso. This trip had certainly been worth taking the gamble of leaving Guatemala and missing the chance to see more of Sarah, a lot more of Sarah. After I put this next job together, and completed it, I would have money to spare when I visited Guatemala.

I spent the night in El Paso and caught up on my sleep. The next morning I spent shopping for parachutes and other supplies I would need and couldn't buy in Mexico. In addition to ten 28-foot personnel parachutes, I bought three 32-footers and some cargo chutes.

I had been thinking of maybe using a 32-footer on some of my jumps into the boondocks. The rate of descent was less and it took a little more effort to steer them, but they let you down easier, and my bones could sure use some softer landings at these high altitudes. But they cost a lot more, as they had to be custom made—something to think about.

I got back to Zacatecas Friday morning and after talking to Fr. Lopez and getting up to speed on what was happening at home base, I called Raul. I had caught him at a good time. He said he would be free for the next week or so, and he was looking for work. We agreed to meet at his hangar tomorrow morning and go over the plan for the jump into Sonora.

Fr. Lopez told me the same thing as Elena had. Things were the same and there were no fires to put out, but someone had been trying to call me from southern Mexico. They couldn't get through because some of the lines were still down because of the storms.

Now would be the time to get my equipment back in order and assemble a couple of new personnel parachutes. My inventory had been wiped out by the Guatemala expedition. I spent the rest of the day at my hangar and caught up on some bookwork that evening.

Raul and I met the next morning to plan the Sonora jump. This one was going to be important, as we both needed the money. Neither one of us was familiar with the area where we would be operating, so we had to study the charts closely. I had the topographical maps the engineer had given me, plus his own hand-drawn maps, and Raul had the latest Mexican government aerial charts, so this was going to be one of our more intellectual operations. I wanted to get the job done and get back here as soon, and as safely, as possible.

I didn't tell Raul anything about Sarah. I was in no mood for any wise remarks from a young, "love 'em and leave 'em," junior aviator. We debated which aircraft would be the best to use. The distance from Zacatecas to the target was about three hundred and fifty miles. Add another fifty miles to be spent scouting for a place when Raul could land to pick me up and another fifty to a refueling station, That would be four hundred and fifty miles, the maximum range of the "Bug," and four hours in the air. It would require good fuel management and good weather but since we were excellent pilots, we could probably shave that and complete the mission.

Then there was Raul's Cessna 180. It was faster and more comfortable and it was a much better aircraft to parachute from, but it couldn't land and pick me up. If we used it, that would mean that Raul would have to fly back to Zacatecas and transfer to the "Bug" and fly back to pick me up, and we had no time certain that I would be ready for pick up.

In the interests of time and money we decided that we would forego the comfort and use the Bug. Raul would fly to the nearest fair-sized town, Nuevo Casas Grandes, refuel and stay there overnight and the next morning, overfly the target and see if I was ready to be picked up. If I was, make the pick up. If not, play it by ear.

I had thought of taking my partner Ace along on this mission, but since there was no indication that I would run into any problems with the natives, I would make the jump without him. I would be taking a minimum of supplies, as I thought I could get in and out in a full day and an overnight. We would leave the cargo container we carried under the aircraft behind, as its drag cut down our airspeed and increased our fuel consumption. I didn't expect that there would be any natives on the ground to steal the cargo, so we could just drop a cargo bundle.

We made plans to take off the first thing Monday morning, so that would leave Sunday to wrap up all the loose ends. I planned to fly to Albuquerque as soon as I got back to Zacatecas, brief the engineer and his staff, and then head for Guatemala and Sarah with a pocketful of cash. How was I going to get to Guatemala? I hadn't figured that out yet, but I would when we returned. I just couldn't wait to get back to that rotten, wet, miserable smelly jungle to see Sarah.

We took off at dawn; I in the back seat and Raul flying from the front. It worked out well. Raul needed more stick and rudder time, and we didn't have to land and change places before I jumped. It was a nice clear day and as we droned northward, my mind was churning over how fast I could finish this inspection and get back to what was foremost in my mind.

As we got closer to the target, I knew that I had better get focused on the jump. For me, a working parachute jump was like a championship football game. I had to psych myself up so that my reflexes were one hundred percent spring-loaded to automatically react to any emergency.

"Ready to play?" It was game time! We started our search pattern and immediately spotted a fairly large river that ran roughly north and south. We followed it in a northerly direction until we ran into a small stream that intersected the river from the northeast. Directly across the river from where the two intersected, a mesa dropped off into the river. This was probably what we were looking for. It was exactly as the engineer had described it to me.

Just to make sure, we flew north for 25 miles and encountered another smaller stream that intersected the main river from the west. We saw a cluster of huts, and we determined from our maps that it was Bavispe. This was just where the engineer said the village would be. We flew back to the intersection, and I told Raul to drop down to one hundred feet. Taking out my camera, I shot a whole roll of film of this location from every angle. I wanted to have these pictures to show the engineer that we had found the spot he described to me. We flew up the tributary for about two miles and turned around and flew back down.

I shot another roll of film at the point that I guessed was a half a mile from the intersection. A canyon ended at the stream and it looked like there was an outcropping on one side of it. This had to be the place. This is where I was going to jump! Now to find a place where Raul could land to pick me up.

Once again we flew north about thirty miles, but we didn't find anything that looked good. Then we flew south and at a bend in the river, there was a level stretch that was clear of rocks, and it looked like it would give us enough space to land and take off. We were still at 500 feet and Raul made two passes. I asked him what he thought. He said, "I can do it, if the ground is not too soft."

"But we won't know if it is solid enough until you are on that ground." I said.

"Then let's try it."

We remained at five hundred feet, and Raul made a slow pass over my chosen drop zone. I tossed out the cargo bundle, and it landed about a hundred feet from the river. I told Raul to climb to twenty five hundred feet, and I would jump from there. I would use a wind drift indicator even though there didn't appear to be any winds to worry about. We circled the area as the indicator floated down and it hit where I had expected it to hit.

I was not wearing a reserve parachute, as it was just something extra to carry. I would have to trust my packing skill and also my body control expertise to prevent any parachute malfunction. I was jumping a 28-foot flat circular canopy and I was going to make the four-line cut after it opened to make the canopy steerable.

The four-line cut is a procedure that makes the standard military surplus parachute canopy steerable, gives the jumper a forward speed of about four miles an hour, and reduces his rate of descent. It is made by cutting four adjacent suspension lines in the back of the canopy after opening.

I first started using it in 1954 after I had broken four suspension lines on an exhibition jump during one of my head-down openings and my boots snapped the four lines. It has proven to be a life-saver to many military pilots.

Raul made a long jump run, and I did not have to tell him to make many course corrections. He was getting to be a very good jump pilot, and he was learning a lot quicker than most pilots. Part of his value was his willingness to take instructions, a trait not common among pilots, especially old pilots.

I freefell about 500 feet before opening my parachute, and everything went as it was supposed to. The opening shock was hard. I had not packed the canopy in the sleeve—I guess I'm a slow learner.My back still hurt like hell from that rough landing in Guatemala.

After checking the canopy for malfunctions, I made the four-line cut and turned toward the place where I wanted to land. The view from up here was spectacular, and I got a much better perspective of the ground below than I had from the airplane. I could now see a prominent outcropping that might be what the engineer was talking about. I was descending at about twelve hundred feet per minute so I had less than two minutes from the time my parachute opened until the time I hit the ground. As I was coming down, I was busy sightseeing and did not notice the ground coming up. I had lost my focus, and I wasn't paying attention to where I was landing. Although my rate of descent was reasonable, I did not have my feet together and my left foot landed on a rock and I twisted my ankle.

"You idiot!" I thought. I wanted to make this inspection as quickly as possible, and dragging a sprained ankle behind me wasn't going to be much help. I had enough experience to know that if I took my boot off to look at the sprain, I would never get it back on until a couple of days later. My leather boot would offer the sprain a lot more protection than a cotton sock, so I left it on.

Raul was circling overhead, and I got on the radio to tell him about the dumb stunt I had pulled. He called back and asked, "What do we do now?"

We agreed that the inspection and the walk to the pickup point was probably going to take a little more time than we thought it would, and the best thing for him to do was to fly to Casas Grandes, stay overnight, then come back about ten o'clock the next morning and see how I was doing. It wasn't likely that I would finish the inspection and hike the twenty or so miles to the pickup point by that time. I told him we would just play it by ear and talk about it in the morning.

One thing was for damn sure. I was going to complete this inspection before I left this canyon, and I would come back with the results so I could pick up the rest of that seven thousand bucks that was still on the table—or die trying. He rogered that and I could hear the sound of that 150 engine as it faded away, and then it was just me, silence and that outcropping.

I had suffered through several bad ankle sprains, and I knew enough to determine that my ankle was not broken, so I could walk on it as long as I could stand the pain. I field-packed my parachute and hobbled over to where I found a tree branch and taking my trusty KA-BAR, I fashioned a crude crutch to help me walk. It was a short distance to where my cargo bundle had landed and when I got there, I fished out my canteen and took a long drink. I wished that I had filled it with whiskey, but it was too late now.

The mouth of the canyon was another short distance, but it took me about ten minutes to reach it. This was going to be a long day. I finally reached the outcropping and when I sat down and took a closer look at it, I was surprised to see that it was a very interesting formation. I could see where it could have attracted the attention of an inquisitive young engineer. There was no evidence that anyone had ever dug into the quartz that was underneath the foot of overburden that covered it.

It took me about an hour to dig through the dirt and clean off the quartz and chip out a representative sample. Damn, that stuff was hard. I should have brought a couple of sticks of dynamite along to help me blast it. I crushed the chunks of rock and quartered the sample, just as the textbook instructed a junior engineer to do.

Looking through my geologist's magnifying glass, I saw flecks of gold, and it looked pretty good, but I wouldn't hazard a guess as to the value of that gold—that would be up to the chemist at the assay office.

Using the same sampling techniques, I went along the formation and collected pieces of the quartz material at ten-yard intervals until the outcropping disappeared into the hillside and I couldn't follow it any more.

I ended up with twelve bags of material, and this was probably the best sampling job I had ever done. I gave it my best shot, even though I was in a hurry to get on the trail walking down the river to the pickup point. As I was working, I came to believe that maybe that short, overweight engineer with the pudgy forefinger just might have been a pretty sharp engineer when he was a young man. He had spotted a gold-bearing outcrop that perhaps even a great field geologist like me could have overlooked.

It was almost dark when I finished sampling and collecting the bags. The total weight of the bags was about 25 pounds, and when you added the weight of my parachute, the supplies, gun, knife, plus the radio, I would be packing about 50 pounds.

I still had a little time left before it got dark so I looked around to see if there was any indication that gold might be found in this area. I dry-panned the dirt in front of the outcropping, and some gold flakes appeared. When I left, I knew that I had given the engineer a fair shake, and I was ready to call it a day.

Now, back to the problem at hand. I had to travel at least twenty miles along the river, and I knew that I wasn't going to be going very fast, so I had better get humping. By now, my ankle was throbbing and my back was feeling about the same, and I wanted to lie down and rest. I knew that wasn't going to work so I unpacked my parachute, rolled up all the other stuff inside the canopy, tied a rope tightly around it, and I had a reasonable back pack.

It took me about an hour to reach the junction of the stream and the Rio Bernardino, and this gave me a clue that I was going to have a tough journey ahead of me before I arrived at the pickup point. I was tired, but I decided to keep on walking.

It was going to be a hot one tomorrow, so it was best that I go as far as I could while it was cool. I walked, or hobbled, on my crutch another two hours before I ran into a rockslide that had washed down from the hillside and forced the river to make a sharp turn. I could hear the water as its speed increased because of the narrowing of the channel, and that gave me cause to rethink the idea of trying to wade across to the other side in hopes of finding a better path.

There was no moon and it was scary dark, and the thought crossed my mind that perhaps the good Lord was telling me that this was a good time to spread out my parachute canopy and wait for daylight. I found a dry place in the sand, unpacked my gear, and made a soft bed of nylon. It didn't take me long to relax and fall asleep to the soothing sound of the flowing San Bernardino. Despite the idyllic surroundings, I only slept a little while before my aches and pains brought me back to reality.

As the eastern sky heralded the coming of a new day, I looked around and took stock of the situation. My fears were confirmed. There was no way I could get to the other side of the river, and I was going to have to pick and crawl my way through this rock pile in front of me before I could start walking again. My ankle was throbbing so I loosened my boot laces. That did little to reduce the pain that was hammering into my brain with each beat of my heart.

I had picked up a lot of sprained ankles in my jumping career, but this was the worst of them all. I was going to build a small fire to heat up my favorite "on the trail" breakfast of thick beef stew and canned peaches, but I didn't think that this was going to work today. The way I felt, I was sure that I would throw it up. I had better start walking. Maybe this will give me some new pain that will take the place of the growing pain in my ankle.

I shouldered my 50-pound pack of samples and working gear, put my makeshift crutch under my right arm and stepped into the sea of rocks, big and small. I had only gone a couple of steps before my feet shot out from under me and I was flat on my back in the slime. It was as if I was trying to walk on a bed of marbles. The pain in my ankle was pushed into the back of my head by a feeling of complete helplessness as my body sunk down into the muck. Using my hands, I inched myself back to solid ground and shrugged off my soggy backpack. I was shivering and shaking as the sun burst out into the eastern sky.

It was clear that I was not going to be able to walk through this rock and mud slide and I knew that I was not going to be able to swim up the river, so the only alternative left was to crawl through this mess. I had better start moving as I had a long way to go and a short time to do it. I cut up my parachute container to make knee pads and, although it only had a few jumps on it, my parachute canopy would have to go to additional padding for my knees. Dragging my ore samples and other gear, I crawled to the part of the rock slide that was up against the cliff and began to inch myself over the rocks.

It was slow going and although my mud-soaked body was chilled when I started, I was beginning to work up a sweat. I stopped to rest at a place where a small stream had intersected the river and as I glanced around, I saw a large chunk of rose quartz in my path. The low, rising sun cast a long shadow of the rock and its first rays caused a rounded corner to glow a dull yellow. My heart skipped a beat! No way, I thought. This isn't the way it is supposed to happen and after all the bad luck I had yesterday and this morning. In disbelief, I inched myself forward and grabbed the quartz rock. I was not going to have to make the standard field tests to determine if this was the real thing, but force of habit caused me to stick the point of my Ka Bar into the soft yellow metal and gouge out a small piece. This was the real McCoy, it was pure gold and I had stumbled upon a rock that was worth a couple of hundred bucks.

Wow! I had never before in my life been this close to instant wealth. My outlook on life changed as I gazed at the rock I held in my mud-stained hand. I visualized that I was enjoying a big, juicy steak dinner sitting across from a beautiful, buxom, brown-eyed blonde and bottle of red wine. Strange, but everything was plausible except the wine. I was strictly a beer drinker.

As the shock began to wear off, my engineering mind took over. Where did this prize come from? My first guess would be that it came from above where I was standing. As I turned the rock over I noted that the normally sharp quartz had rounded corners which told me that it had traveled a long way and probably for a long time. I looked up and all I saw were large rocks mixed with mud and some small trees and bushes. There had to be an outcropping somewhere so I started climbing. I had to climb about a hundred feet before I found another piece of rose quartz—and it was worth the effort. A solid vein of gold, about a quarter of an inch wide, ran down the center of the rock, adding several hundred more dollars to my find. My heart was beating faster, I was hyperventilating and I knew I had better rest and cool it.

I smoothed out a place among the rocks and just plopped down. I was still holding onto my last lucky find and I was mesmerized by that streak of gold. Here I was sitting in the middle of a rockslide on a mountain overlooking the Rio San Bernardino in the State of Sonora in Mexico with the sun beating down, my ankle hurting like hell and me wondering how I am going to handle an event that is going to turn my life in several new directions. My mind was running a mile a minute as I bounced from one option to another. This gold find was going to be huge. Or was it? Maybe it is just a freak gold occurrence—one of a kind. I have to find the source. I have to think things through. Am I legal? I have a Mexican company but it is going to take more than that. I have seen that anything can happen if someone puts the right kind of money in the right place. As soon as the world hears about this discovery, I could have an "unfortunate accident" and the Mexican Government takes over the property or the regional commander or some other official. What if . . . ?

It had been quiet until now—just the background of the river rushing by and the occasional chirping of the birds. Now I hear a steady humming . . . It is the sound an engine and as I look down the river, I see a dark speck that is turning into a red speck and it is the "Bug." It is Raul and he is early. My radio is in my pack and it is several hundred tough, rock-slide feet from me. The "Bug" flies over and beyond me before I reach the radio and turn it on. I try to reach Raul, but all I hear is static. I spread out what is left of the parachute canopy. It is mud-stained but surely he will be able to see it. That's if he comes back. Of course he will come back. He has got to come back. I've got to get back to civilization so I can stake my claim to the biggest gold strike in Mexico—ever.

I get on the radio and keep up a steady, one-sided "conversation." Finally, Raul breaks through. He is breaking up but I read,

"I am having trouble with this damn radio. Also the engine is running rough. Where are you? I cannot see you." I tell him that I am in the rock slide and, as he says "Which one?" he is flying over and is gone. I hear the engine. It is running rough. The "Bug" disappears from sight but in several minutes he is flying over my location. He sees me and waggles his wings. "I see you, amigo. You had me scared for a while. How are you feeling?"

I of course said, "I am feeling great, you clown. How in the hell do you think I feel?"

"Just asking. When I went back to where I left you, I couldn't find you and I got worried. Now that we are hooked up, what's the plan?" I told him I wanted to spend some more time here and he replied, "Very bad idea. The weather guys tell me that a fast moving front is on its way and it will be raining very hard by late afternoon. If it starts raining before I can pick you up, we are in deep trouble. You had better start moving right now."

Damn! What to do? If it starts raining before Raul can pick me up I will be stuck here for who knows how long? I am out of water and food and my ankle is only getting worse. It will probably take me a couple of more hours to find the source of the gold if I can find it without better equipment. It is certain that the source has to be close by. What is certain? If I leave here without finding it, will I be able to find this location again? I am certain that I can. I look up river and I think I see storm clouds forming. That does it! I am out of here.

I told Raul to find some safe place to land out in the desert, see if he could find out what was causing the engine to run rough, go to sleep and come back in about five hours. Keep a sharp eye on the weather and if it looks like it is going to start raining, come get me and we will work something out.

I pick up my samples, now about five pounds heavier, the rest of my gear, and begin working my way through the rocks and mud. An agonizing hour later I had made it through the slide and I was worn out by the effort. I sat down on the sand, recouped my strength and spirits, got up and trudged on.

By nine o'clock the sun was high enough in the sky to make limping around with fifty-plus pounds on my back very uncomfortable. I am beginning to get the picture that I am not going to be able to pack this load for another ten or so miles. I find some shade, break open my pack, cut the samples in half, smash up the quartz without harming the gold and leave everything else but the radio. I am down to about twenty pounds and this load is much easier to handle.

There are probably ten more miles to go. I had steeled myself to the pain of the sprain but now I am beginning to worry that if I kept walking, I might be doing permanent damage to the ankle. But so be it. I had no other option. It was hotter than hell, and getting hotter, but there wasn't much I could do but keep on walking. For the next hour my senses were dulled and I just put one foot in front of the other. I tried to think pleasant thoughts starting with my childhood back in Pennsylvania to the time I met up with Sarah, and what I planned to do when I met Sarah again.

The sun was just beginning to sink below the hills to the west when I heard the sound of the "Bug's" engine. I switched on the radio, and Raul was already trying to talk to me. He said, "Keep on going. You are almost there. Only about a quarter of a mile farther."

I replied, "That's great. The sand I am walking on is solid and that gives me hope that the stuff you will be landing on is also solid."

He continued circling and fifteen minutes later, I stepped into the clearing that we had spotted from the air yesterday morning. I hobbled down the beach for about three hundred yards to check out our proposed landing strip. It was solid, not rock solid, but solid enough to bear the weight of the "Bug" and its crew.

I radioed Raul, "You are cleared to land. The wind is five miles per hour coming from the northeast, and steady." I took off my shirt and held it up as a windsock to show him where northeast was.

Raul made a short-field landing, just to be on the safe side, and rolled up to where I was standing. He moved the front seat up as far as it would go, and I painstakingly climbed in the back. Raul spun the plane around and lined it up for takeoff. He dropped the flaps, stood on the brakes, poured the coal to the big 150, and we made a carrier take off. We were on our way home!

But first, a refueling stop in Casas Grandes. Raul wanted to tell me about the good time he had last night at his motel and asked me if I wanted to stick around and meet some of the girls he had met. I told him to shut up and keep on driving the airplane. I was beat, and I wanted my own bed to sleep in. The sun was setting as we touched down at the airport in Casas Grandes and taxied up to the gas pumps.

Fifteen minutes later, we were back in the air and drilling holes in the sky as we headed southward. I had made a kind of bed, and I moved around until I got relatively comfortable. My ankle was hurting like hell, as was my back, but other than that, all was well. I tried to doze off, but I didn't have much luck. But I got through it and we touched down at the Zacatecas airport about nine o'clock, just after a Western airlines flight had landed. We were in luck, as the runway lights were still on and we did not have to ask the control crew to turn them on for us. That was a "special favor" we would not have to pay for some time in the future.

We unloaded the cargo in my hangar, all except the ore samples. I wasn't going to let them out of my sight. To me, they were like money in the bank. Raul asked me if I wanted him to drive me to the hospital, and I told him no, I could handle it myself. I drove the mile to the hospital in second gear as it was too painful to use the clutch in the Jeep.

When I got to the hospital, the night shift was on duty and I did not know any of the doctors, but I guessed they were as good as my regular ones that treated all my ailments during the day. They asked me if I was new around here and I told them that I was a regular customer, and I could pay my bills. They X-rayed the ankle and said that because it was such a bad sprain, they were going to have to put a cast on it. About that time, I didn't give a damn what they did with it, I just wanted to lie down in my own bed. They gave me some pain pills, put the cast on and said, "Under no circumstances should you walk on this foot for the next several days. If you do, you might cause permanent damage to the ankle."

I said, "Sure." The cast on my foot and leg made it a little awkward to use the clutch, but after a while I got the hang of it, and I didn't run into anything on the way into town.

It was after eleven o'clock when I walked into my hotel room, and I immediately sensed that something was wrong. There was a faint scent of Estee Lauder perfume in the air, and things seemed different. I switched on the light and there, in my bed, was an extremely frightened and extremely naked, Elena. Well, almost naked.

She was wearing my flight jacket, but nothing else. As I quickly snapped off the light, I saw her leap to her feet and try to wrap the jacket around her. I noticed that it didn't fit. It was dark, but not totally dark, and I could see Elena pull the bed sheet up tight around her throat. In a frightened voice she blurted out, "Mi Ingeniero, I am so sorry, Please do not be angry with me. I was lonely, and I wanted to be near you. I am in love with you."

I was in a state of semi-shock and I answered, "You are just a little girl. What do you know about love? You don't know what love is."

She sat straight up in the bed and defiantly said, "I know a lot about love. Ever since the young Padre Portellas came here from Mexico City, I have been reading all the magazines that he hides under his mattress. I read them over many times, and I look at the pictures. I am just as pretty as the señoritas who have their pictures taken without any clothes on. Some of the magazines say, and show pictures of, things the men want their lover girls to do with them and I think I can do those things. I can show you, and I am not a silly little girl.

"I love you because you saved my life and you are kind to my mother and the kids, and you are the only friend we have. My mother, she tell me that I should stay with you, even if you do not want to marry me."

I was embarrassed, and I said, "This is loco. You don't know what you are saying. If someone finds us in here, there will be big trouble. You stay here. Do not go outside! We will talk in the morning."

She cried harder and I was tempted to go to her and put my arms around her to comfort her but something in my mind fairly screamed, "You had better get the hell out of here, fast!"

I stammered, "You stay here. I will stay in the next room. You will be safe."

I still had the bag that contained the ore samples in my hand, and I dropped it on the floor and walked rapidly toward the door of the adjoining room. As I closed the door, I saw that she was crying uncontrollably. She was just a kid, and I knew I had better continue thinking that.

My ankle and my back were no longer throbbing with pain and when I took off my shirt, I saw that I was sweating. I guessed that it was the pain pills kicking in. I put my shirt back on and decided that I would take a shower tomorrow morning. I was beat. I hadn't gotten much sleep the night before, and it had been a really tough day. I needed the sleep. I would keep my clothes and my boot on just in case there were any more surprises tonight.

As I laid down on the bed I thought, "This life down here in old Mexico is sure hard on the emotions."

What Might Have Been

Even though I was back home and my body had taken a pretty bad beating, I did not sleep well. I awoke at about two in the morning, and all was quiet. I cracked open the door and peeked into my room. Elena was gone. I was concerned for many reasons, but there was nothing I could do, at least right now. I went back to bed, but I did not sleep. As the sun was rising, I got up, showered, shaved and went to the six o'clock mass at Santo Domingo. As Fr. Lopez walked down the aisle and passed me, he noticed my crutches and his expression told me he was looking for an explanation.

I waited for him in his office and after greeting me with, "I am glad you made it back," he followed with, "But not without some problems, I see. I thought that you were too much the expert to get injured."

I answered him that even the mighty sometimes fall.

Over breakfast I told him what had happened on this last jump in Sonora and just a little bit about Sarah. I did not tell him anything about my gold find. This will remain my secret while I worked on a plan.

"How is the injury going to affect your operations?" he asked in a concerned voice. "It is going to slow me down somewhat, and I'm not going to be jumping for a couple of weeks. A sprain is not as bad as a break and I will stay off it as much as I can, but there are some important things that I have to do so I will not be sitting on my rear end during this time.

"First, I have to get up to Albuquerque and deliver these ore samples and the inspection report I will be writing this afternoon and collect the rest of the money that is due on my contract. When I come back, I will have the hospital make me a walking brace and it's off to Guatemala.

"I can sit around down there just as well as I can here in Zacatecas and, besides, I can learn a lot about archaeology from a beautiful teacher. This time, I will pay attention," I laughed.

The padre said, "Jim, I believe that you have been bitten by that little winged insect we call the 'love bug,' and I hope that bite does not cause you to do crazy things. We like you the way you are."

I asked the father if I could use his phone, and I called reservations at the airport. They said I could get a flight out tomorrow morning that would get me to El Paso and then to Albuquerque and back to El Paso and to Zacatecas in one day. Now that is the way things should work but rarely did in Mexico.

While I was on the phone and on a roll, I made reservations to Mexico City for the day after tomorrow. When I arrived there, I would see what my options were to go farther south. I went back to my room and wrote my report for the engineer in less than two hours. I made sure that I had a clean and pressed pair of khakis and a clean shirt, and I was ready to go for tomorrow morning.

I looked around for Elena, but I guessed she was hiding from me. That wasn't hard to do as she knew every nook and cranny in the hotel and in the church. I had mixed feelings about talking to her as I knew that it was going to be awkward, but it was going to have to happen. Maybe the sooner, the better.

Since I was going to be gone again tomorrow, I thought I had better check in with the Ace. I started the Jeep in second gear so I would not have to use the clutch, and drove out to Mrs. Martinez's house. In the back of my mind, I thought that I might run into Elena, but I would have to take that chance as I had to visit my partner. When I knocked on the door, I was greeted by Mrs. Martinez, the kids and Ace, being held back on a short leash. "He is my guard," she said.

Ace jumped up on me and tried to lick my face. This mutt was getting downright civilized. Maybe one of these days, I can take him into town and he won't want to fight with everyone he sees. I guessed that being around the kids has smoothed off some of his rough edges, kind of like his master, I mean, his partner.

I kicked Ace around for about a half hour, and he seemed happy and tired when I left. There was no sign of Elena, and Mrs.

Martinez seemed to be friendly, I guessed that she had not talked to her daughter. I went to bed early and got a good night's sleep for a change.

The next morning Fr. Lopez took me to the airport after Mass, and when I got into his truck, he said, "Someone has been trying to reach you by telephone from the southern part of the country, and they are always getting cut off. I understand that the telephone lines down south are still damaged by the storms, and they are having all kinds of trouble." I told him to take a message, and I would call them back tomorrow.

The airlines were on schedule, the customs officials were agreeable, but looked bored as usual, and I was sitting on the edge of that good-looking secretary's desk in the engineer's office and waiting for him to return from lunch at one o'clock that afternoon.

He greeted me with about as much enthusiasm as he could muster after a three-martini lunch. He looked like he would just like to close his office door and go to sleep.

His face brightened when I said, "Well it looks like you had a pretty good eye for gold when you were a young engineer. I think that you may have something here."

I handed him the bag of samples and he undid his tie, unbuttoned his shirt, and pulled out his geologist's magnifying glass. This guy was a hard-core, old-school engineer. Never leave home without your glass.

He picked out one of the larger pieces of quartz I had just happened to leave in a sample bag, held it in his hand and peered through the glass and shouted, "Hot dog, here, take a look at this! See that gold?" The good-looking secretary took the engineer's glass, which was still looped around his pudgy neck and peered intently into the eyepiece. Her face and her hair were jammed into his face, and I could smell her perfume from where I was standing. This guy was more excited by a speck of gold than he was by this beautiful girl. I hope I never get that far into being an engineer.

He yanked the glass back from the lady and said, "Look here. Can't you see the pure gold?"

I assured him that I could and that back then, he had to have a pretty good eye to be able to spot the potential of a formation that was covered by a foot of dirt. He finally looked alert and said,

"Come into my office and tell me about the geologic formations."
To the good-looking secretary he said, "Bring us some coffee."

We went into his office and sat down at the conference table.
I pushed the cup aside and started to tell him about how I got into
the canyon. He stopped me and said, "Don't tell me about that
stuff. I want to hear about the formations, what they were made
of, the dirt and all the important things."

And, again, how smart he was to be able to see through that
dirt and tell that there was gold there. He wasn't interested in
how difficult it would be to get that gold out of there, the avail-
ability of power, the lack of a work force, and all the things that
it would take to make this property a money-making venture.

At the end of an hour's worth of his nit-picking questions, I
came to the conclusion that this guy was just interested in getting
his name on a project that would never even get off the drawing
board before his fat butt was sitting on the beach in some retirement community in Florida. I told him I had to catch a plane,
gave him the report and told him I had to go.

When I got to leave, he didn't offer to shake my hand or ask
what I was doing on crutches or how I brought back the samples.
Did he think that I took a bus or a train down into the bottom of
that canyon of the Rio San Bernardino? Didn't he realize that he
held in his pudgy, little hand an inspection report by the world's
only parachuting mining engineer? One of a kind!

My ego was crushed, but I recovered somewhat when the
good-looking secretary, the sweet-smelling girl, handed me a
check for $3,500. She leaned over and her cleavage was enticing,
and said in a low sexy voice, "You are still on an expense account
and my offer to show you the real Albuquerque after dark is good
until you walk out that door."

Those words pulled me back into the real world, and I swallowed
hard and muttered, "Thank you ma'am, but I have to catch a plane.
Maybe the next time I am back in town."

The trip back to Mexico was as smooth as the one coming up
to Albuquerque. Something must be wrong. This past day or two
have been too smooth. Something told me this couldn't last.

We landed on schedule at the Zacatecas airport, and I didn't
want to bother Fr. Lopez so I bummed a ride into town with one
of the control tower operators. When I got to my room, I saw that

Elena had turned down my bed, and there was a fresh pitcher of water on my night stand. I checked under my pillow and didn't find a bomb. My luck was still holding.

The next morning I was up at six o'clock. I looked out my window, and it looked like it was going to be a gloomy day. The sky was overcast and I couldn't see the sun. No big deal. Today was going to be a down day, and I was going to be busy getting ready to leave for Guatemala.

How long was I going to be gone? I didn't know. I hadn't thought that far ahead. My leg and my ankle and my back hurt, and I went back to bed. I woke up about eight o'clock to the sound of someone banging on my door. When I opened the door, I was greeted by one of the altar boys from Santo Domingo with a message from Fr. Lopez that said he wanted to see me in his office as soon as possible. A telephone call from down south had finally been completed, and they would call back again in ten minutes. I pulled on my clothes, got my crutches and hobbled out the door and walked as fast as I could to the church. Damn these crutches. I'll be glad when I got rid of them.

Fr. Lopez met me at the door and said, "Hurry, we don't want to lose the connection." He handed me the phone and although the sound was poor, I recognized the voice of Steve Powell, the pilot from Merida.

He said, "I have been trying to get you for the past week. I have some bad news for you, buddy. Your girlfriend has been killed."

It took me a couple of seconds for his words to sink in, and I said, "Say again." He repeated, "Your girlfriend, the iron lady from Talco, was killed the day after you left the diggers camp. She drowned while trying to cross the river."

I was dumbfounded. Sarah dead! And that bone-headed pilot called her my girlfriend. Girlfriend, hell. She was my future. She was—right now I was confused. I didn't know what she was.

I asked Steve, "How did it happen?"

He began, "They were crossing the river with an Indian baby that they were taking to the missionary hospital when..." The phone went dead. I banged the receiver on the desk a couple of times, but all I got was a steady hum. I handed the phone to Fr. Lopez and he tried to get someone on the line, but no luck.

From my actions, he knew that something was very wrong, but he didn't know what. He said, "I'll try to get them back on the line, but why don't you sit down in our chapel while I try."

He led me to a small room off of his office and closed the door. It was dark except for two candles burning on an altar, and very quiet. A thousand images were running through my head, but nothing was making any sense. The main thought seemed to be, "What do I do now?" I was so solidly fixed on going to Guatemala in the morning that the thought of changing my ideas of what I planned to do was overwhelming. It was as if an artillery shell had exploded in my face.

A half hour passed before Fr. Lopez entered the room to tell me that they had lost all connections and that the lines had probably been knocked out by the storms. Again. But, he would keep on trying. He asked me if there was anything that he could do for me and I said, "No."

I limped back to my room and picked up the keys to the Jeep. The hotel gofer, Chico, asked me if there was anything that he could do for me and I said, "No." When I got to the garage, I had a hard time getting into the Jeep. That damn cast kept getting in the way. I tried to start the Jeep in second gear, and it did not want to do that. Finally, it turned over and I was driving, in second gear, on the road to—where?

Anywhere, at first, but in the back of my mind I knew that I would end up at the airport. I wanted to go flying. That would clear my head and my thinking. When I reached the hangar, I realized that I did not have the key to the lock on the door. I hadn't paid the monthly loan payment on my airplane, and they still owned it and they had the key. But I did have a hammer in the Jeep. I took out some of my frustrations on the lock, and I beat it to death.

When I tried to crawl into the cockpit, the cast kept getting in my way and it dawned on me that once I did get in, I would not be able to work the rudder pedals with the cast on. My KA-BAR was on the floor in the back seat and with it, and a pair of pliers, I hacked the cast off. My ankle was hurting, but in my state of mind, I didn't care. I cranked up the engine and taxied out on the ramp. I had enough good sense to call the control tower and tell them I was going to take off. "What is your destination?" Philipi, the tower operator asked. "I don't know," I answered.

I took off from the ramp and when I cleared the ground, I pointed the nose of the "Bug" straight up, and it was throttle full forward. I was passing through twelve thousand feet when the engine backfired and it caught my attention. Instinctively, I pulled power and leveled off. I was flying in and out of the clouds, and I was fascinated by the rays of sunlight bouncing off the clouds and something told me to peel off and dive through those clouds and head toward the ground. I was right over the runway and its northern end was growing ever larger in the windscreen of the "Bug" as we hurtled downward.

I pulled back, hard, on the stick and bottomed out at about fifty feet above the ground. Man, that got my attention, and it scared the hell out of me! But since I was down here on the deck, I zeroed in on the control tower and headed straight for it. I thought I could see the whites of the eyes of Philipi and his partner in the tower as I passed a couple of feet to the west of their perch. We were moving as fast as this bird had ever flown, and it screamed as I pulled back on the stick, and we clawed our way up and up. Philipi's shaking voice boomed from the radio receiver, "Señor Hall, return to the field and land immediately."

He had forgotten his English and was yelling in Spanish, but I understood him perfectly, even though his words were garbled. I didn't answer him and kept the throttle full forward. I kept my eye on the altimeter, as I wanted to see just how high this bird could climb. I passed through eighteen thousand and the engine started to miss and as I approached nineteen thousand feet, it quit, cold. My vision was blurring, and I was feeling woozy and guessed that I was becoming oxygen-starved. With the engine dead, the "Bug" scratched at the sky, and as she ran out of steam, she shuttered and fell off on one wing.

At first we fell side to side like a falling maple leaf in the autumn sky back in Pennsylvania and as we picked up speed, we stumbled into a half-assed spin. I jerked the stick back and forth, but nothing happened. Now, I was really scared. My basic flight training back on Guam in the old L-5 had gotten me this far, but I had never been in this situation before. I was an adequate pilot in straight and level flying, but I had never had the training in controlling spins and all that fancy crap, and at this moment, I was in deep trouble and I needed help. When I started on this

flight, I was in some kind of drunk condition, and I wasn't thinking straight but right now, the thought hit me right between the
eyes, "Jimbo, you are going to die. Think, you idiot!"

The engine was not running. Why? Well, when you and Raul
came in from Sonora, you didn't fill up the airplane with gas and
it probably ran out. But hit the starter a couple of times, just for
the drill. I did, and nothing happened. Next bright idea. Move
the stick back and forth, rapidly, and see what happens. Again,
nothing. Next, you are one of the world's greatest parachutists,
reach for your chute. You have often bragged, over a few beers,
that you could jump out of any airplane that flew, and this one
was still flying.

Probably you could have done that, but that was with a parachute, but this time, you ain't got one. Your parachute is back in
the hangar along with two others you just packed yesterday. You
are a complete moron. Sarah is dead, and there is not a damn
thing you can do about it. And you want to stay alive! You have
your whole life to live!

We were rotating faster and faster and as we got down to heavier air, my head went from woozy to dizzy. I slammed the stick
back and forth but still nothing happened. I could hear strange
sounds, and I knew I was pulling a lot of "Gs" and the "Bug" was
pulling the same, and maybe that was enough to tear the wings
off of this old beast. I kept moving the stick and suddenly, with
a loud groan, the gallant "Bug" quit spinning and she leveled out
of the dive—by herself.

I did not have to look at the altimeter to see that we were very
close to the ground, probably less than five hundred feet, and
directly above the runway. It took a couple of seconds for my
head to clear and for me to think, "Boy, that was a masterful feat
of airmanship. I handled that crisis just about as good as Capt.
Chuck Yeager could have done. You should thank God that you
are such a magnificent pilot."

The radio was blaring, "Aircraft zero niner niner, land immediately and report to the airport office. Niner niner, do you read?"

I read, but I was too damn busy trying to get the airplane back
on the ground without further damage to answer, as if I wanted
to. I cautiously moved the stick from side to side and everything
seemed to be OK. I looked around to see if there were any other

aircraft in the pattern, say, like a Mexicana Airlines flight with a hundred people on board. Now, won't that be a helluva way to wrap up this stupid, childish stunt I just pulled? I lined the "Bug" up with the runway and made a credible dead stick landing. I told myself. "Americano, you are one lucky guy."

I climbed out of the airplane and fell flat on my face on the concrete as my left leg collapsed under me. My mind was just beginning to register the fact that my ankle hurt like hell, and I had just done an incredibly dumb thing. As I was getting to my feet, Raul raced up in his truck, followed closely by the fancy crash wagon.

Raul shouted out, "Companero, are you crazy? The aviation people will yank your license and no amount of a bribe will get it back for you. During that dive, I am feeling, as you Americanos say, that you were going to buy the ranch."

I was embarrassed, and I lamely said, "My engine quit. How about helping me get this plane back in the hangar?"

Raul rattled off some Spanish to the crew of the crash truck and they dropped their hoses, turned around and hooked a rope to the landing gear and started to tow it down the runway. I had left the ignition on, and I could hear the tower calling, "Pilot of aircraft zero niner niner, report to the aviation office at once." I was beginning to calm down, and I was shaking. I had run out of adrenaline.

I climbed into Raul's truck, and we followed the "Bug" to my hangar. The crash crew pushed the airplane into the hangar, and they drove off without a word. Their day was ruined. There was no fire to put out, and they didn't have a chance to use their axes. What a disappointment.

When they left, Raul turned to me and said, "What the hell was that all about?" I said to him, quite sincerely, "I really don't know. I guess, I just don't take grief too well. I have a lot of growing up to do. I hope that I live long enough to do it."

I just wanted to get out of there as soon as possible. I picked up a rag from the hangar floor and wrapped it around my left foot. It wasn't exactly as comfortable as a Corcoran jump boot, but at least it would keep my foot fairly clean.

Raul noted the pieces of my cast littering the floor and he remarked, "Was that a good move?" I said, "Probably not, but it

seemed like a good thing to do at the time." As I climbed into the
Jeep to drive away I shouted to Raul, "How about putting a lock
on my hangar door and telling the tower people that the pilot of
Aircraft zero niner niner will talk to them later."

I stopped at the hospital on my way into town and they asked,
"What happened to your cast?" I told them that it fell off and would
they please put another one on. They said, "No can do." They
would have to wait until the swelling went down. Come back and
see them in a couple of days, and by the way, "stay off that foot."
They gave me some more pain pills and two Ace bandages and
sent me on my way. I paused at the front desk and gave Chico
the money to buy me a six-pack of beer and a bottle of imported
Kentucky whiskey, and keep the change. He would probably buy
the cheapest booze on the market, but right now, I didn't care.

When I got to my room I saw that Elena had cleaned up and the
place was spic and span. I tossed my gear on the floor and went
into the bathroom, washed the dirt off my leg and wrapped an
Ace bandage around it. I printed up a sign that said, in Spanish
and English, DO NOT DISTURB!

When Chico returned with the booze, I told him to hang the
sign outside the door as he left and lock the door behind him. I
sat down in my big easy chair, propped my leg up on a pillow,
cracked open a beer, took the cap off the whiskey bottle and
threw it on the floor, just like Hank Henderson used to do when
we were fighting the Japs back in the Pacific, and prepared to
grieve.

Probably not the best thing to do, but it was the best thing
I could think of at this time. I opened the curtains and I was
right this morning when I thought that it was going to be a dark
and gloomy day. A gentle rain was beginning to fall and it was a
suitable time and place to remember Sarah and what might have
been, and what never was.

28
What Next?

Twenty-four hours later, I got up, showered, shaved, put on clean clothes and started a new life. The sun was shining as I walked next door to the church of Santo Domingo. I met Fr. Lopez coming out of the church and he said, "You OK?

"Yep," I answered.

"Where do you go from here?" he asked.

"Right now I really don't know. I think that I'll just hang around and see what happens."

I went down the street to the telegraph office and asked the manager to see if he could get me a line to Merida. A short while later he called me into his office and said, "This is your lucky day. We have your man on the line."

Through the static, I heard a voice, but it wasn't Steve, it was Bud, the flight engineer on the phone.

"Steve ain't here, but I can tell you all we know," Bud said. "The Talco area was hit pretty hard by the storms the night you left. The next morning, from what we were told, the baby that the Iron Lady had delivered the night before got real sick and they decided to take the kid to the missionary hospital about fifty miles from the camp. The lady went with the mother and the father to try to keep the kid alive until they reached a doctor.

"While they were crossing the river, which was now running very fast, the father, who was carrying the baby, lost his footing and the two of them fell into the water. They were washed downstream and the father lost his hold on the baby.

"Your girlfriend let loose of the rope and dived into the river to save the baby. She got the kid and swam to the shore and safety but in the meantime, the mother had lost her grip on the rope and was now being carried down the river. The lady jumped back into the river and tried to save the mother. I guess that she didn't have enough strength left to fight the current and she was washed away and drowned.

"That gal sure had a lot of guts. She was hard-headed and you couldn't tell her what to do. Kind of like you. You two would have made a wild couple."

"Did they find her body?" I asked. "I understand there are crocodiles in the river."

"Yeah," he replied. "The natives recovered the body and they did not want to give her up to the Guatemalan government officials. The natives treated her as a god. They held a big ceremony that lasted several days, with dancing and flowers and all that stuff, and built her a coffin made of mahogany and other fancy woods. It must have weighed a couple of hundred pounds; we had to unload it in Mexico City with a fork lift.

"How did you guys get involved in this operation?" I asked.

"Well, when the baby and her parents reached the hospital and told them their story, the hospital administrators notified the Harvards and they in turn notified the Guatemalan government. Using their pull with the government, the University told the natives that they had to carry the body through the jungle to where it could be picked up by airplane. But they had a helluva time with the natives. They wanted to keep her and build a shrine for her as if she were some kind of deity and they did not want to turn her body over to the officials.

"Finally, the government people paid the natives to form a couple of teams of six men each to carry the coffin about a hundred miles to higher ground where an airplane could land. The Harvards contacted our boss and we got the job of flying the coffin to Mexico City. We did a rush job on the C-122 and hung the engine, slow-timed it, and we made the trip.

"We met her parents in Mexico City and they seemed like good people. A little stuffy and aloof but OK folks. The old man was an American, from the state of Georgia. He had worked for the State

Department in England before World War I, where he had met and married your girlfriend's mother, a rich and high-class lady.

"When the war started, they sent the kid back to the States and she lived in Georgia off and on for the rest of her life. She went to school there and that's where she picked up that southern drawl and the Yankee slang. As far as I know, she is going to be buried back in England, and that's all I know, Jim."

I thanked Bud, hung up the phone and that pretty much ended that part of my life. I think that I'll just stay here in Zacatecas for a while and take it easy.

My ankle improved much faster than the doctor predicted. I was walking without the crutches in less than a week and in another ten days, I was ready to jump. I was beginning to think that perhaps my body was getting used to all the abuse I had been giving it these past few months.

Training for the Jump and No Jump

When Fr. Lopez saw me walking without crutches, he started to bug me about the promise I had made to teach him and Raquel to jump. Now that I had some free time, it's a good time to start the training, he said. I felt as if I was getting backed into a corner, but I guess I might as well get it over with. I had promised, but I kept having this nagging feeling—what if something went wrong and one of them got hurt? I had been parachute jumping for seven years and, although I might act like it was no big deal, it was still dangerous and a person could get hurt, and even killed, if something went wrong.

They were both in good physical condition and, seemingly in sound mental condition, but I had never seen them under severe stress. What if they were in freefall and freaked out and did not pull the ripcord? That would be a bad news situation for all concerned.

The normal procedure when you're training a person to make a parachute jump is to use the static line method. Using this method, the parachute is opened automatically when the student, with a parachute on his back, exits the airplane and a length of rope pulls the parachute canopy from the pack and the stream of air inflates the canopy. That makes sure that you have an open parachute canopy, even if you freeze and fail to pull a ripcord that could normally do the same job as a static line.

In the case of these two students, I did not want to even take the small chance that something might happen to bungle a static line parachute jump and I decided that I would make a "buddy jump" with them. With this method, a skilled instructor gives his student a concise description of what will be happening to his body in freefall and what the student should do to make his body fall in a stable position relative to the ground.

The two will exit the aircraft, usually at 12,500 feet above the ground, with the instructor holding on to the student parachutist's main lift web—the strong vertical webbing extending from the parachutist's shoulder to his leg strap. The instructor will give the student instructions, both physically and verbally, about what he should do to maintain the stable position.

Student and instructor doing a "buddy" jump.

When they reach the correct altitude for the student to pull his ripcord, he will pull it. If he doesn't, the instructor will pull it for him. After the student's parachute is open, the instructor, under an open parachute nearby, will give instructions on steering to a safe landing.

I came up with the idea for the Buddy System when I was the commander of the Survival School at the Air Force Flight Test Center at Edwards AFB in California. In 1962, I was awarded the Leo Stevens Award, the highest award given by the parachute industry, for developing, testing, perfecting and filming the "Buddy System." The mission of a test pilot is to push the aircraft he is testing to its limits, and, frequently, he will do just that. and the aircraft comes apart. He is then forced to eject or bail out to save his life. The death and injury rate for these ejections or bail outs was unacceptable so the Command started to send their pilots to the Army airborne school to learn how to make a successful parachute jump. This proved to be a bad idea because of the high injury rate of broken bones.

The average airborne recruit is in excellent physical condition, but the average pilot is not. The airborne recruit spends many hours running cross country and doing push ups while the average pilot spends his time behind a desk or flying. Also, a static line jump is very different than a free fall.

The answer was to put the pilot into a freefall environment without exposing him to injury or death from tumbling or flat spins and incorrect landings. I have been involved with training more that two hundred Air Force, Navy, British and German pilots and we have never had a death or a major injury. The Air Force has never adopted the buddy system for whatever reason.

The student can be injured on landing, but the chances are minimized by the instructor's calling out the correct landing procedures. The chances of a student being killed on a parachute landing are minimal, but there is the possibility of a broken ankle or an occasional bruise or abrasion.

I was just about to leave my room for a meeting with Fr. Lopez and Raquel at the church when I heard a knock on my door. It was Fr. Lopez and he had a very worried look on his face.

"Jim," he said. "We have a serious problem, and it is my fault. In our culture, a young lady from a wealthy and upper class family

such as Raquel has to have a chaperone with her when she is alone
with a man, or men. This is not going to be possible if she takes this
training and makes a parachute jump.

"What is worse, we are doing it in secret and without the
knowledge and permission of her parents. After much thinking,
and much praying, I might add, I cannot be a part of deceiving
and betraying her mother's trust. So, we are going to have to call
the whole thing off."

I knew this change of plans was going to cause a lot of trouble.
I had to admit that I had not given much thought to the ramifi-
cations of having Raquel's mother as an enemy. One that instantly
came to mind was that she could have her very good friend,
Gen. Garcia, pull my gun permits and, quite possibly, arrange
for his former friend, me, to be the victim of an unfortunate
accident while I was off in the back country. Raquel's mother's
good will is absolutely essential to my wellbeing while I am in
Mexico. Raquel is going to be mad, but I was going to have to
take that chance.

I was right, only to a much lesser degree than I had expected.
She was furious, white-hot furious. I actually believed she could
have killed me on the spot when I told her that I was not going
to train her to make a parachute jump. If we were not in a church
and there wasn't a priest present, I'm sure she would have pulled
her stiletto and at least wounded me. What a temper!

I had never seen a woman so angry. She stormed out of the
church, leaving her older cousin, who had accompanied her, and
Fr. Lopez chasing after her. They couldn't let a single women be
out on the street unaccompanied at night. But God help the mo-
lester who approached Raquel tonight. He would have about a
dozen stab wounds in him before he even had a chance to say,
"Buenas Noches."

There would be no parachuting lessons tonight, and for Raquel,
ever. I was certain that this would end any chance of a romance
between Raquel and me, but it would extend my life while I was
in Mexico. But, most importantly, it would not cause me to violate
a basic tenet of decorum that was essential to maintaining the
structure of upper-class Mexican society.

As a guest of the Mexican people—although I have had a few
problems with some segments of its citizenry since I have been

here in Mexico—I had a responsibility to respect their laws and customs.

When Fr. Lopez returned, he said, "Why don't we postpone the training until next week and wait until things calm down?" I thought that was a great idea. I had dodged another bullet and lived to spend a few more days in Mexico.

El Rey Banquet

Today was going to be a big day for the employees of the El Rey Mining Company, S.A. The company had just ended its first year of operation and the Board of Directors had decided to combine a director's meeting with a banquet at the best hotel in town. Here is a news release that I would have liked to have seen in the Zacatecas Post Dispatch, front page, of course.

"The secretary of the El Rey Mining Company, S.A., headquartered in Zacatecas, announced that the company will hold its annual Board of Directors meeting at the Plaza Hotel today at noon. Immediately following the meeting, an Awards Banquet honoring the outstanding employees of the company will take place in the main ballroom. The Chairman of the Board, Sr. Ruben Hernandez, will be flying in from Juarez, Chihuahua, to preside over the meeting and the guest speaker will be Sr. John Ochoa, the superintendent and director of operations at the open pit activities of the mine in western Zacatecas.

"Sr. Luis Caldron, who heads up the transportation division, will also speak. Sr. Ace Bull Hall, a security expert, will outline the plans for a new system to protect the gold shipments from the property and Sr. Ramon Lopez, noted authority on human relations, will update the attendees and guests on the new additions to the employees health plan.

"There is a possibility that Ingeniero Jaime Hall, consultant for gold mining operations, may drop in later during the meeting."

That is the news release that I had hoped to see, but, unfortunately, it was replaced by the latest breaking news on what was happening in the cold war between the United States and Russia.

Even without the news release, the meeting and the banquet were huge successes. Ruben did fly in from Juarez and he was looking well. He had cut back on his activities and was much more relaxed. The Board of Directors meeting was a formal affair. Big John and Luis had both bought new work clothes and they looked sharp. Luz wore a new dress and the kids, well, they looked like kids.

John and Luis had been told what was going to happen at the board meeting and they were encouraged to voice their opinions. They were, of course, reluctant to speak, and said very little. The meeting was more or less like a family gathering, although a strange one. The people present were from different and varied backgrounds and they didn't know what to expect, but once the meeting got started, everybody was more at ease.

Mrs. Martinez, Elena, and Maria and Jesus attended as special guests, and the kids had a great time showing off their store-bought clothes and interacting with their new friends. Ruben remarked that the operation that started out as an attempt to salvage some good from a very difficult situation was turning out to be a success with promises of a bright future. The educated guess, or hunch, of the company's consulting engineer that an ancient stream could have eroded a goldbearing quartz vein and deposited its contents several hundred feet from the present dry stream bed turned out to be correct, and now the El Rey Mining Company is mining a deposit that everybody else had passed by. This was good luck, but also good geology work on the part of the Ingeniero Hall. The Board declared a dividend and all the directors were handed a check in the amount equal to their shares.

John and Luis didn't quite understand what was going on, but they did realize that for the first time in their lives, they were getting some money that was more than wages. And for the first time in their lives, they were going to start a bank account. The do-gooder in Fr. Lopez was almost uncontrollable and he gushed that only in Mexico can two poor workers, through their hard work and a profitsharing plan, reap the extra benefits they deserve. I didn't bother to tell the padre that this had been going on for some time in the United States. This was a happy event for the people there and I was glad to be a part of it.

Fr. Lopez had arranged for John and Luis to attend a basic Spanish reading and writing class and they had their own tutor when they were in town. Luz is sitting in on some of these classes and Little Jaime can now write his name. I am working on Ace.

John has his driver's license and Luis will get his next week. He will now be in charge of the company Jeep as well as the mules and burros. With my forty percent share of the El Rey gold property, I have established a trust fund, managed by Fr. Lopez, that will give money to good causes, such as paying the rent for the Martinez family and making sure that they have a few extra things that they have never had before.

Maria and Jesus are snapping back from their years of neglect and are rejoining society and playing with other kids and learning to talk. I was glad that I was able to arrange for the operation for Elena. She has so much to offer and she has a family to take care of and God did not mean for her to hide behind a scarf for the rest of her life. All in all, things are going well for my new family in Mexico. I sure had not planned for my life to go in this direction many months ago when Fr. O'Hara and I came to Mexico for a wedding and a fun trip to find a lost gold mine. The next time I get in a philosophical mood, I will discuss this with Fr. Lopez.

Fr. Lopez was becoming a pretty good pilot. I take him up whenever I can and Raul is checking him out in the Cessna 180. I think that he is almost ready to go to Mexico City and take the test for his pilot's ticket.

Now parachuting is another matter. About a month after the blow-up with Raquel, and after she left town, I put Fr. Lopez through my "buddy system" of freefall parachute training. After ten jumps, I'm afraid that he is one of those people who will never master the art of freefall parachuting, and it is an art.

On our first jump, I knew we had a problem. He had an innate fear of falling through the air without an airplane wrapped around him. We made ten "buddy" jumps but I never had enough confidence in his ability to pull his own ripcord to let him go and freefall on his own.

But I will give him a lot of credit for sheer guts. He must have gone through hell on the nights before we were to make a parachute jump. I could see the terror in his eyes as soon as we got in the airplane. It is written that a coward dies a thousand deaths, the brave man but one. But he tried, he tried. We took a break from our practice and no one suggested that we start it again, and so it faded away.

Prospect in Chihuahua

Early one morning I was walking over to the museum to meet with Prof. San Roman, the scuba diver who had lent me the tank I had used when I jumped to deliver insulin to a yacht last year. He had just returned from an unusual diving expedition to the State of Yucatan in southern Mexico, where he and a group of archaeologists from the University in Mexico City had spent a week exploring several ancient cenotes.

A cenote is a natural sinkhole, or sometimes a well, that had a special religious significance to the Mayan people when they ruled the southern part of Mexico and some areas of Central America. Some cenotes are famous as places where they sacrificed virgins to the gods for various reasons. During these ceremonies, items made of gold or silver or stone idols were thrown into the water.

These are the things the archaeologists would be looking for and I, as a scuba diver myself, was interested in what they may have found.

As I was about to enter the museum, Mario came running up to stop me. "Jefe," he breathlessly said, "You have got to see this." He was carrying a brightly-colored, hand-woven cloth bag that had seen many years of use. He opened the bag and showed me three quartz rocks. What instantly caught my eye were the small pieces of gold spread throughout the samples.

At least, at first glance, these dull, yellow spots looked like gold. I always carry a geologist's magnifying glass in my pocket, and sometimes around my neck. It's like a doctor's stethoscope; a professional gimmick that gives you time to analyze something before you have to comment on it. And it usually impresses the natives.

I looked at the specks of material through the glass, dug them out of the rock with my pocket knife and declared, "Si, it is gold."

"Am I not smart, jefe?" Mario beamed.

After I examined the rock, Mario took it and handed it to an elderly Indian who had been walking behind him. The Indian took the rock and put it back in the bag and held it tightly to his side. Mario made a clumsy attempt to introduce the man, but it was evident that he did not speak the Indian's language. The old man made no attempt to shake hands, but made a slight bow and just stood there. Obviously, we are going to have a communication problem.

I asked Mario to tell me the story about these rocks? Where did they come from and who is this man?

Mario explained, as best he could, that the man was waiting for him when he opened the door of the storefront office early this morning. How he got there, Mario did not know. About the only solid information that Mario got from an hour's back and forth interrogation was that his village was located in the sierras and the closest big city was Hidalgo del Parral in the State of Chihuahua. Parral was a very old mining town about three hundred miles north of Zacatecas and the location of some extremely rich gold and silver mines. It was also made famous as the city where the revolutionary guerilla leader, Gen. Pancho Villa, was gunned down 35 years ago.

This guy was a long way from home. How did he hear about us? I had heard about the power of word-of-mouth communication among the poor people of Mexico, but this seemed like a stretch. I had an idea that maybe Prof. San Roman could help us with the language barrier, so I invited Mario, and his friend—I will call him George—into the professor's office.

Prof. San Ramon was a thirty-something guy, in good physical condition, who had been educated in Mexico City. He looked as if he would be at home in the sierras, but for some reason he had turned to the water for his recreation and the southern part of the country, the jungles, for his area of expertise.

I explained to the professor what information we needed and turned the discussion over to him. George understood some Spanish, but the dialect he spoke was unlike any the professor had ever encountered. Mario said that some of his words were kind of similar to his father's tribe, but not enough to make sense. To me, some of his phrases sounded like Tarahumara, but nothing like English.

We must have seemed like a really weird group, muttering sounds unintelligible to one another and trying to come up with some Rosetta Stone that would help us communicate. The professor surmised that George must have come from a tribe that lived in the sierras at the south end of the deep canyons of the Tarahumaras. This tribe had been at war with the Tarahumara Indians until recently and had a very bad reputation for being hostile toward outsiders.

San Roman brought out some topographic maps that showed the country to be generally rugged but with some places where an airplane like the "Bug" could land. The river George mentioned was probably the Rio Turuachi which feeds into the Rio Verde and that is the river that carved the incredibly beautiful and deep Barranca Sinforosa out of the volcanic soil of the Sierra Tarahumara.

This looked like a prospect that could pay off. I asked Mario if he would like to have the job of going back into the sierras with George to bring back some samples of the vein that this quartz rock came from.

He said, "Si, señor." He knew that he would share in the profits if we found a strike and he was willing to take the gamble. Anyway, he had been sitting in the storefront talking to peons who said they had found gold, and he wanted part of the action.

George said that he was sure that he could find his way back to his village, but, just in case, we mapped out a likely route and gave Mario a copy of it. I also gave Mario a thousand pesos and our new, and more powerful radio, as well as a new compass.

Since we knew the rough location and the approximate time it would take for Mario and George to get to the village, I would fly over that area in exactly five days at seven in the morning and establish contact with Mario. Once we were talking to each other, we would work out the details about when and where to pick him up.

It sounded good on paper. It remained to be seen just how it will work out in practice. Mario and George caught the next bus north to Hidalgo del Parral—firstclass, no less. I imagine this is a big thrill for George, and maybe for Mario. Now we would sweat them out for five days.

Five days later, at seven o'clock, I was flying over the Rio Turuachi with Fr. Lopez as my rear seat observer, hoping to pick up Mario on the radio. After zigzagging over the area for about ten

Baranca de Sinforosa

minutes, we made contact with Mario. He had a pile of brush ready and after he lit it, we pinpointed his location. It was just about where we had figured it would be, but the village was half way up the side of the river bank and was small and hard to see from the air. The padre duly noted the location on a map and I told Mario to stand by while we searched the surrounding countryside for a landing site.

Thirty minutes later, we spotted a mesa that looked like it would be a safe place to land. It looked fairly smooth and had no visible obstacles and was about twenty-five miles from the village. But they were tough miles, up and down hills and valleys and across what looked like small streams. It would probably take about two days to make the trip. There was another likely place, about half as far away, but it was on a rugged mesa and there were some small trees that could be a problem on takeoff.

I contacted Mario and gave him the compass heading he would need to reach the first location and told him to leave as soon as he could. I would fly over the area tomorrow morning at ten o'clock to see how he was doing. I would plan to pick him up about eight o'clock the next morning, but that could change, depending on his progress.

Instead of flying back to Zacatecas, we landed at Parral airport and stayed overnight. This would save us about eight hours flying time and allow us to relax for a day. Fr. Lopez had some friends in town and he could stay with them and I would get a room near the airport. I caught up on some reading and finished a report and had a nice day.

The next morning I was over the mesa at 8:30 and Mario was there to meet me. We flew back to Parral and I dropped off Mario and picked up Fr. Lopez. Mario took the bus back to Zacatecas, first class naturally, and Fr. Lopez got a chance to get some night flying. We made a night takeoff from Parral—an important step for an all-weather pilot. I dropped the samples off at the assay office and they guaranteed the results would be ready by late tomorrow afternoon.

The results looked good, but not as good as I had expected. That could have been because of poor sampling procedures and other intangibles that come with the lack of experience. Digging in a solid quartz vein is tough work and it is easy to take short-cuts when the going gets hard. But the results were good enough to say that this property was worth an inspection by an expert, or at least by the guy who was going to make the final decision.

I asked about the people, and he said they seemed to be divided into two sides. Several of the tribe wanted to help him, but the majority were surly and did not seem to want him in their village. The language was still a barrier and he didn't learn anything more about who they were and where they came from. They appeared to be a lazy group and he did not make any friends. But that's not what he went there for.

I needed a prospect I could show to one of several Mexican and American companies that were in the market to spend some venture capital, and this looked like a good one. I had turned down recommending the Conquistador property because any large-scale intrusion on the land in that part of the sierra would displace most of the people who had lived there for centuries and knew no other life than hand-to-mouth farming and goat herding. Although their standard of living was not what we would think of as good, they were doing OK. And who were we to drag them into the twentieth century?

I would take the hit and chalk it up to experience.

29
Jump at
Rio Turuach

Tomorrow would be a slow day and I would spend it getting ready for the jump the next morning. Ace would make the jump with me, as I did not like the reports of the locals not being too friendly. I would plan to spend about a day on the inspection and a day and a half with hard walking and climbing to the pickup point. But I was getting ahead of myself and I had better call Raul to make sure that he is available for Thursday and late Saturday afternoon.

I would make a few changes to the way I had done things. I tried to make use of every new thing I learned on each jump, like taking some canned dog food for Ace, and extra water. I also got Ace a new parachute canopy, as I had cut up his old one to bind his feet on the Conquistador jump and I had left what remained for the natives. I would also take some extra-heavy material to make shoes for him, just in case we ran into any foot problems.

I packed both chutes and we were ready to go. I also replaced the batteries in the portable radio, as I saw how important good communications were in directing Mario to the pickup point. I checked the weather, and from the limited information I could get, there wasn't anything unusual brewing for this time of the year. It had been raining more than the normal amount north of the drop zone but I didn't think it would bother me.

I picked up Ace at Mrs. Martinez's house and he spent the night on his chunk of rug beside my bed. He knew that something was up, but he didn't ask any questions. Just like any paratrooper before a combat jump, his senses were cranked up several notches

and his paws hit the floor about the same time as my feet did when
the alarm clock jangled us awake at 4 a.m. As I pulled on my extra-
heavy canvas pants and boots, Ace went into the bathroom to get
a drink of water from the toilet. I carefully checked the equipment
we were going to take against a check list and stacked it by the
door. Too many times I had forgotten an item that could have been
useful to me, and experience told me that today was going to be
one of those days when I didn't need any screwups. Ace gave each
item a final sniff, and we walked out the door before five o'clock.

At this early hour, Elena was waiting for us at our Jeep and she
said, "Someone has to see the brave warriors off on their mission."
Just a few weeks ago Dr. Mendas had removed the last bandages
that covered Elena's face and finally the world could see a beautiful young lady, whose radiant smile we all knew was hidden behind
that ugly hood, matched her loving and caring disposition.

I was very pleased to see her, and I thought that she was getting
prettier every day. We had a meeting, and we agreed that we
should just be good friends. She was beaming with happiness and
the early morning light made her even more desirable. She hugged
Ace and the battered old fighter smiled and gulped down the two
cookies she offered him. I didn't remind her that paratroopers do
not eat before a jump and Ace didn't mention it and begged for
more. She handed me a small package of cookies and said, "For
you and your piloto. Fly safe and be careful, mi Ingeniero. The
family needs you."

She put out her hand, but I didn't want to shake her hand, I
wanted to hug her and kiss her beautiful lips. She was a truly
lovely young girl and the blonde hair and light blue eyes she
inherited from her German father reminded me of my college
girlfriend—our fraternity chapter's Sweetheart of Sigma Chi back
at the University of New Mexico in '52. But my better and
smarter instincts took over and I just held her hand and said,
"Don't worry, the Ace and I can handle anything that comes up.
We will be back in a couple of days." As she left, I could smell a
lingering scent of Estee Lauder.

My sleepy-eyed pilot, Raul, was finishing his walk-around inspection of the Cessna 180 when we drove up to his hangar. He
stopped to help me hang the cargo container on the bomb shack-
les we had installed under his aircraft. He joked that these early

morning takeoffs were interfering with his social life and he was going to have to tack on a surcharge to any flight when the wheels left the runway before six o'clock. I lifted Ace into the aircraft and hooked up his static line and we were ready to head north to the canyon country of Chihuahua. If Raul had implemented a surcharge, we would have had to pay it, as the 180 was climbing through a thousand feet of altitude into a blazing yellow sunrise at exactly ten minutes to six o'clock.

It was great to be alive on this wonderful day and even Ace concurred as he smiled and snuggled into an old blanket we were using as his bed on any long flight. We were carrying extra oxygen for all three of us, so I stuck Ace's head into a makeshift mask I had designed to fit his flat face, adjusted the elastic strap around his head and turned the valve to give him a steady supply of pure oxygen. He didn't seem to mind it at all, and lay still and in a short while was asleep. This guy was a truly remarkable dog. I was glad that I had found him in that garbage dump and had given him a chance for a second career.

This was great flying weather. Last night a light rain and a slight breeze had scrubbed the sky clean of all the dust and pollution. The wind that rushed by the open door of the aircraft was warm but it was loud, so I covered Ace's head with part of his blanket. I was wearing an old World War II leather flying helmet and ear plugs so I was also comfortable. It was very difficult to talk to Raul because of the noise, but we had gone over the bailout procedures many times so there was no need for future communications. We cruised at about 150 miles per hour and we were over the Rio Tueuachi in two hours.

Once we spotted the river, we had no trouble locating the village. We dropped down to a thousand feet and made several passes, and I could see some people on the ground. But there was no evidence of a fire. Mario had assured me that George understood he was to light a fire and make smoke in order to guide me to the correct village. Also George was to make sure that the dogs were tied up, as Ace was here to work and not to kick the crap out of the local dogs who thought they were tough guys.

To give George time to organize, I decided to show Raul the two places I had selected as the pickup points. We flew over the first mesa and made several approaches and Raul indicated that he would have no trouble putting the "Bug" down and getting it off. He said that he could probably land the 180 if he had to.

The second, or alternate, landing site was a different matter. We made several low and slow passes and Raul said he could land but taking off might be a problem. We returned to the village but there was still no smoke or signs of unusual activity on the ground. I turned it over in my mind. Had Mario really made George understand what he was supposed to do? Had something happened to George? Had they killed him for bringing outsiders to their country?

It was decision time. I was used to making decisions and taking chances, and quickly, but the thought of not having any support on the ground from the locals gave me a bad feeling. But I had a lot of time, effort and money committed to this project, and if I backed away from a deal every time it just didn't feel right, I wasn't going to accomplish much in my life. As the Mexicans say, "No se adventura, No passa la mar." Very roughly translated, "He who does not venture does not cross the sea."

I told Raul to make a long pass at five hundred feet and I would drop the cargo container. The valley carved by the river trended northwest to the southeast, so we made our pass following the river. We dropped the container below the village and about a hundred yards west of the river. As we passed low over the river, I noticed that it was flowing much faster than I had thought and that I could see an occasional whitecap when it passed over a rock. Then I remembered that the weatherman had said that they had received a lot of rain north of the location during the past few days. I made a note to be sure to exit well west of the river. We weren't equipped to go swimming if we landed in the water.

After the cargo drop, Raul pulled up sharply and I did not have a chance to see where the cargo landed, as the tail was in the way. But I was sure that it was well away from the river. There was some smoke visible from fires in the village and that their twisting and turning told me that the winds were going to be squirrelly and unpredictable near the ground. Also, the sun was beginning to heat up the terrain so I had better drop a wind drift indicator at jump altitude to get a more accurate average of the winds all the way to the ground.

We circled at three thousand feet above the ground and I dropped two indicators, just to be safe. I was not going to wear a reserve parachute and I wanted a little extra altitude in case things did not go as planned. The indicators told me that the winds were about ten miles per hour and variable. I had Raul pick a reference point about three miles away and he started his approach as I finished securing my radio case and the rest of my gear.

As usual, Ace was alert and ready for action. I moved in to the open door, tossed my leather helmet into a corner of the airplane, checked Ace's static line, picked up Ace and stood by for Raul's signal to jump. It was show time! Time to put your knees in the breeze, as the 82nd Airborne troops would say.

We passed over the river and a couple of seconds later, Raul's fist slammed down on the dash board and he yelled, "GO!" I pushed back hard and made a strong exit and we were instantly swept toward the tail of the airplane by the slipstream. The static line stretched to its limit and the cover on Ace's parachute pack was violently snatched away and Ace's was torn from my arms. I was falling on my back and I watched Ace's canopy blossom into a beautiful yellow umbrella. I had purchased some new cargo chutes the last time I was in El Paso and I had dyed them various bright colors so I could keep track of the different items on a multiple cargo drop.

I held my back-to-earth position until I was sure Ace had a good chute, then turned over and free fell another five hundred feet. The parachute canopy unpacked smoothly and the opening shock was minimal. I had packed my canopy in the sleeve. I am no longer a slow learner, at least in this area of parachuting. I looked up and checked my canopy for lines over the top or damage. Everything looked OK, so I swung my body back and forth and looked up to check on Ace's canopy. This was the first time we had jumped Ace's canopy, and I was surprised to see that the four slits I had made to make it more stable and give it a forward speed were larger than I had remembered.

I got another shock when I looked down and saw that the river was running much faster that I had expected and was quite a bit wider. My exit spot was closer than I had visualized but, no sweat, I could turn into the wind and make up for that mistake.

I was at about a thousand feet when I checked to see how Ace was doing and I got another jolt. He was almost at the same altitude as I was. This was bad news, as he could not turn into the wind and make up for my mistake.

If he continued on the same course, he was going to land in the river. All he could do was pray, and I had yet to teach him that stuff and I didn't know if Catholic prayers would work for him. If he didn't overshoot the river and landed in it, he was in deep trouble. The parachute would drag him under and he had no way of getting out of it. I had less than a minute to figure out what I was going to do. I could now see that the sandy beach ended about twenty feet from the river and had turned into thousands of rocks churned up by the fast moving river. I quickly spun around and with a stiff wind at my back ran toward the river. I had to land down river from Ace if I had any chance of snagging his parachute and dragging him to land.

With the wind pushing me and with the built-in forward speed of my canopy—I was jumping a hot seven panel TU—and me pulling down on the front risers, I was really moving out. I lifted my feet to clear the rocks which were now a blur beneath me and I smashed down—short! I hit on my back, about five yards short of the river, in the middle of the rock pile. Instantly, I felt a tremendous, searing, jabbing pain in my lower back and the lights went out for a couple of seconds, or maybe more.

When I came to, all I could see were flashes of light and stars flying around and all I could hear was the rushing of the river roaring by. I lay there for a couple of minutes and gradually my head began to clear. My mind was yelling at me, "You've got to get into that river." I tried to get to my feet, but my legs wouldn't work. I rolled over on my stomach, and tried to stand, but nothing moved but my arms. I could feel the sharp rocks with my hands, see the blood oozing through my shirt where my elbows were and feel the blood running down my face from the cuts above my eye, but I couldn't feel a damn thing from the waist down. The top half of my body hurt like hell, but I couldn't feel my legs.

I had been going downwind when I landed, and my canopy had kept on going with the wind pulling it. It was now in the water and was still about three quarters inflated with the lower quarter water-soaked but still floating. I rolled over on my back and a gust of wind filled the canopy and yanked me around, and over the rocks so that my hands were now in the water. I clawed frantically at the mud and rocks and tried to pull myself into the river. That didn't work, but just then another gust of wind inflated the canopy and now I was in the river, floating face down.

I took a quick look upstream to check on Ace and damned if he wasn't about fifty yards from me being swept along by the swift current. I had to do something to intercept him before he raced past me but I couldn't move my legs to swim.

My mind flashed back to when I was working with Dave Burt on his parascuba project in the ocean off the coast of California and I got a lot of experience with parachute canopies in the water. I remembered that the suspension lines on the canopies would float for a couple of minutes before they became water-logged and sank.

My canopy was still inflated but I was not moving. I reached up to the left side of my parachute risers and pulled down the Capewell fitting that attached the risers to the parachute harness and released the two left risers. The risers were under a lot of strain and they leapt forward as if propelled from a slingshot toward the center of the river. It was far enough into the river to tangle with the suspension lines of Ace's parachute and now I was being towed down the river by both parachute canopies.

My canopy was partially deflated and was acting as a brake and Ace drifted into to me. I grabbed him and held on tight. He was trying to swim with all his might, but all this mess was dragging him underwater. I reached down to my right boot and unsnapped the sheath holding my KA-BAR knife. I cut the two main risers on Ace's parachute and it drifted away. But we were still entangled in the mess of nylon cords and fabric of my parachute canopy and the sleeve and pilot chute and bits and pieces of tree branches that were being washed down the river.

I released the other Capewell fitting that was holding me to my parachute canopy. Then I cut away anything that was clinging to me and we were free. I was floating and then I realized that the only reason I was on top of the water was that I was holding on to Ace's parachute harness and my waterproof radio case was acting as a flotation device. I could use my arms, but I still couldn't use my legs. I could have been standing on the river bottom, but I couldn't tell.

Ace was in a panic mode and he was swimming as fast as he could toward the shore. We were about five feet from the shore when my knees starting dragging against the bottom and Ace's swimming couldn't pull me any more. I released my grip on his harness, and he swam away. Good for Ace, bad for me.

My face went under and I got a mouth full of muddy water. I clawed my way forward as best I could and my radio case was helping keep my head out of the water. Finally, I was out of the river and in the rocks. I pulled myself over the rocks and it was tough going.

My elbows and arms were cut and bleeding and they hurt like hell, but I still couldn't feel my legs. I knew that no matter how much they hurt, I had to keep going to where I could rest, collect my thoughts and think things through.

Wounded by the River

I lay on the sand and tried to catch my breath. Ace was about ten yards from me and his sides were heaving up and down and he gulped for air. I yelled for him to come to me as I wanted to snap on his leash before he got distracted and ran off. I had his leash wrapped around my waist and I wanted to get him under control as soon as we landed. We were here to accomplish a specific job and his job was to protect me and not run around looking for something to fight. He was reluctant to move so I shouted to him in my "get your butt over here or I am going to stick my foot up your rear" voice and he pushed himself to his feet and came to my side.

I snapped the leash to his collar and I felt a lot better. I patted him on his face and he cocked his head to the side and looked at me as if to say, "Hey boss, was this the way this thing was supposed to happen, or did somebody screw up?"

If this was his question I would have to answer him, "Buddy, we are a couple of very lucky guys. Just count your blessings and try to learn from your mistakes. The good Lord might be looking the other way on our next jump."

And he might have answered, "What's this WE crap, sarge, I'm hanging up my jump boots just as soon as we get home. My mom dog didn't raise any idiot pups."

Since leaving the airplane, I hadn't paid much attention to our surroundings other than what was important to our immediate survival so when I looked around, I was surprised to see eight or ten guys sitting on their haunches about a hundred feet from us. Ace saw them at the same time I did and he went into his fighting stance and growled and barred his teeth.

These people didn't say a word. They just stared at us. My instant reaction was to reach for the .25 in my shoulder holster. It was still under my left arm and it was wet but I knew that it would work if I pulled the trigger.

I shouted, "Buenas dias." No one moved. No one spoke. They just sat there in a tight group and stared at us. Just then, Raul's 180 roared over us at about five hundred feet, shattering the silence and yanking me back in to the real world of what we are going to do to get out of what I suspected was going to be a very difficult situation. I put a slip knot in the end of Ace's leash and secured him to my left arm. I pulled him close, hit him a couple of times to get his attention, and told him to sit down.

Keeping my eye on the group of men, I unzipped the radio carrying-case and to my surprise it was completely dry. I switched it on and immediately Raul's voice greeted us. He had been trying to reach us and I broke into his transmission by holding down the send button. His voice was coming in loud and clear.

"What's happening down there?"

I replied, "We have some problems here. But it is nothing that we can't handle if we don't screw it up." Fortunately, Raul and I, and Fr. Lopez, had gone through a "what if " drill while drinking a couple of beers about a month ago, and I was sure that Raul still had a rough idea of what we had planned. Only this time we have a really big, "what if " in that I think my legs have been paralyzed and I can't walk.

This thought had been in the back of my mind ever since I had plowed into that rock pile, but I had been ignoring it. Now I had to face it. I told Raul to wait while I tried to stand up. My legs wouldn't respond. I had no feeling from my waist down and I couldn't get up. I knew I should be feeling some pain as my knees were bleeding and I could see the blood oozing through my pants.

I told Raul to circle above me while we worked this out. We had better go over the instructions in both English and Spanish to be sure we both knew what the other was talking about. Raul rogered that and added that we had better hurry up as he was getting low on fuel if he wanted to make it back to the airport at Parral. I told him to listen to my plan, don't interrupt me, and then repeat it back to me. He said "OK" and I outlined my plan.

"First, fly back to Zacatecas and pick up the "Bug." Call Fr. Lopez and tell him what has happened and what we intend to do. Have him alert Dr. Alvarez's clinic and tell him that I think my legs might be paralyzed, so be prepared. Since time is very important, Raul should land at the alternative landing site, if at all possible. I know that there are some trees there, but drop the Cub in, and we will take care of the trees later. Fly to El Rey and pick up Big John. Pray that he is there and not on his way into town. I am going to need lots of help walking. If John is not there, bring back Fr. Lopez. Plan to stay overnight at the landing site. "Good luck, buddy. You don't know how much I am depending on you."

Raul said that he understood and that he had a lot to do to make things square, and I could count on him. He dropped low, made a high-speed pass, pulled up and he was gone. Out of sight and out of sound.

I checked my watch and it was nine fifteen. It was beginning to get hot here on the river and I could tell that it was going to be a long and exciting day at the beach. There were going to be many unknowns and we had better be prepared for them. My first problem: the group of short—I suspected that they were short, but I wasn't sure how tall they were because I had not seen them stand up—darkskinned men who were still sitting on their haunches, just as they had been ever since I first saw them. There were ten of them, I counted twice, and no one talked and no one moved.

I shouted to them, "Hello. Does anyone speak Spanish?" There was no reply. What were their intentions? What did they want? Did they plan to kill me? I didn't have any idea, but I was thinking the worst. If they made a move toward me, my first defense would be

Ace. If that didn't work, I would fire a warning shot—I was sure
the weapon would work after being in the water. If the warning
shot didn't stop them, I still had five rounds in the gun and a clip
with six more. I would wound a couple of them and kill the rest if
I had to. I also had my KA-BAR. It had not tasted human blood
while in my hands, but Brother Honus said that he had used it
many times during the night fighting on Guadalcanal.

That was my battle plan. Pure and simple. I was not going to die
at the hands of some illiterate savages here by some lousy river in
the Mexican boondocks. My defense situation was pretty good as
my back was to the river and I knew that they could not get behind
me. They would have to approach from the front or from the side
and I could cover that. Next problem, since I couldn't move, what
am I going to do about the sun? I was wearing a heavy denim work
shirt and a tee shirt. The shirt would make a good sunshade if I had
something to hold it up. And, looking around, I did. There was a
large tree branch that had been washed down the river and it
would work just fine. I rolled over to the branch and cut off what
I needed, and I built a sunshade.

What about the Ace? He didn't have much hair to protect him
and I didn't want him to get sunburned. He was still wearing his
parachute harness or sling, but that wouldn't protect his head. I
dug a hole for him to lay down in. I wanted him to help, but I had
a hard time explaining to him what I was trying to do, so I gave up
and finished it myself. I cut the harness off him and made him a
sunshade. It worked fine. We were in fair shape, so we settled in
for the day and waited to see what was going to happen.

Now, if we only had some water. There was tons of it less than
twenty feet away, but drinking it would mean instant dysentery.
I had a bout with that stuff when I was in the South Pacific and
I didn't want to battle it now. Also, I didn't want Ace to get sick,
but I knew that it was going to be hard to keep him away from
the water. So, I was alone with my thoughts. Ace was dozing, the
Indians were staring, and the sun was beating down.

This was the first time in a long while I had time to do some
uninterrupted thinking. Since I had a lot of time to think, my
thoughts went back to my first days when Fr. Pat and I came to
Mexico; he to take part in a wedding and me to inspect a potential lost gold mine. Things have sure moved fast since then and I

had met many people on the road to where I am today. Some
good, some bad, but all in all, it has been a very interesting and
exciting journey. To think it might end here in this unlikely place,
in a deep canyon in the majestic Sierra Madres of Mexico beside
a roaring dirty brown river surrounded by probably unfriendly
Indians, was something that I would have never imagined.

And, if I do get out of this place, will I be paralyzed? A cripple,
in the prime of my life. This I did not even want to think about.

Just then there was a commotion up the hill in the village. The
men did not move or speak or turn their heads to see what was
going on. This was a weird situation. Suddenly a cloud of green
smoke rose into the blue sky. It was one of my smoke grenades.
The natives must have broken the lock on the cargo container
and were now rifling through some things from the civilized
world that they had never seen before or tasted.

Tasted? Food. Things like succulent, juicy beef stew in beef
gravy or peaches in thick sweet syrup. I hope these bastards
are enjoying our dinner. Suddenly I am hungry. I hadn't thought
of food all morning, and suddenly I am hungry. So much for
my organized thoughts. Without a sign or a command, the group
rose to their feet and walked away toward the village. I looked
at my watch. It was exactly twelve noon. What did that mean?
Who knows?

The afternoon wore on. The sun beat down and it got hotter.
But there was a good sign. A slight breeze began to move the
swarms of bugs around. I had covered Ace with sand and he
wasn't bothered too much. But they had been feasting on me. My
insect repellent was in the cargo container. I hope the Indians
were now drinking it. I hoped they got real sick and all died. I
had put my mind in neutral for the past few hours, but still on
alert when I heard a disturbance behind me. I rolled over in time
to see three natives in a make-shift boat drifting by. So much for
the feeling that we were safe from attack from the rear.

I had the radio on standby and about three o'clock I began to
pick up some static activity. Ten minutes later I heard the drone
of an aircraft engine and the "Bug" chugged into view. Boy, was
I glad to see that airplane. Raul circled overhead and I picked
him up loud and clear. The radio wasn't working very well unless we were in line of sight range, so I asked him to continue

circling. Raul said, "Jefe, we are back. And Juan is with me. I am going to make a couple of passes at the landing place and try to put her down."

I came back with, "What in the hell do you mean try. Land that thing and send Big John right away. I need him. You always wanted to make a carrier landing. This is your chance. Stick it down and stand on the brakes! Keep in touch with me and good luck."

"I will do my best. Out," he said as he signed off. I could hear the engine noise for about ten more minutes—then nothing. I waited a few minutes and tried to contact Raul, but all I got was static. Did he make it? I kept trying for another fifteen minutes, but got nothing. I shut down, and hoped for the best. I left the radio on stand-by, just in case. All we could do was wait and hope and pray.

Shortly after the "Bug" flew over, the group returned. As I had supposed, they were small guys, not pygmies but they probably stood about five feet four. There were ten of them. I guessed they were the same bunch and they hunkered down a little farther away from Ace and me. Ace must have smelled them as he opened one eye, growled and went back to sleep. It was the same drill. They just sat on their haunches and stared, I kind of laid on my side and looked back, and Ace slept. The sun still blazed away, but some clouds had moved in and we had intermitted shade and, at times, it was almost pleasant.

The hours passed slowly and finally, the sun dropped below the mountains to the west, and the shadows began to move slowly up the canyon. If Big John was coming—and there were a lot of ifs connected with this hope—he had better hurry or he, himself, was going to be in big trouble. It was getting darker and darker as the twilight faded.

Suddenly Ace's ears stood up and he got to his feet and turned his body down river. About five minutes later, I heard the sounds of someone walking on the sand. It was Big John and I was a very happy man. He was carrying something in his arms that was a bright yellow. It was Ace's parachute and it was still wet. "Jefe, I am very glad to see you, he said. I found this parachute in the river and it told me I was close to you."

Ace thought he recognized him, but smelled and sniffed him before he said hello. John had a backpack full of food and water and his .357, plus plenty of ammo. He put down his pack and asked, "Who are those hombres?"

I answered him, "I do not know but I think they are enemies."

"Oh," he said and stuck his pistol into his waist band.

I asked John, "How did Raul land the airplane? Did he hurt it?" He said that Raul did well and he got it stopped before he ran into some trees. As John left, he said that Raul was chopping down the trees.

Ace and I feasted on cold, succulent, juicy beef stew in thick gravy and cold juicy peaches in sweet syrup and cold water. It was dark now and as far as I knew, the little dark men were still out there. I filled Big John in on the situation, and there was nothing else to do but try to get some sleep. John was tired from his hike from the airfield and I suggested that he get some sleep.

I took the first watch and thinking that the change in atmospheric conditions with the onset of darkness might change the behavior of radio waves, I tried to establish contact with Raul. It didn't work, so I turned off the radio to save the batteries.

The nighttime hours passed more slowly than those during the day and my thoughts kept coming back to the possibility that I may be paralyzed and, if so, how was that going to change my life?

The cooking fires in the village began going out just as the moon rose. It was about half full, but it lit up the surroundings and I saw that the little dark men were no longer sitting there staring at us. That was a relief, but we couldn't let our guard down. About ten thirty, I felt myself nodding off and I awakened Big John. I told him to kick Ace if he sensed any trouble, and that would wake me, as Ace was still tied to my wrist. I impressed upon him to "Keep your pistola ready, with plenty of ammunition, but do not shoot to kill unless I tell you to."

It was getting cold, so I took down my shirt from the sunshade, put it on and made sure that Ace's harness was still on top of him. John had hung Ace's parachute canopy over the tree limb at our back and it was almost dry, so I put it over my legs. I would give it to Big John when we changed night guard shifts. I didn't think that I had slept much that night, but I guess that I did as I was refreshed when the first streaks of morning light flashed across the dark sky.

My head hurt, my elbows and arms hurt and my back hurt, but there was still no feeling in my legs. As I checked myself out,

I felt a little guilty as I saw that Ace's parachute canopy was still wrapped around me. John looked miserable and when he saw that I was awake, he got to his feet and moved around to keep warm. I offered the canopy to him but he said no, he was OK. Ace got to his feet, shook himself, said he wanted a drink of water, and he was ready to meet the new day.

"Here goes nothing," I thought, and I tried to stand up. As I feared, I couldn't do it. It looks like Big John was going to have to carry me. My arms hurt, but they were still strong. With John carrying me piggyback, I would have to hold onto his neck. But there had to be a better way.

John helped me get my parachute harness on and using parts of Ace's rig we made a sling that fit under my butt and around John's chest. This was going to be tough on John, but he was a big, tough guy and this was the best that we could do. We were on the trail as the sun rose out of the eastern sky.

As we departed, I noticed that the cooking fires were being lit in the village, but there was no sign of the "group." We left what remained of Ace's parachute canopy as a peace offering to our silent friends—they would find my parachute canopy and sleeve in due time and this would be an additional gift—and I was left with unanswered questions of what happened after George went back to his village.

We traveled down the west side of the river until we found a place to ford to the other side. After about a mile of easy traveling, we started our climb out of the canyon. It was tough going, but we stopped frequently to rest until we were finally at the base of the mesa where Raul had landed the "Bug."

Raul had seen us coming and was waiting for us. Good. We were going to need his help. After an all-out effort, we made it to the top of the mesa and I breathed a mighty sigh of relief when I saw the bright red super "Bug." We all rested under the wing of the Cub, and after about a half hour, we were ready to take off.

Because Raul had to come back and pick up Big John and Ace, we had a weight problem, and maybe a behavioral problem with Ace. So I decided that Ace had better fly back with me. We removed the panel from behind the passenger seat and made a place where Ace could lay down and be tied down. I remembered

Brother Honus's Marine Corps motto, "We leave no man behind on the battlefield," and Ace was surely a warrior as much as anyone in this outfit, and he was going home with us. After we tied Ace down, Big John and Raul lifted me into the rear seat and the cargo parachutes that Raul had brought with him were packed around me to immobilize my lower body.

I had absolutely no idea what damage had been done to my spine or my backbone—I really don't know the difference between the two—since I landed on my back, but I did know that what we were doing had to be done. Big John would stay here on the mesa and Raul would return to pick him up as soon as he dropped me off in Zacatecas. Big John strapped me in tight and Raul cranked up the engine and taxied back as far as he could and lined up for the take off. He extended the flaps, stood on the brakes and ran the engine up to full RPMs. The "Bug" leapt forward and we were rolling down the unimproved strip. Our wheels were still on the ground when we passed the spot where Raul had chopped down the trees—good thing that he did that— and shortly after, lifted into the air. We were airborne and the next stop would be the airport at Parral where we would refuel.

The flight to Parral and then on to Zacatecas was uneventful. We radioed ahead to have the tower call Dr. Alvarez's clinic and have their ambulance standing by and also call Fr. Lopez so he would be sure to meet us. The doctor was there when we landed and gave me a quick examination and a shot before heading into town. On the way, we stopped at Mrs. Martinez's house to drop off Ace. Elena came out to the ambulance and gave me a rose from her garden and said that she would make sure that Ace was fed. This gal sure has a way to a guy's heart.

When we got to the clinic, Dr. Alvarez's nurses cut my clothes off and cleaned me up. The technicians took a series of X-rays— many more than I thought were necessary—but I was glad that they were going overboard rather than being miserly. The X-rays were rushed to the bus station, where they were put on the first-class bus to the big hospital in Mexico City. Dr. Alvarez had a cousin who was an expert in spinal injuries and he had called ahead to have him ready to read the films. By this time, the shot was beginning to take effect and I was falling asleep. Tomorrow morning, we will know much more about my future.

No Decision

During the night, the nurses woke me up a couple of times as they rubbed lotion on my many cuts and scrapes. At five o'clock, I was wide awake in anticipation of the telephone call from the hospital in Mexico City. I hoped that the cousin was an early riser.

Fr. Lopez came over to the clinic right after the six o'clock Mass, but there wasn't much he could do except wait with me. He knew that I was not in any mood for any platitudes or discourses on God's will, so we just chatted about what was going on in the cold war and how Russia was screwing up the world.

Actually at that particular moment, I didn't give a damn about Russia; I just wanted to know if I was ever going to walk again. Dr. Alvarez came into my room at eight and looked me over. Besides the scrapes, I had a fairly large size bump on the back of my head to go with a two-inch gash over my eye and some black and blue patches surrounding indentations left by sharp rocks and massive swelling of my lower back. I asked the doctor to give me some idea of what he saw on the Xrays but he said that was not his field and we would have to wait until the specialist called.

At ten o'clock, the cousin came through and fifteen minutes later, Dr. Alvarez returned to my room. The doctor usually had a solemn expression on his face but today, I think I saw a glimpse of a smile. We were ready and waiting for what was probably the most important words I was about to hear in my short life.

He cleared his throat and said, "I am going to speak in Spanish, as I am afraid that my English is not good enough to be precise and I know that is very important that I do not make mistakes. Fr. Lopez can explain my words to you after I finish. The doctor was not a gifted public speaker, but he sure had my complete interest as I hung on his every word. Addressing me he said, "First, you will be able to walk again, but it is going to take lot of work and at times it will be slow going. Are you willing to work hard?"

"Is the Pope a Catholic?" I said in an attempt to break the tension. "That's an old American joke," I hastened to explain when I noted the curious looks from everyone, including Fr. Lopez.

What I mean is, "Hell, yes, I will do whatever it takes to be able to walk again. What do I have to do and when do we start?"

"We start right away, with you staying in bed and allowing the swelling in your back to go down. The extreme shock and trauma on your spinal cord produced when you landed on those rocks caused a short circuit between your spinal cord and your legs. While the body is figuring out how to make things normal again—I have got to admit, we doctors lack much knowledge on how the spine works—swelling is taking place to protect what the body is doing. As the swelling goes down, the pressure on the spine will be reduced and you will begin to feel sensations again. But you must remain calm and not move around. We will talk more, much more in the next few days. I will give you a shot for your pain and I will see you tomorrow morning."

So, I'm not going to be a cripple after all. In the back of my mind, I still had some misgivings. But right now, I felt great.

"How about a beer?" I asked. Fr. Lopez. He said that was not a good idea. He was probably right, so we forgot about that. The room cleared out, I became sleepy and I went to sleep. I had been awake for about fifteen minutes when a nurse came into my room and said, "There is a señorita, dos ninos and a very ugly perro to see you. Should I send them away?"

"No, no," I told her. "That is my family. Please send them in."

She gave me a strange look, and said, "The perro, too?

"Si, the perro, too."

A few minutes later, Elena, Maria and Jesus, and Ace came in. It was great to see them. Here were four people that really cared about how I felt and how I was doing. Maria held on to Jesus with her right hand and she had a bouquet of pretty flowers in her left. She dragged Jesus up to the bed and placed the flowers at my feet. Jesus had two cookies in his right hand and placed them besides the flowers. As if on cue, they stepped back and said, in English, "Hi Jim."

I replied, "Hi kids. How ya doing?"

I was greeted with silence as I supposed that they had exhausted their English vocabulary. Elena said that she was glad to see me and hoped I got well real soon. She blushed when I told her that she got prettier each time I saw her. Ace stared at me and the cookies with a look that seemed to say, "How about sharing with me, partner? We're buddies, ain't we?" I tossed him one of the cookies and it shattered on the polished floor, but all was not lost as he dropped his flat face and suctioned up the crumbs up like a Hoover vacuum cleaner.

We struggled through a conservation, and when they left I was glad that they had visited me. I asked Jesus where his little, dirty white bear was and all I got was a blank stare. Hopefully, he didn't need that bear for security anymore.

I slept through the night and the first thing I did when I woke up the next morning was to test my legs. I still couldn't move them but, and maybe it was my imagination, I thought that I could feel some sensation below the waist. That sensation was pain, but I was feeling pain all over my body, so how could I tell? The nurses had stopped giving me pain pills, so I guess I would start pinching my legs and see if I could feel that.

Dr. Alvarez's cousin was probably the best spine doctor in Mexico and he took a special interest in my case, but all he could tell me was just be patient and let nature take its course.

And I did. As the swelling in my back went down, the feeling in my legs returned along with a world of pain. Within a week I was able to use a walker, graduated to hanging on to a nurse and finally I was on my own.

This bump on my road of life scared the hell out of me and gave me a brief glimpse of what it would be like to be a cripple. Was this going to affect my willingness to take the big chances that had placed me above most of the other guys in what was dangerous work? I would have to give that some serious thought, but first, I had to get well and get over this damn pain. I did know that life for the next couple of months was going to be different from what I had planned.

Dr. Alvarez came in to see me that afternoon and we went over the steps that I should be taking on my road to recover. The first part of my treatment was to stay in bed for several days and get the feeling back in my legs. I should wear a back brace and in a few weeks, we would evaluate the situation. Maybe surgery, but it was too early to tell. I had had a close call and for the first time in quite a while I began to think about the chances I had been taking. Were the risks I was taking to find the lost gold of the Conquistadors worth it?

Right now, I really didn't want to think about the future. I just wanted to roll over and go back to sleep. Dr. Alvarez said that I was having an amazingly rapid recovery and in two weeks I was feeling as good as new. Life was good and I now had time to think and do some serious reading and maybe smell the roses. I was becoming good friends with Prof. San Roman of the museum and he was teaching me about the early civilizations that once ruled southern Mexico and Central America and Fr. Lopez was telling me tales of the Catholic church in the New World since the time of the Conquistadors.

This stuff was all good to occupy my mind in the short term, but as I looked down the road, I was beginning to think that my future was probably going to be back in the States.

Looking at the options on the table, the most interesting one was the possibility of a television series. I was not a big enough egotist to think that I could compete with the Hollywood con artists and sharks like Marv, but even a chunk of that action was big bucks and a lot of adventure. Also, I would like a chance to meet the "girl" again. I had my degrees in engineering and geology, but working in those fields on a day-to-day schedule would bore the hell out of me.

How about the military? I had been promoted to captain in the Air Force Reserve but I was not a West Pointer or a graduate of the new Air Force Academy, so my chances of getting to the top in this profession were not too good. I could hope for a couple of wars, but I understand that a guy could get killed in that occupation while climbing to the top. Perhaps I should just wait a couple of weeks and see how things work out. Maybe now might be a good time to take a break and go to the beach and relax.

It will give me time to work on a plan to figure out how to return to the gold discovery on the Rio San Bernardo and break the news to the world.

The days passed slowly and the "cousin's" therapy routine seemed to be working and day by day I was getting the strength back in my legs and the pain was less and less. Then, one day, I said, "I'll do it. I'll head south to Acapulco, lie on the beach, take in the sun and some of the action that is non-existent here in the provincial city of Zacatecas."

I put a rather large and overdue check in the bank, paid all my bills except the loan on the "Bug," and was square with everybody when I boarded the plane for Mexico City.

30
Vacation
in Zihuatanejo

I said goodbye to Elena and the kids and told Ace to watch over
them. In addition to some books I had been wanting to read,
I took two main parachute back packs just in case I had a
chance to make some water jumps. I took the 28-foot blank gore,
as I didn't want the hassle of re-attaching the suspension lines
after I had made the four line cut and I took a 32-footer in case
I got a jump for pay and I had to land on hard ground while my
ankle was still feeling bad. I was also wearing a back brace and
if I used one of Istel's new sleeves, I felt sure that it would help
take some of the "fun" out of the opening shock after a long delay.
I also had a new sleeve shipped to me while I was in the hospital
and my hat's off to the Russian or Frenchman who invented it. I
was ready to get back in the air.

One good piece of good news I had received before I left was in
a letter from Dave Burt. He was now in California and his health
was getting better day by day. His father had pulled some strings
in the Mormon community in Mexico City and had received permission to fly him back to the States before the hospital officials
had a chance to move him to a charity hospital where they probably would have amputated his leg.

The newest antibiotics and advanced surgery had allowed him
to walk around on crutches and work full speed on his parascuba
concept—he was able to make water jumps off the beach in Santa
Monica—and he was getting interest from the Navy in San Diego.
He had met some jumpers at the drop zone at Elsinore, California, and was putting together a team to break into the motion

picture stunt business in Hollywood. Bob Sinclair was going to
come down from Alaska when the weather got too much for him
and I would complete the team when I got enough good sense to
give up on Mexico.

Part of the good news was that I was going to be able to get
back some of the money I had paid to the hospital in Mexico City
for Dave's medical care. That meant that I could pay off the bank
and that I would own the "Bug" once more. No more having to
go by the bank and get the keys from that good-looking secretary. Oh well, there has to be a downside to all things.

Beach Cottage

I changed planes in Mexico City and hopped a flight to Acapulco.
But I didn't stay there. A new resort was being developed at a little town called Zihuatanejo, about eighty miles north of Acapulco
on the Pacific coast. It promised to be much more laid back than
Acapulco and I would have a better chance to lay around on the
beach. I rented a cottage on the beach, complete with a maid to
keep the place clean and cook for me and my guests whenever
we got hungry.

Ah, this was the life. I quickly found out that the action was at
the headquarters clubhouse about four hundred yards from my
cottage. They had a little dune buggy that ran between the cot-
tages and the lounge, so I never had to walk anywhere unless I
wanted too. The resort had good food, a bar and lots of tourists
coming and going so there were always new people to talk to.
My ankle was quickly healing and walking in the sand did it a lot
of good and made it stronger. There was a scuba diving school
located on the beach, so I had a chance to keep current in a sport
that I had a small part in starting in the States several years
earlier. The locals who were running the school were marginal at
best, and more interested in chasing after the American girls than
they were in maintaining a safe school, but I didn't tell them that,
as the fact that I was young and good looking and had plenty of
money was reason enough for them to hate me.

At dinner one night, I met an old guy who ran a sightseeing
business from a dirt strip east of the village. By the end of the
evening, we were old buddies and I had made a new friend. He

was one of the first guys to get a Mexican pilot's license and had
accumulated almost ten thousand hours of light airplane flying
time. I told him that I was going to want to make some parachute
jumps into the bay once my ankle got better and he said that he
would fly me. This was a lucky find, as some pilots, especially old
pilots, did not want to drop would-be parachutists as they might
screw up and cause his airplane to crash.

My new friend had one bad habit, I discovered as we stood up
to leave the lounge. He could not hold his liquor and he fell flat on
his face when he tried to walk and passed out. I gave the bartender
twenty pesos to get him back to his room safely. The bartender
took the money, said thanks, but revealed that a servant came
every night and took him back home.

He said the man's name was "Avion,"—that's "airplane" in
Spanish—and he was his best customer. "He comes in here every
night. He is a man of many troubles," the barkeep said.

A couple of days later, my ankle was feeling better and things
were getting dull so I asked "Avion" if he would take me up in
his plane to make a parachute jump. He said, "Seguro, Senior
Paracaidista." He picked me up in his old Jeep at ten the next
morning—I wanted to make sure that he was going to be sober
while he was flying me—and we drove out to the dirt strip he
called his airport. I was surprised, and pleased, to see that he was
flying a fairly new Cessna 180. It was clean, had a low-time
engine and looked like it was well maintained. I should have
known that he didn't get to be an old pilot with thousands of
hours of flying time by being a bold pilot, especially in Mexico.
He was all business and listened intently while I outlined the
correct procedures we both should follow.

We took off and he gave me a sight-seeing tour of the area and
I could see that this place had the potential to give Acapulco some
stiff competition. We called the control tower at the commercial
airport and requested permission to make a parachute jump over
the bay. Our request caught the operator unaware and after a
long pause asked, "Who is your pilot?"

"Avion" was well known to them and since they couldn't think,
on short notice, of anything that was illegal, they had to grant
permission. This was new and uncharted territory; I could almost
hear the tower operator thinking that this was an area where

an enterprising minor official might be able to supplement his meager wages by suggesting that a small payment would expedite receiving permission to jump while the aircraft was circling the drop zone.

I would give Maj. Morales a call as soon as I got back to the resort and ask him to nip this idea in the bud. This airspace was part of Manny's patrol area and I was sure that he had some say on what goes on in it. I could see that it was a plus to have good relations with the Mexican military.

We made a couple of dry jump runs over the bay at five thousand feet and I jumped and made a fifteen second delay and opened at three thousand feet. I wasn't wearing a reserve parachute, as that was just something more that had to be washed out, dried and repacked. The bay was packed with power boats, yachts and all kinds of swimmers and there was quite a bit of excitement when I splashed down.

I had my pick of eight or ten boats that wanted to pick me up and I chose the one that contained four young, beautiful bikini-clad girls. I soon learned that they were part of an all-girls traveling softball team from Beverly Hills, California. They told me that this was their last night of vacation and they were going to have a beach party tonight, and I was invited. When I got to the shore I was surrounded by a group of people who said that they had never seen a parachute jump before and would I tell them when I was going to jump and then do it again? I told them that I might do it again tomorrow morning, but that I had to wait until the parachute dried.

Two of the kids who worked at the resort volunteered to wash the parachute out in fresh water and dry it in the shade if I would give them each a peso. I did and told them to keep an eye on the chute, as I didn't want any souvenir hunters cutting a piece of it off. Several of the onlookers asked me if I would train them to make a parachute jump and I had to tell them no as I did not have the permission of the officials to train people.

But this gave me an idea. That afternoon I put in a call to Maj. Morales and he was very glad to hear from me. When I told him where I was, he said, "Strange coincidence, we are flying a mission tomorrow that will take us to a village north of where you are in the State of Michoacan and on the way back, if we have to spend some extra time looking for the place, we might have to land at the airport there to refuel. "

"We have pretty good intelligence that there is a large area where some bad guys are growing marijuana and the department is interested in making a statement so we might have a chance to use the new machine guns we have recently installed on our T-6s. Anyway, there is just a chance we have to stop for gas at your airport about four o'clock tomorrow afternoon. Bring a six-pack. With any luck at all, we might have something to celebrate."

I went back to my cottage and worked on my tan and waited for the dark and the beach party. The party had been going on for a couple of hours before I arrived at eight o'clock. It was an all-girl affair, as the team's chaperone had had a run-in with some of the local Latin lovers who had tried to forcefully put the make on some of her young charges. The hot dogs were good and the beer flowed freely and it was almost like a beer bust back on the beach at Malibu.

It was close to ten o'clock and the chaperone was going to tell the girls that it was time to wrap it up, when the team's catcher, a buxom blonde, took off her bathing suit and yelled, "Let's go skinny dipping." The rest of the group stripped to the skin and headed for the water. The chaperone shrugged her shoulders, slipped out of her suit and said, "Care to join us?"

What could I do? I knew that the swimming would be good for my injured ankle, so I joined them. The following scenes showed me that these California girls came in many shapes and sizes, and were very different than the females I had sneaked a look at in the National Geographic magazines as a kid. It was a very interesting experience for a country boy from the hills of Western Pennsylvania.

After a half an hour, it was time to bid the Beverly Hills "Lambs" softball team a fond farewell, go back to the resort and catch the dune buggy back to my cottage.

The evening was a welcome break from what was becoming a rather dull existence. The next afternoon I was at the commercial airport when a Mexican Air Force AT-6 made a low pass down the runway, pulled up in a steep bank and landed right in front of the airport terminal. The engine wound down and backfired, the canopy slid back and out stepped the "Mexican Red Baron," Maj.

Manny Morales, complete with white scarf and leather flying helmet, big goggles and a .38 revolver in a shoulder holster and a .45 automatic on his hip. As he hopped down off the wing of the T-6, he gave me a huge abrazo.

"Amigo," he shouted above the noise of a twin engine cargo plane that had just taxied up and parked beside us! "You should have been there! You would have enjoyed it. It was almost like being back in the Philippines during the 'Big One.'"

Out of the corner of my eye I could see the blackish grey powder burns surrounding the machine gun ports in the wing of the airplane. He continued, "It felt good to get some of those narc bastards. Our intel said these guys were from the same bunch of scum that killed your friend in Sinaloa."

I shook his hand and sincerely thanked him. He smiled and said, "Our public relations guys are going to have a helluva time covering this one up, but our orders were to make sure this operation was shut down once and for all. There are some people in our organization that are not completely in favor of what we are doing, so I might take a few hits on this one."

I told him, "That's OK, Manny, you can always go to work for me."

He laughed and replied, "No thank you, señor. I will not work for a crazy man who cuts up his parachute."

He introduced me to his rear-seater, a guy named Rudolpho, who had that same killer look in his eyes as did Manny's former partner, Joe. He was wearing a shoulder holster with a .38 revolver in it, and carrying a .45 on his hip. As we walked to the terminal, Rudolpho didn't have anything to say. I thought I would not want to meet up with him in a dark alley or even on a side street without Ace by my side.

After a pit stop, we sat down on a couch in the lounge, where I had stashed a sixpack of Corona beer, Manny's favorite. While we were drinking our first beer, an official-looking guy approached and greeted Manny warmly. Sure enough, he was an official—no less than the chief of aviation for this region. Manny introduced us, and asked him to join us, but he did not offer him a beer.

Then Maj. Morales said, "My very good companero, Ingeniero Jamie Hall, has a Mexican parachuting license and is visiting here on vacation. He would like to have permission from your office to make some parachute jumps in the bay. Can you make sure that he is not hassled by the tower people when he requests clearance to make a parachute jump? He assures me that he will abide by all our rules and not endanger the lives of any of the citizens on the ground."

The official smiled and said, "Most certainly, major. I will tell my people to treat him as if he were one of us. Any friend of the Mexican Air Force is a friend of mine."

It appeared that Manny had some kind of hold on this guy, so I thought that I would ask another favor from him. "Can I have your permission to make some parachute jumps with some of the other American tourists who are staying here?" He didn't hesitate and replied, "Of course, Ingeniero,"

The chief of aviation said goodbye and as he walked away, Manny raised his beer and said, "See, companero, we military guys stick together."

By the time we had finished another beer, the ground crew had completed refueling the AT-6 and it was time for the Red Baron to take off. When we got to the aircraft, the civilian crew was standing at attention and saluted as Manny and Rudolpho approached.

The people around here seemed to have a fear of the military, especially officers. I am glad that the relationship between the military and the civilians in the States is a lot different. As the major jumped up on the wing he turned and said, "I still have to show you the real Acapulco after dark. Maybe the next time."

He got into costume, climbed into the cockpit, cranked up the engine, saluted and said, "Companero, until we meet again. Be careful, aviation is a dangerous business."

Now, there was a guy who made up for all the bad experiences I have had with some of the male members of this society. I would go to war with him. Anywhere, anytime.

Student Jumps in the Bay

The next morning when I went to the beach, I announced, "I have received permission to take a select few students up for a parachute jump. Are there any adventurers among you who would like to make a safe parachute jump?"

Three young guys immediately raised their hands. I said, "It will cost you fifty bucks, American, paid in advance."

Two said OK, but one said he would pass. So I had my first students.

Since I was in charge, I was making the rules. First, I didn't want anybody getting hurt, especially me. Second, I didn't want to waste any time giving them paratrooper training, like running and push ups and how to do parachute landing falls. So we would land in the water and I would use the "buddy system" to train them. This method of instruction did not require a person to be in excellent, or even good, physical condition.

It was easy to train military pilots, as they were well above the intelligence and learning ability of the average civilian and most of them realized that this was another way of increasing their chances of staying alive while performing a very dangerous job.

I didn't really know what to expect with taking an off-the-shelf civilian up on a "buddy system" jump, but I did know that I could handle it. My first order of business after getting up in the morning was to pack the two parachutes, catch the dune buggy to the resort headquarters, have a cup of hot tea, exercise my ankle and my back, swim for about a half hour and meet my student for the day. I would give him, and sometimes several onlookers, fifteen minutes of what he should be doing on his upcoming parachute jump. That consisted of: this is a parachute, this is how you put it on and this is the ripcord and this is how you pull it.

I will tell you how you will get out of the airplane and stand on the small step that "Avion" has built, how you will grasp the wing strut and hold on to it for dear life to keep from being blown off by the seventy mile an hour slip stream—this was called the "poised exit"—and how you will wait until I slam into you and knock you off the step and into empty space. I will now be right beside you, holding onto the left main lift web of your parachute and trying to keep you from curling up in a ball, which is natural for a first time freefall jumper, as you are scared out of your wits and thinking, "I am going to die."

We are now falling through space at seventy miles per hour and our airspeed will increase to about one hundred and twenty miles per hour and we will continue at that speed until we crash into the earth, or water, if we fail to pull our ripcords. Remember where the ripcord is?

Once we hit 120, I will yell at you to arch your back and spread your legs like a flying squirrel, and if we both do everything right, we will be falling face to earth in what is known as the stable position. I am still beside you, yelling into your ear to arch. If you do not arch, we will be staggering through the sky and not enjoying the freefall experience, as you will be wondering why in the hell you ever decided to do this crazy thing.

If we are able to stable out, then we will be falling face to earth and as things settle down, we can make a few gentle turns and enjoy the view and maybe even manage a smile before it's time to pull the ripcord and open your parachute. We have fallen two miles through space in what, to you, on your first jump, will think is a very short time, but it was actually a full minute.

I will drag you close to me, and shout in your ear "pull" and with the speed of light, you will reach over with your right hand to grab the ripcord.

Too late! I will already have your ripcord in my left hand and we will pull it together. I will hang onto your ripcord, as you would have probably dropped it after your chute opened if I let you pull it, and I will need it when I repack your parachute. You will experience an opening shock that will range from mild to "what the hell hit me" depending on several things. However, the opening shock will be much gentler than it was just a few months before because of the invention of a new device called the sleeve.

You are now drifting down toward the ocean at about sixteen feet per second if everything is all right. First, look up and check the condition of your parachute canopy and see if there are any rips, tears or suspension lines over the top of the canopy. If there are, you have a malfunction and you have a problem. If the canopy has rips or tears, there is nothing that you can do about it but curse. If you have a lineover, you can try to shake it loose, but don't get too excited. That's why we are jumping over water. The water is a lot softer than the ground. Next, look down and locate my parachute canopy. Reach up and pull the correct riser to turn your parachute canopy to follow the direction that I am drifting. Pull the toggle to inflate your life preserver.

Enjoy the view and whatever sensations you have at the moment. Usually, relief is a good place to start. You can make turns and slips and swing back and forth, but before you enter the water, try to make sure you land close to me, as I can help you if you become entangled in the parachute canopy and are drowning. When you hit the water, swim upwind away from the canopy and tread water and wait for the pick-up boat to snatch you from a watery grave.

Hopefully, a beautiful young, hero-admiring girl will be driving the boat and after we retrieve the parachutes, she will serve us a free bottle of beer. We will return to the beach to the cheers of your friends and later, when you return to your home town, you can tell the locals about how you made a death-defying leap from two miles high and survived.

I will return to the resort, have the bellboys wash the salt water from the chutes, hang them up to dry in the shade and have an early lunch, partially paid for by your fifty bucks.

I hate to say it, but I could have strapped a parachute on a bag of cement and made a successful parachute jump with it. However there was one loud-mouthed, fat guy from New York City that did give me some trouble. He was one of those guys who couldn't keep his mouth shut during the instructions, and once we bailed out of the airplane, he panicked and went completely ape. He tried to grab me around the neck—I guess he was like a guy who thought he was drowning—and he fought me all the way down to about six thousand feet before I reached over and pulled his ripcord. He was upside down when his parachute opened and he got wrapped up in his canopy and got a pretty severe opening shock.

I opened my chute right away so I could be close enough to yell instructions to the dumb jerk. I unhooked my chest strap and threaded both ripcords through it, as I sure didn't want to lose them. As I looked up, I could see that he had a malfunction; a couple of suspension lines over the top of his parachute canopy. This is called a Mae West, as it resembles a large brassiere, something that a jumper might admire on a woman. In this case, it can be very dangerous, as it can greatly increase your rate of descent by decreasing the diameter of the parachute canopy and giving you a much smaller chute.

As we descended toward the ocean, I yelled to him to turn his parachute canopy away from the shore and follow me. We had opened high and if there was a breeze blowing toward the beach, he would likely land on the hard ground or the parking lot and bust his butt. I didn't want that to happen. as it would mar my safety record. He was hanging limp in the harness and was probably too frightened to function. I was jumping the 32-foot canopy so I was descending at a slower rate than he was and he soon passed me.

I considered running into his canopy and jarring loose the lines that were over the top of his canopy. But I dismissed that idea because if I ran into him, there was a good chance that I would go through his suspension lines and collapse both canopies and we would streamer into the ground, if we were unlucky to be over land, or into water if we were over the ocean, and impact hard enough to kill us both. I pulled down hard on the right risers and went into an extreme slip to get below him and show him the direction he should be traveling. But he just hung there like a sack of crap and let the wind push him whichever way it was blowing.

Fortunately, the wind was blowing us parallel to the beach, but we were going to touch down a long way from the spot that I had picked out. He passed me again and although my arms were getting tired from holding the slip, I pulled down harder.

I had to land near him. This basket case would probably drown if there was not someone there to help him. He splashed down first, but I was right on top of him. Naturally, he did not activate his flotation gear and the thrashing of his arms caused the floating suspension lines to cling to his body. The harder he struggled, the tighter the lines wrapped around him and the weight of the sodden nylon parachute canopy was dragging him under.

Luckily, I had not inflated my Mae West, so I was able to swim through the mess and pull the lanyard that blew up his life preserver. I had my KA-BAR knife, but I did not want to cut any of the suspension lines to free him, as I needed this canopy for future jumps. The thought struck me that he might drown if I could not keep him afloat until the pickup boat arrived, but he was still attached to the canopy and I needed it if I wanted to stay in business, so I would try hard to save him. However, his loss would not affect the human race all that much.

It took the boat another five minutes to reach us and I had trouble pushing the fat clown up and into the boat. He was shivering like a wet dog and he was muttering to himself. It took a while to untangle the mess without cutting any of the lines. Between carefully separating the water-soaked suspension lines and drinking two beers, mine and the student's—he didn't deserve to have a beer—I managed to save the equipment.

My student didn't say a word on the way back to the beach. I can image what kind of story he is going to tell his psychiatrist when he gets back to the big city.

I Meet the Three Ladies

I was having a sandwich at the lounge when "Avion" came into the dining room leading three women. They were obviously American, well-dressed, well-built, about thirty six or maybe thirty seven, and all beautiful. I could see that they were rich and upper class. I stood up and walked over to greet them and as they shook my hand and smiled and showed perfect teeth, I picked up a different fragrance from the perfume that each one wore. There was rose and a scent that I did not recognize and there was Estee Lauder and when I smelled that, I knew that I was going to like at least one of these young ladies.

There was a tall one, named Robin, a medium one named Buffy and a small one named Markey. Markey did most of the talking and I soon found out she was a writer. They had just returned from a sightseeing trip and they were flushed with excitement. "Avion" must have pulled out all the stops and showed them the countryside at low level and high speed. I asked them to sit down and they gracefully accepted. They ordered margaritas and took off their sandals, as if they were going to stay a while.

"Avion" ordered a beer and we settled in for a pleasant conservation about life in Mexico in general and what "Avion" and I did for a living in particular. I think they thought we were two local characters, kind of country bumpkins, that could add some flavor to their vacation. They asked, "Is parachuting very dangerous? We saw the jump this morning and it did not seem to go very well."

"Avion" said, "It is muy peligroso, very dangerous."

"Not so, I said. "It is very safe if you know what you are doing.
A case in point is this morning. I ran into a difficult and unexpected
situation, but I overcame it without too much trouble because of
my skill and experience. With some modesty, I can say that I have
made almost every mistake in the book and I have survived. That's
not saying that there is not something lurking around that could
kill me, but every day I get smarter."

Robin, the tall, blonde, extremely good-looking one, said, "Are
you ever going to get smart enough to quit?"

I laughed and replied, "Probably not as long as I am the best
in the field."

She countered, "Maybe you are the best in your field because
you are the only one in that field and you have no competition."

She smiled sweetly, and took a sip of her margarita. I had to
admit she had me there. Now, there was a lady I would like to
know better. Buffy made some excuse to take Robin and "Avion"
to the patio to look at something on the beach and after they left,
Markey drew her chair closer to mine and said, "This might sound
kind of kinky or weird, but your pilot told us you have done everything, but have you ever made a parachute jump in the nude?"

This surprised me and I gave her a strange look and said,
"Well, no, but I don't think that it would be too much different
from jumping with your clothes on. It would probably be uncomfortable at altitude or landing in the trees, but no big deal."

"Has it ever been done before?" Markey asked.

"Beats me," I answered.

Markey drew her chair a little closer and said, "Buffy and I have
this crazy idea. Tomorrow is going to be Robin's fortieth birthday
and she has always wanted to make a parachute jump. Back home,
when we put together the idea of celebrating her big Four Oh, we
decided to go south to Mexico, rent a motor schooner—Buffy's
parents own one and she knows how to run one—take it out to sea
and lay around in the nude under the full moon and get drunk on
champagne. When we saw you guys jumping this morning, we
thought, why not put a little excitement into the celebration and
fulfill her dream of making a parachute jump at the same time?
You could take off late tonight and jump after midnight and start
the next phase of her life with something very unusual."

Markey was getting excited and grabbed my arm and asked, "Is this something we could do?"

I said, "Sure, this sounds like a jump that could be very interesting." Her cherub face broke out in a mischievous grin and she said, "How much would it cost? We will pay anything you ask."

I immediately answered, "I will do it for free. I can chalk this one up as an experimental jump. You know, anything to promote the research on what effect the lack of clothes has on a female body falling in space."

"Oh, we want you to be in the nude, too. That's part of the plan to give her something extra special."

I said, "I'm going to have to think this one over. I will tell you tonight."

"Please, Mr. Parachutist, your pilot said that you could do anything," she pleaded.

"OK," I said. "You've got a deal."

"Absolutely fantastic," Markey said. "Tell me how we can make this happen."

"First," I said, "Let's meet here at the resort at ten thirty tonight and then drive to the airport. I will give Robin the standard fifteen minute instructions on what she is supposed to be doing during this parachute jump. It's pretty simple stuff—she seems like a quick study and will grasp the fundamentals in half that time. Then I will pack the parachutes and this will give you guys a chance to see what one looks like, close up, and show you how it works so that you can speak intelligently about it when you are telling the Ladies Garden Club about making a parachute jump in Old Mexico. Then we will jump and land in the ocean."

She laughed, jumped up and gave me a big hug. "This is really going to be fun," she said. She was wearing the rose.

Robin, Buffy and "Avion" came back to the table and asked, "What's so funny. Let us in on the joke." As they turned to leave, Markey said, "I'll brief the girls on the way back to the beach and you tell your pilot what we plan to do." The girls looked puzzled and Markey grabbed Robin by the arm and led her to the car. As they drove off, she shouted, "We will see you back here at ten thirty." I replied, "Count on it. And bring a couple of blankets to keep us warm and prevent "Avion" from having a heart attack when he sees what we are up to."

I could hear them giggling and laughing as the car disappeared. I told "Avion" what we had planned and at first he seemed shocked but, when it sunk in, he laughed loudly and said, "I am looking forward to this."

I returned to my cottage and spent the rest of the day catching up on my reading, something I hadn't been able to do since I left Zacatecas. The dune buggy picked me up and dropped me off at the resort at ten thirty and the ladies were there. We drove to the airport and "Avion's" hangar where I gave the free fall instructions to the very attentive Robin and her giggling buddies and gave them a crash course on the different parts of a parachute rig and how it works.

After this, we were ready to suit up in our parachutes, or rather, in this case, to suit down, before we climbed into "Avion's" Cessna. The ladies went to one corner of the hangar where Robin took off her clothes and I went to the opposite corner to strip down and put on my parachute. We met under the wing of the airplane, both wrapped in our respective blankets and I said, "I don't know of any way I can put this parachute on you unless you drop that blanket.

She said OK and let the blanket fall to the hangar floor. My God! What a body. She didn't seem embarrassed or self-conscious, as if this was an everyday occurrence for her. I imagined that my face turned beet-red and I tried to glance away. I had yet to get used to seeing a naked woman, and probably never will.

Buffy and Markey doubled over with laughter and said, "Do you want us to help you?"

"Yep," I gulped. We put the parachute on Robin and I ripped up my shirt to make padding to put under the leg straps of Robin's parachute harness to protect against the bruises that the opening shock of the parachute could cause to delicate flesh like that fabulous flesh on the insides of Robin's beautiful legs.

Markey put the blanket around Robin and we two climbed into the rear of the jump airplane and "Avion" slid into the pilot's seat. The ladies said that it was OK for me to wear my back brace. That didn't count as an article of clothing, but part of my equipment. They both kissed Robin and me and then ran to their car with our clothes bundled under their arms and sped off to the beach and their schooner.

Parachuting for Gold

As soon as we gained altitude, "Avion" called the tower at Zihuatantejo for permission to make a parachute jump into the bay and it was granted right away. The aviation boss had passed the word that we were some part of the Mexican Air Force and we were to be granted special consideration. It was eleven thirty when we took off so we could burn some time sightseeing while we climbed to jump altitude and the girls got back to their boat. Our plan was to move the schooner out of the harbor about a half mile from the other craft so it would be a clear target. When they got to the target area, Buffy would turn on all the lights on the boat, including two large battery-operated lamps we had borrowed from the resort. We had no radio—I had left my set back in Zacatecas as I had never imagined I would be in this situation—so we had to rely on our understanding of the agreed-upon instructions.

It was an absolutely beautiful full moonlit tropical night and the Cessna pushed through scattered clouds as we climbed to twelve thousand five. As the moon reflected from those dark clouds, it was suddenly brought back to me that it was exactly two months ago tonight these scattered clouds were passing over me about 600 miles south of here in Guatemala. It was 600 miles in distance but a world away in time when the storm had stopped and Sarah and I could see the moon through the clouds as we walked back from the pump house to her hut, and suddenly, she took my hand and gave me that million dollar smile.

These thoughts were causing me to lose my focus and I was smart enough to realize that I always got into big trouble when this happened. My focus should be on this beautiful naked lady who huddled under a blanket next to me in the rear seat of a Cessna 180 aircraft that was now flying two miles high above Zihuatanejo Bay in the State of Guererrero, Mexico.

I looked at her and she had the blanket pulled up, tight, under her chin and she was shaking, either from the cold or from fear— I didn't know which—but she was not smiling. "Avion" had started a long jump run and I peered out the open door to get my bearings. We were right on course and up ahead I saw the lights of a single boat all alone in the dark ocean. That was our target.

A couple of minutes later, "This is it! It's show time!" I hit "Avion" hard on the shoulder and that was the signal for him to pull back the power and slow the airplane down. I lifted the edge of Robin's blanket and with my right hand took a firm grasp on the left lift web of her parachute harness and yelled "Let's go!" As I tossed my blanket, the coldness of the wind surprised me and I instantly decided that I was not going to let her stand outside on the step in this biting cold while I worked my way out the door and got into position to jump. The seventy mile an hour wind was going to be brutal on her naked body.

Who in the hell thought of this stupid stunt anyway? I pulled her close, her eyes were as big as saucers, and I kissed her, hard. I didn't intend to do that. I picked her up by the parachute harness and pushed her out the open door and we were falling down, into the inky, unfriendly darkness of the night. We were tumbling over and over and I felt my grip on Robin's parachute harness starting to slip and I panicked. I wrapped my arms tightly around her and this was the worst thing I could have done if I wanted to gain control of these two falling bodies, but I desperately wanted to hang on to her. I couldn't take a chance of her getting ripped from my grasp and falling free toward the ocean. I was afraid that she wouldn't pull her ripcord and I would wake up every night for the rest of my life regretting that I was so damn stupid to take this little girl up on a stupid parachute jump and hurl her to her death.

While I was training military pilots how to parachute using this "buddy system" method of instruction, if I let a million-dollar Air Force test pilot slip out of my grasp and be on his own on his first free fall parachute jump and maybe fall to his death, it was just part of the chances he took when he entered the program. But to let a girl who had placed her trust in me die because of my incompetence was unthinkable.

We continued tumbling and falling faster and faster and soon we had reached terminal velocity, 120 miles per hour, and it was cold. I screamed in her ear to arch. I pushed my right arm under the webbing of her parachute harness and grabbed the other lift web with a death grip and stuck out my left arm and spread my legs. Robin made a valiant effort to arch her back and thrust out her arms and legs and between the two of us we gained a stable, but tenuous, flying position.

By the time we were under control and I had a chance to look down, see the boat and gauge our altitude, I guessed we were at about five thousand feet. But this was no time for guessing. Judging altitude over water was much different than judging altitude over land. I did not want to take a chance of our smashing into the water at more than one hundred miles an hour.

I looked over to see sheer terror on her white face and my heart went out to her. Gone was the wise-ass, confident, arrogant woman of the world. Right now, she was just a very frightened little girl enjoying an exciting birthday gift from her best friends— the bastards!

When I looked into her eyes I was tempted to ask, "Are we having fun yet?" But I said to myself, "You are a stupid jerk. Your ego wouldn't let you pass up this stunt. You might kill this precious, beautiful human being. Don't take any more chances, pull that ripcord!"

In one motion, I grabbed her ripcord, worked my arm out from under her parachute harness, screamed in her ear to pull, and she was gone, snatched away from me at 120 miles per hour. I don't know if she pulled her ripcord or I pulled it, but it ended up in my hand and out of the corner of my eye I saw her parachute begin to blossom. I waited a second and pulled my ripcord, as I wanted to open my parachute as close to her as possible. I got a normal opening shock but I felt the leg straps dig into the bare skin on the insides of my legs.

After things settled down, I stowed the ripcords, rocked my canopy back and forth and saw that Robin had a good chute and was about two hundred feet above me. With the difference in the size of our canopies, she was descending a little bit faster than I was. That was great, as we would splash down at about the same time. We had exited the aircraft sooner than we should have, and that put us upwind from our target so I turned my canopy and ran toward the boat. There would not be much time for sight-seeing; we had to catch that boat. I yelled to her to pull down on her right riser and turn to follow me. Also, pull the toggles on your life preserver to inflate it, now!

We were fast approaching the boat and I was relieved to note that the wind and the forward speed of our canopies were going to put us very close to the schooner. I slipped my canopy to increase my rate of descent to make sure that I splashed down before Robin did and I was successful. My feet hit the water and I was out of my parachute harness and swimming toward her when she splashed down. The surface wind had caught her canopy and was dragging her away from me and I yelled to her to pull her riser release. All I got was a mouth full of water and she was getting farther away from me. I had to catch her! She didn't know what she was doing. She would drown, just like Sarah!

I had not inflated my life preserver, so I was swimming as fast as I could, but I couldn't stop her. The bottom of her canopy was beginning to soak up water and she was going under. This slowed her down and finally I was able to grab her foot. I worked my way up her body and reached the canopy release and popped it. We drifted to a stop and I inflated my life preserver. Her head went under the water and I realized that her flotation gear had not been activated. I pulled the toggles and she rose to the surface. I held her tight, and she was very cold, and kind of trying to laugh.

In a small, weak voice she said, "Boy, that was fun."

I thought to myself, "Right, girl."

Within a few minutes Buffy and Markey pulled up in the launch and I helped them lift Robin into the boat. They hugged her and wrapped her in a big bathrobe while I went after the parachutes. I couldn't afford to lose either one of them, so I worked as quickly as I could to keep them from sinking.

It took me about five minutes to retrieve them and put them in the boat and return to the schooner. When we got to the schooner, the girls took Robin on board and disappeared below deck and left me to struggle with the wet parachutes. When I got on board I called down to the cabin and asked them to send up a blanket for me.

"Men get cold, too," I said.

They did better that that; they sent up a blanket and it was wrapped around Robin. She opened the blanket and her arms, and drew me inside with a huge hug. She had warmed up quite a bit since I held her in the water and she showered me with passionate kisses. I was pleasantly surprised to discover that she was the one who was wearing the Estee Lauder.

I remembered the scientific study done by the Human Behavior Department of the University of Southern California that found some females were sexually aroused after experiencing a stressful situation, and Robin had certainly gone through one. However, if she had anything romantic on her mind, she had better count me out, at least until I warmed up. The chilly 120 mile per hour trip through the atmosphere had shrunken my extremities and I would have really been embarrassed if she had chosen to take advantage of this beat-up parachutist.

The girls produced three air mattresses, more blankets, a heavy bathrobe and two giant bottles of champagne. So we all stretched out on the mattresses, Robin and me in our bathrobes and Buffy and Markey in nothing. The champagne was passed around and we proceeded to celebrate Robin's fortieth birthday.

The ladies were in high spirits and having a great time reminiscing about how they had first met, five years ago, liked one another, pooled their resources, tried several businesses and failed at all of them, and finally hit upon the idea of starting a high-end, high-class, exclusive travel agency to cater to the rich of San Francisco. They laughed as they recalled scams they pulled on some of their wealthy patrons in the Bay area. They chattered away and didn't seem to remember I was there.

From what I gathered, all three of them came into the group from failed marriages and had a bitter view of all males. Robin had been the head nurse of a hospital in San Marino and found the work too confining for her rebellious nature. Buffy was the only child of a banker from Marin County and had grown tired of living off her father's wealth. Markey was a Phi Beta Kappa from Stanford University, turned political reporter and now was a successful short story writer, and a man-hater.

But they all seemed to like me and took me to their bosoms, so to speak. They had gotten into the nude scene during their frequent trips to the French Riviera and they liked it. Their sculptured bodies were a result of a personal trainer, female, of course, a lot of work and occasional surgery.

We polished off the two bottles of champagne and Buffy came up with two more giant ones and when they were finished, Buffy and Markey went below deck to go to bed. The moon had slipped behind the clouds and Robin turned on a small radio that picked up a station in far away Acapulco. Frank Sinatra was crooning all the popular love songs of the day and Robin and I talked about many things, most of it, as I remember, rather incoherently, and I was getting toasty warm and I had taken off my back brace and was about to make a move on my parachuting companion, when Markey stuck her head up out of the stair well and said, in a super sweet voice, "Time to go to bed, big sister. The birthday party is over."

The lovely Robin got to her feet, leaned down and kissed me on the lips, draped her bathrobe over me, and glided toward the open hatch. Frankie was crooning a Jerome Kern tune from the twenties and it seemed to be just right for the situation. His velvet tones drifted over the scratchy Mexican airwaves, "Some day when I'm awfully low, And the world is cold, I will feel a glow just thinking of you, And the way you look tonight."

Mr. Sinatra, I wouldn't take your millions for the chance I have had to be with these three lovely ladies and remember just how they looked tonight. Robin turned, stood there in the bright moonlight, blew me a long kiss and disappeared down the stairwell, out of my life and into my dreams.

The rising sun woke me and my head hurt. Mexican beer I could take, but that French champagne was too much for me. I put Robin's bathrobe over my head and went back to sleep.

Several hours later, the smell of Robin's perfume was in my nostrils as I opened my eyes and I looked up into her beautiful face. She offered me a cup of steaming coffee, but I said no thanks and just held her hand. My head hurt, but just looking at her made my day, even through she was wearing a conservative sunsuit with a large red bow across her chest. As she knelt down in front of me, she leaned over and said, "I owe you one, Buddy, and I will pay you back. Thanks. That was one helluva trip. I'll never forget it. I really, really hope that we will meet again." She leaned over and gave me a kiss—on the forehead. I thought, "That's not much for scaring the hell out of me last night. And more than a couple of times."

The irresistible trio dropped me off at the resort lounge about ten o'clock. I had to get the parachutes washed out in fresh water and dried in case I have another jump later this evening. The ladies were off for a day of shopping in Acapulco and then they were to catch a flight back to San Francisco. Before they left, Buffy tried to stuff a roll of bills in my pocket, but I said, "No, thank you. This experience was something that money couldn't buy. You beautiful ladies have shown this country boy that, just maybe, there can be a heaven on earth." I did accept her business card and when I tried to put it in my shirt pocket, I realized that I wasn't wearing a shirt and that rag had been sacrificed to help protect those beautiful legs of the lovely Robin.

I left the chutes with the bellboys and walked back to my cottage. My ankle was almost better. I could probably walk to San Francisco.

Two days later, I was having lunch at the lounge when the owner approached me with a box in his hand. "This was delivered for you this morning," he said. I walked back to my seat overlooking the beach and while drinking a cup of hot tea, I opened it. In the box was a large gold alarm clock mounted on a gold plated base on which was inscribed, "Much love and kisses to our favorite paracaidista. When this clock wakes you up in the morning, think loving thoughts of your 'Three Little Bares.' Jim, you're no Goldilocks, but you can sleep in our bed any time."

And under the lettering were etched three little bears, holding hands. I laughed out loud. So that was the tattoo I had seen on the left breasts of Robin, Buffy and Markey.

I stayed at Zihuatanejo for another three days, made two more parachute jumps and had enough of the lazy good life. It was time to go back to Zacatecas.

31
The Third Man

It was time to go back to work, so the next day Luis and I headed for the El Rey Mine. When we arrived at the mule way-station at San Mateo we were met by Dog and his pack and I guessed that they smelled the scent of Ace as they barked and leapt at the Jeep.

Luis was in his glory as he assumed the official title and duties of "wagon master" and supervised the choice of animals and the loading of our gear. The old man smiled and remarked on how much Luis had changed since he first saw him the day we rented his mules and from the day when we came back from El Rey and Luis was almost dead. Luis was having a good time bossing the boys around and as I sat down in the shade, the old man approached me. He seemed very nervous and asked me to follow him to a grove of trees behind his shacks.

What I saw surprised me. It was a late model Ford with the state of Chihuahua license plates on it. I asked the viejo, "Que paso? What does this mean?"

He explained that a city man came into his place three days ago. He guessed it may have been one of the guys who rented his mules the day we first went into El Rey, but he couldn't remember, He looked scared and said he just wanted to rent one mule for the day. He didn't want my son to go with him as he would be back before nightfall. If anybody asked me, he wanted me to say that I had never seen him. He also wanted me to hide his car. He did not ask any questions and I was scared when I saw that he was wearing a pistola in his belt. He did not return that day and I have not seen him again.

"What should I do?" he pleaded and I saw fear in his eyes.

Rats! I sense trouble here. "I will take care of this matter," I told him. "And if anyone else comes looking for me or the stranger, come for me right away."

Damn it! If it ain't one thing it's another. My mind was working fast. This was probably the third man from Juarez and, if it was, we were in for some big trouble.

A thousand "what ifs" raced through my mind. The bottom line was this could only end with somebody getting hurt or killed. I parked my Jeep beside the Ford and removed the rotor from the distributor on the engine and I did the same to the other car. These two vehicles are not going to be used by anyone but me, so I eliminated one problem. I cleaned out anything of value from the Jeep, put on my shoulder holster, and stuffed a box of bullets in my pocket. I wasn't going to be caught again without my weapon.

I had the old man bring out his biggest, most gentle mule for me to ride and I pulled my back brace up as tightly as I could around my body. I gulped down a pain pill that Dr. Alvarez had given to me and we started up the trail to El Rey with the hope that the doctor would not have to treat any gunshot or knife wounds when I returned.

Luis led the way, but I didn't want to tell him anything about what was going to happen until we got out of sight of the old man and his sons. About an hour and a half into our ride, and on a ridge with a commanding view of the countryside, we pulled off the trail and I told Luis we were going to have some trouble. A look of fear came over his face as he probably remembered the last time he was on this trail.

I told him I was going to leave him and the pack mules hidden off the trail and I was going on to El Rey by myself. If I didn't return within six hours, he was to go back to the old man's shack, rent a horse and get to a telephone and call Gen. Garcia's office. Tell him I was in trouble with the guys who had tried to kill you and me and I need help right away. He should wait and return with the general's men.

Luis had a very scared but excited look on his face, and as I looked back, he was hobbling the mules and unloading the supplies. My plan was to circle around and approach the house from above. From there I could observe what was going on and decide what to do.

I was in place for about ten minutes when I saw Big John come out of the house. After several minutes, he went back in and all seemed normal. I drew my .357 and approached the house. When I was within fifty yards, I called out to Big John to come outside. He did, and after asking him if every thing was OK, he advanced and said, in a very worried voice, "Jefe, we have had some very bad troubles."

Just then, little Jaime came out of the house and I could see that he had been crying. I was both worried and relieved as I asked him what happened.

"Ace dog has been killed." Little Jaime started crying and Big John told him to go back in the house.

"Tell me what happened," I asked again.

John looked solemn and said, "Three days ago I am up on the hill getting some logs to finish the corral and when I return and go in my house I am surprised by a man with a pistola. He wanted to know where the boss was. I told him you were in the city and he got very mad. He wanted to know where his two friends were. I tell him, I do not know your two friends. He grabbed Jim and say he is going to kill him if I do not tell. Ace jump on him like a tigre and bite him on the arm. He shoot two times and knock Ace down.

"Ace is hurt but he jump at him again and bite him and chew on his arm. He shoot Ace again, and Ace fall down. I have a knife and I stab him. He fall down and I stab him again. He is dead and Ace is dead. Jim hold Ace but he does not move. Poor Ace. Jim lose his friend."

Little Jaime starts to cry again but Luz makes no move to comfort him and stands there stonefaced. Big John continued, "I dragged the bad hombre outside and I wonder, what am I to do? I think about the big holes in the ground up on the hill. I put him on the mule and tie him down and take him to a big hole up on the hill. I throw him down in the hole and I throw his pistola too. Nobody see me."

So we don't have to worry about where the third man is anymore. I asked John, "Are you sure that nobody can see him, the body?"

"Si, jefe, the hole is very deep. I will show you."

I said, "OK, John," as I looked around the house to see if there were any visible signs that would indicate that the guy had been here. I saw none and breathed a sigh of relief.

"Where is Ace?" I asked.

"He is in your house. Jim sleep with his head on his friend until it is time to go to bed. We put him in your house as Jim not want him to be outside where it is cold. We put the canvas over him to keep him warm.

What do I do? First, I will see that the body is well out of sight. Then we will bury Ace and I will go get Luis and return to camp with the supplies. We will not tell Luis anything about what has happened, ever. Then I will go back into town. Probably my best move is to get an audience with Gen. Garcia, with no aides present or within earshot, and tell him the whole story and let him handle it. If I have the general figured out, he will say, "Case closed. The guy never existed, anyway, not in my region of responsibility."

But now what do we do about the car? I imagine that the general could turn this matter over to one of his senior staff officers and the colonel could tow it away, or better yet, jump it, do a simple rehab and change a few serial numbers and the Ford would be out on the streets of Mexico City working as a taxicab in no time. And every one should have made a few bucks on the deal, and life goes on, except for the third man.

We climbed on the mules and we were at the mine shaft that Big John had chosen in less than thirty minutes. He was right about no one ever seeing the body. However, for my own peace of mind, I tossed a big rock down the hole, and after ten seconds when I didn't hear it hit bottom, I was satisfied that it was deep enough. Just to be sure, we pushed in a couple of tons of rock from the lip of the shaft.

When we got back to El Rey, Big John dug a hole about four feet deep next to the house, and we wrapped Ace in a piece of canvas and prepared to send him to his god.

I knew nothing of Ace's background, but from what I could imagine, he was born into a family of middle-class dogs, well, maybe upper middle-class, as he was almost pure pit bull. It was reasonable to assume that he had several brothers and sisters and he was the youngest of the family as evidenced by his independent manner. This attitude probably caused him to get into a lot of street fights, which brought him to the attention of the people who staged professional dog fights.

He was drafted into their Army and served with distinction until one night, during a match, he was caught with a hard hay-maker from a big Staffordshire Terrier and a claw ripped open his left eyeball. That lucky punch ended Ace's fighting career, as he couldn't see to defend himself and the terrier mauled him with-out mercy until the handlers dragged the badly wounded dog from the ring and tossed him into the garbage.

The next morning, Ace and I met at the Zacatecas town dump and we had been partners ever since. That was more than a year ago and we fought a lot of battles and won them all; at least we walked away from them all with our honor and pride and lived to fight another day.

I felt really bad that I wasn't here by his side to help him fight his last battle. I knew I had lost a close personal friend and com-rade when I gently patted down the last shovel full of Zacatecas soil on his grave.

Ace died as he had lived—a fighter until the last. He had three bullet holes in his white and black hide and he died with a smile on his face. I felt that as an airborne warrior, Ace deserved a symbol of his dedicated service. With two pieces of a packing crate I fashioned a crude cross and drew a pair of paratrooper wings on it.

Ace had completed his five basic parachute jumps, but he also had a combat jump at the Conquistador Mine and another one in Chihuahua so he rated two combat stars on his wings. Little Jaime had picked a bunch of wild flowers to be placed on the grave and I chose a buttercup to represent the combat stars and centered them on the silver parachute on his wings. He had also received wounds on his paws while crossing the Bolanos River and paid with his life in the firefight with the Juarez Nazi so he deserved the purple paw with one oak leaf cluster, so a twig of purple sage brush and a brown leaf would serve as this decoration.

For valor above and beyond the call of duty while giving his own life to save the life of a comrade, he deserved the Distinguished

Service Cross. The deep gash on my elbow that I had picked up on the Turuachi jump was beginning to bleed through a bandage so I would take the red and white gauze and combine it with the blue denim of my shirt to make the ribbon that held the silver cross. The silver cross would come from the rosary I always carried in my pocket.

I hammered the wooden cross into the freshly dug-up earth, and I saluted my partner, Private Ace Dog, while Big John, Little Jaime and Luz stood at attention. So Ace went to the airborne trooper's heaven with his comrades from the battles of Normandy, Nijimegen, the Rhine, Bastogne, Corregidor and Korea.

As I left to bring back Luis, I saw Little Jaime watering a small clump of grass he had placed on Ace's grave as a tribute to his friend. As my personal hero, U.S. Marine Corps Sgt. Honus Hall would have said, "Ace did real good for a 'girl'." Yes, Ace was a girl.

Luis saw me coming and met me at the bottom of the hill. We unloaded the supplies and Luis took over my tent. Before I left to go back into town, we established that Big John was the boss of everything, except the animals. Luis' stint as "wagon master" had increased his self-worth in his own eyes, but I didn't want him to give Big John any lip.

Earlier, I had explained to Big John what had happened on the jump in Chihuahua and that I would probably have to return to the States for further medical treatment, While I was gone, Fr. Lopez was to be in charge of all my affairs and the padre would take care of all my business stuff concerning the operation at El Rey and Big John was still be in charge of the operations. I also assured John that he would still have fifteen percent of the operation and Luis still had his five percent.

When I got back to the old man's shack, I told him that the man who owned the Ford had gone back to the city and had given the soldiers permission to take it away. And be very careful that his kids do not steal anything from the car because if they do, the soldiers would get very mad, and it is bad to get the soldiers mad at you.

I drove back to Zacatecas, arriving before five o'clock. The general was still in his office and it was a good time to have my audience with him. No one else was around so I was sure that no one else overheard our conversation. He greeted me warmly and thanked me again for my performance. I told him the entire story of the third man and he agreed "case closed." He knew just the colonel to give the Ford to and before I left, he offered me a drink from a freshly opened bottle of Jalisco tequila. He patted the bottle and said, "I drink nothing but the most expensive. I am, as you Americanos say, back in the big bucks."

32
Good Bye to Raul and the Bug

r. Lopez, Prof. San Roman and I were having lunch at our favorite restaurant when one of Gen. Garcia's captains pulled up in a military Jeep and without getting out of the vehicle, shouted, "The commander wants to see you right away! Come with me. Please do not delay."

I looked at the padre and he said, "You had better go. As we know, when the military calls, we must respond."

I detected a hint of sarcasm in his voice, and maybe a touch of fear.

"We will keep your food warm." I climbed into the Jeep and the captain floored it. The captains were always nervous when the general barked, but this time this one appeared scared out of his wits. This must be important. We skidded to a stop at the headquarters building and the captain jumped out and ran and held the door open for me. I was moving slowly and the driver was shifting from one foot to the other as he encouraged me to hurry. When I entered the old man's office, he was pacing the floor and I immediately saw that the scars on his neck were a blood red. He was really angry. He didn't bother to ask me to sit down, but shouted to me, "What in the hell was your amigo, the young pilot, doing in Chihuahua?"

His question caught me by surprise and I replied, "As far as I know, he had a contract to fly a group of anthropologists in and out of the Tarahumara Indian country. I was letting him use my airplane as he would be landing and taking off from small dirt landing strips and his airplane was too big to safely operate in those conditions. The general stopped his pacing, sat down at his big desk and slammed his fist down, hard. "Well, your amigo has been killed and your fine airplane has been smashed up!"

Wow! That was a blow to the gut. My good friend, my jump pilot—you don't get much closer than that—was dead and my number one investment destroyed. I was having difficulty processing that information.

He yelled at me, "Did he ever have anything to do with drug smuggling?"

I immediately answered, "Hell no. He hated anyone who he thought had anything to do with the rotten business. We would sometimes run into guys in the sierras that we thought might be growing the stuff, but we always steered clear of them. They all carried guns and acted a little crazy."

"Send in Capt. Salas," the general barked to his aide. Capt. Salas must have been standing right outside the door, as he instantly entered the room and snapped a salute to the general. The old man didn't return the salute and told the captain to tell his story to the Ingeniero. Salas stood ramrod straight, and then assumed parade rest and began his narrative.

He had just returned from a quick trip to Chihuahua on the orders of Gen. Garcia to conduct an inspection of an accident involving an aircraft from Zacatecas. Three days ago, Gen. Garcia had received an angry telephone call from his counterpart in the State of Chihuahua, Gen. Rodrigues, who wanted to know why an airplane from Zacatecas carrying papers signed by Gen. Garcia that gave the pilot permission to fly anywhere in Mexico, was flying in his area of responsibility in the remote regions of the State of Chihuahua? The captain was aware that Gen. Garcia and Gen. Rodrigues were not exactly good friends because Gen. Rodrigues had recently lost a large sum of money to Gen. Garcia because of a bet during the commanders' conference and he was told to be very careful when in the State of Chihuahua.

The captain said he reported to Gen. Rodrigues' office and was flown to a small dirt airstrip in the Tarahumara Indian country and showed the remains of a single-engine airplane. The pieces of the airplane were all mixed up and Rodrigues' men, three conscripts and a sergeant, said that the Indians had stolen everything of value except a large amount of drugs that were still in a pile in the center of the airplane wreckage. The drugs seemed out of place among the twisted pipes and engine parts, but the soldiers said that was exactly were they had found them.

"What happened to the pilot?" I asked the captain, hoping that there was a small chance that Raul had survived. The captain replied, "The soldiers told him that the Indians who found the crash said the airplane driver was dead and that they did not take anything from him."

"What happened to the body?" I pressed the captain. He hesitated before answering and glanced at the general. The general growled, "Tell him everything."

"Gen. Rodrigues sent a staff officer, a lieutenant who was a very good friend of mine at the officer's candidate school, to the crash and he was to interview the Indians who were at the airstrip, take pictures and bring the body back to Chihuahua City. He told me in deep secrecy that the body had been shot in the head two times, but he did not put that in his report. He also told me that the Indians said the pilot had a bad argument with the city men in the other airplane at the airstrip and the guys pulled guns and pointed them at the pilot and told him to leave. As the airplane was running down the airstrip, the city men got rifles out of their airplane and shot at the pilot's airplane. The airplane got up in the sky a little bit and then fell into the canyon.

"The Indians wanted to run to the crash but the city men told them to stay where they were and took the mules to the crash. When the men returned, they took some of the packages the Indians had sold to them, put them on a mule and went back to the crash. They returned in a hurry and got in their airplane and left."

The captain looked over at the still red-faced general and said, "I told my friend I would not tell his secret, but I am loyal to my general and I must tell him everything in case he needs to protect himself."

Gen. Garcia had calmed down a little bit and dismissed the captain. He opened a desk drawer and pulled out a bottle of the prime Jalisco tequila. He looked at me and gulped down a big swallow of the fiery liquid.

"I know that you don't like this stuff, but I do. So I will drink it. Sit down. I wanted to get your comments. I felt pretty sure that your amigo was not involved in drugs, but I wanted to make sure before I do some harm to Gen. Rodrigues. Rodrigues will do anything to discredit me. But he knows that he can only go so far. I have too many connections in high places in Mexico City. I do not like him, but he is not a very bad man, he is just stupid and weak and a poor commander. He has some staff officers who are involved with this drug problem and it is becoming a dangerous cancer in our great country. He had better take drastic action or he may find himself in some very bad trouble.

"Ingeniero," the general said in a serious tone, "I have been paying more attention to you than you might realize. I sense that you think that our way of doing business with bribes and gifts and special privileges and favors is wrong. But, for those of us who fought for our country, we deserve these things. I believe that I deserve the good life and as long as you are my friend, you will benefit from my being in power. But there are some things that I cannot fix. I cannot bring your pilot friend back to life and, under the circumstances, there is no way you will get your airplane, or the money you had spent for it, back. The people who took both from you are out of reach.

"I am not a philosopher, I am a simple soldier. I am not religious. I lost all ideas of the goodness of man when I saw how both sides of the revolution used God to justify their atrocities. I believe in fate and destiny and I say to you, as an old soldier to a young man who has some experience as a combat soldier, stop and think about where your life is going and if you should be doing something to change its course."

We shook hands and saluted and I walked through the big oak doors of his office and out into the parking lot. He had a grim look on his face and I knew that some heads were going to roll, literally, and I knew that he was not going to lose any sleep over it. I didn't think that I could ever be that kind of commander and I didn't think that I would like to serve under him, but I liked him.

When the Jeep arrived back at the restaurant, Fr. Lopez and Prof. San Ramon were just getting up from lunch. The padre said, "We didn't think that you were coming back for a while and that you military men were solving all the world's problems.

"I told Elena to take the rest of your lunch home to feed their new puppy."

"Thanks, padre," I said. "All the conversation with the general did was give me a few more problems to think about. If you don't mind, I am going to walk back to the hotel by myself and let you two intellectuals solve the problems of the world while I try to deal with the day to day stuff that, right now, has me totally confused."

33
Decision Time

When I got back to my hotel, Mario was waiting for me at the front door. He greeted me with, "Jefe, do I have a great deal for us? It is a gold prospect over near the Nayarit border, far away from the villages in Indian country. It hasn't been visited since the time of the ancient ones. The Indians said that they could see the gold in the rocks. We are the only miners that can get to it."

I said to him, "Good work, Mario, but some things have changed and we might have to rethink some of our operations. Keep working and talking to people, but don't make any promises."

I entered my room and I could see that Elena had been there and had straightened things up on her break and the room looked warm and cozy, but I felt a chill in the air.

Something was missing. It didn't seem comfortable. I saw one edge of the old carpet that Ace used as his mattress sticking out from under my bed and Raul's New York Yankee's baseball cap hanging from the clothes rack on top of one of my World War II flying jackets. Things that shout out, "Welcome home trooper. Take your boots off and unwind. You are safe and secure here."

But I was uneasy. So many things had happened in these past few weeks, and I hadn't been able to sit down and sort them out. I sat down on my bed and I guess I had dozed off when I was awakened by a knock on my door.

It was Fr. Lopez and he said, "It's going to be a nice evening. Why don't you join me for a walk and we can talk over some things that seem to be bothering you?"

It seemed to be a good idea, so I said, "Fine, let's go." As we walked out into the plaza it was just getting dark and the streets were becoming deserted as the people were going home and gathering their families for supper. The padre said, "You look like you are in a reflective mood, and so am I. Let's go to a place where I sometimes visit when I want to do some really deep thinking. Follow me."

I replied, "Lead on, padre."

We crossed the plaza and walked along the church wall until we came to a small passageway. We followed it and stopped at a steep stairway that led straight up. We climbed the stairway for several stories and encountered a narrow ladder.

"It's a hard climb from here on. Do you think that your leg can take it?" the father asked.

"Of course," I answered. "I'm right behind you."

It was a tough climb and after about fifty feet of using muscles that I hadn't used for a while, I was getting winded and stopped to rest and look down. Mistake, I forgot that I was afraid of heights and a jolt of fear went though my body. I clutched the side of the ladder. I was glad that the padre was above me, as I sure didn't want to show him any sign of fear and let him think that a little thing such as climbing a ladder could faze me.

I sucked it up and continued climbing and in about twenty more feet, I was at a small ledge that circled the bell tower of the church. Fr. Lopez had slid to the right side of the ledge and I moved over to the left. We both kept one hand on the ladder, just in case. A sudden noise and rapid movement almost caused me to lose my grip on the ladder as a flock of pigeons arose from inside the bell tower and scattered into the fading light.

"Well, Jim, how do you like my roost?" the padre asked, and I could see that he was also winded and looked a little apprehensive.

"Great view," I replied. And it sure was. We could see for miles, over the city and down into the far valleys. The street lights in the downtown part of the city were coming on, one by one, and in the suburbs and the slums the lamps of the poor people were being lit. We both withdrew into the innermost corners of our minds and all was silent except for the background noise of the city streets and an occasional honking horn or the bray of a donkey.

Right now, I am feeling down. This morning I had been told that a friend, a very good friend—more than that—he was my jump pilot and absolutely essential to my business, had been murdered and my most valuable monetary asset was destroyed and there was no chance of getting any of my money back.

Less than six months ago, an old buddy from the war, and a fellow engineer, had been killed just for being in the wrong place at the wrong time and not knowing the people he was there to help. On top of all this, the sudden death of a lady who could have been the love of my life and a serious, career-ending injury plus the loss of one of the best friends I had ever had, my dog and partner, Ace, had put me at a low point in my life.

I have stumbled on what may or may not be a fabulous gold deposit. But, I am hesitant to tell the world as I fear that I might be killed when many people learn of my secret.

I had been in Mexico for a year and a half and my emotions had been on a roller coaster ever since I pulled up to that military checkpoint in Chihuahua that June day in 1956. It has been one high after another, with a few lows in between, but all in all, good stuff. I came down here to make money and to have adventure and I have done both. I have made better than average wages and I sure have had my share of adventure. From guns being shoved in my gut to face-to-face confrontations with bandits to drug smugglers to revolutionaries to insanely jealous Mexican boyfriends with knives. Now, this! It was time to take a look at what I have been doing down here, south of the border, and as the general said, "is my life going in the right direction?"

First. I should look at my work. In the past eighteen months, I have carved a niche in the field of mining, although a minor one, and it has been at a high cost to my body and my mind. My business, and the chances of a making a big strike is getting better every day, but will a big break come before I make a mistake that could prove to be fatal? I am now without an airplane and a pilot and my funds are low, but, perhaps, money is not the only thing in life. I have experienced every emotion known to man. From love to hate to fright to anger and everything in between.

My love life has been a crazy mess ever since I crossed the border. My first misstep was my attraction to the lovely, hot

blooded, fiery, but cold and calculating Raquel, the rich virgin of
the romance novels who desperately wanted to marry an Americano who was a professional like, say, a doctor or a lawyer or an
engineer and leave Mexico behind. She was the prize, the best
the city of Zacatecas had to offer so I pursued her, and almost
caught her but then discovered that the prize was not going to
be worth all the downsides that came with it. Now I am living in
an uneasy truce.

Then I fell in love with an older lady archeologist who was my
dream girl, but probably more in my dreams than in reality, and I
lost her in a tragic accident. Then came Elena, who fell in love with
me because I had a chance to help her and I did. In between was
Tina the Temptress, the good looking secretary at the engineer's
office, the girl on the Hollywood yacht who wiped the blood from
my face and recently, the voyeuristic encounters with the "Beverly
Hills Lambs" and the unforgettable "Three Little Bares."

But perhaps the most love I saw down here was that in the eyes
of the little Mexican kids when I was dressed up as Santa Claus or
Rudolph the Red Nosed Reindeer and brought them presents from
the sky. I experienced fear from the meeting with the rattlesnake
on the mountain side in the Tarahumara Indian country when he,
or she, or it tore a chunk out of my arm; the Alacran scorpions
who sunk their deadly stingers in my hand in Chihuahua; looking
down the barrel of the .30-0-6 rifle in the hands of a fear-crazed
little wimp named Julio, the chance of bleeding to death after a
beating by drug dealers in Zacatecas, the parachute jump in the
tropical storm over Guatemala; looking into the marijuana-induced
vacant stares of Nicaraguan rebels who wanted our money, our
watches or our lives and, probably my most fear was the fear of
failure when I almost lost my grip on the beautiful Robin during
the midnight jump from two miles high over Zihuatanejo Bay.

A sadness to me was that sometimes, in the back country, I
would encounter a poor Mexican laborer who had entered the
States illegally and had worked hard in the fields and been cheated
out of his wages by a rancher, or a farmer, usually a Texan, and the
laborer would want to harm me, or kill me, to avenge his hatred
of the Texans. This always ended in violence but so far, I have
managed to stay alive. But this always caused hard feelings among
the local people and most of them are good people.

Where do I go from here? I had made up my mind and I reached over and touched the padre on the shoulder and said, "Let's go down."

I Leave Mexico

The next morning I was waiting in the Santo Domingo Church when Fr. Lopez and his servers came down the aisle to the altar. I sat over to one side so that I could see and hear the Mass, but also where I could work on my checklist for things that I had to do during what promised to be a very busy day. When the padre finished saying the Mass and walked back down the aisle to return to his office, he glanced my way and indicated that he wanted to see me. I nodded my head and several minutes later I was in his office waiting for him to change into street clothes.

As we strolled toward our favorite restaurant, the padre said, "I feel that you have made your decision."

"I have," I replied, "but before I discuss it with you, let me first tell you of several important things that have happened since last we talked. As we entered the restaurant to sit down for breakfast, we noticed that Elena was now in charge of the operation and was skillfully and efficiently seating people and taking their orders. She greeted us with a shy smile and said, "I feel very good. Now I am making money and helping support my family and getting a chance to practice my speech." It made me proud that I had done something that was going to help one of the poor people of this country work her way up the ladder of success.

After the father had a cup of coffee and I had some tea, I told him what had happened at the El Rey mine, how the third man's life had ended and how Ace had given his life to save the life of Little Jaime. I told him that I felt no sorrow at all at the death of the scum from Juarez and I knew that I should not ask, or expect, the forgiveness of God for the part I will play in covering up the man's death. The death of my companero, Ace, was much more important to me than the passing of this fellow human being. To add to my misfortune, yesterday the general told me that my pilot, Raul, had been murdered up in Chihuahua and my airplane destroyed and there is nothing I can do about it. Life has come crashing down on me these past few weeks.

I asked him the question, "Am I now paying the price for my past sins, or is it fate? Does your direct line to the Pope or to God say what fate is? For the first time in my life I am looking for answers, and I am not finding any."

"You have caught me off guard and I do not have any pat solutions for you," the padre said. "I'll give it some thought and we will talk it over tomorrow."

"No can do, Father," I said. "At this time tomorrow, I will be in California, starting a new phase of my life. My body and my mind are badly in need of repair and I do not have any idea how long that will take. But be assured, my friend, that I will come back to visit you and the others I leave behind as I am also leaving part of my heart and many responsibilities in Mexico. I will be counting on you to make sure that what good I have done here in your country will continue."

Last night before I went to bed, I had written out what was kind of my last will as to what should happen to the assets I will leave in Mexico. I wanted Fr. Lopez to be my executor and have complete control over the 40 percent share that I owned of the El Rey Mining Company and the shares of several other properties in which I had an interest. I wanted him to make sure that the shares of El Rey owned by Big John and Luis were protected and that they retain their jobs and that the bungalow I owned serve as a home for Mrs. Martinez, Elena and Maria and Jesus, rent and tax free, for as long as they wanted to live there. Above all, he was to serve as an advisor and protector of these poor people as long as they needed him.

The padre said that all my requests were what the Lord told him to do every day and that he would gladly do what God demanded.

The deal was sealed. We shook hands and had two businessmen who were having breakfast at the table next to ours witness the document to make it legal.

It was time to go but we lingered over our half-eaten breakfasts and made small talk for the next fifteen minutes. We both knew that this was a parting and that we had to go our different ways. This simple, but very complex, religious man and I had built up a trusting friendship over the past months and I was going to miss his wise counsel.

Finally the padre stood up and said, "You call it." This was going to be, at least for a while, the last time we would go through the ritual of flipping a coin to see who pays for the breakfast. I took a quarter from my pocket and said "tails" as I tossed it in the air. It landed heads. That damn two-headed coin of mine had just cost me another bet.

As we walked toward the door, Maria and Jesus ran out of the kitchen and held on to Elena's starched apron.

"She is pretty in her new clothes," Maria proudly announced.

"She sure is," I said. And I meant it. I was looking at a very grown-up little girl now, but it was too late. My life was taking a new direction and my future was back in the States. Fr. Lopez turned and headed back to Santo Domingo Church and I got in the Jeep and headed for the airport. I drove through the gate and crossed the ramp to my hangar. I unlocked the door for the last time and stuck the lock in my jacket pocket—something to remember Raul by. There in a corner were my only remaining airborne assets—two personnel parachutes, three 16-foot cargo chutes and a dummy bomb container. I tossed them in the back of the Jeep, walked out and left the door open. Nothing left here but a lot of happy memories, and nobody could steal them.

Things were very quiet in Raul's hangar. His Cessna 180 sat silent and alone and part of an engine cowling lay under a wing and several small parts were soaking in a pan of gasoline—just as he had left things. Just as if he would be back to finish the job. But he would not be back, ever. How sad, how very sad. I looked in the right side door of his airplane and saw one of my parachutes. It had been carelessly tossed in the back seat by a pilot dumb enough to think that he would never use it, but smart enough to keep it handy, just in case. That was my pilot. That was Raul Parra, the young pilot who will never have a chance to grow up.

I took the parachute and headed back into town. I stopped at Mrs. Martinez's bungalow and gave her the parachute. I told her to cut it up and make a wedding dress for Elena, and maybe one for Maria—use the rest of it for the kids to play with. The little pup—they had named him Benito, after the peace-loving priest who started the Mexican revolution—played at my feet and chewed on the cuff of my pants. I reached down and petted him and he rolled over on his back and kicked his feet in the air and asked for more. He was mostly Labrador retriever, with all the good traits of gentleness and love of that breed; just what Maria and Jesus will need as they grow up. Ace, the fierce warrior, had protected our family but his time had passed and his blanket had been cast aside and no trace of him remained. Just as well. Ace's role as a full participant in some pretty hairy adventures had come to an end just as his partner was about ready to hang it up and give up his aerial assaults on the ancient gold mines of the Conquistadores and start doing it the old fashioned way, by Jeep and then burros and mules to get into the real tough places.

Technology was on the march and soon those new machines called helicopters were going to replace me and my World War II equipment. I took one last look at the hangars, the runways and the control tower, got in the Jeep and drove back into town to the bank. I went into the president's office, wrote him a check for the remainder of the loan on the "Bug"—I heard a sigh of relief as I closed his office door—withdrew all but a thousand pesos from my account, said goodbye to the good-looking girl who handled the keys to the "Bug" and told her how much I regretted not being able to take her for a moonlit flight in the air machine. Maybe when I return...

I spent the rest of the afternoon writing letters to Fr. Lopez, Elena, Raul's mother and father, although I had never met them, Big John and Luz and Little Jaime, and Maria and Jesus and dog Benito. I hoped that if they couldn't decipher my Spanish writing they could at least be able to understand my feelings and guess that I was trying to tell them that I was very happy to have met them and that I would always remember them.

Luis was in town to pick up supplies for the mine and he came by my hotel at six o'clock to drive me to the airport. He had just visited his girlfriend and I could see that he was in love, or at least he thought he was. He was dressed in new khaki pants and the latest in sport shirts and he was smiling and whistling He had sure come a long way from being a homeless ward of the church and living on the streets. Both he and Big John had been taking Spanish lessons and Luis was getting to be a pretty good speaker. He thinks that he might even run for the city council one of these days.

As a shareholder in the El Rey Mining Company, a member of management and a worker, he feels that he can represent both sides of the business to the community. He is even sounding like a politician.

He dropped me off at the gate of a new small airline that was flying routes between the smaller cities and Juarez and as we said goodbye I handed him the letter I had written to Fr. Lopez and asked him to deliver it to the padre as soon as he got back into town. I also handed him the keys and the title to my Jeep.

"This is a wedding present, my friend. I hope that you can handle it as well as you do a mule," I said as I shook his hand. I think he was crying as he slowly drove away from the gate. I had made friends with the pilot of the aircraft and as I boarded I asked him to do me a special favor. He said, "You bet, we are a new airline and we have to take care of our passengers."

We took off on time and at exactly eight o'clock we were flying over the Church of Santo Domingo in downtown Zacatecas and the pilot told the co-pilot to lower the landing lights. If things were going according to schedule and as planned, and for once in Mexico I was hoping that things were, Fr. Lopez would be reading the letter that Luis had delivered to him.

It said:

"ESTIMADO PADRE RAMON:
LOOK UP, MI AMIGO. I AM ON THAT AIRPLANE THAT
IS FLYING ABOVE YOU, BUT I WILL BE BACK; COUNT ON
IT. THIS IS JUST ¡ADIOS! AND NOT GOODBYE."

"INGENIERO JAIME HALL"

About the Author

Jim Hall's incredible parachuting career started, and almost ended, on a bright early March morning in 1949 in the skies above northern Sonora, Mexico. On this, his first parachute jump, everything went wrong but he escaped serious injury. He limped away from a very hard landing with little more than a few bumps and bruises. He came away, however, with an intense desire to learn more about this new adventure.

Now, 60 years and 1800 successful parachute jumps later, Jim has decided to write about his early days as the world's first parachuting mining engineer. He was born into a miner's family in the rolling hills of the coal fields of northern Appalachia at the start of the Great Depression. Like his brothers and his cousins before him, he was destined to spend his life digging the black gold from the hills to supply the steel mills of Pittsburgh. All this changed when fate intervened and the Japanese bombed Pearl Harbor.

The young men of the region were scattered all over the world to defend the country. Jim became one of them when he joined the Army Air Corps in 1943 at the age of 17. By the War's end, he had flown a combat tour in B-29s bombing Japan, received a battlefield commission and returned home looking for more adventures.

He took a stab at becoming a Catholic priest, quickly learned that was not a fit for him, and enrolled at the University of New Mexico to start a new life.

In his first engineering class at the University, he met a former paratrooper who had two parachutes and was looking for a partner to join him in making exhibition parachute jumps at fairs, rodeos and air shows. Jim became that partner.

Before he could be trained, the opportunity to visit a remote gold deposit in Mexico came up and the enthusiasm of youth overruled good sense. Jim made his first parachute jump without training. He would not make this mistake again, and for the next four years, he made a very good living by smart parachuting and learning from other barnstormers and military paratroopers.

When he graduated in 1952 with a double degree in engineering and geology, he put aside his parachutes and devoted his efforts to learning everything he could about mining from the grass roots up. He held jobs from hard rock miner up to mine foreman and worked in most of the major mining areas in the western United States.

In 1956, during a trip to Mexico he decided to combine his two areas of expertise and become the world's first parachuting exploration mining engineer. This was before the new machine, the helicopter, was used to gain access to the remote regions of the world. Jim saw the parachute as a unique way to use his talents to re-visit long-lost gold mines discovered by the Spanish Conquistadors more than 400 years ago in old Mexico.

In *Parachuting for Gold in Old Mexico*, Jim Hall takes the reader on a remarkable journey. You will learn:

- What it feels like to parachute into the high sierras and deep canyons in the central region of Mexico where these lost gold mines were located;
- How he interacted with native people who had never seen a white man before and who were terrified and mystified by the appearance of a man and his dog as they fell out of the sky;
- About his relationship with the Mexican government and local officials, the Indians in their remote villages and the ordinary Mexican people, both good and bad.
- About exhibition parachute jumping on the beaches of Acapulco and onto soccer fields in other major Mexican cities;
- How he met the young revolutionaries Fidel Castro, Che Guevara and Raul Castro as they raised their army in

southern Mexico, and how he volunteered to lead their 82-man army into Cuba but was stopped at the last minute by the American Embassy in Mexico City; and

- About some of the interesting and intriguing "behind the scenes" activities that went on in Mexico during the middle fifties; about his near fatal brush with Nicaraguan guerrillas and his hair-raising parachute jump into the teeth of a hurricane in Guatemala.

Injuries and opportunities caused him to return to the States in 1958 where he joined with top exhibition parachutists Dave Burt and Bob Sinclair, to form the world's first professional parachuting company, Para Ventures, Inc. The company was a magnet for adventurers from all over the globe with its headquarters located on the main stem of the world's entertainment capital, Hollywood Boulevard.

Jim was its Director of Operations, and the company operated the world's largest commercial sport parachuting facility; it was based at the Elsinore Para Center, midway between Los Angeles and San Diego. In 1963, Para Ventures merged its operations and personnel with Parachuting Associates, dropped its sport parachuting activities and concentrated on TV commercials, motion pictures and Air Force-related test work.

In 1961, Jim was co-creator of the television series, *Ripcord* that put Sky Diving before millions of viewers for the first time. The story line was based on Jim's adventures in Mexico and the show served as a proving ground for many of the advancements in free-fall parachuting and air-to-air photography.

In 1962, Jim was awarded the Leo Stevens Medal, the parachuting industry's highest award, for his development of the "Buddy System" of free-fall parachuting instruction that teaches aircrew members to safely make a parachute jump from high altitudes.

In 1964 he was part of the elite team of parachutists who created the Air Force Academy's Airmanship Free-Fall Parachuting Program.

In 1965, he live-tested the F-106 zero-zero ejection seat and in 1967, he wrote and directed the Air Force's definitive training film on how to survive an ejection or bail-out.

He retired from the Colorado Air National Guard as a Brigadier General in 1981 and was awarded the Air Force Legion of Merit. Jim was inducted into the Colorado Aviation Hall of Fame in 1985. He lives in Aurora, Colorado, with his wife and two children.

Jim Hall can be contacted at:

Parachuting Associates
PO Box 461377
Aurora, CO 80046

Info@ParachutingAssociates.com
www.ParachutingAssociates.com